LEAN HOSPITALS

Improving Quality, Patient Safety, and Employee Engagement

Third Edition

Endorsements

Lean Hospitals, Third Edition – Mark Graban

"Leaders of today's healthcare organizations are on a continuous journey to improve results, requiring a relentless focus on improving the underlying process of care delivery and leadership practices. Mark has written a book that provides compelling ideas to help create better places to work, practice medicine and receive safe, high quality care."

Quint Studer
Founder of Studer Group, a 2010 recipient of the Malcolm Baldrige National Quality Award, Author of Hardwiring Excellence: Purpose, Worthwhile Work, Making a Difference and Results That Last: Hardwiring Behaviors That Will Take Your Company to the Top

"Mark Graban's book has documented what is now happening in hospitals all across America as we learn to apply the Toyota Production System methodology to healthcare. This book lays out the nuts and bolts of the Lean methodology and also describes the more difficult challenges, which have to do with managing change. Graban's book is full of wins—these are the same type of wins that are happening at ThedaCare every day. I wish I could have read this six years ago, as it might have prevented some of the mistakes we made in our Lean transformation journey."

John S. Toussaint, MD
President/CEO
ThedaCare Center for Healthcare Value

"Mark Graban is the consummate translator of the vernacular of the Toyota Production System into the everyday parlance of healthcare. With each concept and its application, the reader is challenged to consider what is truly possible in the delivery of healthcare if only standardized systems borrowed from reliable industries, were implement. Graban provides those trade secrets in an understandable and transparent fashion."

Richard P. Shannon, MD
Executive Vice President for Health Affairs
University of Virginia

"There is an enormous shortfall between the healthcare we receive and what we actually get. Mark Graban explains how those in the system can make care delivery better for everyone –patients, providers, and payors."

Steven J. Spear
Sr. Lecturer at MIT Sloan School of Management and Sr. Fellow at the Institute for Healthcare Improvement Author of The High Velocity Edge

"Mark Graban has been tirelessly studying the application of Lean to healthcare, with an emphasis on respect for the people served by the system as well as the people who provide excellent care. He has an accurate sense of how things work in health systems, which makes his work more meaningful for people who want to make them better."

Ted Eytan, MD

"The medical community has a tremendous opportunity to learn methods and techniques to improve the quality and efficiency of care and reduce costs, while at the same time engaging the staff in these efforts. Mark Graban has deep experience applying Lean in the healthcare field, and in his book provides an outline of how to transfer concepts originally developed in manufacturing into the unique environment of medical care. Don't miss the opportunity to learn and apply some great ideas in your organization."

David Meier
Co-Author of the best selling books The Toyota Way Fieldbook and
Toyota Talent

"The concepts outlined in this book are the most powerful tools that I have ever encountered to foster innovation, ownership, and accountability at the front line staff level. This is a must-read for any leader n today's increasingly complex healthcare industry."

Brett Lee, PhD, FACHE
Market Chief Executive Officer
Tenet Healthcare

"The Institute of Medicine (IOM) calls for systems in healthcare that support continuous learning and process improvement, and highlights waste as a fundamental obstacle to attaining highly reliable and value-based healthcare systems. Lean is a proven way to eliminate waste, while hardwiring systems to ensure sustainability. Eliminating waste and engaging employees are the key to value-based medicine, where waste is identified and eliminated, and value emanates seamlessly from continuous process improvement in the rich environment of a continuously learning organization. *Lean Hospitals* is a foundational text for understanding the concepts and application of continuous process improvement in a healthcare environment, and provides practical guidance and concrete examples to eliminate waste and increase value to the customer."

Beverly B. Rogers, MD
Chief of Pathology, Children's Healthcare of Atlanta
Clinical Professor of Pathology, Emory University School of Medicine

"Mark Graban's book will leave you with an appreciation for what Lean is and what it can do for your healthcare organization. Since the original edition in 2008, I have conducted *Lean Hospitals* book studies for all my staff. Everyone gets a personal copy of *Lean Hospitals* for the study and to keep as a reference. I look forward to the 3rd edition. It's my Lean bible."

Jim Adams
Admin Director of Laboratories
Children's Healthcare of Atlanta

"It's obvious that Mark Graban has spent time in the trenches of healthcare and understands the complexities of applying the Lean philosophy and tools to that environment. If you want to improve your chances of surviving in today's healthcare system (both literally and figuratively), read this book."

Dean Bliss
Former Improvement Advisor
Iowa Healthcare Collaborative

"Graban provides a helpful translation of the terms, practices, and tools of Lean thinking into hospitals' everyday situations and challenges. His book illustrates Lean's elements with many actual examples of Lean applications in typical hospital practices and procedures. Graban's book should definitely be on the reading list for those who want to bring the benefits of Lean thinking to healthcare."

David Mann
Principal, David Mann Lean Consulting

"Lean healthcare is becoming a global movement. The reasons given are overrun costs, errors that compromise patient safety, time of patients wasted, and general bureaucratic inefficiency. Healthcare is different than car making. This is true but many, many hospitals are learning from Toyota and making remarkable improvements. The two pillars of the Toyota Way certainly fit the healthcare environment—Respect for People and Continuous Improvement.

Unfortunately, the remarkable improvements are in specific areas and seem difficult to sustain because of a mysterious ingredient, which the folks at Toyota seem to understand quite well--humans. Healthcare exists to serve humans and humans provide the services. Humans are far from perfect. Toyota's system is actually designed to support the development of people, not to provide a quick fix set of technical solutions, and this takes time and patience.

Many healthcare consultants have rebadged themselves as Lean consultants and do not understand the real thinking behind the Toyota Way. Mark Graban is an exception. He has worked hard to study the philosophy and stay true to the thinking of Toyota. His book is a welcome translation of the Toyota Way into language any healthcare professional can understand."

Jeffrey K. Liker
Professor, University of Michigan
Author of The Toyota Way

LEAN HOSPITALS

Improving Quality, Patient Safety, and Employee Engagement

Third Edition

MARK GRABAN

Foreword by John Toussaint, MD

CRC Press
Taylor & Francis Group
Boca Raton   London   New York

CRC Press is an imprint of the
Taylor & Francis Group, an **informa** business

A PRODUCTIVITY PRESS BOOK

CRC Press
Taylor & Francis Group
6000 Broken Sound Parkway NW, Suite 300
Boca Raton, FL 33487-2742

© 2016 by Mark Graban
CRC Press is an imprint of Taylor & Francis Group, an Informa business

No claim to original U.S. Government works

Printed on acid-free paper
Version Date: 20160429

International Standard Book Number-13: 978-1-4987-4325-9 (Paperback)

Visit the Taylor & Francis Web site at
http://www.taylorandfrancis.com

and the CRC Press Web site at
http://www.crcpress.com

Printed and bound in Great Britain by
TJ International Ltd, Padstow, Cornwall

Contents

Foreword

I have now studied over 160 organizations in 16 countries in the last five years looking for the "Toyota of healthcare." Unfortunately, I haven't found it yet. But I have seen legitimate attempts at applying Lean principles in every type of healthcare setting. And this is a significant change since Mark Graban's book was first published in 2008. As we have learned more about successful Lean transformations, we have been able to identify the core elements of that success.

That's important because as we surge toward 20% of the U.S. gross domestic product being spent on healthcare, we now have a big problem that probably could have been avoided by Lean thinking, but now must be solved by it. Our status in the world economy depends on our ability to manage healthcare costs. Other countries are faced with similar healthcare financial burdens. While costs in the United States are significantly higher, no country is happy with its current cost curve.

Lean thinking changes all "conventional healthcare thinking," and that is good because we need a complete transformation in our industry if we have any hope of improving patient value. In this book, Mark has written about some of the new thinking that is at the core of Lean with new and improved healthcare system examples.

In the work I do at the ThedaCare Center for Healthcare Value, we are using the principles in this book to explain the framework for changing the system. It starts with the principles that then inform systems—systems such as the Lean improvement central office, the Lean management system, leadership standard work, and behaviors required for success. As Mark points out, this is learning by doing. Doing work that matters is critical. So another important construct is the "model cell." The model cell has two distinct and almost contradictory roles. It is a testing center where people can experiment with ideas, embrace failure as a path for learning, and put new concepts into action. It is also the demonstration exhibit—the results of your finest efforts to create a new care delivery ideal state. It is how you will sell Lean healthcare ideas and spread these new methods to the rest of the organization.

Since 2009, I have worked with many organizations in the Healthcare Value Network (learn more at createvalue.org/networks/healthcare-value-network/). These organizations are led by the serious few leaders who have proven Lean works in healthcare. The question today is not "does Lean work in healthcare?" but "how do you do it?" Leaders who are curious can visit Seattle Children's Hospital, the Palo Alto Medical Foundation, or HealthEast in St. Paul, Minnesota, and see daily improvement in action. They can visit Winona Health Services in Minnesota to understand how to eliminate wasteful budgets and move to rolling forecasts. Or travel to Salem Health in Oregon and see how the analytics team has partnered with operations to improve patient safety. The question is how are *you* going to do it? I believe starting with Mark Graban's updated book *Lean Hospitals* is a good first step.

Mark knows what he is talking about. He has dedicated his career to learning and teaching the Lean methodology to healthcare professionals, and this book is a testament to that. Mark includes new learnings and examples that give the book more depth, with the intent to try to help us all deliver lower-cost and higher-quality patient care—better value.

But, you must also know that you cannot learn Lean from books alone. Books are for creating a framework of thinking. The only way to know, however, is to go to the *gemba*, which means the place where the work is done and observe, learn, and experiment. If a leader is not spending a minimum of 20% of their day at the *gemba*, the leader will never learn or be able to apply Lean. The more often executives go to the *gemba* the less time they spend firefighting, because they are getting upstream of patient complaints and problems, which leads to defect avoidance and more time for improvement.

This is not an easy journey, however. It is difficult to break down the traditional healthcare notions that everything is done by committee and the most powerful people win, squelching the ideas of the frontline workers (nurses, doctors, technicians, etc.), who actually understand the problems and can craft the best solutions.

This book lays out the nuts and bolts of the Lean methodology and describes the more difficult challenges, which have to do with managing change. *Lean Hospitals* is full of wins—these are the same types of wins that are happening at Healthcare Value Network members every day. I wish I could have read this in 2004, as it might have prevented some of the mistakes we made in our Lean transformation journey at ThedaCare.

These new mindsets, along with the Lean techniques described here, are the keys to reducing errors, freeing up more time for patient care, improving patient flow, and reducing caregiver burnout. That's exactly what our patients expect.

John Toussaint, MD, CEO
ThedaCare Center for Healthcare Value

Preface

This is a book I feel privileged and honored to write (and update), as it would have been hard to imagine my career would bring me into healthcare after a decade of working in the manufacturing world. My undergraduate education was in industrial engineering, which was always focused on factory production and business issues. In some eerie foreshadowing, my senior group project at Northwestern University was done at a local blood banking and distribution operation, something that seemed like a poor fit for a "manufacturing guy" at the time. Little did I know I would run across blood banks again about 10 years down the road. When I got started in healthcare in 2005, I also didn't know that I'd then spend another 10 years (and counting) working with people to help improve healthcare.

Back in 2005, and even when the first edition of this book was published in 2008, the vast majority of healthcare leaders and professionals didn't know about Lean or were barely aware of it. Conversations in those years were often about convincing people that Lean could work in healthcare. Ten years later, awareness about Lean is much higher, to the point where there are some risks created by Lean being trendy. The risk is that Lean is just a superficially understood buzzword instead of being something that people are studying deeply and putting into practice through structured experiments and reflection. Lean is powerful, but it's not a quick fix or an easy answer for what ails healthcare. There have been many success stories, answering the question of "will Lean work in healthcare?" The key question now is "how do we help as many organizations as possible be successful with Lean?"

My own personal story somewhat parallels the movement of Lean thinking and practices across industries. How did I get to this point, transitioning from manufacturing into healthcare? I hope you'll indulge me in a bit of autobiography, as I hope you might see parallels in your own organizations and career.

After growing up near Detroit, Michigan, I was somewhat skeptical of career paths in the automotive industry, but I took a job with a General Motors plant that said (during college recruiting) it managed under the Deming philosophy. That was a real attraction for me, as I had been exposed to Dr. W. Edwards Deming by my father, and I might have been the only college kid to read Deming's *Out of the Crisis* over a winter vacation for fun. Unfortunately (and ironically), the Deming philosophy was really just a sign hanging on the wall, as the plant management operated under the very traditional auto industry management approach—far from Toyota ideals (which were influenced heavily by Deming).

So there I was, a 21-year-old engineer, working in an environment in which managers yelled and intimidated; employees were not listened to, as they were the source of the problems (being unfairly labeled as "lazy" or "careless") in the eyes of management. I was first introduced to the sad command of "check your brain at the door," as many workers claimed to have been literally told this. Most employees cared about quality and had pride in their work, building premium Cadillac engines, but management wanted them to keep the line running at all costs. Production quantity trumped quality, and both results suffered under that old management system.

From this experience, I learned that the problems at the plant were not the fault of the workers; it was a management system problem. It was not even that the individual managers were bad people; the problems were in the system they were taught and the expectations they were given. Seeing so many disgruntled employees created a deep empathy in me for those who are mistreated in the workplace, any workplace. Our results in quality, cost, and productivity were lousy, and nobody was sure if our plant had much more than a few years left to live. This old way of managing was not doing much good.

While I had gained some awareness and basic knowledge about Toyota and Deming in college, I learned firsthand from some incredible mentors I had at General Motors. These experts took me under their wing and used the plant, full of its problems and waste, as a teaching opportunity. We observed the process, seeing lots of waste, and talked to the people working in it. My mentors talked about how things should be, and we tried implementing small improvements, but the overall environment was still pretty unwelcoming to any major change.

While the prevailing management method and results left a lot to be desired, our plant manager was finally replaced—as it was more likely the poor results, not the outdated management method that did him in. Our new plant manager, Larry Spiegel, was an outstanding leader who was one of the first General Motors managers to be trained in the Toyota Production System at New United Motor Manufacturing Inc., the General Motors-Toyota joint venture plant in California. You can hear him speak a bit in the "This American Life" radio episode titled "NUMMI" if you search for it online—it's a great listen.

The new plant manager spent much of the time over the first few months just walking and looking through the factory, often alone, stopping to talk with employees. He wanted to see problems firsthand and make sure the employees knew he knew what the problems were. Spiegel stood in front of the entire plant, all 800 employees, and told them the problems were not their fault—it was the management system. The management system was going to change, and everyone, if they participated, would see better results. The old blaming and finger pointing behaviors were ending—slowly.

With the new leadership and the rejuvenated Lean coaches, we conducted a lot of training and started implementing many improvements with the production workers. The plant, over the course of just a few years, went from being the worst auto plant in the United States (or so the plant manager argued, having data to back his claims) to being in the top quartile of its peer group. It was a great transformation story. But, sadly, the plant was closed in the aftermath of the General Motors bankruptcy. It's a cautionary tale that having great Lean operations and a Lean culture can't always protect people from a bad business model and higher-level problems.

Thanks to the urging of one of my General Motors' mentors, Steve Chong, I left to attend the Leaders for Manufacturing program at the Massachusetts Institute of Technology, where I took some courses on Lean and had a chance to first meet Jim Womack, one of the world's leading Lean gurus. Later, after finishing graduate school, I was working in Phoenix, Arizona, and was part of an informal network called the Valley Lean Council, a group of Lean zealots from different companies who met quarterly to compare notes and tour a facility. One of those tours was a hospital in Scottsdale, Arizona, that was using Lean methods to improve its emergency department. That was my first exposure regarding the applications of engineering to healthcare since my senior project, and it really piqued my interest. Shortly thereafter, my wife had a new job offer in Texas, which put me in the job market.

I was very lucky to then receive a phone call from a Johnson & Johnson recruiter, who was looking to fill a consulting position in the ValuMetrix Services group, a consulting arm with Ortho Clinical Diagnostics, which helped hospitals learn and implement Lean and Six Sigma. By far, the Lean work I have done in hospitals has been the most rewarding, most exciting, and most gratifying work I have ever done. It is not always easy, but anything worthwhile has to be a bit of a challenge.

One thing I was surprised to see, and maybe should not have been surprised by, was that the human dynamics in a hospital can be similar to those in a factory. After all, it is just people being people. Medical technologists said things I remembered production associates saying, that their supervisors did not listen to them and never saw what the problems were. Suggestion boxes had locks, and nobody could find the key. I saw people bandaging the process instead of being able to stop to fix the problem so it would not occur again. I saw people who were stressed out and no longer enjoyed their work. The motivation for improving the management system for the sake of the employees was the same, sometimes sadly so.

What is different, however, is the deep and intense passion for helping patients. I mean no disrespect to the medical community when I point out problems and waste, since our physicians and surgeons do amazing work that saves many lives and improves many more. There are many brilliant people, most of whom are trying their hardest in often heroic fashion—yet the system is broken. We need to get the medical practitioners on board and collaborate with them in Lean, since Lean will support them in being able to spend more time doing what they went to medical school for and less time on the problems and the frustrations. The Lean thinkers and the process improvement specialists cannot do it all themselves, but there is amazing potential to improve the healthcare system in ways that the clinicians and caregivers generally have not been doing. We cannot blame them, as most doctors received as much process improvement training as I received anatomy training, and pharmacists received as much training on inventory management as I received on formulating intravenous solutions. For this to work, we all have to partner up, put our egos aside (if need be), and be willing to admit what we know and what we do not know, figuring out how to combine our knowledge in a way that works.

This book is intended to help answer the question "What is Lean?" for an audience of hospital or healthcare leaders, managers, physicians, and employees. One assumption is that hospital readers know what their problems are and are looking for new ideas and approaches. So, I have tried not to be encyclopedic in my documentation of the problems facing patients and hospitals. Rather, I have tried to capture some particular issues that can be addressed with Lean (while highlighting a few that are somewhat out of scope for Lean).

I have tried, also, to summarize some of the key problems for readers who are new to healthcare, including those who are following my career path of transitioning from manufacturing to healthcare improvement. To those readers, I hope you will find confidence that your methods and experiences can be helpful to hospitals, provided you are respectful of how this environment is different. Hospitals are much more mission based, and profit is not usually a priority (of course, before Lean, many factories seemed to have been run as if profit were not a priority).

This book is also not meant to be a comprehensive "how to" guide, as far as the details of how to implement specific Lean tools. There are many existing books, including the Productivity Press Shopfloor and Operator series of books on topics like 5S, *kanban*, and other Lean tools that can be adapted to hospital settings. The tools are the same; the key is why you use them and what you are working to improve, so that is the focus of this book. In recent years, we have seen the publication of healthcare-specific books on Lean tools, as well as new books that share the broader transformational experiences of hospitals like ThedaCare, Seattle Children's Hospital, Denver Health, and Virginia Mason Medical Center.

This book also generally limits its scope to hospital and health system operations instead of the global issues of healthcare. It is not possible to include examples of every possible application of Lean, so the exclusion of a department or patient pathway should not be considered an indication that Lean does not apply. There are many forms of waste to be found throughout healthcare, and Lean methods can be applied to ongoing health maintenance, prevention, and primary care relationships, but those topics are left for somebody else's book, including those now being published about Lean in primary care, emergency medicine, and other more specific settings.

Since Lean concepts are very interconnected and mutually supportive, it was a challenge to create a linear structure (a book form). I hope the book is helpful and inspires you to take action, to learn more, and to share what works (and what does not work) with your colleagues in the industry—and to learn from others outside of healthcare.

I thank all of those who have mentored me and taught me about Lean throughout my career, including Sid Siddiqi, Glen Elmore, Rich Rachner, Paul Scheel, P. L. Godwre, Blake Headey, Mike Santarelli, Pascal Dennis, Mark Spearman, Stan Gershwin, and Steve Graves.

I owe a debt of gratitude to Dean Bliss for referring Productivity Press to me in the first place. Dean has been a regular reader of my blog (www.leanblog.org) and knew of my work in hospitals. This would have never happened without his help and support.

I also thank my former leaders and colleagues at ValuMetrix Services for supporting the initial efforts for this book and lending their assistance. Thanks to Rick Malik, Steve Friedland, Jo Ann Hegarty, Jamie Miles, Audrey Knable, Lewis Lefteroff, Ken LePage, Shana Padgett, Norka Saldana, Chetan Shukla, and Susan South, among others, for your help, insights, and encouragement. I was truly fortunate to be part of such a strong team so dedicated to improving healthcare. Thanks to everyone in our group and those who previously worked for us and taught us, especially Charlie Protzman and Mike Hogan, for building a foundation for our current and future success. Not all of the examples in this book are from my firsthand experience, so I am not trying to take credit for all of the fine work these other Lean change agents have done before me.

Thanks also go to those who helped me visit their organization or reviewed drafts and gave input, including Theresa Moore, Amy Sigman, Travis Beamish, Scott Ovenden, Marta Kartov, Jim Adams, Lee Fried, Dr. Ted Eytan, Andrew Castle, Joe Swartz, Bart Sellers, Michael Lombard, David Meier, Jamie Flinchbaugh, Gwendolyn Galsworth, Naida Grunden, and Norman Bodek. Special thanks to Jeff Maling and Bryan Lund for their tireless research efforts about the early uses of Lean and the Training Within Industry methodology in healthcare. Thanks also to Mike Wroblewski for finding a great example of Henry Ford and a "Lean hospital" from 1922. Special thanks go to Dr. Sami Bahri, the "world's first Lean dentist," as the innovative Lean work in his dental practice is quite an inspiration to me. I could not have done this without the efforts and dedication of my wonderful clients, leaders, and project team members, especially Jim Adams, Dr. Beverly Rogers, Stephanie Mitchell, Dr. Mark Pool, Robin Aldredge, and Kim Morris. It is an honor to work with each of you and to support your important missions. There are too many other stimulating people I have worked with to mention them all, but if you have worked with me before, please forgive me for not mentioning you here (and forgive me for the moments I did not live up to the leadership ideals laid out in the book).

I absolutely appreciate the efforts of Cheryl Fenske, who assisted greatly with editing and helped to focus my writing as I went. Thanks also go to my acquisitions editor, Kris Mednansky, for bringing this opportunity to me and for helping to keep me calm as deadlines approached. Thanks also to the original publisher, Maura May, for her support and assistance.

In many of the years since the publication of the first edition, I have been fortunate to work with the Lean Enterprise Institute, a non-profit education and research institute. I have been honored to be part of the team that has helped build our Healthcare Value Network, a collaboration of North American hospitals that are committed to improving healthcare using Lean thinking as well as sharing their lessons learned with other members and the broader healthcare world. Many thanks go to Helen Zak and Dr. John Toussaint for their leadership and inspiration and to the entire team for the learning opportunities that I have been able to use to advantage. My gratitude also goes to the groundbreaking leaders in these network organizations, including but not limited to Dr. Jack Billi, the late Dr. Michel Tétreault, Dr. Dean Gruner, Dr. Zeev Neuwirth, Barbara Bouche, Paul Levy, Alice Lee, and Amir Rubin.

I thank my parents, Bob and Marlene Graban, for their love and support—in particular, their support of education throughout my life, from preschool to graduate school, and the sacrifices they made to create opportunities for me along the way.

I also thank my in-laws, Charlie and Debbie Gowder, for sharing their daughter and their love with me. To my wife, Amy, thank you for your love and support, which never end. Beyond our love and friendship, I am always inspired by your drive, intellect, and professional success. I am proud to be your husband, and I am very happy you are my wife. Thanks for being my supporting partner in making this book happen.

Mark Graban

Author

 Mark Graban is an internationally recognized expert in the field of "Lean healthcare," as a consultant, author, keynote speaker, and blogger. Mark is also co-author, with Joe Swartz, of the book *Healthcare Kaizen: Engaging Front-Line Staff in Sustainable Continuous Improvements*. He has been recognized twice (for this book and *Healthcare Kaizen*) as the recipient of the prestigious Shingo Research & Professional Publication Award.

Mark is an experienced change agent, with a background in industrial and mechanical engineering and an MBA from the MIT Sloan Leaders for Global Operations Program. Prior to healthcare, Mark worked in multiple industries, including automotive (General Motors), electronics (Dell), and industrial products (Honeywell). At Honeywell, Mark was certified as a "Lean expert" (Lean Black Belt).

Since August 2005, Mark has worked exclusively in healthcare, where he has coached Lean teams at client sites in North America and the United Kingdom, including medical laboratories, hospitals, and primary care clinics. Mark's motivation is to apply Lean and Toyota Production System principles to improve quality of care and patient safety, to improve the customer/patient experience, to help the development of medical professionals and employees, to make healthcare more affordable, and to help build strong organizations for the long term.

From June 2009 to June 2011, Mark was a senior fellow with the Lean Enterprise Institute, a not-for-profit educational organization that is a leading voice in the Lean world. In this role, Mark also served as the director of communication & technology for the Healthcare Value Network, a collaboration of healthcare organizations from across North America, a partnership between the Lean Enterprise Institute and the ThedaCare Center for Healthcare Value. Mark continues as a faculty member for the Lean Enterprise Institute and the ThedaCare Center.

In June 2011, Mark also joined the software company KaiNexus to help further their mission of spreading continuous improvement, while continuing his other work and activities. He also serves on the board of the Louise H. Batz Patient Safety Foundation.

Mark was raised in Livonia, Michigan, and currently resides in Texas with his wife, Amy.

To interact with Mark, please visit www.LeanHospitalsBook.com or www.MarkGraban.com.

Chapter 1

The Need for Lean Hospitals

Better Results with Lean

"Lean" is a process improvement methodology and, more importantly, Lean is a leadership style and a management system. Lean has been embraced by hospitals and health systems since the 1990s, especially so in the past 10 years. The Lean approach is powerful, but it is not a quick fix. Lean promotes a new way of thinking and a different organizational culture, requiring change and participation from everybody at all levels. The practical methods and tools used within this broader framework have led to measurably better performance in areas such as patient safety, quality, waiting times, cost, and employee morale in healthcare organizations around the world.

Lean is not something you simply implement this year or in a few short years. Lean is an approach that you practice diligently, improving and learning more over time. Lean doesn't mean being perfect or completely free of waste, since no organization ever reaches those heights. But a "Lean hospital" is one where leaders have a humble, inquisitive mindset and a management style that allows for the reinvention of aspects of healthcare delivery and creates a culture of continuous improvement.

Why Do Hospitals Need Lean?

Taiichi Ohno, one of the creators of the Toyota Production System, wrote that organizations must "start from need" and that "needs and opportunities are always there."[1] In 2014, John Shook, CEO of the Lean Enterprise Institute and the first American to work for Toyota in Japan, said we should start by asking, "What is the purpose of the change and what problem are we trying to solve?"[2] John Toussaint, MD, former CEO at ThedaCare (Wisconsin), emphasizes that Lean activity must be "focused on a ... problem that is important to the organization."[3]

Today, the need for Lean in healthcare is very clear in terms of underperforming performance metrics and general dissatisfaction. Hospitals face a growing number of external pressures and challenges as well. Hospitals do many wonderful things, including saving lives. But, a senior leader at a prestigious university hospital summarized their internal challenges by lamenting that "we have world-class doctors, world-class treatment, and completely broken processes."

So, how can an approach called Lean help healthcare organizations? On first hearing the word, people might complain that they are already understaffed and do not have enough resources. Of course, being Lean means having the *right* staffing levels and resources to do quality work in a way that's not too stressful. The everyday use of the term *lean* and countless newspaper headlines reinforce what are often negative connotations about not having enough resources. Rest assured, the approach presented here is not about mass layoffs. Lean is very different from traditional "cost-cutting" methods that have been tried in multiple industries, including healthcare. The idea of "preventable" errors may also bring skepticism, as employees and physicians believe they are already being as careful as possible. Hospitals using Lean methods do not improve quality by asking people to be more careful any more than they improve productivity by asking people to run around faster.

Lean is a tool set, a management system, and a philosophy that can change the way hospitals are organized and managed. Lean is a methodology that allows hospitals to improve the quality of care for patients by reducing errors and waiting times, which also results in lower costs. Lean is an approach that supports employees and physicians, eliminating roadblocks and allowing them to focus on providing care. Lean is a system for strengthening hospital organizations for the long term—reducing costs and risks while also facilitating growth and expansion. Lean helps break down barriers between disconnected departmental "silos," allowing different hospital departments (and sites within a health system) to better work together for the benefit of patients.

How a Lean health system respects and supports staff:

- Focuses on their safety and well-being
- Ensures people have what they need to do the work
- Doesn't put people in a broken process
- Doesn't drive cost-cutting through layoffs
- Doesn't overburden people
- Has proper staffing levels
- Gives help and support when needed
- Doesn't blame people for systemic errors
- Lets people do meaningful work
- Lets staff work to their level of licensure
- Listens and engages people in improvement

Someone might ask how Lean methods can help solve the everyday, nagging problems that so many committees and teams have already tried fixing. Lean is not a silver bullet, but it is different in that people learn how to look at the details of processes instead of jumping through the same proverbial hoops every day. The people who do the work help fix things where the work is actually done, instead of relying on experts to tell them what to do. Lean helps leaders see and understand that it is not the individuals who are broken, but the system itself. This happens in a way in which the system can actually be fixed, improved, or reinvented in small, manageable bites, with managers and staff working together. The Lean approach also requires the continued learning and professional development of employees, for their own sake and the sake of the organization.

A Renewed Sense of Purpose

People in healthcare are driven by an important mission and a strong sense of purpose. The everyday problems, waste, and broken processes interfere with what healthcare providers and employees want to do: provide the best possible care to patients and keep people healthy. These problems can also leave people short on time, interfering with their ability to provide a caring environment for their clinical care.

Dr. Jacob Caron, an orthopedic surgeon and former chief of the medical staff at St. Elisabeth Hospital (Tilburg, the Netherlands), is one of their leading advocates for Lean. During a 2009 presentation at a Dutch Lean healthcare symposium, his title slide read, "Lean and Loving … a mission impossible?" To hospitals like St. Elisabeth, an important motivation for reducing waste is to free up time for clinicians. This newly found time is used not only for better clinical care and improved responsiveness to patient requests but also for what St. Elisabeth describes as "loving care."[4] When nurses are not scrambling to find supplies and medications, they can take time to talk with patients, answering questions and alleviating anxiety they might have about their hospital stay. In 2015, Dr. Caron said, "Our quest has developed further in a growth process for our coworkers and ourselves. Lean still influences my work as orthopaedic surgeon and medical specialist on quality and safety, as well as my behavior as a person."[5] The combination of efficiency and caring has led to results including orthopedic waiting times being reduced from "several months to four weeks."[6]

Lean Methods Are Not New to Healthcare

While Lean has been used formally in healthcare for a relatively short time, industrial engineering (often known as management engineering in healthcare) has been used for a century to improve hospitals.

Frank and Lillian Gilbreth, sometimes known from the original 1950 version of the film *Cheaper by the Dozen*, were two of the original "efficiency experts" of the late nineteenth and early twentieth centuries, with many of their methods influencing the later development of Lean. Outside of their primary factory work, the Gilbreths published many studies in medicine, being among the first to demonstrate that industrial engineering methods could be applied to hospitals. One innovation from the Gilbreth studies was a practice we take for granted today—having a surgical nurse hand instruments to surgeons as called for, instead of the surgeon taking time away from the patient to search for them and retrieve them.[7]

In 1922, Henry Ford wrote about efforts to apply his production methods to a hospital in Dearborn, Michigan. Ford said, "It is not at all certain whether hospitals as they are now managed exist for patients or for doctors. … It has been an aim of our hospital to cut away from all of these practices and to put the interest of the patient first. … In the ordinary hospital the nurses must make useless steps. More of their time is spent in walking than in caring for the patient. This hospital is designed to save steps. Each floor is complete in itself, and just as in the factories we have tried to eliminate the necessity for waste motion, so we have tried to eliminate waste motion in the hospital."[8]

Almost a century later, nurses around the world still spend more time dealing with waste in the workplace than they spend at the bedside—until Lean is employed to help. This long history suggests that there are long-standing systemic problems in healthcare that have not been solved by old approaches. Virginia Mason Medical Center (Seattle, Washington) has increased the amount of time that nurses are able to spend at the bedside from 40% to almost 90%, which improves job satisfaction and patient care.[9]

Toyota's Role in Popularizing Lean

Toyota Motor Corporation is sometimes known as "the company that invented Lean production."[10] Toyota developed the Toyota Production System over many decades, starting in 1945.[11] Inventing and refining a new production system was not an overnight success story, nor will be your hospital's Lean transformation, as changing old mindsets and organizational cultures takes time. Saying that Toyota "invented" Lean is not exactly accurate, as Toyota learned from and was inspired by many others, such as the writings of Henry Ford, the nineteenth-century Scottish self-help author Samuel Smiles, and the restocking practices of American supermarkets.[12] Toyota was also heavily influenced by the visits of Dr. W. Edwards Deming, as the president of Toyota said in 1991, "There is not a day I don't think about what Dr. Deming meant to us. Deming is the core of our management."[13]

Toyota took some aspects of the Ford approach, but created its own management system, using and inventing methods that fit its needs and situation. In 1945, Toyota set out to improve quality, while improving productivity and reducing costs, as the company was very cash poor and had a small Japanese market in which to sell cars. Crisis and hardship forced Toyota to be creative and innovative; it did not set out to create a production system per se. Toyota was focused on improving its business, and that turned into a management system that became the way they conduct business every day, as opposed to being a short-term program. It is critical for hospitals to follow Toyota's model of adapting what you learn from others and developing methods that solve the problems in your organization, without blindly copying the practices of factories or other hospitals. Lean is a new way of thinking and not just a simple to-do list of tools to implement.

> The CEO of Virginia Mason Medical Center, Gary Kaplan, MD, FACP, FACMPE, FACPE, says, "If your leaders think this is just another improvement method, a program or initiative, you'll never achieve the long term success this management method offers. This is not something you do in addition to other work; it is how we work. The guiding principle of 'patient first' known and committed to by everyone in the organization provides long term thinking…perfection is a pursuit not a finish line. Knowing we're getting closer every day is what matters and what the executives need to recognize and reward."[14]

Origins of the Term *Lean*

While the concepts came to us via Toyota, the term *Lean* is credited to John Krafcik, part of the research team at the International Motor Vehicle Program[15] at the Massachusetts Institute of Technology (MIT). That team, led by James P. Womack, Daniel T. Jones, and Daniel Roos, studied the global auto industry in the late 1980s, looking for practices that led to Japanese success. Through their research, they disproved their hypothesis that all Japanese automakers were doing things differently—it was primarily Toyota. The term *Lean* was coined to describe a system that managed to get by with half of just about everything—physical space, labor effort, capital investment, and inventory—and far fewer than half the defects and safety incidents. The term described the results, but the word has also entered the language as a description of the method. In recent years, Toyota has acknowledged that the word Lean is basically a synonym for the term they prefer, the Toyota Production System.[16] If people in your organization react negatively to the word *lean*, that invites a conversation about what the Lean methodology really is, or it creates an opportunity to give it your own label, such as "loving care" or "the ThedaCare Improvement System."

The early spread of Lean started in the auto industry, where it was easy to see the direct applicability of the Toyota method and, more important, there was a strong recognition of the need to improve. Western automakers typically focused on copying tools and practices that could easily be seen with the naked eye, such as *kanban* cards (a method for moving parts to assembly lines), as discussed in Chapter 6. Even though Toyota started sharing its tools through publications and open tours (even allowing competitors to visit its factories), the unseen management system or "the soul" of Toyota was (and still is) harder to copy or emulate.[17] The other automakers found it more difficult to challenge their existing management systems and thought processes; it was easier to adopt a tool like *kanban* or 5S and to say "we are doing Lean" than it was to fully adopt the Toyota model. Hospitals that say they are doing Lean should reflect on whether they are using an occasional Lean method or project or if they are embracing the holistic management system and culture of Lean.

I often get asked, "How many hospitals are implementing Lean?" That's a difficult question to answer for a number of reasons. First, there's not public reporting about the use of Lean methods. Secondly, there is wide variation in what it means for an organization to be "using Lean"; they could be using a tool like 5S in a few departments, or they could be aiming to transform their culture and leadership system. Or, a health system might be somewhere in between, using a broader set of Lean practices, training many people, and running many Rapid Improvement Events (RIEs). Practicing Lean or choosing to do so should be based on problems you need to solve rather than doing something because it is popular.

Lean Is Proven to Work outside Automotive Factories

Lean eventually spread beyond the automotive industry, as other manufacturing sectors adopted the methods in their factories. Manufacturers also began to understand that Lean was not just a factory system; it was also a business system, incorporating all aspects of bringing a product to market, including design, supplier management, production, and sales. For example, the Toyota Product Development System[18] was renowned for bringing new cars to market twice as fast as their U.S. competitors (half the time, indeed "Lean" by the MIT definition). In recent years, "Lean Startup" concepts have helped with the development of new products and services in startups and large companies, alike.[19]

Because every type of organization—including health systems—should be concerned with issues such as safety, cash flow, customer satisfaction, and quality, Lean methods and philosophies are being used, at least to some extent, at some banks, schools, retailers, software companies, airlines, government agencies, and the military, as well as the dominant coffee sellers in the United States (Starbucks)[20] and Canada (Tim Hortons)[21]. In non-profit settings, Toyota staff and leaders helped the New York City Food Bank's staff and leaders improve their operations and helped them provide meals to more people in the aftermath of Hurricane Sandy.[22]

Toyota University, in California, has coached some surprising students, including the Los Angeles Police Department (LAPD), in problem-solving methods that come from the factory floor. This has helped the LAPD manage its jails more effectively. A Toyota coach said, after the training classes, "What I saw was a commonality in human behavior, a commonality in some of the issues and challenges that every company faces."[23] We all have problems to solve, and we are all looking for better ways to lead and manage employees.

Lean Is Helping Hospitals Improve

It is difficult to pinpoint exactly when hospitals started looking outside the industry for Lean ideas. Some hospitals started experimenting with Lean methods in the 1990s, in some cases with help from Michigan automakers. Seattle Children's Hospital can trace its Lean journey to early discussions in 1996 with consultant Joan Wellman, who had previously worked with Boeing.[24] In 2001, *USA Today* reported on a study conducted by the Robert Wood Johnson Foundation that looked across hospitals for leaders, those who did things dramatically differently from other hospitals. Foundation executive vice president Lewis Sandy said, "We want to see a Toyota in health care. That's been one of the barriers in health care. No one can point to a health system and say 'That's how it ought to be done.'"[25] The motivation was clear that hospitals had to look beyond their peers to find solutions to widespread systemic problems.

Is there "a Toyota of healthcare" today? Is there a hospital with half the cost and half the defects of other hospitals? Some have made significant progress in this direction, and there are now many examples of the positive impact Lean is having in hospitals throughout the world. As a sample, Lean methods have resulted in the following improvements:

Safety and Quality

- Reduced central-line-associated bloodstream infections by 76%, reducing patient deaths from such infections by 95% and saving $1 million—*Allegheny Hospital, Pennsylvania*[26]
- Reduced hospital-acquired infections, saving 57 lives, reducing intensive care unit (ICU) length of stay, and reducing costs by over $5 million over two years —*University of Pennsylvania Medical Center*[27]
- Reduced readmission rates for chronic obstructive pulmonary disease (COPD) patients by 48%—*UPMC St. Margaret Hospital, Pennsylvania*[28]
- Reduced falls by 22%, reducing costs by more than $500,000—*Hanover Regional Medical Center, North Carolina*[29]
- Reduced pressure ulcers by 56% in three pilot areas over two years, with a 30% decrease system-wide—*BJC Healthcare, Missouri*[30]
- Avoided 87 readmissions for congestive heart failure in 12 months across four hospitals, saving $830,000—*Four hospitals in California*[31]
- Reduced sepsis mortality from 24% to 9%, reducing the average cost per case from $15,772 to $12,771—*Presence Health, Illinois*[32]

Waiting Times and Length of Stay

- Reduced patient waiting time for non-emergent orthopedic surgery from 14 weeks to 31 hours (from first call to surgery); improved inpatient satisfaction scores from 68% "very satisfied" to 90%—*ThedaCare, Wisconsin*[33]
- Reduced emergency patient length of stay by 29% and avoided $1.25 million in new emergency department (ED) construction—*Avera McKennan, South Dakota*[34]
- Reduced waiting times for screening colonoscopies from six weeks to less than 24 hours while reducing cost per patient by 9.5%—*Palo Alto Medical Foundation, California*[35]

■ Increased the percentage of atrial fibrillation patients treated within 40 days from 11% to 94% *HealthEast, Minnesota*[36]

Flow

■ Reduced turnaround time for clinical laboratory results by 60% in 2004 without adding head count or new instrumentation; further reduced times by another 33% from 2008 to 2010—*Alegent Health, Nebraska*[37,38]

■ Reduced instrument decontamination and sterilization cycle time by 54% while improving productivity by 16%—*Kingston General Hospital, Ontario*[39]

■ Reduced late surgery starts from 50% to 30%, reduced rescheduled procedures from 20% to 4.4%, while increasing cases per month from 329 to 351—*New York City Health and Hospitals Corporation*[40]

■ Reduced operating room (OR) turnover time from 60 minutes to 30 minutes, increased utilization rates from 25% to 65%, and achieved 100% on-time starts in a pilot area—*Guangdong Provincial Hospital of Traditional Chinese Medicine, China*[41]

Satisfaction

■ Improved patient/family satisfaction rates in the Neonatal Intensive-Care Unit (NICU) from 45th percentile to 99th percentile—*Franciscan St. Francis, Indianapolis*[42]

■ Improved physician satisfaction from 63rd percentile to 87th, being highest rated in overall care among 170 California medical groups for two consecutive years—*Sutter Gould Medical Foundation, California*[43,44]

■ Improved ED patient satisfaction from 5th percentile to 98th percentile in just four months (through door-to-doc times falling from 67 to 18 minutes)—*Sumner Regional Medical Center, Tennessee*[45]

Financial

■ Bottom-line benefit of almost $200 million over seven years, while achieving "the lowest observed-to-expected mortality among the academic health center members of the University Health system Consortium in 2011" and avoiding layoffs—*Denver Health, Colorado*[46]

■ Avoidance of $180 million in capital spending through Lean improvements—*Seattle Children's Hospital, Washington*[47]

■ Improved operating margin by 44%, from 1.70% in fiscal year 2011 to 3.06% in fiscal year 2014—*HealthEast, Minnesota*[48]

Problems in Healthcare

Before taking a deeper look at this approach, let us begin by practicing a good Lean habit—starting by defining the problems that hospitals and health systems are trying to solve. There are many long-standing problems that hospitals face, a list too long to present here. Lean is not about fixing any one major problem within healthcare; it is about solving the critical few strategic issues, along with the hundreds or thousands of little problems that plague hospitals each day. Some systemic problems in our health systems are important, but probably outside the scope of Lean, such as dysfunctions in insurance or payer models. Rather than just debating political solutions, we can take action and improve now, regardless of the payer system in our country. We can improve the delivery of healthcare, if we start learning and start taking action today.

Do you have any of these problems in your hospital?

- Deliveries of supplies delayed because of improper ordering
- Mix-ups in getting supplies
- Articles returned by other departments because they were not made correctly
- Employee difficulty in handling new-type equipment
- Limited storage space (linens and supplies) not properly used
- Safety equipment not being used
- Minor injuries or illnesses not reported
- Correct procedures not followed
- Employees leaving to go to other hospitals
- Employees passing the buck—let the other person do it

Are these modern hospital problems? Yes, but these were also problems in 1944, as documented by the training materials for hospitals provided by the U.S. Training Within Industry (TWI) Program.[49] TWI was halted after World War II ended, so the methods disappeared from hospitals, as well as factories, but became very influential to Toyota and the development of Lean.[50]

Hospitals everywhere, even across different countries, tend to have the same problems because they were often designed from the same template and are managed the same way. Physical layouts share similar characteristics, possibly given to them by architects with a poor understanding of the details of the hospital's work. Processes were often developed using the same paradigms, or they were just allowed to evolve without structure. Copying other hospitals and their "best practices" might bring incremental (or temporary) improvements, but we can use Lean concepts to drive more dramatic (and more sustainable) improvements by looking at our own processes and management approach in a new way, engaging our own employees to identify waste and develop their own solutions. In the Lean mindset, we have to be open in our recognition of problems as the first stage of improvement.

When asked what is needed for improvement, hospital employees and managers often answer, "We need more money, more space, and more people!," something that budgets often don't allow. Even if adding people were guaranteed to help, we live in a world of finite resources, including shortages of nurses, medical technologists, and other key clinical professionals, in some locales. If we cannot afford more resources, working harder is not usually an option. Lean thinkers do not blame a lack of hard work for problems at their hospital. We have to improve the system, and sometimes that means that people expend less effort because their work is easier, which leads to improved outcomes for all.

The late Michel Tétrault, MD, was the CEO of St. Boniface General Hospital (Winnipeg, Manitoba) and a great Lean leader. In 2010, he commented about three things that kept him up at night. They were

1. "Being able to find an adequate workforce, to get the people we need to serve all the patients that come to our door" because of an aging population and all of the retirements from the workplace.
2. "The sustainability gap of the cost of health care, and this is a worldwide phenomenon. It's neither only [an] American nor [a] Canadian [problem]. How do we address that?"
3. "Our patients, our communities, our funders, whether they be private funders or public funders, are [increasingly] scrutinizing how safe and reliable our health care actually is and how good our outcomes are."

Lean helps address all of these concerns. As Tétrault said, "One way or another, we have to find a way to demonstrate that we're providing better value, that we're providing safer, more reliable health care with better outcomes at a reasonable cost."[51]

Price Pressures and Cost Challenges

Healthcare costs are increasing rapidly, as U.S. healthcare insurance costs are increasing at a rate higher than inflation. As of 2012, healthcare spending consumes 17.9% of the United States' gross domestic product (GDP), reaching levels of over $2.8 trillion per year.[52] Per-capita spending in the United States is the highest in the world and is much higher than comparable industrialized countries. Even with that high spending, too many patients are harmed by preventable medical errors, and the United States lags in many key quality measures. The high spending does bring a great deal of innovation and technology, which can improve care and save lives, but the cost increases are not sustainable.

In an attempt to rein in higher spending, governments or private payers often propose cutting reimbursement rates. In doing so, they are changing the price paid but not the underlying costs in the system. Price cuts by payers might also, unfortunately, encourage traditional, dysfunctional cost cutting by healthcare organizations, in which layoffs and the closure of units and elimination of services might harm quality or reduce the level of care provided to a community. Lower prices without corresponding cost reductions will hurt hospital margins, which can slow future investment or jeopardize a hospital's financial future, unless a health system is able to reduce costs by using Lean as an alternative method.

In some countries, lower government budgets mean less care and fewer patients being served, unless the actual efficiency of care delivery is improved. Rather than reducing spending by slashing payments or rationing care, Lean methods enable us to reduce the actual cost of providing care, allowing us to provide more service and care for our communities. A hospital that saves tens of millions of dollars by using Lean methods to avoid costly expansion projects is a hospital that costs society less, while providing the same levels of care, if not more care to more people, with better quality.

Cutting prices also risks driving some physicians out of the market for some patients, as evidenced by the increasing, yet currently small, number of American doctors who opt out of the Medicare and Medicaid systems or stop taking on new patients under those programs.[53] Unilaterally slashing prices to hospitals or providers is, unfortunately, more reminiscent of the supplier management practices of the Big Three automakers, who traditionally demanded annual price reductions from their suppliers, squeezing many of these suppliers to the point of bankruptcy or forcing them to reduce quality.

In comparison, the Lean approach, as demonstrated by Toyota, is more of a partnership between customer and supplier working together to identify true cost savings, often achieved through quality improvement. These cost savings are shared, benefiting both parties, as Toyota and its suppliers operate in an atmosphere of trust and long-term relationships. In healthcare, payers and providers should strive to have relationships more like Toyota and its suppliers, rather than squeezing their suppliers—the hospitals, clinics, or physicians. In some American states and Puerto Rico, health insurance companies or employers are working directly with hospitals on Lean improvement efforts, sharing the benefits.[54]

In the Lean approach, companies are taught that prices are set by the market and that a primary way to improve one's profit margin is to reduce your own controllable costs. Healthcare is often a strange and highly regulated "market," but this is still a useful concept. This thinking flies in the face of older "cost-plus" thinking, by which we look first at our own costs and set prices based on a desired profit margin. The reality is that most companies, whether manufacturers or hospitals, do not have market power to set prices as they wish. Many health systems have focused on growth and increasing market share, through acquisitions to get better price leverage against payers (who are also merging and trying to gain leverage by getting larger).

Larger health systems still have big opportunities to reduce costs by improving flow and improving quality. Or they can find ways to add more value to their services, so that the market might increase or at least maintain what it is willing to pay. No matter how dysfunctional healthcare markets might be, we should focus less on the unfairness of what is paid to us and more on what we have control over—our costs. One study estimated that 13% of a hospital's costs are due to "inefficient practices within control of the hospital,"[55] while other estimates were closer to 20%.[56]

Employee Shortages

Hospitals in some locations suffer from widespread employee shortages, particularly for nurses, pharmacists, and medical technologists. In the United States, nursing vacancy rates averaged 8.1% as of 2008, and the shortage was expected to grow to 260,000 registered nurses by 2015.[57] In 2010, 34% of hospitals reported unfilled pharmacist positions.[58] In situations like these, hospitals are often forced to hire costly temporary agency or "traveler" staff, further cutting margins. This is also a problem in the United Kingdom, where the National Health Service (NHS) trusts in England spend over £1 billion a year on agency nurses, a number that continues to grow.[59] If agency nurses cannot be found (or paid for), hospitals are sometimes forced to shut down units, reducing the extent of care they can provide to their community and the amount of revenue received by the hospital.

Nursing shortages can lead to overworked conditions that harm quality, patient and staff safety, and employee morale. Highlighting the connections among employees, patients, and quality, studies show that overworked, tired, or stressed employees are more likely to make mistakes that could harm patients.[60] Understaffed pharmacies, imaging departments, and laboratories might have slower response times, which could delay care or put patients at risk. Physicians who are unhappy with poor service from staff or ancillary departments might react by moving their patients to a competing hospital, thus exacerbating the revenue problem.

Quality and Patient Safety

While there are differences in the healthcare systems across different countries, there are some universal problems that affect patients: preventable errors that lead to injury and death. It is imperative that we examine and understand the details of how healthcare is delivered, implementing processes that support safe, efficient, high-quality care. Lean provides a great way to accomplish this.

Other than focusing on some high-profile incidents, the media often overlook the quality problems with the delivery of care in the United States. Many Americans know the numbers of the uninsured—approximately 41 million, even with more receiving coverage under the Patient Protection and Affordable Care Act of 2010, or "ObamaCare."[61] Far fewer know the estimates of how many patients die as the result of preventable medical errors each year (different studies place the number anywhere between 44,000 and 440,000) and from preventable infections (estimated at about 100,000).[62,63,64]

Quality and patient safety are not concerns just in the United States. The Canadian Institute for Health Information estimated that as many as 24,000 Canadians die each year due to medical errors, such as surgical errors, medication errors, and hospital-acquired infections, which is a similar per-capita rate as the United States. The Canadian Auditor General estimated that one in nine hospitalized patients will acquire an infection during a stay.[65] In the United Kingdom, the Royal College of Physicians estimated that medical errors contribute to the deaths of almost 70,000 patients per year, and Britain's most senior doctor warned that the risk of dying from a preventable hospital error is one in 300, a similar risk as in the United States.[66] It is estimated that 850,000 British patients are the victims of errors that lead to permanent or moderate injury in 200,000 of those cases. The NHS estimates that half of the errors are preventable, again about the same as U.S. estimates.[67,68] Other countries face the same challenge.

In comparison, with advances and systemic improvements in aviation safety, passengers in the general public take it for granted that they will arrive safely at their destination; we should hope for similar advances in healthcare so patients can take it for granted that they will not be harmed in hospitals. In fact, in recent years, hospitals are learning safety and quality lessons from commercial aviation, such as the use of checklists and "crew resource management."[69] Some patients blindly trust the healthcare system, assuming they will receive perfect care each time. Lean methods can help us work toward making that goal a reality.

Good Quality Costs Less

As in other industries, many in healthcare have assumed there is an inherent trade-off between cost and quality; they think better quality must automatically cost more. Patients and payers often make this same assumption. It is true that some methods for improving the quality of patient outcomes might cost more, such as new technologies, treatments, or medicines. Hospitals do have many opportunities, however, to improve the quality of healthcare delivery methods and processes in a way that also reduces costs. Across all U.S. hospitals, there is a large cost-saving opportunity that results from preventing errors and improving quality. For example, preventable adverse events from medication errors are estimated to cost health systems $4 billion per year.[70] Again, a similar opportunity exists around the world.

David Fillingham, former CEO of Royal Bolton Hospital NHS Foundation Trust in the United Kingdom, has said, quite simply, "Good quality costs less."[71] This was proven to be true as a result of Bolton's Lean improvements; the hospital reduced trauma mortality by 36% and reduced a patient's average length of stay by 33%. ThedaCare documented similar results in cardiac surgery; mortality fell from 4% to nearly zero (11 lives saved per year), with a length-of-stay reduction from 6.3 to 4.9 days, and 22% lower cost.[72] It might sound too good to be true, but many hospitals are proving that you can simultaneously improve quality, access, and cost.

Lean teaches us to see quality improvement as a means to cost reductions, a better approach than focusing directly and solely on costs. Bill Douglas, chief financial officer at Riverside Medical Center (Kankakee, Illinois), summed it up as the hospital began its first Lean project by saying, "Lean is a quality initiative. It isn't a cost-cutting initiative. But the end result is, if you improve quality your costs will go down. If you focus on patient quality and safety, you just can't go wrong. If you do the right thing with regard to quality, the costs will take care of themselves."[73] Riverside's laboratory, for example, had previously focused primarily on cost, using layoffs and other traditional cost-cutting methods, but the lab's quality of service did not improve. Through their initial Lean efforts, reducing errors and improving flow led to getting test results to physicians 37% to 46% faster, while improving labor productivity.[74] The lab's improved service helped reduce length of stay in the ED, which allowed Riverside to postpone a $2 million expansion.[75] Riverside has since spread Lean and continuous improvement to many areas including pharmacy, inpatient care, and primary care clinics, as discussed more in Chapter 12.

Interconnected Benefits

Many of the goals and benefits of Lean are interconnected, as illustrated in Figure 1.1. Lean organizations view cost and financial performance as the end result of doing everything else well.

Improved employee engagement, through the *kaizen* style of continuous improvement, can lead to better safety and outcomes, patient satisfaction, and lower cost in direct and indirect ways. For example, higher employee engagement can reduce voluntary turnover rates, which can improve quality while reducing the cost of hiring and on-boarding new staff. Improved patient satisfaction and quality can lead to more patients choosing the health system (given that data are publicly available), which can improve the bottom line. Reducing costs can allow a health system to offer lower prices, which can lead to higher volumes as, for example, American employers start to steer employees to get care in "center of excellence" sites that have higher quality and lower cost.

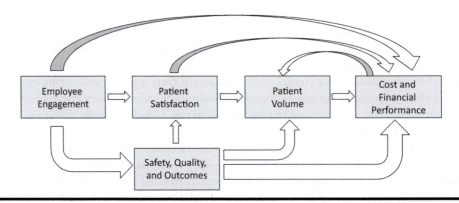

Figure 1.1 Connections between different goals and measures.

Again, Lean is about solving problems that matter and improving performance; problems that matter to patients, to staff, to physicians, to payers, and to healthcare organizations.

A Snapshot of Department Success: Laboratory, Children's Health Dallas

Improvements made in the laboratory at Children's Health, formerly Children's Medical Center (Dallas, Texas), help illustrate how Lean can provide benefits to all stakeholders—patients, employees, physicians, and the hospital itself. The lab's leadership team was first exposed to Lean in August 2006 when they saw a presentation by Seattle Children's Hospital, an early adopter of these methods in healthcare. The lab had previously been studying system dynamics through Peter Senge's seminal work *The Fifth Discipline* and had high-level goals of becoming a "learning organization."[76] Lean provided a means for operationalizing this philosophy in a practical way, according to Jim Adams, the senior director for lab operations from 2005 to 2011.

Prior to Lean, benchmarking data seemed to confirm the view that the lab was good, if not above average. For example, the lab reported 90% of stat test results within industry-accepted time limits. However, an initial assessment by outside Lean consultants in November 2006 helped Adams realize that the lab had actually long been experiencing, in his terms, "delusional excellence" because the benchmarked labs had the same waste built into their own physical layouts and processes; therefore, they had similar results. Instead of feeling good about exceeding benchmarks, the lab started looking at their true potential—to be the best lab they could possibly be for their patients.

The consultant's analysis, later repeated by medical technologists as they learned to observe and better understand their own work, showed that 70% to 94% of typical turnaround time performance was time when the specimen was sitting and waiting. The new challenge became minimizing that waiting time. Instead of thinking that benchmarks showed they did not need to improve, the team learned they had large opportunities to reduce turnaround times by 50% or more, providing better service to patients, ordering physicians and departments that relied on accurate and timely test results.

A formal Lean project was initiated in March 2007, which the author led. In contrast to the common week-long Lean events that are used in many hospitals (more on this in Chapter 12), a team was formed to work on a 12-week "Lean transformation" project that focused initially on the end-to-end flow of clinical lab testing. This team consisted of four medical technologists and two lab assistants from various parts of the department. This group was dedicated full time to the improvement and redesign efforts, learning deeply about Lean principles, analyzing their current state, and working with the larger group of colleagues to transform both the physical space and their processes in an integrated way.

As another early step, the lab's leadership initiated discussions with internal customers and learned that particular tests were deemed crucial by the ED for the sake of prompt diagnosis and improved patient flow. They were sometimes surprised to learn that tests the lab thought not to be time-critical were, in fact, considered to be so by the ED. It became more important to the lab to improve the relationships with those who ordered tests and used test results—a key part of the customer- and patient-focused Lean approach. With this better customer understanding, success would be defined by their customers' needs rather than being defined within the lab and their assumptions.

In another example of better understanding customer needs, the lab had been having difficulty meeting turnaround times for complete blood count (CBC) tests with what's called a "manual diff." The lab was "killing ourselves" trying to improve turnaround time performance. The ED told the lab that the only urgent part of the result was the basic CBC, not the more time-consuming manual diff counts. As the ED explained, "We don't need that right away; we can wait on the manual," so the lab focused their improvement energy on areas that would more directly benefit their customers.

The full-time project team learned and used the analysis methods outlined in Chapter 4 to trace the flow of testing work from specimen collection through the reporting of test results. As in most hospital situations, the flow moved across multiple roles in many different departments. The team focused on improving the overall flow rather than looking merely to optimize their own departmental definition of success.

While there was a longer-term initiative to fully redesign and reconstruct the physical layout of the laboratory (an effort not fully implemented until late 2010), the lab's leadership team, including Dr. Beverly Rogers, then the chief pathologist, helped everyone understand that Lean was not a one-time project. Rather, it would become a new management system and a new way of life. Instead of putting all of their hopes on the major redesign, the lab started to take action to make immediate improvements.

Steps were taken to improve specimen flow through small, incremental changes. The blood gas analyzers, used for critically time-sensitive tests, were moved to be much closer to the tube station, where specimens arrived. This reduced average turnaround times for those tests from 20 minutes to about 5 minutes. The "front end" of the process (the nonclinical area where specimens were received, labeled, and prepped) was reconfigured. Instead of two separate work areas about 25 feet apart (a distance that encouraged batching and time delays), the preanalytical area was set up as four identical, separate "flow benches" where one person could do all of the work on a single specimen without the extra movement and delay. This reduced the average turnaround time for chemistry and hematology tests by 43%.

As the team observed and even videotaped their colleagues in the lab, they helped identify waste (as described more fully in Chapter 3) and took initial countermeasures that could reduce wasted walking and motion in the lab. The lab implemented basic methods including 5S and *kanban* (see Chapter 6) to help ensure that supplies and test reagents were always available at the right locations in the right quantities, reducing the amount of time that highly trained technologists spent hunting and gathering. In the first year of the *kanban* system (a system for planning and restocking inventory and supplies), the lab reduced spending by $80,000. As staff productivity improved, thanks to the waste reduction efforts and new "standardized work," as discussed in Chapter 5, the lab was able to reduce labor costs by $147,000 in the first year, through attrition and reduced overtime, without laying anybody off.

Adams and Dr. Rogers also continued the shift toward a Lean culture, educating all staff members about Lean principles, involving them in the improvement work, and continuing group book discussions on titles like *The Toyota Way*. This talk of Lean culture, such as focusing on processes and systems instead of blaming individuals for problems, was invigorated by a number of management practices, which are described more fully in Chapter 11.

Within the lab, daily 10-minute stand-up meetings were held to review performance measures, enabling staff members to talk about their ideas for improving the process. These ideas were tracked on a simple bulletin board; an approach that was far more visual and more interactive than their old suggestion box. As new ideas were implemented, regardless of how small, recognition was given through the documentation and posting of the changes on a "*kaizen* wall of fame," which created positive reinforcement that led to more *kaizen*, or continuous improvement, as described more in Chapter 11.

Denver Health (Colorado) has embraced Lean and continuous improvement, first under CEO Patricia Gabow, MD, and continuing under their new CEO, Art Gonzalez. Gonzalez said, "Essentially, we use lean to apply the scientific method to the practice of process improvement. That means we do a little bit here and there and it all adds up to significant improvements." Elizabeth Fingado, their director of Lean systems improvement, says they look for areas where the hospital's costs are higher than their reimbursement rates. She explains, "We're teaching every individual unit how to approach their biggest opportunities for improvement. So, if we have a priority this year to decrease costs by 2%, we will allow each unit to do it in their own way. We give them the tools to do it and teach them ways of thinking about how to do it in a way that makes sense in their area. Then they can deploy lean locally. If we do that throughout the hospital, we can find savings across every unit."[77]

Managers from different areas now meet for a daily huddle to review the hospital's patient census, along with the status of key areas, including staffing levels. Kenny Carr, vice president of clinical and support services, says the huddles "help gel the overall Lean communication together. It's been phenomenal." Leaders have visited from other departments, and that huddle, along with the visual status board, is being adopted in areas including the emergency department, operating rooms, and pharmacy, says Carr.[78]

Adams reflected on their experience, saying "There was a growing recognition among lab users in the hospital that the lab was focused on understanding and meeting their particular needs. The nurses and physicians started working with the lab staff in a more respectful, collegial way. We felt more a part of the team caring for the patient."

As the clinical lab was implementing Lean practices and management methods, leaders and team members introduced these approaches and mindsets to other parts of the lab, such as microbiology, blood bank, and anatomic pathology. The histology department created a new process layout with improved co-location of sequential steps, which improved flow and reduced turnaround times. "There was no flow to start," says Elma Cortinas, anatomic pathology lab manager, but with the new layout, turnaround times for gastrointestinal (GI) specimens were reduced dramatically.

The positive impact of the cultural transformation was illustrated by the results of a staff engagement survey, comparing "pre-Lean" numbers to 12 months after the Lean education and improvement efforts started. As shown in Table 1.1, scores increased in key questions (on a 1-to-5 scale, with 5 being highest). Every single question on the engagement survey showed an improvement, highlighting the benefits of a Lean environment.

As an additional sign of meaningful culture change, two of the lab's Lean team members accepted lab supervisor positions after repeatedly turning down the opportunity in previous years. They each took on the role because the lab's leadership had successfully redefined the role of a supervisor from being a directive "boss" or "cop" to being a coach and teacher, working with team members to make patient-focused improvements that created a better workplace. Adams commented, "Both have thrived and are effective as supervisors in the Lean culture."[79]

Even as the major reconstruction project has been completed, the lab sees Lean as its culture and a key part of its ongoing improvement efforts. It is not "complete," as this improvement is never ending. After years of planning and waiting, the new clinical "core lab" layout was finally implemented in late 2010, as a major step function improvement. Evidence of this mindset and

Table 1.1   Improvement in Employee Engagement Scores at Children's Health Dallas

	Before Lean	12 Months after Starting
3. I have the opportunity to do what I do best every day.	3.11	3.92
8. I feel free to make suggestions for improvement.	2.84	3.48
10. I feel secure in my job.	2.32	3.42
13. Stress at work is manageable.	2.43	3.23
17. I am satisfied with the lab as a place to work.	2.51	3.43
18. I would recommend my work area as a good place to work to others.	2.38	3.46
Grand average of all questions	2.96	3.69

culture shift includes the medical technologists quickly coming up with ideas for tweaking that new layout after they started working in it. Traditional cultures might not look for input, leaving well enough alone with the new design. Instead, the Children's Health lab leaders listened and allowed staff members to experiment and make changes to the standardized work and layout based on data and their firsthand experiences.

As lab leaders reflected on their first years of Lean, lessons learned included ensuring that consistent, continuous education about Lean principles and methods takes place, especially in roles with traditionally high turnover; staff members know how key performance measures, such as turnaround time, are aligned with end patient needs—that this is about improving care, not just hitting numbers; and people do not assume that methods like 5S and standardized work are meant to be controlling and that managers constantly reinforce the importance of staff engagement in continuously improving these standards.

As of 2015, the *kaizen* wall of fame is still active, as staff are being engaged in continuous improvement throughout the lab. "We still have a good culture of continuous improvement, as we help new staff realize they have a voice," says Amy Sigman, the current lab director. She adds that examples of improvements that are used in new employee orientation illustrate that "anything small" is an idea worthy of mentioning in huddles.

The *kanban* system is still active as the method for ordering supplies, which helps them "not run out of chemicals," says Sigman. Updated standardized work documents and daily assignments of individuals to certain roles are still posted daily in the core lab. A 5S holding area is still used for staff to place items that are no longer needed, and "5S sweep" events are held quarterly to give special attention to ongoing 5S improvements.

After eight years of practicing Lean, "the spirit is still there," says Carr. If "leaders all decided tomorrow to stop doing Lean," he guesses that the lab staff would continue with Lean practices because it has helped them better serve their patients while improving quality.

Carr reflected further on their progress, saying:

> Healthcare has changed so much in the past five years, especially pediatric medicine. Because we adopted Lean, we were more prepared to take on challenges associated with change. We've been able to address things and improve earlier compared to others.
>
> We've asked hard questions up front, focused on performance metrics and asked, 'What are our staff doing that adds value to the overall patient experience?' Looking

at it through that lens bought up some hard questions about how to be efficient, rather than just saying 'you need to do more.' When we look at the process, we realize that just because we've done it that way doesn't mean we need to keep doing it that way.

Now, physicians never say they have a problem with the lab, and there's a lot of pride in that. It's nice to step back and think about how far we've come. We've done a lot and continue to improve on that journey we started.

While Children's Health was named "Medical Lab of the Year 2009" by a major trade publication,[80] it is the culture change and the willingness to never be satisfied and to continue learning that makes it more likely to again be a lab of the year in the future.

From Departmental to Hospital- and System-Wide Success

Lean is not just a methodology that can impact individual departments. Lean can become part of the hospital's core strategy and day-to-day operating approach, as illustrated by examples including ThedaCare, Virginia Mason Medical Center, Seattle Children's Hospital, and Denver Health.

The story of Avera McKennan Hospital and University Health Center (Sioux Falls, South Dakota) is highlighted in Chapter 12, as their initial Lean projects, which also started in their laboratory in 2004, eventually became a management system and daily improvement methodology for the entire hospital and have started spreading through the broader Avera system.

At Avera McKennan, Lean methods are now taught to all employees in all departments, and their Excellence in Service and Process program has become a cornerstone of the hospital's strategy and vision. Their goals are not timid, as they state, "Through service and process excellence, Avera McKennan will lead the nation in high quality, affordable health care."

The leadership and passion started with Fred Slunecka, formerly the regional president of Avera McKennan Hospital and now the chief operating officer of Avera Health, and his people throughout the facility. To Slunecka, it is "a moral imperative" to streamline processes and eliminate waste, as "30–40% of all health care is waste—pure and simple." The motivation for improvement came from a realization that government reimbursement was increasing 2%–3% a year, while the hospital's costs were increasing 5% a year. "We absolutely have got to do a better job," said Slunecka, and the hospital set out to do just that. Even with the talk of financial needs and motivations, the patient is at the center of their improvements. "The goal is a seamless patient experience, marked by great service, quality care and efficiency," says Kathy Maass, their director of process excellence. "Lean is about examining the patient care process step by step and redesigning it around the patient to eliminate waste. Employees become involved in the solution at the most grass-roots level," Slunecka said.

This is the potential of Lean hospitals: strategically redesigning the physical space and processes that provide patient care, while engaging all healthcare professionals and leaders in neverending continuous improvement.

Reflecting further in 2015, Slunecka says,

> After over a decade of trial and error, American healthcare organizations are finally understanding the need to adopt Lean principles. It is only through rigorous attention to work redesign and eliminating variation that we can provide the safe and reliable care that our patients deserve.

I believe that, for the last decade, most healthcare organizations viewed Lean as a tool without a major purpose. Today's focus on value requires that organizations embrace Lean to assure our patients receive what they deserve: safe and highly reliable patient care.

The historically slow adoption of Lean has probably been due to the amount of time and energy needed to change a single process in a single organization. The juice, as we say, was not often worth the squeeze. Today, the largest organizations are developing highly reliable practices and then disseminating them across all their many hospitals. Now the juice is worth the squeeze. The rapid development of 'service lines' is helping to assure that practices are quickly disseminated.

When our revenues were based on volume, quality and value took a back seat. As we confront 'star ratings' and payment penalties we are now focused on safety and quality. I believe that can only enhance the adoption of Lean over the longer term."[81]

Conclusion

Hospitals and their processes are full of waste and inefficiency through no fault of the talented, caring, and hardworking people who work there. The problems that hospitals face could be discouraging—unless we also had a proven methodology for driving sustainable quality and process improvement. That could be overwhelming if we did not have others to learn from and to model our own improvement after—both Toyota and our hospital colleagues who are blazing the Lean trail.

Lean can be described in a simple way: Lean is working. In one way, Lean is about looking at how we do our work and figuring out ways to improve how that work is done. Lean is about improving quality and productivity. Lean is also about learning to fix problems permanently instead of hiding them or working around them.

In another sense, Lean is proving to be an effective methodology for improving patient safety, quality, and cost, while preventing delays and improving employee satisfaction. It can be done. Lean is working; it is effective. Lean helps save money for hospitals, while creating opportunities for growth and increased revenue. Lean methods can benefit everyone involved in hospitals. Understanding Lean principles is just a starting point. The real challenge is finding the leadership necessary to implement these strategies and to transform the way your hospital provides care.

Virginia Mason's Kaplan says, "If you want this to last, to sustain and not just be seen as another management program or initiative, it has to be the way you work, the way you do everything. Culture change comes from the CEO's commitment to work differently and to model a long-term commitment to 'better never stops.'"[82]

Those of us who have seen leaders successfully use Lean in many hospitals realize this is not an academic exercise or easy. Lean methods allow us to improve how hospitals are managed today. Lean methods let us improve quality now. But, Lean requires vision, leadership, and persistence. We have scattered instances of Lean success and significant results in hospitals throughout the world. As the science fiction author William Gibson wrote, "The future is already here—it's just not very evenly distributed."[83]

Lean Lessons

■ Lean methods started in factories but have proven successful in many functions in many industries, including healthcare.

- Quality improvements are a means to cost reductions.
- Productivity improvements and cost savings can be accomplished in ways other than layoffs or head count reductions.
- Lean is focused on patient safety, quality of care, and improved service, not just efficiency, cost, and productivity.
- Improving the system, rather than working harder, is the key to Lean improvements.
- To make major changes, you often have to start with smaller steps.
- Hospitals cannot just copy others; they need to think through their own improvements after learning Lean concepts.

Points for Group Discussion

- Are rising healthcare costs having an impact on your hospital's quality of care?
- How can better quality cost less?
- How does personal satisfaction on the job have an impact on productivity and quality?
- What are the biggest problems your department faces? Your hospital? Your health system?
- Why does a hospital typically have departmental silos?
- Are there situations in which your departments or processes are not as patient focused as they could be?
- Why have other improvement methodologies or programs not achieved lasting benefit? How can your organization avoid repeating the same mistakes?
- What percentage of leadership time is spent expediting, firefighting, or working around problems?
- How can our Lean efforts be oriented around the mission and purpose of our organization and our people?

Notes

1. Ohno, Taiichi, *Toyota Production System: Beyond Large-Scale Production* (New York: Productivity Press, 1988), 1.
2. Rapoza, Joshua, A Lean Transformation Model Everyone Can Use, January 23, 2014, http://www.lean.org/LeanPost/Posting.cfm?LeanPostId=135 (accessed March 30, 2015).
3. Toussaint, John, *Management on the Mend* (Appleton, WI: ThedaCare Center for Healthcare Value, 2015), 29.
4. Graban, Mark, Lean is "Loving Care"? 2010, http://www.leanblog.org/2010/01/lean-is-loving-care/ (accessed March 26, 2015).
5. Caron, Jacob, personal correspondence, 2015.
6. van Ede, Jaap, Lean Maakt St Elisabeth Ziekenhuis 'Reactiever', April 2012, http://www.procesverbeteren.nl/LEAN/lean_st_elisabeth_ziekenhuis2.php (accessed September 12, 2015).
7. Weinger, Matthew B., Jason Slagle, Sonia Jain, and Nelda Ordonez, "Retrospective data collection and analytical techniques for patient safety studies," *Journal of Biomedical Informatics*, 2003, 35: 106–119.
8. Ford, Henry, and Samuel Crowther, *My Life and Work* (Garden City, NY: Doubleday, Page and Company, 1922), 219.
9. AAMC Readiness for Reform, Virginia Mason Medical Center, Applying LEAN Methodology to Lead Quality and Transform Healthcare, Undated, https://www.aamc.org/download/278946/data/virginiamasoncasestudy.pdf (accessed March 30, 2015).

10. Liker, Jeffrey K., *The Toyota Way: 14 Management Principles from the World's Greatest Automaker* (New York: McGraw-Hill, 2004), cover.

11. Ohno, Taiichi, *Toyota Production System: Beyond Large-Scale Production* (New York: Productivity Press, 1988), 3.

12. Ibid., 97.

13. Stratton, Brad, "Gone but never forgotten," *Quality Progress*, March 1994, https://deming.org/content/gone-not-forgotten (accessed March 26, 2015).

14. Kaplan, Gary, personal correspondence, September 2015.

15. Womack, James P., Daniel T. Jones, and Daniel Roos, *The Machine That Changed the World: The Story of Lean Production* (New York: Harper Perennial, 1991), 13.

16. Toyota, Toyota Production System, http://www.toyota-global.com/company/vision_philosophy/toyota_production_system/ (accessed September 12, 2015).

17. Taylor, Alex, "How Toyota defies gravity," *Fortune*, December 8, 1997, http://archive.fortune.com/magazines/fortune/fortune_archive/1997/12/08/234926/index.htm (accessed March 26, 2015).

18. Morgan, James M., and Jeffrey K. Liker, *The Toyota Product Development System: Integrating People, Process And Technology* (New York: Productivity Press, 2006), 1.

19. Ries, Eric, *The Lean Startup: How Today's Entrepreneurs Use Continuous Innovation to Create Radically Successful Businesses* (New York: Crown Business, 2011), 1.

20. Jargon, Julie, "Latest Starbucks buzzword: 'Lean' Japanese techniques," *Wall Street Journal*, August 4, 2009, http://www.wsj.com/articles/SB124933474023402611(accessed September 12, 2015).

21. Morison, Ora, "Tims' efficiency drive gives birth to 'lean' machine of innovation," *The Globe and Mail*, http://www.theglobeandmail.com/report-on-business/careers/management/tims-efficiency-drive-gives-birth-to-lean-machine-of-innovation/article4435812/ (accessed September 12, 2015).

22. Graban, Mark, Video: Toyota Helps a NYC Food Bank & Hurricane Sandy Victims, http://www.leanblog.org/2013/06/video-toyota-helps-a-nyc-food-bank-sandy-victims/ (accessed September 12, 2015).

23. Spector, Mike, and Gina Chon, "Toyota University opens admissions to outsiders," *Wall Street Journal*, March 5, 2007, http://www.wsj.com/articles/SB117286364032225058 (accessed March 26, 2015).

24. Wellman, Joan, Howard Jeffries, and Pat Hagan, *Leading the Lean Healthcare Journey* (New York: Productivity Press, 2010), 1.

25. Appleby, Julie, "Care providers slam health system," *USA Today*, May 9, 2001, p. A01.

26. McCarthy, Douglas, and David Blumenthal, Committed to Safety: Ten Case Studies on Reducing Harm to Patients, The Commonwealth Fund, http://www.commonwealthfund.org/publications/fund-reports/2006/apr/committed-to-safety--ten-case-studies-on-reducing-harm-to-patients (accessed March 26, 2015).

27. Martin, L. A., C. W. Neumann, J. Mountford, M. Bisognano, and T. W. Nolan, Increasing Efficiency and Enhancing Value in Health Care: Ways to Achieve Savings in Operating Costs per Year, IHI Innovation Series white paper (Cambridge, MA: Institute for Healthcare Improvement, 2009).

28. California Health Advocates, Creative Interventions Reduce Hospital Readmissions for Medicare Beneficiaries, October 7, 2010, http://www.cahealthadvocates.org/news/basics/2010/creative.html (accessed March 26, 2015).

29. Barto, Jack, CEO Blog: Avoiding Patient Falls: Where Patient Safety Meets Cost Reduction, http://www.nhrmc.org/body.cfm?id=2293&action=detail&ref=1085#sthash.JYEqkbCA.dpbs (accessed September 12, 2015).

30. Lean Tools Used to Reduce Pressure Ulcers, http://www.hret-hen.org/index.php?option=com_phocadownload&view=category&download=1305:barnes-jewish-christian-hospital-saint-louis-mo&id=283:pressure-ulcers-case-studies (accessed February 14, 2016).

31. Wu, Shinyi, Pai Liu, and David Belson, "Multiple-hospital Lean initiative to improve congestive heart failure care: A mixed-methods evaluation," *Journal of the Society for Healthcare Improvement Professionals*, http://www.jship.org/articles/vol-3-articles-october-2013/multiple-hospital-lean-initiative-to-improve-congestive-heart-failure-care-a-mixed-methods-evaluation-2/ (accessed September 12, 2015).

32. Rice, Sabriya, Learning to Be Lean, http://www.modernhealthcare.com/section/learning-to-be-lean (accessed October 22, 2015).

33. Toussaint, John, and Roger Gerard, *On the Mend: Revolutionizing Healthcare to Save Lives and Transform the Industry* (Cambridge, MA: Lean Enterprise Institute, 2010), 29.

34. ValuMetrix Services, Avera McKennan, Case Study, http://www.valumetrixservices.com/sites/default/files/client_results_pdf/CS_Avera%20McKennan_ED_OC4047.pdf (accessed March 26, 2015).

35. Maser, Ben and Osman Akhtar, PAMF's Ambulatory Surgery Center: A value stream approach to improvement, Presentation at 2015 Lean Healthcare Transformation Summit, June 2015.

36. Healthcare Value Network, Healthcare Value Network Members Share New Quarterly Results, http://www.prweb.com/releases/2015/06/prweb12793784.htm (accessed February 14, 2016).

37. ValuMetrix Services, Clinical Laboratory Improves Turnaround Time by 60%, Case Study, http://www.valumetrixservices.com/sites/default/files/client_results_pdf/CS_Alegent_Lab_OC4029.pdf (accessed March 26, 2015).

38. Ford, Anne, "Thanks to weak economy and more, efficiency is king," *CAP Today*, April 2010, http://lnbg.us/20T (accessed March 26, 2015).

39. Lefteroff, Lewis, and Mark Graban, "Lean and process excellence at Kingston General," *SME Lean Manufacturing* 2008, 53.

40. Rice.

41. Guo, Jinshai, Shijun Ma, and Xun Zhang, Lean Management to Transform a Chinese Hospital, http://www.planet-lean.com/lean-management-to-transform-a-chinese-hospital (accessed October 27, 2015).

42. Graban, Mark, Gemba in the NICU: More Notes from Our "Kaizen Live" Experience at Franciscan, http://www.leanblog.org/2015/05/gemba-nicu-notes-kaizen-live-experience-franciscan/ (accessed September 12, 2015).

43. Graban, Mark, Podcast #230—Paul DeChant, MD, MBA on reducing burnout through Lean, http://www.leanblog.org/230 (accessed September 20, 2015).

44. Consumer Reports Health How Good is Your Doctor? Special Report for California Residents, February 2015.

45. No author, "Slash door-to-doc time, boost patient satisfaction with staff-driven improvement effort," *ED Management* 2011, 23(6): 70–71.

46. Gabow, Patricia, *The Lean Prescription: Powerful Medicine for an Ailing Health System* (New York: Productivity Press, 2014), xix.

47. Weed, Julie, "Factory efficiency comes to the hospital," *New York Times*, July 10, 2010, http://www.nytimes.com/2010/07/11/business/11seattle.html (accessed March 26, 2015).

48. Healthcare Value Network, Healthcare Value Network Members Share New Quarterly Results, http://www.prweb.com/releases/2015/06/prweb12793784.htm (accessed February 14, 2016).

49. United States, *Hospital Adaptation for the Job Instruction Manual*, August 1944, Subgroup 211.22.3 General Records of the Training within Industry Service, Records of the War Manpower Commission (WMC), Record Group 211, National Archives Building, Washington, DC, http://chapters.sme.org/204/TWI_Materials/National_Archives_March_2006/Job_Instruction/Hospitals/Materials-Hospitals.pdf (accessed March 26, 2015).

50. Dinero, Donald A., *Training within Industry: The Foundation of Lean* (New York: Productivity Press, 2005), 48.

51. Graban, Mark, Podcast #232—Remembering Dr. Michel Tétrault, http://www.leanblog.org/232 (accessed October 7, 2015).

52. The World Bank, Health Expenditure, Total (% of GDP), http://data.worldbank.org/indicator/SH.XPD.TOTL.ZS (accessed March 31, 2015).

53. Wasik, John F., Are Doctors Really Ditching Medicare? http://www.thefiscaltimes.com/Columns/2013/09/04/Are-Doctors-Really-Ditching-Medicare (accessed April 6, 2015).

54. Torinus, John, *The Company That Solved Health Care* (Dallas, TX: BenBella Books, 2010), 159.

55. Zuckerman, Stephen, Jack Hadley, and Lisa Iezzoni, "Measuring hospital efficiency with frontier cost functions," *Journal of Health Economics* 1994, 13(3): 255–280.

56. Vitaliano, Donald F., and Mark Toren, "Hospital cost and efficiency in a regime of stringent regulation," *Eastern Economic Journal* 1996, 22(2): 167–175.

57. American Association of Colleges of Nurses, Fact Sheet: Nursing Shortage, http://www.aacn.nche.edu/media/factsheets/nursingshortage.htm (accessed March 26, 2015).
58. Halvorson, Deanne, "Pharmacy salary and staffing supplement," *Pharmacy Purchasing and Products,* November 2010, http://www.pppmag.com/article/796/November_2010/Pharmacy_Salary_Staffing_Supplement/ (accessed March 26, 2015).
59. Donnelly, Laura, "NHS spending on agency nurses triples in two years," *The Telegraph,* http://www.telegraph.co.uk/news/nhs/11391273/NHS-spending-on-agency-nurses-triples-in-two-years.html (accessed April 6, 2015).
60. Gaba, D. M., and S. K. Howard, "Fatigue among clinicians and the safety of patients," *New England Journal of Medicine,* 2002, 347: 1249–1255.
61. Tavernise, Sabrina, "Number of Americans without health insurance falls, survey shows," *New York Times,* http://www.nytimes.com/2014/09/16/us/number-of-americans-without-health-insurance-falls-survey-shows.html?_r=0 (accessed April 6, 2015).
62. Committee on Quality of Healthcare in America and Institute of Medicine, *To Err Is Human* (Washington, DC: National Academies Press, 2000), 1.
63. Allen, Marshall, How Many Die from Medical Mistakes in U.S. Hospitals?, http://www.propublica.org/article/how-many-die-from-medical-mistakes-in-us-hospitals (accessed October 27, 2015).
64. Clancy, Carolyn, "Reducing health care-associated infections," *AHRQ,* April 1, 2009, http://archive.ahrq.gov/news/speech/test040109.html (accessed March 30, 2015).
65. Morgan, Gwynn, "Private sector health care: Think quality, regulation," *Toronto Globe and Mail,* April 16, 2007.
66. Hall, Sarah, "Medical error death risk 1 in 300," *The Guardian,* November 7, 2006, http://www.guardian.co.uk/society/2006/nov/07/health.lifeandhealth (accessed March 30, 2015).
67. "Medical massacre," *Guardian Unlimited,* March 5, 2001, http://www.theguardian.com/theguardian/2001/mar/05/guardianleaders (accessed March 30, 2015).
68. Committee on Quality, *To Err Is Human,* 26.
69. Gawande, Atul, "The checklist," *The New Yorker,* December 10, 2007, http://www.newyorker.com/magazine/2007/12/10/the-checklist (accessed March 30, 2015).
70. Zajac, Andrew, "FDA seeks to reduce drug dosage errors," *Los Angeles Times,* November 5, 2009, http://articles.latimes.com/2009/nov/05/nation/na-fda-drugs5 (accessed March 30, 2015).
71. Fillingham, David, presentation, First Global Lean Healthcare Summit, June 25, 2007.
72. Toussaint and Gerard, *On the Mend,* 3.
73. Graban, Mark, "Riverside Medical Center puts Lean in the laboratory," *SME Lean Manufacturing,* 2007, p. 56.
74. Ibid., 53.
75. ValuMetrix Services, For Riverside Medical Center, Lean Is Not Just about Better ROI, Case Study, http://www.markgraban.com/wp-content/uploads/2015/09/CS_Riverside_Lab_OC10114.pdf (accessed September 15, 2015).
76. Senge, Peter, *The Fifth Discipline: The Art & Practice of the Learning Organization* (New York: Doubleday Press, 1994), 14.
77. Burns, Joe, Lean Lifts Clinical and Financial Processes, http://www.healthcarefinancenews.com/news/lean-lifts-clinical-and-financial-processes (accessed October 27, 2015).
78. Carr, Kenny, personal correspondence, August 2015.
79. Adams, Jim, and Mark Graban, "CMCD's lab draws on academics, automakers, and therapists to realize its own vision of excellence," *Global Business and Organizational Excellence,* 2011, 30(4): 12–28.
80. Bersch, Carren, "Winning teams: A common vision yields uncommon results," *Medical Lab Observer,* 2009, 41(4): 22, 24, 26–28, http://www.mlo-online.com/features/2009_april/0409_lab_management.pdf (accessed March 30, 2015).
81. Slunecka, Fred, personal correspondence, October 2015.
82. Kaplan, Gary, personal correspondence, September 2015.
83. Gibson, William, NPR Talk of the Nation, The Science in Science Fiction, November 30, 1999. http://www.npr.org/templates/story/story.php?storyId=1067220 (accessed March 30, 2015).

Chapter 2

Overview of Lean for Hospitals and Health Systems

What Is Lean?

Countless books have been written on Lean, creating many frameworks and definitions, some of which are shown in Table 2.1. It is difficult to have a single succinct, yet comprehensive, definition, but we can learn something from each definition. Lean is both a tool set and a management system. Lean is a method for continuous improvement and employee engagement. And, Lean is an approach that allows us to solve the problems that are important to us as leaders and as an organization.

One succinct definition used by many instructors at the Lean Enterprise Institute is: "Lean is a set of concepts, principles, and tools used to create and deliver the most value from the customers' perspective while consuming the fewest resources and fully utilizing the knowledge and skills of the people performing the work." How can healthcare deliver the most value to patients while using the least possible resources and maximizing the use of our people's skills and knowledge? That is the primary question when it comes to Lean healthcare.

Ohno's Definition of Lean

Toyota's Taiichi Ohno, who along with Shigeo Shingo was one of the primary creators of the Toyota Production System (TPS), defined Lean in terms of business goals that included more than the factory. Ohno wrote, "All we are doing is looking at the timeline from the moment a customer gives us an order to the point when we collect the cash. And we are reducing that timeline by removing the non-value-added wastes."[1]

In this context, *waste* has a specific definition, being any problem that interferes with people doing their work effectively or any activity that does not provide value for the customer, as we discuss more in Chapter 3. A hospital could view the timeline described by Ohno as, for example, the time between a patient feeling symptoms and actually receiving care, ending at the point when the hospital gets paid (if it is a fee-for-service model). A similar definition could be created

Table 2.1 Definitions of *Lean*

Framework	Definition
Toyota Triangle[a]	Lean is an integrated system of human development, technical tools, management approaches, and philosophy that creates a Lean organizational culture.
Toyota Way pillars[b]	Lean is about continuous improvement (*"kaizen"*) and showing "respect for people."
"Fixing Healthcare from the Inside, Today" (Spear)[c]	1. Work is designed as a series of ongoing experiments that immediately reveal problems. 2. Problems are addressed immediately through rapid experimentation. 3. Solutions are disseminated adaptively through collaborative experimentation. 4. People at all levels of the organization are taught to become experimentalists.
Shingo model[d]	Ideal results require ideal behaviors; beliefs and systems drive behaviors; principles inform ideal behaviors, with the guiding principles being: 1. Lead with humility 2. Respect every individual 3. Focus on process 4. Embrace scientific thinking 5. Flow & pull value 6. Assure quality at the source 7. Seek perfection 8. Create constancy of purpose 9. Think systemically 10. Create value for the customer

[a] Adapted from Convis, Gary, Role of Management in a Lean Manufacturing Environment, Society of Automotive Engineers, http://www.sae.org/manufacturing/lean/column/leanjul01.htm, accessed December 20, 2007.

[b] Adapted from Ohno, Taiichi, *Toyota Production System: Beyond Large-Scale Production*, New York: Productivity Press, 1988, p. xiii.

[c] Steven J. Spear, "Fixing healthcare from the inside, today," *Harvard Business Review*, Reprint #1738, September 2005, p. 5.

[d] Shingo Institute, The Shingo Model™ Is Not Just Another Initiative; It Is a New Way of Thinking, http://www.shingoprize.org/model.html, accessed September 3, 2015.

for countries or situations that have set budgets or capitated payment systems: "All we are doing is looking at the timeline from the moment a patient needs care to the point where they receive that care. And we are reducing that timeline by removing the non-value-added wastes."

Ohno's definition shows Lean to be a time-based approach; reducing delays leads to better quality and lower costs. Toyota's website defines the Toyota Production System as having two pillars: "just in time," which means improving flow so we can provide the right care at the right place at the right time, and "jidoka," or the idea of building in quality at the source.[2] Better flow leads to better quality and vice versa.

Lean is very different from traditional cost-cutting, which is often done by slashing hospital budgets, head count, and services. Ohno was focusing on flow, not efficiency, per se, where efficiency is defined as the ratio of outputs over inputs. Efficiency-based management systems focus on doing more or keeping everybody and every resource as busy as possible, which interferes with flow, as will be discussed more in Chapter 9. Flow is improved not by working faster, but rather by reducing waste.

Lean Thinking

The book *Lean Thinking* defines the term *Lean* as follows: "In short, Lean thinking is Lean, because it provides a way to do more and more with less and less—less human effort, less equipment, less time, and less space—while coming closer and closer to providing customers with exactly what they want."[3]

The five key principles of *Lean Thinking* are

1. "Specify what creates **value** from the customer's perspective
2. Identify all steps across the whole **value stream**
3. Make those actions that create value **flow**
4. Only make what is **pulled** by the customer just in time
5. Strive for **perfection** by continually removing successive layers of waste"[4]

It is important to define Lean in terms of the goals and objectives of a health system. Like other types of organizations, hospitals have the need to do more work with less (or more work with the same number of staff). Providing patients (customers in the healthcare context) with exactly what they want includes the right care that is done right the first time. Patients also expect a caring environment, and many want increasingly hotel-like service. Patients want efficient, cost-effective care, but they also want perfect care that does not harm them in the course of their hospital visit. From a broader perspective, patients want to be kept healthy by their healthcare providers, providing new challenges for how hospitals integrate into the broader system. Lean is not just about the "less and less"; it is sometimes about the "more and more"—we should not lose sight of trying to provide more value and more service to patients and our communities.

The Toyota Triangle: Tools, Culture, and Management System

Figure 2.1 describes the Toyota Production System (TPS), along with the "house" diagram of Figure 5.1. The diagram shows that TPS is an "integrated system of three key elements: philosophy, technical, and managerial roles, all focused on people development," says Jamie Bonini, vice president of the Toyota Production System Support Center (TSSC), which works with manufacturers, non-profits, and health systems. The model starts with people and human development in the middle, as "people are the most valuable resource," says Bonini. That is surrounded by a balanced approach combining technical tools (what we do), managerial tools (how we manage), and philosophy (what we believe). All of this, taken together, will become our organizational culture, or a TPS culture of improvement.

Human Development

First, look at the middle of the triangle in Figure 2.1. It is no accident that diagrams like this from Toyota place people in the center. Toyota leaders like to use the phrase "Build people, not just cars,"

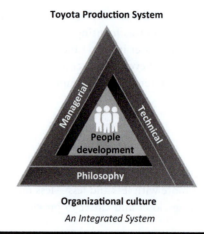

Figure 2.1   The Toyota "Triangle" depiction of the Toyota Production System.

meaning that developing its employees is the key to improving its products and processes.[7] If you visit a Toyota plant or other organizations in Japan, you will hear leaders emphasize that the primary goal of improvement work is learning and the development of people, with the secondary goal being the impact that improvement might have on performance. This sits in stark contrast to the priorities in most Western organizations, which tend to look first (or primarily) at return on investment, or ROI.

Human development, in the Lean approach, means putting in place "a solid framework for cultivating capable leaders and for providing employees with necessary practical skills."[8] A fundamental challenge for hospitals is developing broader leadership skills throughout the organization, not just our skill with Lean methods. ThedaCare is one example of a health system that has provided more training and coaching on basic supervisory skills and leadership fundamentals in addition to training on "Lean leadership." Far too many health systems struggle because they throw talented individuals into management roles without teaching them how to manage or coaching them over time.

Philosophy

The base of the triangle is philosophy: What do we believe as an organization, and what is our purpose? What is described as the TPS philosophy often comes from what we have learned about Toyota—it is their company culture we describe. Bonini says the core of their philosophy has four points:

1. Customer first; provide customers with what they want, when they want it, and in the amount they want it
2. People are the most valuable resource; deeply respect, engage, and develop people
3. Continuous improvement (kaizen); engage everyone each and every day
4. Shop floor (gemba) focus: go to where the work is done to find and solve problems[9]

Toyota's philosophy also includes commitments to their "long-term contributions to society" and to "company economic performance and growth."[10] Having a long-term focus is a frequent theme, as principle 1 of *The Toyota Way* states a company should "base your management decisions on a long-term philosophy, even at the expense of short-term financial goals."[11] ThedaCare has embraced the long-term view as a part of their Lean transformation. Dean Gruner, MD, MMM, their president and chief executive officer (CEO), says "the simplest way we do this is through our 'true north' metrics, where we include one-year and five-year targets," starting every bi-monthly review with a look at their progress.[12]

Hospital mission and values statements often sound like Toyota's, as many state that their top priorities include safety, employee engagement, continuous improvement, and stewardship toward their communities and the environment. However, can hospital employees walk through the hospital and go through their workday feeling like those values are lived and practiced every minute? Is patient safety really a top priority as so many health systems state publicly? Perfectly living up to those ideals can be a challenge in any organization, even Toyota, considering we are all human, and we do not always behave in accordance with our stated standards. Recognizing that, leadership has a responsibility to set a good example and to insist that others live up to the organizational ideals and philosophy every day. If our values state that we respect and value people, a traditional non-Lean top-down command-and-control management system that barks orders and tells employees to stop complaining is not consistent with those values.

As a hospital, we have to make a choice: are we going to implement isolated or limited Lean methods within the context of our existing culture, or are we going to examine what needs to change with our culture? Health systems that have transformed their management system and culture have greater and more sustained success than those who run a few projects or implement a Lean tool or two. ThedaCare (Appleton, Wisconsin) and Virginia Mason Medical Center (Seattle, Washington) are two leading examples of hospitals that have gotten great results by working toward a Lean culture throughout their organizations for more than a dozen years.

Many hospitals have an existing philosophy about patients and employees that is conducive to adopting the tools and management system of Lean. Other hospitals, those that do not live up to the ideals and goals of their own values, may struggle with Lean if they expect to find a simple cure-all for their workplace culture woes. That said, trying some of the Lean tools may lead to new ways of viewing and working with people; as the expression goes, "People are much more likely to act their way into a new way of thinking, than think their way into a new way of acting."[13] Saying "our culture is not like Toyota's" should not be an excuse for not trying Lean, but health systems should recognize that the need to change the culture will require additional time, leadership, and effort.

Lean concepts might seem simple, but a Lean transformation takes many years. Dr. W. Edwards Deming said, pithily, "[Change] does not happen all at once. There is no instant pudding." One architect rightfully complained of hospitals that wanted quick easy answers, saying "I can't design a magically Lean hospital for them."

Technical Tools

The technical side of Lean is the tools and methods that we implement and use. You may know of Lean by some of the specific methods that you have seen hospitals use, shown in Table 2.2, including *kanban*, 5S, A3, error proofing, and visual management. The development of these tools was born from the underlying philosophy, including the idea of making work easier for staff and putting the customer first. As Womack says, these tools are "necessary, but not sufficient" for transforming an organization.[14]

Table 2.2 Selected Lean Tools or Methods

Lean tool or method	Definition
Kanban	Japanese term meaning "signal," a method for managing inventory
5S	Method for organizing workplaces to reduce wasted time and motion for employees, making problems more readily apparent
A3	Structured problem-solving methodology, tracked and reported on an A3 sheet of paper (11 inches by 17 inches)
Error proofing	Method for designing or improving processes so errors are less likely to occur
Visual management	Method for making problems visible, providing for fast response and problem solving

Talking about a single tool or a collection of tools does not accurately define Lean. Lean is not just "a toolbox," and it diminishes the power of Lean to categorize it as "one of the tools in our improvement toolbox." It is easier to define and copy tools, but to get the full impact of Lean, you have to work at adopting and practicing the full management system. The right tools in the wrong culture might not lead to the right results. A new tool in the old culture might just frustrate people or create more dysfunction.

Dr. Jack Billi is Associate Dean for Clinical Affairs at the University of Michigan Medical School, and Associate Vice President for Medical Affairs at the University of Michigan Health System. He once commented, "We all want to use Lean thinking as a fundamental business strategy, a holistic model of approaching our work … Of course, everyone [normally] focuses on the tools. We all want to make sure that Lean is more than just the application of simple tools, because you only get so far using the tools.

On the one hand, first we actually train people in all the tools. If we're doing a program, we'll train them about the tools because until they understand the tools, it's very hard for them to see how this fits together as a holistic problem solving model. The tools are really powerful. On the other hand, if they just stop with the tools then they can only go so far."[15]

Managerial Methods

Beyond philosophy and technical tools, Lean also challenges how we manage people and systems. Leadership and management skills are important for implementing Lean methods. Without leadership, employees might not understand why improvement is necessary and why Lean methods can help. Once Lean methods have been adopted, consistent leadership and a management system are required to sustain those improvements (and continue improving).

Bonini says the role of a leader is to "develop people to surface problems and to solve problems, to better serve the customer." He adds that the four roles "that a leader must play in a Lean transformation" include:

1. Show passionate commitment for improvement and TPS
2. Learn TPS principles well enough to teach them to others (the basic principles and the details)
3. Build an organizational culture that surfaces and solves problems
4. Be active in the *gemba* (go and see, or *genchi gembutsu*)[16]

Gary Convis, a retired Toyota senior vice president who had been one of the top-ranking Americans in the company, wrote that the "managerial culture for TPS is rooted in several factors, including developing and sustaining a sense of trust, a commitment to involving those affected by first, teamwork, equal and fair treatment for all, and finally, fact-based decision making and long-term thinking."[17]

ThedaCare's leaders have worked diligently to create new management methods as part of their Lean culture. Part of this evolution is a shift from a command-and-control environment where "leaders talk about how to make their wishes—our commands—known to employees" to a workplace where respect is shown to each individual by listening, asking for employees' opinions, seeking their help when there are problems, and providing training so staff can drive improvement in their own areas.[18]

Kim Barnas, president of the ThedaCare Center for Healthcare Value, writes, "the leader [in the new system] is more of a Zen master. Even if we 'know' the answer, our conclusion is less valuable than a team's investigation into root cause, learning the tools, applying the logic, and applying their own solution. Instead of rapping out answers, we have now become listeners. We may suggest tools to apply and offer inputs, but we do not have the answer. Answers are the province of teams, applying tools in a standardized process."[19]

The "Toyota Way" Philosophy

The simplest, and possibly the most elegant, definition of Lean comes from Toyota, in two parts:[20]

1. Continuous improvement
2. Respect for people

Ohno described this: "the most important objective of the Toyota system has been … consistently and thoroughly eliminating waste. The concept and the equally important respect for humanity that has passed down from the venerable Sakichi Toyoda (1867–1930) … are the foundation of the Toyota production system."[21] This respect extends to all stakeholders—customers, employees, suppliers, and the communities in which Toyota operates.[22] These principles go hand in hand. Because we respect people, we are driven to improve continuously. Because we respect people, we engage staff, physicians, and patients in the improvement process. Respect for people is the reason for continuous improvement, and it is also the way improvement happens.

These are not new concepts in the Lean approach; however, many organizations that have attempted to adopt Lean have focused only on the elimination of waste. Leaders, however, do not get very far by forcing people to change. To be successful, we must focus on both aspects equally—continuous improvement and having respect for people. Using Lean to make quality and productivity improvements that result in layoffs would be an example of not maintaining this balance. A growing number of healthcare organizations have publicly stated policies about not using Lean to drive layoffs.[23] It's understandably difficult to get employees to embrace Lean if they fear for their jobs.

Continuous Improvement

While many associate Lean with projects or weeklong events, the greatest potential comes when every person in the organization is engaged in improving processes every day. The Japanese word *kaizen* is often used to describe continuous improvement, sometimes translated as small changes or change for the good.[24] These improvement efforts regularly focus on reducing waste that exists in the patient's care or in people's work. Masaaki Imai defines *kaizen* simply as "everyday everyone, everywhere improvement." Contrast that to organizations where improvement is only the responsibility of experts, consultants, or managers, or where improvement only happens through sporadic projects or committees.

The term *waste* (also described using the Japanese word *muda*) has its own unique definition when used in association with Lean. In healthcare settings, waste can be defined as any activity that does not help patients or does not move them toward being diagnosed, treated, or discharged. One example of waste is time spent waiting—waiting for an appointment or waiting for the next step in the patient's treatment. Another example of waste would be activities or errors that harm a patient. We take a deeper look at waste in Chapter 3.

Dr. Donald Berwick, former president and CEO of the Institute for Healthcare Improvement and former administrator of the Centers for Medicare and Medicaid Services, argued that hospitals are full of waste, but the actual extent is unknown. Berwick claimed that 20% to 30% of the total expenditure of healthcare in the United States—about half a trillion dollars—is waste.[25] David Sharbaugh, director of quality improvement at Shadyside Hospital (Pittsburgh, Pennsylvania), said, "It's not unrealistic at all to consider 40% and 50% waste in the healthcare system."[26] Waste, to some extent, is present in every hospital process and organization. That is not an indictment of our people; it is just recognizing the system in which we work.

Continuous improvement methodologies have often been used in systems that are already stable and relatively free of waste. Leading hospitals are using Lean principles to completely redesign or radically overhaul their processes and space, working to create this stability. Beyond this redesign, or before it, Lean healthcare organizations create an environment for continuous improvement through their management mindsets and their mechanisms for engaging staff members, as covered in more detail in Chapter 11.

Respect for People

A display in the visitor center of a Toyota plant in Japan highlights "respect for people" and says, "There is no limit to how far human wisdom can be developed. Within the company, we continually aim to achieve mutual understanding, fulfill mutual responsibilities, and combine the power of our individual employees. Respect for people is the attitude that regard's people's ability to think most."

When leaders at Toyota talk about having respect for people (or, originally, "respect for humanity"[27]), this might have a different meaning than what traditional organizations might mean by respect—after all, what leader would say they do not respect their people? Respect does not mean that managers give employees latitude to do their jobs however they please, out of a sense of trust, as long as the results are good.[28] In a hospital that uses Lean principles, managers and leaders frequently verify the details of how work has been done. This is done out of respect for the patient (to ensure proper outcomes and quality) and can be done in a way that still shows respect for the employees.

In Lean organizations, respect does not mean that managers and leaders are always nice to their employees or that people avoid conflict with each other. Our goal is not simply to have happy employees, as that could be accomplished in any number of superficial ways that might be costly to the hospital or might not improve patient care. Respect, in a Lean context, means a number of things, including challenging people and pushing them to perform to the best of their ability, in a constructive way.

Respect for humanity also recognizes our human limitations and failings, such as our propensity to get fatigued or distracted, leading to errors and defects. When a problem occurs, a Lean leader looks first at the system and processes rather than blaming an individual. Gary Convis, formerly the president of the Toyota plant in Kentucky, said, "You respect people, you listen to them, you work together. You don't blame them. Maybe the *process* was not set up well, so it was easy to make a mistake."[29] Sir Liam Donaldson, the former chief medical officer of England, expressed a similar idea, saying, "Human error is inevitable. We can never eliminate it. We can eliminate problems in the *system* that make it more likely to happen."[30]

Respect does not mean leaving employees alone to struggle with problems or their heavy workload. Lean "is a system that demands employees do their best, but does not overwork them. The sense of trust created between management and the workers can promote efficiency and at the same time a relaxed feeling."[31]

Japanese not only has a word for waste (*muda*), but also has specific words that describe overwork (*muri*) and uneven workloads (*mura*). Having respect for people means we do not allow our employees to be overworked or overburdened. Lean is not about pushing people to work too quickly or to be in two places at the same time. One hospital employee, when first hearing about Lean, joked about the need for roller skates so they could zip around faster. Lean thinkers, instead, would ask why employees have to travel such long distances and would search for ways to eliminate the need for moving faster.

Part of the approach to respect people is that we engage and trust our employees to participate in solving problems and eliminating waste. It is not the job of leaders to solve every problem for the employees. As we discuss throughout the book and in Chapter 11, improvement needs to be a partnership between employees and managers. We are not looking to create a system in which managers do all of the thinking, problem solving, and system design, with employees just mindlessly following instructions.

Employees in hospitals report feeling more fulfilled when they are allowed to spend more time on their primary patient care work, whether this is direct patient care or work that indirectly supports patient care. We have a great systemic advantage in healthcare—the intrinsic motivation of our employees is the desire to help people, a desire that led so many to healthcare. It is our job, as leaders, to make sure that intrinsic motivation is not eroded over time through frustration and burnout. The late Peter Scholtes liked to ask about the so-called deadwood in our organizations, pointing out how we most likely hired "live wood and killed it."[32]

It is because of the notion of respect for people that we work tirelessly to create an environment in which our "live wood" (our employees, our most important assets) is supported and allowed to grow instead of getting frustrated and leaving the profession or jumping to a competing hospital. Brand new live-wood employees might make a suggestion the first time they face a problem, like a missing surgical instrument. When their suggestion is not taken or when the problem is not fixed, they might understandably get frustrated and give up, turning into deadwood that no longer tries to fix the source of the problem.

Both of these concepts—continuous improvement and having respect for people—are indispensible elements of Lean. When applied to the healthcare industry, respect for people includes respect for our patients, our employees, our physicians, our community, and all stakeholders of the hospital. Respect for people is not just a matter of treating people nicely; it can impact patient safety and outcomes. A study suggests that patients who "indicated they rarely received respect from hospital staff were two and a half times more likely to experience a preventable medical error than those who felt they were usually treated with respect."[33]

John Toussaint, MD, the former CEO of ThedaCare, described how Paul O'Neill, former CEO of Alcoa, taught him three key questions to ask as a test of whether your environment is conducive to respect for people:[34]

1. Are my staff and doctors treated with dignity and respect by everyone in the organization?
2. Do my staff and doctors have the training and encouragement to do work that gives their life meaning?
3. Have I recognized my staff and doctors for what they do?

Four Organizational Capabilities for Lean

Professor Steven J. Spear described Lean as a rational and scientific approach, one that hospital employees can readily embrace, as many of them are scientifically trained. If we have respect for people and fully involve them in improvement rather than relying on a few experts, this should be the case. Spear outlined four organizational capabilities in the article, "Fixing Healthcare from the Inside, Today," and elaborated on them in his book, *The High-Velocity Edge*.[35,36]

Capability 1: Work Is Designed as a Series of Ongoing Experiments That Immediately Reveal Problems

There are three key elements in this statement. First, "work is designed" means that the way we do things is not random, inconsistent, or haphazard. The Lean concept of standardized work (discussed in Chapter 5) means that work should be designed, by both the employees and their leaders, rather than allowing common practices just to develop. A director of patient safety at a hospital lamented that this is not always the case in hospitals, saying, "Our blood administration system is complex and it just sort of evolved on its own. There are many inefficiencies and opportunities for error."

Hospital employees need to standardize key processes and tasks for the sake of improving patient safety, preventing time delays, making work easier for employees, and reducing costs. We don't standardize for the sake of standardizing or because "Lean says we should standardize." When different nurses treat the same patient on different days, having standardized methods helps ensure a consistent experience and consistent care for that patient. As a patient in an outpatient cancer treatment setting complained, "Things work differently every time I come here." For example, some staff allowed late patients to be fit in immediately, while others made them wait until an open chemotherapy slot was available, even if the delays were not that patient's fault. This might not have necessarily impacted their clinical care or outcomes, but it caused frustration nonetheless and could have harmed patient satisfaction scores.

Second, standardizing our work does not mean procedures are carved in stone. The Lean concept of *kaizen* means that we have an obligation to find new ways of improving our work. There is a Toyota expression that says each person's job is not just to do the work but also to find a better way of doing that work. That said, we have to take care that "ongoing experiments" do not mean chaos or a shift back to everybody doing tasks their own way. For example, if we have a standardized method for inserting a central-line catheter, we need to experiment with improving this carefully and in a controlled way.

The third element is that we need to structure work in a way that problems are made readily apparent so they can be fixed as quickly as possible. Simple methods, such as visual management, give us tools to make problems apparent. They allow us to tell when needed supplies or equipment are out of place, allowing us to more proactively solve and prevent problems. Rather than waiting for supplies, such as blankets, to run out in an inpatient unit, simple visual indicators and controls can help us see that we are running low—because we have used more than usual or because the delivery of new blankets has been delayed. We often do not have visibility to these problems because supplies are hidden behind closed cabinet doors or in drawers. When it is safe to do so, Lean concepts would call us to keep supplies visible (and to have a standardized process for checking the inventory levels), which can prevent waste, problems, and frustration. Visual management and the *kanban* system for managing supplies are discussed in Chapter 6. There is also an important leadership component to this, as we must create a safe environment where staff can speak up and make problems visible rather than being pressured into hiding or ignoring them.

Capability 2: Problems Are Addressed Immediately through Rapid Experimentation

In a Lean environment, we make problems visible and apparent because we recognize that it is normal to have problems, therefore it's acceptable, as long as we are working to fix them. The typical mindset in the automotive industry was that problems should not be revealed to your boss because either you would get yelled at or you would receive unwanted attention and management-driven "solutions" that might not help. There is a famous Toyota story about Japanese executives visiting American managers at their then newly opened factory in Georgetown, Kentucky. The Japanese executives asked what the top problems were, and an American manager replied, "There are no problems." A Japanese executive replied, "No problems is a problem."[37] If a manager says there are no problems, it more likely means that a manager is unaware of the problems or is afraid to speak up. That management problem is one of the problems we are trying to change in a Lean transformation.

When a problem is discovered, the focus is placed on solving that problem immediately, at the place the problem occurs and with the input of (or a reliance upon) the people who are struggling with that problem. There is a Lean expression that problems are not solved in conference rooms; problems are solved at the *gemba*, the Japanese term for the actual place where work occurs.

For example, if nurses are forgetting to send medications home with discharged patients, the team would not just hang signs telling nurses to be careful. Instead, the team might change where the medications are stored so they are more likely to be seen during the discharge process. The team might also develop a standard checklist, a form of "standardized work," for nurses to follow during each discharge that includes a medication reminder. They might even print the checklist on the envelope that is used to hold information and belongings for the patient. With the Lean approach, problems are solved more quickly, and we are more likely to get to an effective countermeasure through rapid experimentation, following W. Edwards Deming's plan-do-check-act (PDCA) cycle. When problems occur, it is better to try something to see if it works rather than taking a long time to develop the "perfect" solution.

The roots of the continuous improvement approach can be traced back to the PDCA cycle (also called plan-do-study-adjust, or PDSA) that Deming taught to the Japanese after World War II. In the PDCA approach, we consider any new and improved condition to be the new starting point for future improvements, never being satisfied with our performance.[38]

The PDCA cycle, as shown in Figure 2.2, is meant to parallel the scientific method, in which any proposed change is merely a hypothesis that is presented for testing. Through small-scale trials, we are able to see if the process change leads to the expected results, and we can respond accordingly. If the expected results do not come, we can challenge our initial hypothesis and put aside the proposed change or go back to try another alternative (or we can go back to the original process). If the expected results do materialize, we can formalize that new process and spread the changes into other areas. The PDCA cycle requires a return to the plan phase, either to find a new method for improvement or to find a new problem that needs to be solved, via the PDCA process.

Traditional management approaches often assume that success is guaranteed when changes are made and either do not test to see if the expected results were achieved or will go out of their way to defend or rationalize the lack of results out of a fear of failure. A healthy Lean culture does not expect people to succeed 100% of the time. An expectation of 100% success

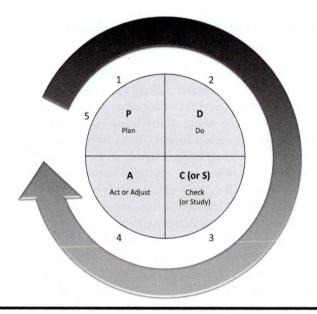

Figure 2.2   The PDCA (or PDSA) cycle.

helps lead to a risk-averse culture in which a fear of failure will lead to a lack of experimentation and a lack of improvement.

Capability 3: Solutions Are Disseminated Adaptively through Collaborative Experimentation

Local improvements made in one area need to be shared with other departments or areas to prevent everyone from having to go through the same improvement cycles on their own. We can view this in terms of our different inpatient units and floors throughout the hospital. Although we might have differences between specialized units, certain core processes can be standardized, such as how to handle pharmacy orders. When a *kaizen* improvement is made in one unit, we need a mechanism for sharing that improvement across all units.

An adaptive dissemination is different from a traditional rollout of a new best practice that was perhaps developed in one unit. People often complain of being "rolled over" when they are forced to take a new practice that might not meet the exact needs of their unit. Health systems, like ThedaCare, are learning that the Lean model leads to a more nuanced approach. Instead of each unit or hospital completely duplicating improvement efforts, the second unit might receive the process that the first unit created—considering that process to be a starting point for future improvement. The second unit does not force fit the new process without thinking; rather, it is free to adapt the process as needed for its specific patients. If the second unit finds an incrementally better way, it is obligated to share that improvement with the unit that originally developed that new method.

This collaboration and sharing could also extend to other hospitals in our system or other hospitals in the same city. The Pittsburgh Regional Healthcare Initiative is an example of hospitals working together on issues of patient safety, sharing information for the benefit of the patients and the community. The global healthcare industry has a great opportunity to create communication methods and infrastructures that allow hospitals to cooperate and share improvements across city, state, or country boundaries, for the sake of patients. Since 2009, the Healthcare Value Network, a collaboration of the Lean Enterprise Institute and the ThedaCare Center for Healthcare Value, has extended that sharing and learning to over 60 hospitals and health systems across North America.[39]

Capability 4: People at All Levels of the Organization Are Taught to Become Experimentalists

While Spear and other Lean thinkers talked about letting employees at the lowest level of the organization solve problems, we cannot just throw people into teams without arming them with the skills and methods for effective problem solving. Many hospital systems, such as Avera McKennan (Sioux Falls, South Dakota), are giving initial Lean training, including that for problem-solving methods, to all employees at the hospital. Continued coaching, training, and mentoring are required, whether coming from outside consultants, internal process improvement leaders, or the direct line management and leaders themselves.

Just putting a group of employees together to come up with solutions may lead to solutions along the lines of what we have already tried in the past, or simply asking people to be more careful or try harder. The Lean methodology helps employees see their work and processes through fresh eyes, allowing them to see problems they could not have seen before and to have new ways of solving those problems. This is not meant to be a criticism of the employees' intelligence or creativity but merely a recognition that one responsibility of hospital leaders is to provide for the ongoing training and development of their employees.

Four Rules in Use for Lean

A growing number of hospitals are using concepts from Spear's earlier article, written with H. Kent Bowen, called "Decoding the DNA of the Toyota Production System."[40] The rules are also presented in the healthcare improvement methodology called "adaptive design."[41]

The rules are as follows:

Rule 1: All work shall be highly specified regarding content, sequence, timing, and outcome.

Rule 2: Every customer-supplier connection must be direct, and there must be an unambiguous yes-or-no way to send requests and receive responses.

Rule 3: The pathway for every product and service must be simple and direct.

Rule 4: Any improvement must be made in accordance with the scientific method, under the guidance of a teacher, at the lowest possible level of the organization.

Lean and Other Methodologies

Lean does not exist on a process improvement island, so it is common for organizations to combine and incorporate other methodologies with Lean. This is often done under a banner of "process excellence" or "operational excellence" labels that give a health system flexibility to incorporate new methods without inadvertently signaling that older methods are going away. Each methodology adds some new wrinkle or element that can be viewed as additive to Lean.

Total Quality Management (TQM) gained popularity in the 1980s and 1990s as an approach for process improvement. Many organizations utilize the "seven basic QC tools," such as Pareto charts and fishbone diagrams, as a continuation of earlier programs, even if they no longer use the TQM label. Some Japanese hospitals are now discovering Lean tools and management practices as an extension of 20-year-long TQM efforts that rely on six-month "quality circle" team projects. Nerima General Hospital (Tokyo) has pursued a process they call "Medical Quality Improvement," based on TQM, for about 20 years. They have recently added Lean methods, like 5S, on top of existing quality circle projects.

The U.S. government's *Malcolm Baldrige National Quality Award* framework was a product of the TQM era, with different recognitions still being given at the state and federal level. Baldrige is a "comprehensive framework for performance excellence" that endorses Lean and other methods for process improvement.[42] Henry Ford Health System (Dearborn, Michigan) and Sharp HealthCare (San Diego, California) are two national recipients that utilize Lean and Six Sigma frameworks. Mary Greeley Medical Center (Ames, Iowa) received the highest state-level recognition in 2014. Karen Kiel-Rosser, their vice president and chief quality officer, says, "Baldrige and Lean go hand in hand, where Baldrige defines what the organization needs to do and Lean defines how."[43]

Six Sigma is a "disciplined, data-driven approach and methodology" for improving quality and processes by reducing defects and variation.[44] The term refers to six standard deviations around a mean, where reaching that level means only 3.4 defects per million opportunities in a process.[45] Six Sigma is known for the DMAIC model, of define, measure, analyze, improve, and control. Those who are trained and certified in Six Sigma practices receive "belts" of various colors, signifying their level of knowledge and experience. Created at Motorola as an extension of TQM, Six Sigma was popularized by General Electric (GE) and was introduced to healthcare in the mid-1990s through GE Healthcare. Some organizations, like ThedaCare and Virginia Mason Medical Center, follow Toyota's example by eschewing formal Six Sigma, as they combine Lean and the seven basic tools of TQM. Other health systems utilize both Lean and Six Sigma, often under the banner of "Lean Six Sigma" or "Lean Sigma." Some differentiate Lean as being something you can teach to everybody and use as a management system, while giving detailed Six Sigma training to a small number of experts who are utilized to solve particularly difficult quality or process problems. Well-known health systems that use Lean Sigma include Cleveland Clinic and Johns Hopkins.

The ***Magnet Recognition Program***® "recognizes healthcare organizations for quality patient care, nursing excellence, and innovations in professional nursing practice."[46] Hospitals receive Magnet designation as the result of having elements of transformational leadership, structural empowerment of nurses, and innovation and improvement. The "unit-based council" approach for shared governance and decision-making can incorporate Lean methods to provide a more structured approach for problem solving within Magnet. For example, a unit-based council at INTEGRIS Baptist Medical Center (Oklahoma City, Oklahoma) used Lean methods to "help improve the discharge process for moms and babies."[47] Other hospitals have taken time that had been carved out for Magnet prep and rededicated it to ongoing *kaizen* improvement efforts after the Magnet designation has been achieved.

The ***Studer Group*** is a well-known and widely used consulting firm that coaches health-care executives and leaders. Many of their approaches and principles are very compatible with, if not similar to, Lean. For example, Studer Group's Evidence-Based Leadership[SM] is "built conceptually around the idea that process improvement methods are most successful when they are not stand alone items but rather are built on a foundation of aligned goals and aligned behaviors" and "then those aligned goals and aligned behaviors serve as a sustainer to Lean results," says Clay Linkous, a Studer Group leadership coach.[48] Also, Studer's "Rounding on Staff" is very similar to a Lean *gemba* walk and standardized work audit. The AIDET® approach is an example of standardized work (discussed more in Chapter 5) for interacting with patients and families.

The phrase ***High Reliability Organizations (HROs)*** refers to industries or settings that have achieved incredibly high levels of safety, including nuclear power plants, air traffic control systems, and aircraft carriers. Studying HROs led to the discovery of some key cultural principles that are being embraced by some healthcare organizations. Key HRO principles include having a preoccupation with failure (thinking about what could go wrong), a reluctance to oversimplify complex situations, sensitivity toward (and a focus on) operations, a commitment to resilience, and deference to expertise (the people who do the work). Lean helps provide what HRO calls a "robust process improvement" model and is very complementary with aspects of an HRO culture or a "safety culture."[49]

TeamSTEPPS is a healthcare teamwork and patient safety improvement system that was developed by the U.S. government and modeled after ***Crew Resource Management*** practices in aviation. TeamSTEPPS, like Lean, aims to provide "higher quality, safer patient care" by system-atically improving teamwork and communication in medical teams. For example, TeamSTEPPS not only encourages surgeons and others in the medical hierarchy to listen to all members of the healthcare team, but it also teaches staff a specific four-step method for how to speak up and raise a concern.[50] Organizations such as Ohio State Wexner Medical Center and Miami

Children's Hospital have combined Lean and TeamSTEPPS into an integrated methodology. A group of pilots at the firm LifeWings have combined the approaches in an approach they call "LeanSTEPPS."[51]

When errors do occur, many healthcare organizations use the ***Just Culture*** approach to strike the balance between learning, reflection, and disciplining individuals (when warranted). Healthcare organizations often err by jumping to punish individuals for problems caused by bad systems or broken processes; however, organizations also need to avoid being "blame free" or never holding individuals accountable for their decisions. The word "just" is used to suggest that our reactions to errors and harm must be "just" to those providing the healthcare and those receiving the care. See Chapter 8 for more on this approach.

Healthcare organizations are realizing that instead of asking "Which methodology is best?" they can ask "How can we best combine these approaches into a system that best serves the needs of our patients, our staff, and our health system?"

What Lean Is Not

It is easy, unfortunately, for someone with a little bit of new knowledge to either take actions or say things that are not in line with the spirit or philosophy of Lean, but they call it "Lean" anyway. For example, if a hospital leader is accustomed to giving top-down orders, blaming people, and balancing the budget through layoffs, there is a risk that they will take an isolated Lean tool or method and use it for the existing agenda. But that's not really Lean.

Based on lessons and books from Toyota's leaders, along with other recognized Lean experts, we can outline a few misperceptions, as shown in Table 2.3.

Conclusion

It can be difficult to present a single definition of Lean that is succinct, yet complete. Lean is a set of concepts and tools that allow people to improve patient care (reducing harm and waiting times). Lean is a management approach and philosophy that fosters the full engagement of our employees and physicians in continuous improvement toward a goal of perfection. Lean gives us ways to precisely define how our work is done, without stifling creativity or our professional judgment. Lean organizations can improve quality and cost without asking people to work harder or to be more careful. Lean is not a silver bullet or a magic fix. As one hospital CEO said to the hospital's leadership council, "Lean is very simple, yet very complicated at the same time." That is very true, as a small set of simple-sounding principles can indeed be challenging to implement.

Lean Lessons

- While its roots may be in manufacturing, Lean can be successful in other industries, including healthcare.
- Lean is an organizational culture that develops from an integrated system of tools, management practices, and philosophy.
- Developing employees, their careers, and their talents is important for Lean to succeed.

Table 2.3 Misperceptions and Reality about Lean

Misunderstanding about Lean	Truth about Lean
Misunderstanding: Lean is only for speed (or efficiency or cost).	Lean is focused on both flow and quality. Flow is improved by reducing delays, not increasing how fast the work is done. Cost is an end result of better flow and better quality.
Misunderstanding: Lean is just a toolbox; use the tools that you need to solve a problem.	Lean is an integrated and holistic system. The tools are most effective when in the context of the philosophy and management practices.
Misunderstanding: Use Lean to address a quality problem and you'll make bad stuff faster.	With Lean, you would error-proof the process to prevent errors from being passed on, or you would stop the line since quality is a top priority.
Misunderstanding: Lean is a group of best practices that you can copy from another organization.	Lean practices and lessons are transferrable, but Lean requires thinking, creativity, and experimentation.
Misunderstanding: Lean is just a bunch of events or projects.	Events and projects are helpful, but Lean is also a management system, and smaller improvements should happen daily, involving everybody.
Misunderstanding: Lean says we should _____.	Lean is a set of principles rather than a dogmatic set of practices that must be followed.
Misunderstanding: Lean is just another name for continuous improvement; it's just a process improvement methodology. It's just PDSA.	Lean has a set of technical methods along with an underlying philosophy and a management system.
Misunderstanding: Lean is a great way to reduce head count through layoffs.	Lean organizations make layoffs an absolute last resort.
Misunderstanding: It's Lean to "staff to demand" each hour of the day, sending people home early as needed.	Lean organizations aren't horribly overstaffed, but leaders don't send staff home early or tweak schedules every hour. They instead focus their energy and time on continuous improvement, making good use of any extra time.
Misunderstanding: Lean always means fewer employees.	Lean organizations have the right number of people necessary to do the work the right way, with some extra time available for continuous improvement and development.

(Continued)

Table 2.3 (Continued) Misperceptions and Reality about Lean

Misunderstanding about Lean	Truth about Lean
Misunderstanding: Lean turns people into robots.	Lean engages every employee in defining how their work is done and how to improve it.
Misunderstanding: Lean means every patient must be treated the same.	Lean organizations recognize there is variation in patient or customer needs and allow physicians and staff to use judgment as needed.
Misunderstanding: Lean would be easier if we were Japanese.	Not all Japanese companies or hospitals have a Lean culture. In a Lean culture, people are more likely to speak up and point out problems than they would be in a typical Japanese company.
Misunderstanding: Lean is only about the mass production of thousands of identical widgets.	Most manufacturing produces a high variety of different products through flexible processes, which is a better parallel to a hospital in some ways.
Misunderstanding: We have to do everything identically because Lean says to standardize.	Standardization is done to ensure quality or prevent problems; it's a means to an ends. We standardize what makes sense, leaving in flexibility where necessary.
Misunderstanding: Every patient is unique, therefore standardized work isn't appropriate.	Patients can benefit from defined care pathways and physician standardized work, while leaving room for flexibility and clinical judgment.

- Continuously improving and having respect for people are equally important and mutually supportive.
- Work should be designed, rather than letting methods evolve.
- "No problems is a problem"—we have to be open about having problems.
- In a Lean culture, new methods are not spread by forcing them onto other units.
- Our goal is to have all of our employees participate in solving problems and eliminating waste.
- Lean can be combined with complementary methodologies.

Points for Group Discussion

- If asked "What is Lean?," what is your best 30-second answer?
- What has to change and be implemented to create a Lean culture?
- How can we develop leadership skills in employees, from top to bottom?
- If the first principle of *The Toyota Way* is taking a long-term view, how can we hope to be successful with Lean if our thinking and decisions are still driven by short-term demands?

- Are there ways in which people in our hospital have previously not shown respect for people? What is the impact of this? How can that be addressed?
- Why do some hospital employees get burned out or cynical over time?
- What methods or practices have just evolved in your area, rather than being designed?
- What conditions and mindsets would you expect to be necessary to have everybody participating in continuous improvement?
- How do you strike the balance between not reinventing the wheel yet not blindly copying other units or other hospitals?
- Are there any misperceptions that we have heard about Lean in our organization? If so, how does that occur, and what can we do about that?
- How can we combine Lean with existing methodologies or other approaches that our organization is adopting?

Notes

1. Ohno, Taiichi, *Toyota Production System: Beyond Large-Scale Production* (New York: Productivity Press, 1988), 6.
2. Toyota, Toyota Production System, http://www.toyota-global.com/company/vision_philosophy/toyota_production_system/ (accessed April 2, 2015).
3. Womack, James P. and Daniel T. Jones, *Lean Thinking* (New York: Free Press, 2003), p. 15.
4. Lean Enterprise Research Center, What Is Lean Thinking? http://www.leanenterprise.org.uk/what-is-lean-thinking/what-is-lean-thinking-and-key-lean-thinking-principles.html (accessed September 16, 2015).
5. Convis, Gary, Role of Management in a Lean Manufacturing Environment, Society of Automotive Engineers, http://www.sae.org/manufacturing/lean/column/leanjul01.htm (accessed March 26, 2015).
6. Bonini, Jamie, Lean Healthcare Transformation Summit presentation, June 2014.
7. Liker, Jeffrey and David Meier, *The Toyota Way Fieldbook,* New York: McGraw-Hill, 2005, p. 242.
8. Public Affairs Division and Operations Management Consulting Division, *The Toyota Production System, Leaner Manufacturing for a Greener Planet,* Toyota City, Japan: Toyota Motor Corporation, 1998, p. 7.
9. Bonini.
10. Jeffrey K. Liker and David Meier, *The Toyota Way Fieldbook,* New York: McGraw-Hill, 2006, p. 26.
11. Jeffrey K. Liker, *The Toyota Way,* New York: McGraw-Hill, 2004, p. 71.
12. Gruner, Dean, personal correspondence, 2015.
13. Ulrich, Dave, *Delivering Results: A New Mandate for Human Resource Professionals,* Cambridge, MA: Harvard Business School Press, 1998, p. 179.
14. Womack, James, 2014 Lean Healthcare Transformation Summit presentation, June.
15. Graban, Mark, Podcast #110, Dr. Jack Billi, Lean and medicine, http://www.leanblog.org/110 (accessed September 12, 2015).
16. Bonini.
17. Convis, Gary, Role of Management in a Lean Manufacturing Environment, Society of Automotive Engineers, http://www.sae.org/manufacturing/lean/column/leanjul01.htm (accessed December 20, 2007).
18. Toussaint, John and Roger Gerard, *On the Mend: Revolutionizing Healthcare to Save Lives and Transform the Industry,* Cambridge, MA: Lean Enterprise Institute, 2010, p. 122.
19. Barnas, Kim, *Beyond Heroes: A Lean Management System for Healthcare,* Appleton, WI: ThedaCare Center for Healthcare Value, 2014, p.118.
20. Liker, Jeffrey and Michael Hoseus, *Toyota Culture: The Heart and Soul of the Toyota Way,* New York: McGraw-Hill, 2008, p. xxvii.

21. Ohno, *Toyota Production System*, p. xiii.
22. Toyota Motor Corporation, CSR policy, corporate website, http://www.toyota-global.com/sustainability/csr/csr/ (accessed March 25, 2015).
23. Graban, Mark, "How Lean management helped hospitals avoid layoffs," *Fierce Healthcare*, October 1, 2010, http://www.fiercehealthcare.com/story/how-lean-management-helped-hospitals-avoid-layoffs/2010-10-01 (accessed March 25, 2015).
24. Graban, Mark and Joseph E. Swartz, *Healthcare Kaizen*, New York: Productivity Press, 2012, p. 4.
25. Pear, Robert, "Health official takes parting shot at 'waste,'" *New York Times*, December 3, 2011, http://www.nytimes.com/2011/12/04/health/policy/parting-shot-at-waste-by-key-obama-health-official.html?_r=0 (accessed April 2, 2015).
26. Louis M. Savary and Clare Crawford-Mason, *The Nun and the Bureaucrat*, Washington, DC: CC-M Productions, 2006, p. 26.
27. Liker and Hoseus, *Toyota Culture*, 326.
28. Womack, Jim, Respect for People, monthly e-mail letter from Lean Enterprise Institute, December 20, 2007, http://Lean.org/Community/Registered/ShowEmail.cfm?JimsEmailId=75 (accessed March 26, 2015).
29. Rode, Jenny, "Breaking the rice ceiling," *Battle Creek Enquirer*, http://www.battlecreekenquirer.com/apps/pbcs.dll/article?AID=/20060212/NEWS01/602120304/1002 (accessed September 15, 2015).
30. Szabo, Liz, "Global goal: Reduce medical errors," *USA Today*, http://usatoday30.usatoday.com/news/health/ 2005-08-23-medical-errors_x.htm (accessed September 12, 2015).
31. Japanese Management Association, *Kanban Just in Time at Toyota: Management Begins at the Workplace*, New York: Productivity Press, 1986, p. xv.
32. Scholtes, Peter R., *The Leader's Handbook: Making Things Happen, Getting Things Done*, New York: McGraw-Hill, 1997, p. 331.
33. Szcerba, Robert, Consumer Reports Study: Demanding Respect from Doctors May Save Your Life, http://www.forbes.com/sites/robertszczerba/2015/01/19/consumer-reports-demanding-respect-from-doctors-may-save-your-life/ (accessed October 27, 2015).
34. Toussaint, John, presentation, Lean Healthcare Transformation Summit, June 2009.
35. Spear, Steven J., *The High-Velocity Edge: How Market Leaders Leverage Operational Excellence to Beat the Competition*, New York: McGraw-Hill, 2010, p. 22.
36. Spear, Steven J., "Fixing healthcare from the inside, today," *Harvard Business Review*, Reprint #1738, September 2005, p. 5.
37. Shook, John, presentation, First Global Lean Healthcare Summit, June 25, 2007.
38. Deming, W. Edwards, *Out of the Crisis*, Cambridge MA: MIT CAES Press, 1982, p. 88.
39. Healthcare Value Network, Network, http://createvalue.org/networks/healthcare-value-network/ (accessed April 2, 2015).
40. Spear, Steven and Kent H. Bowen, "Decoding the DNA of the Toyota Production System," *Harvard Business Review* 1999, 77(5): 97–106.
41. Kenagy, Charles, *Designed to Adapt: Leading Healthcare in Challenging Times*, Bozeman, MT: Second River Healthcare Press, 2009, p. 1.
42. National Institute of Standards and Technology, Improvement Tools, http://www.nist.gov/baldrige/improve.cfm (accessed September 12, 2015).
43. Graban, Mark, Podcast #218—Karen Kiel-Rosser, Baldrige & Mary Greeley Medical Center, http://www.leanblog.org/218 (accessed September 12, 2015).
44. iSixSigma.com, What Is Six Sigma? http://www.isixsigma.com/new-to-six-sigma/getting-started/what-six-sigma/ (accessed September 12, 2015).
45. iSixSigma.com.
46. American Nurses Credentialing Center, ANCC Magnet Recognition Program, http://www.nursecredentialing.org/magnet.aspx (accessed September 12, 2015).
47. INTEGRIS Baptist Medical Center, 2011 Nursing Annual Report, http://integrisok.com/upload/docs/Baptist/INTEGRIS%20NURSE%20AnnualReport%202011.pdf (accessed September 12, 2015).
48. Linkous, Clay, email correspondence, 2015.

49. Chassin Mark R. and Jerod M. Loeb, "High-reliability health care: Getting there from here," *The Milbank Quarterly* 2013, 91(3): 459–490.
50. Agency for Healthcare Research and Quality, TeamSTEPPS®: National Implementation, http://teamstepps.ahrq.gov/about-2cl_3.htm (accessed September 12, 2015).
51. Graban, Mark, Podcast #195—Steve Montague, Lean + TeamSTEPPS for Patient Safety, http://www.leanblog.org/195 (accessed October 7, 2015).

Chapter 3

Value and Waste

Waste: A Global Problem with Local Solutions

A 2012 report from the Institute of Medicine (IOM) estimated that about one-third of healthcare spending in the United States—a total of about $765 billion a year—is "waste." Some of that waste is driven by broader societal issues, such as fraud or a lack of health insurance, but many of the categories of waste identified by the IOM can be addressed through Lean, including "inefficiently delivered services" ($130 billion) and "unnecessary services" ($210 billion).

While the United States and other countries try to address systemic waste through payment reform and other national initiatives, health systems can take action locally to reduce large amounts of waste. In 2011, when Dr. Don Berwick was the administrator of the Centers for Medicare and Medicaid Services (CMS), he said healthcare transformation "won't yield to a massive top-down national project." Instead, he proposed, "Successful redesign of health care is a community by community task."[1] Let's start by identifying and reducing or eliminating waste that we can affect locally.

Reducing Waste Is a Better Goal Than Reducing Cost

Healthcare organizations have focused on trying to reduce costs for a long time, but costs keep rising. Lean provides a different way to look at cost by not directly focusing on it. As author John Kay writes, "Strange as it may seem … winning decisive battles or meeting global business targets are the type of goals often best achieved when pursued indirectly," an idea he calls "obliquity."[2] As an example of this, Patrick Hagan, former chief operating officer of Seattle Children's Hospital, said, "We rarely talk about cost. We talk about waste, quality, and safety and we find our costs go down."[3]

Lean hospitals focus on reducing waste, not cutting costs. Reducing waste leads to lower costs and better performance across the board, but without causing side effects or dysfunction. Lean organizations also focus on the customers (the patients) and the value that is being delivered to them. In this way, Lean is focused not on doing less but rather on delivering the right amount of value. If we are reducing waste, we can often provide more value while expending less effort and less cost. As the Lean Enterprise Institute teaches, "The core idea is to maximize customer value while minimizing waste. Simply, Lean means creating more value for customers with fewer resources."[4]

Cost is important, of course, to Hagan and all hospital leaders; however, Lean thinkers see cost as the end result of all of our systems and processes. Improving quality and patient safety leads to lower costs. Increasing patient flow and patient satisfaction can positively affect the bottom line.

Viewed as an end result, cost is not something that can be directly impacted, at least not without causing other things to get worse. Health systems have typically focused on direct "cost-cutting," which means layoffs and the scaling back of services provided to our communities. Focusing only on cutting costs can also hurt safety and quality, patient satisfaction, and employee morale. As Dr. Berwick commented, "Costs should not be reduced by eliminating any helpful care or by harming a hair on any patient's head."[5] Lean helps us accomplish that goal.

Traditional healthcare cost-cutting also often doesn't reduce costs in a sustainable way. For example, Gary J. Passama, chief executive officer (CEO) of NorthBay Healthcare (Fairfield, California), recognized that their system had three cycles of layoffs over a decade that were driven by financial pressures. However, Passama realized, "After a year or so, the employee count [was] back up and the savings evaporated."[6] Passama concluded, "There has to be a better, longer lasting and less traumatic way to deal with such fiscal situations." In 2012, Passama and NorthBay started a Lean program as a "better, longer lasting, and less traumatic" way of reducing costs.

What Is Waste?

What are the problems and annoyances that constantly appear, interfering with our work and the best patient care? In Lean, we call this *waste*. Dr. Berwick describes waste as "needless hassle" and "what does not make sense in our health care system."[7]

Hospital workdays are full of interruptions, miscommunications, wasted motion, and work-arounds. Employees and leaders often think their job, or the value they bring to an organization, is their ability to put up with problems or to fight fires. When supplies are missing, we run to find them. When our workspaces are badly designed and workloads are high, we walk faster and try harder. When orders do not arrive from a physician's office, we make multiple phone calls to track them down. It's good, in a way, that people make this effort. But, they shouldn't have to. These extra efforts do not prevent the same problem from reoccurring. Instead of pointing at workarounds and heroic measures as "our job," we might do better by viewing waste as something to reduce or eliminate, so we can spend more time doing our real work—caring for patients.

Learning to separate motion (the things we do) from value (the things we do that help the patient) is a critical step in the Lean journey. Instead of defining our jobs in terms of "this is what we do" or "this is how we've always done it," Lean gives us a framework for determining what we *should* be doing and how we should be doing it. Hospitals can learn how to free up time in ways that do not cut corners on quality or care that is needed by the patient.

Hospital employees typically spend a high percentage of their time on wasteful activities. For example, medical/surgical nurses in hospitals around the world typically spend only about 30% of their time on direct patient care, including

- Nursing procedures
- Hygiene and toileting

- Administering medication
- Giving medical guidance

And the studies that generated those results were done before the widespread adoption of electronic medical record (EMR) systems. EMR systems may solve some problems, but new technologies sometimes create new forms of waste and keep providers away from the bedside even more than before.

Seattle's Virginia Mason Medical Center has used Lean methods to increase nursing time at the bedside from about 33% to 90%.[8] The National Health Service in the United Kingdom has taught Lean methods to nurses and hospital staff through its Releasing Time to Care program.[9] On average, time at the bedside increased from 35% to 55% across 19 NHS Scotland hospitals that implemented the program.[10] Hospitals in the United States are using a similar approach called Transforming Care at the Bedside (TCAB), which sets a goal of increasing bedside time from 30% to 70%. One system that adopted TCAB reported the time nurses spent in patient rooms increased from 2.5 hours in a 12-hour shift to 6.5 hours, resulting in a 32% reduction in falls and a 17% reduction in medication errors. Nurse turnover rates in TCAB hospitals fell by nearly 20%, suggesting that an environment with less waste and more time for patient care is more rewarding for staff.[11]

When employees, departments, or hospitals are overworked, we need to reduce waste instead of just asking for more resources and people. Reducing waste, by improving processes, also allows us to take on more work without adding head count, doing so in a way that does not stress our employees. Reducing waste also provides time for people to do their work the right way— providing high quality and great service to patients instead of being pressured to cut corners due to a lack of time. Eliminating waste allows us to reduce costs, provide more service, improve quality, and improve employee satisfaction—it is good for all of our hospital stakeholders.

What Is Value? Start with the Customer

If waste is an activity that does not add value, what is value? In *Lean Thinking*, Womack and Jones stated, "Value can only be defined by the ultimate customer."[12] What does that mean for a health system that is practicing Lean? We need to start by asking the question, "Who is the customer?" In a hospital setting, we might have many customers for any given activity or care that is provided. The most obvious "ultimate" customer is the patient. Most work activities and priorities should be centered on that customer. In general, Lean will support a health system's efforts at delivering more "patient-centered care."

Others who might be viewed as customers might include the patient's family, physicians, hospital employees, and payers. Each of these different stakeholders might define value in a different way. For example, a family member of a patient undergoing outpatient surgery might find value in knowing and understanding the exact status of the patient at all times, reducing the amount of worry during the patient's time in the hospital.

There may be times when we think of an internal customer in a process, or the person who receives our work. For instance, a physician, working on behalf of the patient, is the primary recipient of a pathologist's report. When a patient's biopsy is sent to the lab, the pathologist might also think about the physician's needs and quality criteria, as well as the patient's. The ordering physician might have specific requirements for how the information should be presented and structured in the pathology report.

In any process, the person doing the work should think about the ultimate end customer but can also do his or her work in a way that allows the "downstream" recipient of the work to be a more effective partner in the total patient care effort. Internal customer needs must be in alignment with the end customer, the patient. Discussion of internal customer needs should not distract from the needs of the ultimate customer, as an organization might run the risk of becoming too inwardly focused instead of being properly patient focused.

One of the Lean thinking principles that is questioned or gets confusing in hospitals, at times, is pull. The idea of pull is more straightforward for materials management, as described in Chapter 6, about *kanban*, as supplies are pulled only when they are needed in the right quantities, as opposed to being pushed regardless of need, such as a "standing order." Hospitals sometimes think they already have "pull" in the sense that a patient might be kept in the emergency department (ED) until an inpatient room has been vacated. People often say the empty room "pulls the patient from the ED." That's not really pull.

Back in factory settings, the customer always pulls in the sense that the customer makes a request for what is needed. Activity is generated by customer need, not based on when it is convenient for the factory or machine availability. In a hospital setting, when a patient needs a bed, the patient should be able to figuratively pull that resource, rather than having to wait, even though it is the patient who is being moved to the bed.

The real question is not "push versus pull," but more about how to improve poor flow that causes patients and care to be delayed.

Some have argued that patient flow actually improves when the ED pushes patients so that they wait in the hallway of an inpatient unit instead of the hallway of the ED. Moving a patient to a unit without a bed is thought to create incentives for inpatient unit personnel to complete the discharge process for other patients earlier, freeing up the room. That mindset assumes that employees are purposefully slowing the discharge process, which is not always true. Ultimately, bad flow is bad flow, and shifting where the patient waits does not fix the root cause of the issue or the need to keep the patient in the most appropriate location for their needs. The goal is the right care at the right place at the right time.

How Do We Define Value in a Broad Sense?

Dr. Don Berwick, in his 2009 keynote address at the Institute for Healthcare Improvement annual forum, asked about our health and our healthcare, "What do we really, really, really want?" Dr. Berwick proposed he wants "safe, effective, and evidence-based medicine" for his own care. What he "really wants" is to be active and to participate in recreational activities and meaningful family events.[13] Michael Porter suggested that patients value three levels of care: survival and the degree of recovery, the time required to get back to normal activities, and the sustainability of said treatments.[14]

From a patient perspective, it can be argued that "value" means not just providing efficient, safe, and effective episodes of care when it is needed. Rather than being merely reactive, patients might value a healthcare system that helps keep them healthy and provides a longer life with a higher quality of life. The ultimate value of Lean might be to think through these high-level questions rather than just focusing on tweaking today's healthcare delivery models. Porter wrote that value at a high level should be based on results, not activity, and should be measured as "the ratio of successful patient outcomes achieved to the total cost of care for the patient's medical condition."

Dr. John Toussaint and others define value as an equation of quality divided by cost. We increase the value provided to patients and society by improving quality and reducing cost. Those two goals are often viewed as trade-offs, but Lean shows us how to improve both simultaneously. Dr. Toussaint and his ThedaCare Center for Healthcare Value promote payment reform as an important complement to the use of Lean to redesign care. Toussaint writes, "When physicians are paid per-patient, per-month, however, they will quickly learn to use an array of professionals to keep people healthy," instead of just treating patients after they get sick.[15]

Trends toward "value-based purchasing" (VBP) and other new reimbursement models of paying for outcomes and quality are in line with this thinking and with Lean principles. Capitated payment systems, diagnosis-related groups (DRGs), and accountable care organizations (ACOs) are examples of systems that attempt to pay for results or outcomes instead of paying for activity, often known as "fee for service."

Hospital executives realize this is the future of healthcare. Chris Van Gorder, CEO of Scripps Health[16] (San Diego, California), said, "We should be compensated for results, not just for doing something." Dr. Gary Kaplan, CEO of Virginia Mason Medical Center, commented, "I'm encouraged by the early pay-for-value work" and said that the trend toward VBP is "a good thing" because the current fee-for-service model drives higher costs of care.[17] More hospitals realize that keeping patients out of the hospital is going to be the goal in the future, by keeping people healthy and providing more care at home.

The broader health system (including the government and other payers) often saves money in the short term, but spends more in the long term. One example might be refusing to pay for monthly nutritional counseling sessions (at $100 each) that might help keep somebody healthy while approving larger payments for bariatric surgery (at $15,000) or an amputation (at $30,000).[18] Helping a patient stay healthy (and keep a foot) arguably provides more value at a lower cost. Geisinger Health System CEO David Feinberg says, "I think my job ultimately is to close every one of our hospitals [except for complex surgeries that require hospitalization]. Because we should take care of you at home." In coming years, health systems will be challenged to deliver value and care in new locations and innovative ways.

What if some emergency care could be delivered in the field, without the extra transportation to and from the hospital? Pilot programs in Mesa, Arizona and Anaheim, California are sending nurse practitioners out with paramedics to respond to medical 911 calls. An estimated 35% of calls are "deemed non-urgent and low in severity," such as minor stomach pain, not requiring a trip to the ED. Todd Newton, regional chief of emergency medicine for Kaiser Permanente, says, "They don't have to come in. They don't have to wait. They are being treated in a comfortable setting. It opens up our beds for people who really need them. Everybody wins."[19] Expected benefits include shorter waiting times, lower cost, better care, and a more comfortable setting at home. Even though the average EMS call time for these patients increases from 15 minutes to 50 minutes, the EMS team is more available for other patients since they are not tied up waiting for their patient to be brought into the crowded ED.

How Does Lean Define "Value?"

Within the context of these big picture questions, the Lean methodology gives us some specific rules to use in determining what activities are value-added (VA) or non-value-added (NVA). The three general rules that must be met for an activity to be considered value-added are[20]

1. The customer must be willing to pay for the activity.
2. The activity must transform the product or service in some way.
3. The activity must be done correctly the first time.

All three of these rules must be met or the activity is non-value-added, or waste.

Rule 1: The Customer Must Be Willing to Pay for the Activity

Thinkers with diverse backgrounds such as Porter and Womack agree that value must be defined from the customer's perspective.[21,22] This idea is less complicated in manufacturing. Think of buying a car. If you don't want a sunroof, you can choose to not get a sunroof, thereby not paying for a sunroof. If you don't value a car at all, you can often avoid buying a car. You might instead choose to pay to use a bus, taxi, or ride-sharing service, since what you really value, in terms of an outcome, is getting from point A to point B, safely and conveniently.

In healthcare, this question of willingness to pay quickly gets complicated, as patients often have no choice but to receive care. Additionally, the person receiving the care is most often not the person who is paying. Given the potential for different definitions of value from different customers, how can we agree on value? Often, the providers of a service assume what is valued or not valued by customers. One method for determining what customers value is to ask them. Some hospitals are beginning to formally involve patients and their families in improvement efforts, including asking patients to help define value for their care and the overall services provided by the hospital.[23]

With the first rule, we can start with the patient as customer. A medical professional might think, "Our customers do not always know enough to answer that question! They do not appreciate everything we have to do for them." That might be true; sometimes, customers or patients have to be educated. Hospital employees, caregivers, or leaders cannot assume that any activity that we do is automatically value-added because of our job title or because a certain activity has always been done or done a particular way.

A patient who comes in with a suspected hip fracture would value the steps directly required for comfort, diagnosis, and treatment. Time spent directly with caregivers, such as nurses and surgeons, would be valued. The patient having to give the same triage information to three different people would be waste the second and third times. Having X-rays reviewed would be valued, but time spent waiting because the radiologist is too busy would be considered waste. Education about how to reduce future falls at home might be valued, as well.

Rule 2: The Activity Must Transform the Product or Service in Some Way

The original manufacturing definition for the second rule described changing the "form, fit, or function of the product,"[24] meaning there was a physical change that brought the product closer to its final state. For example, installing a car door changes the product in a value-added way as customers are willing to pay for doors, and the product changes from a doorless chassis to one with doors. Time spent moving doors in the factory, repairing them, or waiting to assemble them would be non-value-added because nothing is changing with the product.

Depending on the situation, the "product" in a hospital might be the patient, a radiology order, a medication, or a laboratory specimen. *Product* is admittedly an insensitive term for patients and is usually avoided. Consider the process by which a patient's blood is tested for potassium levels. The product takes many different forms. The step of physician order entry changes the product from a thought in the physician's head to an order in the hospital electronic medical record and electronic health record (EMR/EHR) system.

The phlebotomist's activity of collecting the specimen changes the product from an order in the system to a tube of the patient's blood. This fits both definitions (it is valued by the patient and changes the product), so it can be called value-added, assuming the work is done properly.

The definition of the second rule can be adapted slightly when we are working with a patient instead of a product. We might define this rule as "The activity must move the patient closer to their ideal health and quality of life in some way." Value-adding steps in patient care might include broad categories of

- Providing comfort for pain
- Stabilizing the patient
- Diagnosis
- Treatment
- Education
- Activities that maintain health and quality of life

If an activity moves the patient from one state to another, in the direction of the desired final state (such as reducing their pain), we can say the patient has been changed in a value-added way. Diagnosing the hip fracture, alleviating the pain, and fixing or replacing the hip would be value-added steps without much controversy.

Merely moving the patient from point A to point B is considered non-value-added. People might question this, pointing out that patients have to be moved from their room to the radiology department to get a computed axial tomographic (CAT) scan. That is true, but we would consider the CAT scan itself to be the value-added step, as it moves the patient from the state of an undiagnosed condition to a state at which a diagnosis could be made. Moving the patient to radiology might be considered "required waste," as discussed further in this chapter.

Rule 3: The Activity Must Be Done Correctly the First Time

An activity might meet the requirements of the first two rules, but if something was done incorrectly, requiring rework and additional motion, we do not get credit for doing the same activity twice as double the value-added time.

There are far too many examples of things not being done right the first time in departments throughout the hospital. A physician might write a prescription for a medication for which the patient has a known allergy. This motion and time, along with the time taken by the pharmacy tech who prepared and labeled the medication, along with the time of pharmacist who caught the error, would all be considered waste. If the prescription had been written correctly, that would be considered a value-added step. In that example, the outcome was correct, and the patient was not harmed. But, the value was delivered in a way that was wasteful. A Lean process would help prevent errors from occurring in the first place, as discussed further in Chapter 8.

In another example, the final minutes of a surgical procedure would not be value-added if an error occurred in the counting and verification of sponges used during the procedure. If the patient's incision is closed (what would be a value-added step) with a sponge left inside the patient, the activity of reopening the patient's incision would be considered waste. If we have to reopen the incision to remove the sponge and reclose the incision, we cannot claim the extra motion and time were value-added. Again, it is far better for all involved to devise systems that prevent such an error.

Hospitals and surgeons have often been paid for non-value-added work because of the activity that was done, rather than the value. For example, a study published in 2007 by the Leapfrog found only 32.3% of hospitals were in "full compliance" with practices that prevent surgical site infections. Preventable infections were, at the time, adding $15,000 to the patient's bill.[25] Would you pay more for a new car if it had been damaged and then repaired in the factory before you received it? Of course not.

This is changing, through new guidelines issued by the U.S. government and the CMS. CMS, followed by some private payers, no longer pays for certain types of errors or rework—care not done correctly the first time.[26] These so-called "never events" include procedures that are done to remove objects left inside patients, preventable infections, air embolisms, and falls. Hospitals have previously tried to reduce these errors and the resulting rework because it is the right thing for the patient. These new payer expectations are an attempt to create more of an incentive for improvement. Lean thinkers are working diligently to make sure these events go from commonly occurring to never occurring.

Examples of Value-Added and Non-Value-Added Activities

Value-added and non-value-added activities can be viewed from the perspective of products, patients, employees, or caregivers. Table 3.1 shows some examples of value-added and non-value-added activity for different roles in various hospital departments.

When categorizing what people do, the distinction between value-added and non-value-added activity is not to be mistaken for a value judgment of individuals or specific roles in an organization. The intent is not to say that surgeons—the people or the role—are value-added, and operating room technicians are non-value-added. The judgment of value-added versus non-value-added is based on the work being done at a given moment. We all have moments in our day that are non-value-added. If the surgeon is standing in the operating room waiting because somebody had to run off to find a missing surgical instrument, that is certainly non-value-added time. The presence of waste does not indicate that an employee is bad or not working hard. On the contrary, waste causes people to work too hard as they fight problems that interrupt their value-added work. Waste tends to be driven by the system and the design (or lack of design) of our processes.

Table 3.2 shows some examples of value-added and non-value-added activity for different departments and products in a hospital.

The distinction between value-added and non-value-added work is not always straightforward and obvious in hospitals. In one hospital, the team debated if nurses' charting activities were value-added. One side made the argument that charting did not directly care for the patient, so it should be considered non-value-added. The other group argued that charting was value-added because it passed along information that helped a physician make decisions about a patient's care. A middle ground was reached that some charting was value-added (because it did have an impact on patient care), but wasted time caused by system problems was non-value-added. The practice

Table 3.1   Value-Added (VA) and Non-Value-Added (NVA) Examples for Different Roles in Hospital Departments

Department	Role	VA Activity Example	NVA Activity Example
Operating room	Surgeon	Operating on patient	Re-opening a patient to retrieve a retained item
Pharmacy	Pharmacy technician	Creating an intravenous formulation	Reprocessing medications that were returned from patient units
Inpatient unit	Nurse	Administering medications to a patient	Copying information from one computer system into another or to paper
Radiology	Radiology technician	Performing magnetic resonance imaging procedure	Performing a medically unnecessary scan
Laboratory	Medical technologist	Interpreting a test result	Fixing a broken instrument
Nutrition services	Dietary staff	Preparing food for a patient	Stacking and restacking plates and trays

Table 3.2   Value-Added (VA) and Non-Value-Added (NVA) Examples for Different "Products" in Hospital Processes

Department	"Product"	VA Activity	NVA Activity
Emergency room	Patient	Being evaluated or treated	Waiting to be seen
Clinical laboratory	Patient specimen	Being centrifuged or tested	Waiting to be moved to the next station as a "batch"
Pharmacy	Prescription	Medication being formulated or prepared	Being inspected multiple times
Perioperative services	Sterilized instruments	Time when instruments are being sterilized	Instruments being sterilized repeatedly without ever being used from a standard kit
Nutrition services	Patient food tray	Time when food is being cooked or tray is being assembled	Being reworked because the tray was made incorrectly

of "overcharting" or putting more information than is necessary for patient care might also be considered waste.

Ultimately, it can be an academic exercise to categorize an activity as value or waste. Rather than arguing for hours about the classification, it is more important to ask if we can eliminate that step or find a better way. Looking for waste is meant to be a way that leads to improvement by challenging existing practices.

Learning to Identify and Describe Waste

To help identify waste, having specific shared terminology can help. Ohno defined seven types of waste, while later publications often listed eight types.[27] These definitions have been adopted as a useful framework for viewing waste in hospitals. Sometimes, the terms are used verbatim; sometimes, they are modified. Having complete agreement on the exact terms is not crucial, as Toyota did not intend this list to be all-inclusive or to be something that could not be changed. Consistent terminology does, however, help us communicate within our organization and across the industry. The types of waste are summarized in Table 3.3.

Table 3.3 The Eight Types of Waste

Type of Waste	Brief Description	Healthcare Example
Defects	Time spent doing something incorrectly, inspecting for errors, or fixing errors	Surgical case cart missing an item; wrong medicine or wrong dose administered to patient
Overproduction	Doing more than what is needed by the customer or doing it sooner than needed	Doing unnecessary diagnostic procedures; producing medications that are not used before the orders change or patient is discharged
Transportation	Unnecessary movement of the "product" (patients, specimens, materials) in a system	Poor layout, such as the catheter lab being located a long distance from the ED; patients moving from building to building to receive cancer treatment
Waiting	Waiting for the next event to occur or next work activity	Employees waiting for a patient, information, or work to do; patients waiting for an appointment, care, or discharge
Inventory	Excess inventory cost through financial costs, storage and movement costs, spoilage, wastage	Expired supplies that must be disposed of, such as out-of-date medications
Motion	Unnecessary movement by employees in the system	Lab employees walking miles per day due to poor layout; walking to find missing supplies, equipment, or medications; unnecessary clicks in an EMR system
Overprocessing	Doing work that is not valued by the customer or is caused by definitions of quality that are not aligned with patient needs	Entering data into a computer system that is never seen or used; Excessive warnings in an EMR system that physicians and nurses just click through
Human potential	Waste and loss due to not engaging employees, listening to their ideas, or supporting their careers	Employees get burned out and stop giving suggestions for improvement or quit their job

Waste of Defects

Defects can be defined as any work activities that are not done right the first time. This might include a form that is not filled out properly or dropping food on the ground in the cafeteria. More serious defects in a hospital setting, however, can cause injury or death. The Institute of Medicine estimated that 400,000 "preventable drug-related injuries" occur in hospitals each year, leading to $3.5 billion in unnecessary costs.[28] Each of these is likely caused by one or more defects, with causes including illegible handwriting (or misclicks in an EMR system), misplaced decimal points, or defects in the process for getting medications to the patient.

In one case that received much media attention, three babies died after they were given adult doses of heparin in the newborn intensive care unit (ICU) of Methodist Hospital (Indianapolis, Indiana).[29] There were numerous "process defects" that led to these deaths, including the stocking of adult doses of heparin by a pharmacy tech in the newborn ICU drug cabinet. In another process defect, nurses did not verify the proper doses before administering them, fully expecting that adult doses would not be in the newborn ICU.

The patient deaths were caused by a number of process defects, miscommunications, and errors—nothing that can be traced back to a single person or a single point of failure. Focusing on the process does not mean that people should never be held accountable. The nurse, in this case, violated hospital policies by not verifying the dose. It is overly simplistic, however, to think that firing or punishing an individual would keep this error from occurring again. This exact same set of process defects led to another high-profile, but non-fatal, overdose case, with the twin babies of actor Dennis Quaid, this time at Cedars-Sinai Hospital in California.[30] We need to ask why multiple nurses violated policies, looking for systemic causes such as overwork, poor lighting, or ineffective training. Defects, and steps that can be taken to prevent them, are covered in more detail in Chapters 7 and 8.

A defect does not necessarily have to cause harm to be considered waste. A defect could be counted even if an error is caught by somebody later in the process, such as a "near miss" or a "good catch." Process defects include things that go wrong that lead to rework or workarounds. For example, if a nurse or phlebotomist draws blood from a patient and there is a problem with the specimen, the failed draw attempt and the time required to have drawn the specimen are considered waste. The defect slows the product (the patient specimen and the test result) and wastes time for the employees.

Some problems could be characterized as "process defects," as something that goes wrong can lead to wasted motion and overprocessing. For example, one hospital's anatomic pathology lab improved the way it organized and stored tissue slides that had already been read. In some cases, a pathologist has to review and re-read a slide. Before the improvements, staff could not find some slides, meaning that the tissue block (if it could be found) would have to be recut, meaning more time, labor, and cost (not to mention delays).

Waste of Overproduction

Overproduction can be defined as producing too much of a product (more than the customer desires) or producing earlier than it is needed by the customer. Waste of overproduction can be defined more easily using a manufacturing scenario. If you are in the market for a new car and visit a dealer, much of the inventory you see sitting on the lot is overproduction—and you often get a discount as a result.

Studies show that "20 to 50 percent of hospital lab tests are completely unnecessary," as the need is generally not questioned after being ordered by residents or physicians.[31] Unnecessary tests do more than overproduce information that might not be medically useful or increase costs; they can also cause patients to become anemic if too much blood is drawn. University of Utah Health Care started requiring residents to justify each test, and the hospital saved $200,000 a year as unnecessary tests were reduced. Reducing waste is good, but a Lean thinker would ensure that physicians are not being pressured into not ordering tests that could be helpful for the patient.

Hospital pharmacies produce (by formulation or delivery) medications for internal customers (nurses and patients). Delivering medications too early can be considered overproduction when some medications end up being returned to the pharmacy because orders changed or the patient was discharged. At Riverside Medical Center (Kankakee, Illinois), 480 medications were returned to the pharmacy each day (more than one per admitted patient). "That's dollars just sitting there [in the returns bin]," said Lori Warren, pharmacy operations manager.

The overproduction of medications led to other types of waste, as pharmacy employees spent a total of 11 hours per day processing returned medications. The improved process delivered medications more frequently during the day, adding more transportation and motion, but with the trade-off of reducing the reprocessing work by 10% and helping ensure the right medications were available when needed. Adding delivery labor, along with other improvements that were made, reduced the total labor required and overall costs, a common theme with Lean in healthcare.

In many cases, hospitals can avoid the overproduction of doing more than necessary for effective patient care. Some laboratories have phlebotomists draw "just-in-case" tubes from inpatients to have extra specimens in case unplanned testing is required after the draw. Labs often find the extra tubes are rarely used (less than 10% of the time), resulting in wasted time, motion, and materials. Looking at trade-offs with the types of waste, it might be easier to rationalize the just-in-case tubes when a trauma patient arrives at the ED, as having the tubes already drawn can prevent waiting time in providing care. Or, it is possible that drawing a "rainbow" of tubes in advance of orders being written is a workaround for laboratory turnaround times being longer than desired. A better systemic fix might be to improve the flow of the lab testing to reduce the need for that overproduction.

One hospital's chief clinical officer discovered that the quality department was "overproducing" information in terms of reports. He found more than 320 different reports were generated on a daily or annual basis, an "astronomical number," as he described it. This happened, in part, because there was no formal process for evaluating requests for reports, as every request was accepted, even if it ended up duplicating an existing report. The CCO questioned the quality of many of these reports (were they full of defects or just not useful?) and if they were even read by anybody. He initiated a process to reduce unnecessary reports and to make sure there was a customer specification for any report that was to remain. He was surprised to learn that there was no formal process to obsolesce a given report, so that had to be created as well.

Charting too early, before the care is provided, is another example of overproducing of information, and it introduces the risk of defects in care. If a nurse in a unit records medication administration for multiple patients in advance, as a batch, the nurse might think they are saving time and being efficient. However, defects can occur if the nurse gets sidetracked or distracted and the medication is not given as planned, especially if it is close to a shift change and the next nurse thinks the patient received their last dose.

In a rural African vaccination clinic, a nurse was observed filling out paper immunization records for a number of babies, doing the work in a large batch before the vaccines were given. Unfortunately, the clinic then ran out of vaccine doses partway through the session (inventory waste that leads to the waste of waiting and additional transportation waste for the mother to bring the baby back). Defects were also created, as the now inaccurate vaccination record might have not been corrected if the mother left in a hurry, possibly causing a baby to not get that dose, even during their next attempt.

Reducing Unnecessary Care

Unnecessary medical care could be considered a costly form of overproduction. Nearly one-half of surveyed physicians admit that "their patients receive too much medical care."[32] While some surgeons get convicted for intentional, fraudulent excess, more common and systemic causes of unnecessary care include a lack of prevention, not following current clinical best practices, defensive medicine, or overdiagnosis. Some medical situations won't have a clear pathway. For example, Dr. Atul Gawande talks about situations where a microcarcinoma is unlikely to cause harm. Should it be removed or just monitored?[33] Questions of clinical "standardized work" are probably best resolved by physicians and clinical experts, not a hospital's Lean department, as discussed more in Chapter 5.

In England's National Health Service (NHS), experts estimate that one in seven "hospital operations and medications" are "not necessary," costing the nation more than £1.8 billion a year, or about 1.6% of their annual spending, in addition to subjecting patients to unnecessary risk. Surveys showed that one-half of NHS hernia surgery patients showed their procedure had "no effect or had even made things worse." NHS England also estimates that one in 20 hospital admissions are not necessary.[34]

Some hospitals, including Virginia Mason Medical Center (Seattle, Washington), have made attempts to reduce the overproduction of radiology and other diagnostic procedures. Virginia Mason started a program in which clinicians decided they would first refer patients with certain types of conditions to physical therapy before approving radiology procedures. This less expensive therapy was expected to be more beneficial than a diagnostic procedure. Unfortunately, Virginia Mason sacrificed revenue because the insurance payers would have likely paid for the magnetic resonance imaging (MRI) or other radiology procedure. This illustrates one of the dysfunctions of a payer system in which hospitals are often paid for their activity instead of for patient outcomes. Virginia Mason was trying to be responsible in how it spent other people's money, but reducing that overproduction harmed the hospital in the short term. Virginia Mason responded by proposing a savings-sharing arrangement with insurers and payers, getting higher reimbursements for physical therapy so both parties could benefit from the waste reduction.[35]

ThedaCare is one of many health systems that have reduced the occurrence of labor being induced or a C-section being scheduled before 40 weeks. Often, these early births are requested by the mother or physician for a non-medical reason. One East Coast hospital reported that some mothers requested "cute" delivery dates, such as Halloween, their own birthday, or New Year's Day. By reducing avoidable early births, outcomes are improved. At ThedaCare, the average number of days spent in the neonatal ICU fell from 30 days to 16. Due to the predominant fee-for-service payment model, revenue fell by one-half.[36] Thankfully, ThedaCare is willing to do the right thing, even if there is a short-term financial penalty to them.

One health system's world-renowned neurology department unfortunately made all but the most urgent patients wait a long time for an appointment in the clinic. When patients were seen, the neurologists often concluded that the referral from primary care had been unnecessary or inappropriate. While they could bill for seeing the patient, their own sense of intrinsic motivation to help patients made them feel like the appointment slots were wasted. Each inappropriate referral meant patients who really needed the consult had to wait. The neurology department created better guidelines that they used to educate other physicians about when to refer patients to neurology (or not). This could be considered a form of clinical "standardized work," as will be discussed further in Chapter 5.

One could argue that the overutilization of diagnostic procedures or other care should be categorized as overprocessing instead of overproduction. But again, it is less important to have 100% agreement on the classification than it is to develop patient-focused process improvements as a result of discovering that waste.

Waste of Transportation

Waste of transportation refers to excess movement of the product through a system. Some amount of transportation might well be necessary given the context of the current hospital layout. For example, blood specimen collections are done in an inpatient's room. For ideal flow, the specimen would be sent immediately to the lab for testing; however, in many cases, that specimen is carried in a tray from room to room as the phlebotomist collects more specimens. In their attempt to reduce wasted motion, transportation and waiting times have been increased for the specimen and the patient. See Chapter 9 for more on improving flow.

The waste of transportation can apply even to patients. One hospital was using Lean methods to improve patient flow through its operating rooms, and followed patients from arrival to surgery. During the course of her visit for a procedure, one 74-year-old woman walked the equivalent of five and a half football fields. The redesign of the hospital was going to more carefully take patient walking distances into account to reduce that waste.

Given the opportunity, we might reconfigure the hospital layout in a way that reduces transportation distance for patients or specimens. More likely, we might use our understanding of transportation waste to improve the design and construction of a new facility.

Park Nicollet Health Services in Minnesota built its Frauenshuh Cancer Center based on the idea of reducing patient transportation time and distance. Rather than making sick patients expend their limited energy by walking between areas and buildings (often through the snow), the new center was designed so that patients remain in a single room for their nurse and doctor visits, lab draws, treatment, and other support services—everything but radiation treatment. "Where care comes to you" becomes both a design principle and a marketing slogan, and a great example of patient-centered care.[37] Virginia Mason Medical Center had similar goals with their Floyd & Delores Jones Cancer Institute, as "all cancer services are brought directly to the patient in his or her private treatment room" with their new design, saving 500 feet of walking and hours of time for patients.[38]

Waste of Waiting

Waiting time can be defined, simply, as time when nothing value-added is happening. It is easy for most to see the lack of activity as a type of waste. Patients wait—and wait—for the next step in their patient pathway (waiting everywhere, not just in waiting rooms). Employees wait because of systemic problems or because of uneven workloads. Lean methods can help reduce both types of waiting.

Patients and Products Waiting

Patients are often unaware of waste or risks associated with the waste of defects. However, the waste of waiting is obvious since they directly experience it, whether that means waiting for an appointment or waiting once they arrive.

Patients often wait for appointments in physician clinics or for procedures due to poor flow caused by preventable process problems or by poor scheduling practices. Hospitals might not have previously focused on reducing this waste if they had been more concerned about maximizing the use of particular hospital resources, such as MRI machines, beds, or physicians. For example, the old practice of having all surgical patients arrive at 6:30 a.m. for "as follows" procedures helps ensure the surgeons and operating rooms are fully utilized, without delays between. One physician observed that, when he was a patient, an orthopedic surgeon asked 35 patients to all arrive at 8:00 a.m., when they clearly weren't going to be seen at the same time.[39] Lean helps us see that this is not a patient-centered approach. Moving to give each procedure a scheduled time and having a patient arrive 90 or 120 minutes before their time reduces patient waiting and improves patient satisfaction, but creates some risk of lower surgical utilization if there are cancelations or no-show patients. As in other situations, these risks must be balanced, or we are challenged to find a creative solution that reduces all types of waste in a process.

Patients are not the only product that waits in a hospital process. Physical products, such as tubes of blood for the laboratory, pharmacy orders and medications, and instruments to be sterilized, also spend a high percentage of time waiting instead of having value-added work performed on them, as is discussed more in Chapter 4 on observing process flows. This waiting is often due to batching within or between departments; lack of first in, first out (FIFO) flow; or the product waiting on employees who have multiple responsibilities, often in the name of being kept busy and fully utilized.

New London Medical Center is a ThedaCare-affiliated critical access hospital. As part of the system's work to improve "door-to-doc" time for Code STEMI (segment elevation myocardial infarction) patients, they originally focused on reducing the "door to transfer," meaning the time that elapsed before the patient was transferred to Appleton Medical Center, some 20 miles away by car. Because time is so critical in these situations, patients had been transported by helicopter. The transportation is "necessary waste," since a small hospital like New London typically does not have a cath lab as would a larger hospital. For other types of care, the emergency department determines if the patient should stay or should be transported, based on their needs and condition.

For the Code STEMI patients, who always had to be transported, the hospital realized that the patient was waiting for the helicopter to arrive, with time ticking away (and "time is muscle" when the heart is concerned). An analysis showed that immediately loading the patient into a waiting ambulance and driving took the same amount of time as did waiting and flying. So, transportation was switched to the less expensive method, since it did not affect the quality of care. A New London leader said, "What patients care about is getting the care; they don't care about the helicopter." Patients who arrive at New London now get the catheterization within 90 minutes approximately 95% of the time, with an average of 75 minutes.

Employees Waiting

Employees are often put in the position of waiting instead of being able to perform value-added work. Common causes of employee waits can include process defects, delays in upstream processes, uneven workloads, and low patient volumes.

Many departments have uneven workloads, including radiology, the ED, or operating rooms. While we want to level workloads and prevent process defects that lead to employee waiting time, there are some cases when the waste of waiting is necessary, or at least preferable to other types of waiting. When we have unpredictable or unscheduled demand, such as in an ED, the prudent approach might be to err on the side of having employees waiting, being ready to go when needed. Choosing to selectively spend more on "excess" labor can sometimes reduce overall system cost and performance. Hospitals need to evaluate employee waiting on a case-by-case basis, understanding which waiting has a root cause that can be eliminated and which is helpful in preventing patient care delays. In many cases, waiting time can be replaced with productive activities, such as problem solving and continuous improvement work instead of just sending people home. See the book *Healthcare Kaizen* for an in-depth discussion of how to capitalize on free time and engage staff in improvement.

Waste of Inventory

All inventory, such as materials, supplies, and equipment, is not inherently wasteful. *Excessive* inventory is waste, meaning we have more inventory than is needed to perform our work properly and provide the right care at the right time. When inventories are too high, the hospital's cash is tied up in the inventory sitting on shelves, or excess inventory may expire, including supplies and medications.

Many manufacturing companies harmed themselves by thinking Lean meant keeping inventory low as a primary goal. A Lean approach first takes care of customer and patient needs but does so with the lowest possible inventory levels, given the current system, including the effects of variation. We should not take the current system as given; we want to look for root causes that lead us to hold inventory so we can eliminate those problems. One root cause might be unreliable vendors whose time required to replenish inventory varies (due to transportation delays or infrequent shortages).

Having too much inventory wastes space and cash, but running out of inventory can result in preventable harm to patients or, perhaps, less than ideal care if a less-effective medication is used. Additionally, reacting to inventory shortages leads to additional wasted motion, costs, and expediting. Employees might have to make additional unplanned trips to stockrooms, or they might have to place expensive expedited orders from vendors, sent via overnight shipping. In a Lean environment, keeping the right supplies and inventory on hand ensures the right patient care can be delivered while reducing costs and waste for the hospital. One hospital used Lean to reduce medication stockouts by 85%, while also reducing the total amount of inventory on hand.[40] It is not uncommon to see million-dollar cost reductions in hospital-wide inventory improvement efforts while also increasing the availability of supplies, as discussed in Chapter 6.

In some cases, improved inventory management can help reduce other types of waste. One hospital was working on improving the adherence to their method for inserting central lines, with the goal of reducing infections. To properly perform the work, a technician or nurse had to gather and bring ten separate items to the patient's room, including drapes, gloves, the line, and sutures. If one item, such as a drape, were forgotten, there would be a temptation not to walk back to the inventory storage area. This would reduce the waste of motion but might also create a process defect (not following the standardized work), which can lead to an infection. By purchasing a new stock item, a central-line kit that combined all of those individual supplies, the risk of forgetting or not being able to find an item was eliminated (as long as the kit was kept in stock). This eliminated the need for extra motion that would have been needed to properly insert the central line and encouraged staff to use the best-known methods for the benefit of patient safety. In addition to benefiting patients, it is likely that the increased cost of buying a kit would be more than offset by the cost savings of not having to treat these infections that would have likely occurred.

Waste of Motion

While the waste of transportation focuses on the product (including the patient), the waste of motion refers to those doing the work. Hospitals should reduce the amount of motion required by employees to get the work done. This provides numerous benefits, including reducing the physical fatigue of employees and freeing more time for value-added work, including more and better patient care. As one hospital CEO said, "Nobody should go home hurting at the end of the day."

Wasted motion in a hospital setting is often most obviously seen as unnecessary walking. Walking is often considered part of the job, but it is rarely a value-added activity. One example of walking as value might be a nurse or technician walking with a rehabilitating patient down a hospital corridor. More often, walking is waste that can be reduced by improving workflows, along with the layout and organization of supplies and equipment. The goal is not to have stationary employees who never move, as that would cause other problems, but to reduce or eliminate unnecessary motion and walking.

At one hospital, a finance director had an employee who would constantly run back and forth through the billing office. The director used to think, "We need more people like that," meaning highly motivated employees willing to go above and beyond to get work done. After starting to learn and practice Lean, the director realized that the running was actually a sign of waste in the process. The director started to ask the employee to identify root causes of the running, discovering it was a combination of a bad physical layout (certain frequently needed files were located across the office) and overburden, or "*muri*," in Japanese. By adjusting workloads and changing layouts, the employee no longer had the need, or felt the time pressure, to run.

Our search for wasted motion should not be limited to walking, but walking is usually a good place to start. With the advent and spread of EMR/EHR systems, clinicians often rightfully complain about software being too difficult to use. For example, one physician reports that "It's not uncommon to traverse ten menus to order a routine laboratory test." He also complains about wasted motion for residents, pointing out they "can spend two hours each morning just aggregating numbers from various clinical information systems into a usable format" such as a Microsoft Word document.[41] As with walking, some time spent interacting with a computer is necessary, but a Lean approach to EMR/EHR system design and selection would strive to reduce time and motion spent on clicks and accessing multiple screens. These improvements would also reduce waste for nurses, who sometimes create their own paper-based "cheat sheets" by writing down information from various EMR screens.

Waste of Nursing Motion

Beyond waste caused by computers, nurses typically walk many miles per day, much of it unnecessary. This can be seen in settings as varied as EDs, inpatient units, and cancer treatment centers. Data collected, with electronic pedometers, at one hospital showed a medical/surgical unit nurse consistently walked 3.5–4.5 miles per 12-hour shift. Data collected at an outpatient cancer treatment center showed that nurses walked at a pace of 4.2 miles per day. A general, broad time and motion study suggests that nurses walk a median of three miles per day[42] (another study says four miles)[43], suggesting the norm is "the professional nurse who is constantly moving from patient room to room, nurse station to supply closet and back to room, spending a minority of time on patient care activities and a greater amount of time on documentation, coordination of care, medication administration, and movement around the unit."[44]

Walking is often driven by the layout of the area. If the nurses' station is at the end of a long hallway, nurses will walk more than if the station were in the center of a cluster of rooms (or the nurses will avoid walking, staying at the nurses' station, which can negatively impact patient care and satisfaction). Keeping nurses closer to the patients not only reduces walking but also allows for faster response and closer monitoring of patient needs. For example, Avera McKennan hospital (Sioux Falls, South Dakota), has built a new ED layout, driven by Lean principles, that has all the patient rooms located around a central nursing station. Other hospitals have a larger number of decentralized nurses' stations located throughout a unit, in close proximity to a smaller group of rooms. Or, others have nurses rely on individual workstations located outside a room or two rooms. A Lean hospital would need to consider pros and cons of decentralized stations and the potential effect on teamwork and other factors or results. As with lower inventory, less walking should not be a primary and singular goal. That said, taking steps to reduce walking can help solve important problems and meet critical goals.

Nurses in one inpatient unit reported having to walk more because of a change in the location of supplies. In the past, many frequently needed supplies had been kept in multiple locations throughout the unit or in patient rooms, where it was convenient for nurses and helped improve care and service. In the name of materials efficiency, a central automated supply cabinet was installed, and most of the supplies were consolidated in that cabinet.

While the hospital kept a tighter control on inventory levels, and the single cabinet made it easier for the materials department to restock supplies (saving money in that department's silo), the nurses disliked walking to the far end of the hallway every time they needed an item. The central cabinet or stockroom often leads to nurses hoarding supplies in drawers, lockers, or pockets, a practice that can create other problems. The hospital started reconsidering the value of the central supply cabinets, rationalizing which items really needed to be under such tight control and which items could be stocked in more convenient locations, as they had been before. Once again, we can see trade-offs in different types of waste. If items are inexpensive and do not take up much space, it might reduce the total waste in the system to store them in more locations or in each patient room.

Hospitals need to improve the system rather than just lecturing nurses that walking is bad. Nurses (and other employees) are often good at reducing their own walking but in ways that could be considered a workaround with ill effects. In one hospital unit, lift assists for patients were located in a closet on a different floor because their unit did not have enough storage space. Because it was inconvenient and time-consuming to go get the proper equipment, nurses often lifted patients without the assist, which increased the risk of employee injuries and patient falls. To reduce walking and to ensure that proper practices were followed, the unit freed space, using the 5S process, and relocated the lifts to the unit.

Waste of Overprocessing

Waste of overprocessing is described with many different names and is sometimes called the "waste of processing itself." *Overprocessing* refers to doing something to a higher level of quality than required by the customer or doing unnecessary work. One example might be found in the laboratory. Many blood specimens need to be centrifuged before they can be analyzed. At some point in the cycle, the blood has separated into its components (plasma, red cells, and white cells). After this separation is complete, additional centrifugation provides no additional separation, or value. The blood is no longer being transformed; it is just being spun longer. Laboratories sometimes find that centrifuges are set at times that are longer than recommended or required, either due to an error or from habit.

Often, overprocessing results from miscommunications in the handoffs between people or departments. In one hospital, a surgery project uncovered that one employee spent three hours a day folding towels after they came back from the laundry, unaware that nurses upstairs were immediately unfolding them and laying them flat. The wasteful folding step was discontinued.

The billing department division of one home health product could be characterized as a classic batch-and-queue process. Individual employees each did small portions of work in the overall flow; a patient record would be handled by seven or eight employees from the receipt of the order to the receipt of cash from the payer. Piles of charts, or batches, were usually passed between workers, leading to the waste of waiting and long delays between steps.

The entire process was observed by a Lean coach. The coach watched the first employee go through the chart, taking out duplicate paperwork and placing it in a bin to be shredded. That employee said the extra copies were unnecessary, just making the chart thicker, so they were removed to save storage space. The coach then observed the next worker and noticed that the first step was to go make a few copies of some of the forms in the chart, walking right past the employee who had thrown out the "extras." It was obvious that each employee meant well, but neither understood how her work fit into the entire process. The coach asked them to stop their work and to explain to each other what they did. They soon realized the waste—that throwing away and re-creating copies was overprocessing. Immediately, the employees changed their process to avoid this waste.

Waste of Talent

Waste of talent, the eighth type, is not always recognized in Lean literature. Some sources only list the first seven and justify this by saying the waste of human potential is embedded in the other types of waste. If highly skilled employees are forced to search for supplies, we are not getting the most out of their potential, and they are not doing any work that can develop their skills or career.

Those who do list this as a separate category of waste emphasize the importance of people in the system. Lean is not just about managing equipment or processes; it is about managing, leading, developing, and inspiring people. This is particularly true in a hospital, when our people (and their performance) are our primary product to the patients. Employees are our primary cost driver (typically between 50% and 60% of a hospital's revenue)[45] and a major driver of patient satisfaction through their daily interactions.

One form of wasting talent is healthcare professionals not working up to their level of licensure. For example, we often see nurses doing work that could be done by nursing assistants or housekeepers. Pharmacists might do some work that could be done effectively and with high quality by pharmacy techs. There are many levels of waste that come from, for example, a nurse dragging a bag of dirty linen down a hallway instead of housekeeping. For one, that nurse is being kept away from patient care and tasks that can only be done by the nurse and her level of skill. Secondly, the nurse is paid a much higher hourly rate than a housekeeper, so it's not a good use of hospital funds. Third, the nurse might get frustrated by having to always do unfulfilling work and might quit, which can have a huge cost to the organization.

It's reasonable to occasionally expect a higher-skilled employee to be a team player by helping out with lower-skilled work. But, if the nurse is always having to do work that should be done by others, a Lean thinker would investigate to see why support staff are not doing that work or if those positions are understaffed. If so, adding more housekeepers might be a good way to reduce overall system costs (as a result of better patient care and lower nurse turnover).

With the adoption of electronic medical records, some physicians question whether time spent typing into a computer is a good use of their skills and time, especially if they are slow typists. Some health systems use lower-paid "scribes" to work alongside physicians, doing much of the computer work, freeing the physicians to focus on their work and decision-making. One emergency room physician explained that he was willing to pay a scribe out of his own pocket because the time saved meant seeing more patients each hour, which leads to shorter waiting times and higher reimbursement to the physician. Of course, if computer systems are slow or difficult to use, use of a scribe might be a "short-term countermeasure" in that it makes things better, but doesn't get to the root cause of the problem. On the other hand, many scribes are early medical students who receive important development opportunities in the process.

In other ways, the waste involved in "not utilizing the talent inherent in your workers" harms patients, the organization, and the employees themselves.[46] It is a common lament in the manufacturing world that management quite literally told workers to "check their brains at the door." This is often subtly told to healthcare professionals. Employees may fall into a cycle in which they feel like they are not listened to, so they quit trying to improve the system in which they work. There is incalculable waste when employees just show up, do their jobs (as told to or as they have always done it), and go home.

At the start of one consulting engagement, a laboratory technologist complained, "Nowadays, I feel like a robot." Having more than 25 years of experience in the field, the employee complained that what used to be challenging, scientific work had become an exercise in loading tubes into a machine and hitting the start button. Ironically, employees are often concerned that Lean efforts, including standardized work, will turn them into unthinking robots. In this case, though, the employee had been playing no role in improving the process. Managers rarely asked employees their opinions or ideas on improving the department. Through Lean management approaches, employees can have their intelligence and creativity utilized in a productive way, even if the details of the work itself have become highly automated.

One aspect of respect for people is engaging employees' minds in continuous improvement. How many problems could be solved permanently if we just asked our employees what we should do? At one hospital, a nurse commented that their initial Lean work led to "the first time in six years that anybody has asked me what I think about anything." Many organizations are stuck in the outdated philosophy that managers must design the system, and workers should just execute the process, no questions asked. Managers often fear losing control or power by engaging employees in improvement. But our patients and our healthcare systems deserve no less than to have everybody working on improvements. This is discussed more in Chapter 11 and in the book *Healthcare Kaizen*.

There's Not Always an Easy Answer

The Lean methodology gives us a framework to help identify and discuss waste. When faced with situations where the perceived trade-offs between types of waste are controversial or when the actions to take are unclear, people often ask, "Is it Lean to _____?" or "Does Lean say to _____?" Which type of waste is worse? Deciding what to do requires judgment or creativity to break those trade-offs to reduce both types of waste.

There are times when we discover apparent trade-offs between different types of waste. For example, when residents or nurses are exhausted toward the end of long shifts or during a double shift, errors are more likely to occur. Reducing the length of shifts and preventing double shifts would likely reduce errors; however, shorter shifts means more handovers between providers, so people might push back and say that more handovers means *more* errors as the result of miscommunications or the provider not being familiar with the patient and their condition. Lean thinking challenges us to find a creative way to break the trade-off. If more handovers are problematic, why do we assume that miscommunications *have* to occur? Instead, we can improve and standardize the handover process, giving us the dual benefits from shorter shifts and better handovers.

In one example, Royal Bolton Hospital NHS (England) used Lean to improve the daily handover process in a respiratory unit that previously had a high mortality rate and excessive length of stay. By analyzing their current processes and adding, among other practices, daily multidisciplinary boards, less time was spent on handovers, yet communication improved and providers had more time out in the wards. Bolton went from higher-than-expected mortality to 10% lower than expected. In addition, length of stay was reduced by about 50%, while improving patient satisfaction.[47]

What's more important than "what Lean says" is the goals you are trying to accomplish and what the team and leaders decide to do. Rather than having the "right" answer thanks to Lean, part of the Lean mindset and process is to do our own analysis and consider our next steps. It's more likely that we can discover the right answer (or the best answer for right now) through the plan-do-study-adjust or PDSA process. Instead of being given an answer, Lean thinkers are comfortable with the process of figuring out an answer, being willing to test an idea that turns out to not really be an improvement.

What Non-Value-Added Activities Are Required?

If waste is bad, can we completely eliminate it from our workday? The answer is usually "no." Some activities don't add value to the patient but are required by regulators or the government. In the course of a given day, time spent walking might also fall into a category called "non-value-added, but required." A nurse might have to walk 100 feet to a medicine cart, but that does not make that walking time value-added. We might not be able to reduce that waste today, but we could next month if we change the system. What if the medicine cart were relocated so that it reduced walking time for all nurses in the unit? What if a second cart was added? What if more patient-specific medications were kept in a locked cabinet in the patient's room?

We might look at nurses and decide what portion of their walking is necessary in the current system and how much can be eliminated. Ideally, all of a nurse's patients would be in adjoining rooms, reducing the need to walk between far ends of the unit. Keeping patients clustered together would also allow faster nurse response. There are conflicting objectives that keep this from happening, such as the need to evenly distribute patient acuity levels and nursing workloads. It might be preferred to have a nurse work with the same patients as much as possible to reduce the number of handoffs and for the comfort of the patient; however, as patients are discharged, newly admitted or transferred patients might be put wherever a room is available. Quickly, we might end up with scattered patient assignments. Moving patients creates additional work and might be disruptive to the patient. Reassigning patients might require additional work for the nurses and creates risks for errors due to miscommunication.

Some people call this activity category "business value-add" or "enabling activities," rather than non-value-added. Those terms somewhat skirt the issue and might make the waste seem more acceptable, leading to less urgency for change. It is preferable to call this "non-value-added, but required" or "required waste" because the negative connotation helps emphasize that this waste should be reduced or eliminated if possible. Again, leaders need to emphasize to their employees that identifying non-value-added activities is not a criticism of the people doing the work.

There are many common hospital activities that are certainly required but cannot be considered value from the patient's perspective. For example, registration and billing paperwork does nothing to directly diagnose or treat a patient; however, the paperwork is required so the hospital can get paid, and it might be necessary to get payer authorizations to provide certain care to the patient. This paperwork might be very necessary, but that does not mean we should categorize it as value. When staff members say "we have to do that step," it may very well be required waste—having to do it does not equal value. Finally, categorizing something as waste does not mean we can or should eliminate that step. We might be able to improve the way it is done so that less time or money is wasted.

One common controversy that arises in discussions of value-added or non-value-added activity involves quality inspections. Granted, inspection steps are intended to protect the patient from harm. The medication administration process has multiple inspection steps, such as

- Pharmacists verifying prescriptions for proper dosing and interactions
- Pharmacists double-checking the work of pharmacy technicians who pulled medications to match the order
- Nurses double-checking that the right medication is being given to the right patient

From a Lean perspective, these inspection steps are most often categorized as required waste. Why would a process step that is intended to help the patient be considered non-value-added? Rather than saying we should stop doing those inspections, Lean thinkers would consider them to be non-value-added because they are only necessary given the existing process is not perfect and might be prone to error. Lean thinkers would always aim to find ways of preventing errors from occurring rather than using inspections or double-checks to find them after the fact. Hospitals should not eliminate inspection steps until error proofing is put in place, as described in Chapter 8. If the error proofing cannot be deemed 100% effective, then inspection steps might still be used to protect the patients.

Case in point: Toyota assembly plants, even in 2015, have brightly lit final inspection areas at the end of their assembly lines. Why? Even with their focus on "built-in quality" and error proofing, they have decided that inspection (catching problems) is better than letting those through to the customer. It's not ideal, but it's the best, most practical decision for today. But one should still continue efforts to create that perfect defect-free process for a number of reasons, including the fact that inspection is never 100% effective. As Dr. W. Edwards Deming said, "Cease dependence on inspection to achieve quality. Eliminate the need for massive inspection by building quality into the product in the first place." That is, of course, easier said than done.

Non-Value-Added, Pure Waste

As opposed to required waste, which we have to tolerate until we can change the system, "pure waste" includes activities that can be eliminated today without causing any other problem or side effect in the system. Pure waste often includes the waste of defects or the waiting that is caused by habitual batching of work or care.

Some walking or motion is required waste, but some of it can be easily categorized as pure waste. Nurses and medical assistants in one primary care clinic complained that they were walking or waiting too much (causing patients to wait) because they only had one digital thermometer to be used across ten exam rooms. Once this was discovered, everybody on the team and in management agreed that the time spent searching or waiting was pure waste. They immediately bought nine more thermometers, to keep one in each exam room. This, along with a number of other improvements, allowed the clinic to see more patients per day and become profitable after years of losses.

For a clinic setting, Table 3.4 shows a list of activities in a patient visit and how those might be categorized as value, required waste, or pure waste.

Table 3.4 Value and Waste in a Patient Visit

Step	Category	Rationale or Questions
Patient fills out forms at front desk	Required waste or pure waste	Some information might be required, but some might duplicate existing information or be completely unnecessary
Walk to waiting room	Pure waste	Could develop a process that allows patient to go directly to a room
Wait in waiting room	Pure waste	Redesign workflow so this isn't necessary
Walk to scale	Required waste	Could be reduced by relocating scale
Get weighed by medical assistant	Value	If that information influences clinical care
Walk to exam room	Required waste	
Get blood pressure and temperature taken	Value	If that information influences clinical care
Wait in exam room	Pure waste	Work to minimize by changing workflows
Describe symptoms to nurse or medical assistant	Value or pure waste	Does this really influence care?
Wait in exam room	Pure waste	Work to minimize by changing workflows
Describe symptoms to physician	Value	
Receive diagnosis and treatment advice	Value	Why the patient is there
Walk to front desk	Required waste	Can co-pay and scheduling be done in the exam room?
Pay co-pay	Required waste	Could that have been done when the patient checked in to reduce a potential wait at this step?

The boundaries between these categories are sometimes unclear. For example, weighing a patient might not have any benefit for a dermatology patient who is having a mole examined, whereas it might very much be a value-added step for a patient with chronic diabetes. Rather than arguing too long about the categorization of a step as value or waste, or as required waste versus pure waste, such time and energy might be better spent discussing what steps can be reduced, simplified, or eliminated.

Conclusion

Learning to identify waste, through our definitions of waste and the types of waste, and going to the *gemba* to identify waste are good starting points (to be discussed more in Chapter 4). Training people and making lists of waste might create awareness, but we need the courage to take action and lead efforts to improve the system and eliminate that waste.

We say "courage" because the mere act of identifying waste can be risky behavior in the wrong environment. Often, when we point out waste, people take it personally, especially if they created the existing system or have been working in it long enough. We have to be careful how we point out waste so we do not turn people against our efforts. Focusing on the waste and describing waste in terms such as "This process seems to have a lot of wasted motion" brings a different response than saying "You are walking too much." When we personalize the waste, intentionally or not, people will get defensive and often attempt to rationalize the existing process. People usually have pride in the way they do their work, even if it is full of waste. Managers might also take it personally if they perceive their department is being criticized, which can interfere with acceptance of improvements.

Employees often define their value as their skill in working around broken processes and making things happen; being the hero, if you will. The nurse who knows where to run to find a blanket when they seem to be unavailable might be praised as a hero for making that extra effort to get the job done. When focusing on waste, we would ask why the same nurse is making the same heroic run every day. We would improve the system so that blankets were available at the right place and in the right quantities, thus avoiding the need for heroic efforts. The nurse might resent this improvement, as it has robbed the individual of a source of pride and recognition.

Recognizing all of this, we cannot dance around the topic of waste. We must point it out. We cannot accept excuses for the waste that is in the system. Keeping with the theme of respect for people, we should not point fingers of blame, asking, "Whose fault is it that the system is this way?" It is helpful to state that we do not care why the system is the way it is today, but we need to focus on the future and work together on improvements.

Lean Lessons

- Value is defined by the customer.
- Waste interferes with us doing our work.
- Not all activity is value.
- Waste tends to be driven by the system and the design in our processes.
- Not all waste can be eliminated; some of it is required to make the system function.
- Just because we have to do something does not make it value.
- Quality is a primary goal of Lean, not just efficiency.
- Patients should not have to pay for defects or rework.

- The primary goal is not low inventory, but rather having enough inventory to efficiently do our work, without having too much.
- To drive problem solving and continuous improvement, focus on the process.
- Don't argue too much over whether something is waste or what type of waste it is. Focus on what you can and should improve, stop doing, or do more of.

Points for Group Discussion

- Who are our customers? Is the customer always right in a hospital setting?
- How do our patients define value? Have we talked to them about this? What steps in our process are value-adding?
- How can we reduce delays in one part of the process without negatively impacting another part?
- Which types of waste are most prevalent in your department or hospital? Can you find an example of each?
- Are there times when we make the patient wait for the benefit or convenience of everyone else in the system? What can we do to change that?
- Are there times when the desires of "internal customers" are out of alignment with patient needs?
- How far are our employees walking on an average day? What can do we do to reduce that?
- What are some reasons we might err on the side of having too much inventory rather than too little?
- In the clinic example of Table 3.4, how would you categorize those steps? What questions would you ask as a result?

Notes

1. Fleming, Chris, "Berwick Brings The 'Triple Aim' To CMS," Health Affairs Blog, http://healthaffairs.org/blog/2010/09/14/berwick-brings-the-triple-aim-to-cms/ (accessed February 4, 2016).
2. Kay, John, Obliquity, http://www.johnkay.com/2004/01/17/obliquity (accessed September 12, 2015).
3. Hagan, Patrick, Presentation to Healthcare Value Network visitors, February 3, 2011.
4. Lean Enterprise Institute, What is Lean?, http://www.lean.org/whatslean/ (accessed September 12, 2015).
5. Fleming.
6. Passama, Gary, Reading My Mind, http://www.northbay.org/blog/ceo/2012/Reading-My-Mind.cfm (accessed September 12, 2015).
7. Fleming.
8. Kenney, Charles, *Transforming Healthcare: Virginia Mason Medical Center's Pursuit of the Perfect Patient Experience* (New York: Productivity Press, 2010), p. 122.
9. National Health Service, *The Productive Ward: Releasing Time to Care,* http://www.institute.nhs.uk/quality_and_value/productive_ward/case_studies.html (accessed March 26, 2015).
10. Health Improvement Scotland, Releasing Time to Care, Making our Priorities Possible, Final Report, http://www.healthcareimprovementscotland.org/his/idoc.ashx?docid=091a7fae-3f68-4606-b1b0-7e98278ac7b2&version=-1 (accessed September 15, 2015).
11. Zimlich, Rachael, Hospitals Resolve to Increase Nurses' Time at the Bedside, http://healthcaretraveler.modernmedicine.com/healthcare-traveler/content/modernmedicine/modern-medicine-feature-articles/hospitals-resolve-increa?page=full (accessed September 12, 2015).

12. Womack James P. and Daniel T. Jones, *Lean Thinking,* New York: Free Press, 2003, p. 16.

13. Berwick, Donald, 2009 National Forum Keynote Video on Demand, http://www.ihi.org/education/AudioVideo/WIHI/Pages/default.aspx (accessed March 26, 2015).

14. Porter, Michael, "What is value in health care?" *New England Journal of Medicine,* December 8, 2010, http://www.nejm.org/doi/full/10.1056/NEJMp1011024 (accessed March 26, 2015).

15. Toussaint, John, *Potent Medicine: The Collaborative Cure for Healthcare,* Appleton, WI: ThedaCare Center for Healthcare Value, 2012, p. 84.

16. Weaver, Christopher, A *Health-Care Model in Coal Country,* http://www.wsj.com/articles/a-health-care-model-in-coal-country-1443407522 (accessed October 7, 2015).

17. Conn, Joseph and Michael, Sandler, CEO Power Panel Poll Finds Broad Support for Value-Based Pay, http://www.modernhealthcare.com/article/20150502/MAGAZINE/305029987/ceo-power-panel-poll-finds-broad-support-for-value-based-pay (accessed September 12, 2015).

18. Toussaint, 71.

19. Smouse, Becca, Cities Put Nurse Practitioners Alongside Paramedics, http://www.usatoday.com/story/news/nation/2015/08/09/fire-departments-pilot-nurse-practitioner-programs/30886395/ (accessed October 8, 2015).

20. Sayer Natalie J. and Bruce Williams, *Lean for Dummies,* Hoboken, NJ: Wiley, 2007, p. 51.

21. Porter, What is value.

22. Womack, James and Daniel T. Jones, *Lean Thinking,* New York: Free Press, 2003, p. 28.

23. Landro Laura, "Hospitals boost patient power as advisors" *Wall Street Journal,* August 8, 2007, http://www.wsj.com/news/articles/SB118652860268491024 (accessed March 26, 2015).

24. Flinchbaugh, Jamie and Andy Carlino, *The Hitchhiker's Guide to Lean: Lessons from the Road,* Dearborn, MI: Society for Manufacturing Engineers, 2005, p. 14.

25. Infection Control Today, Leapfrog Group Survey Reveals 87 Percent of U.S. Hospitals Don't Take Recommended Steps to Prevent Avoidable Infections, http://www.infectioncontroltoday.com/news/2007/09/leapfrog-group-survey-reveals-87-percent-of-u-s-h.aspx (accessed September 12, 2015).

26. Studer Group, It's Now or Never: Resources to Ensure That Never Events Never Happen Again, https://www.studergroup.com/special/complimentary-resources (accessed March 26, 2015).

27. Liker, Jeffrey K., *The Toyota Way: 14 Management Principles From the World's Greatest Automaker* (New York: McGraw-Hill, 2004), pp. 28–29.

28. Stencel, Christine, Medication Errors Injure 1.5 Million People and Cost Billions of Dollars Annually; Report Offers Comprehensive Strategies for Reducing Drug-Related Mistakes, *National Academy of Sciences,* July 20, 2006, http://www8.nationalacademies.org/onpinews/newsitem.aspx?RecordID=11623 (accessed March 26, 2015).

29. Davies, Tom, "Fatal drug mix-up exposes hospital flaws," *Washington Post,* September 22, 2006, http://www.washingtonpost.com/wp-dyn/content/article/2006/09/22/AR2006092200815.html?nav=hcmodule (accessed March 26, 2015).

30. Tiernon, Anne Marie, Families Upset over New Heparin Overdose Cases, MSNBC Online, November 22, 2007, http://www.wthr.com/story/7394819/families-upset-over-new-heparin-over-dose-cases (accessed March 26, 2015).

31. Kolata, Gina, "What are a hospital's costs? Utah system is trying to learn," *New York Times,* http://www.nytimes.com/2015/09/08/health/what-are-a-hospitals-costs-utah-system-is-trying-to-learn.html (accessed September 12, 2015).

32. Welch, H. Gilbert, There Is Such a Thing as Too Much Medical Care, http://www.sciencefriday.com/blogs/ 03/06/2015/there-is-such-a-thing-as-too-much-medical-care.html?series=33 (accessed September 12, 2015).

33. Perry, Susan, How an "Avalanche of Unnecessary Medical Care" Is Harming Us—And What Can Be Done About It, https://www.minnpost.com/second-opinion/2015/05/how-avalanche-unnecessary-medical-care-harming-us-and-what-can-be-done-about (accessed September 12, 2015).

34. Mendick, Robert and Laura Donnelly, One in Seven Treatments Not Necessary, Warns NHS Chief, http://www.telegraph.co.uk/news/health/news/11733871/One-in-seven-treatments-not-necessary-warns-NHS-chief.html (accessed September 12, 2015).

35. Hoangmai H. Pham, Paul B. Ginsburg, Kelly McKenzie, and Arnold Milstein, Redesigning care delivery in response to a high-performance network: The Virginia Mason Medical Center, Health Affairs web exclusive, *Health Affairs*, 2006, 26: w532–544, http://content.healthaffairs.org/content/early/2007/07/10/hlthaff.26.4.w532.full.pdf (accessed March 26, 2015).
36. Toussaint, *Potent Medicine*, 67.
37. Park Nicollet Health Services, Everything to You at Park Nicollet Frauenshuh Cancer Center, video, http://www.youtube.com/watch?v=PUre7cMDYd4 (accessed March 26, 2015).
38. Virginia Mason Medical Center, Virginia Mason Production System, https://www.virginiamason.org/vmps# Benefits (accessed October 21, 2015).
39. Freyer, Felice J., "It costs you $43 every time you wait for the doctor," *The Boston Globe Metro*, https://www.bostonglobe.com/metro/2015/10/05/study-puts-dollar-value-time-spent-waiting-for-doctor/If7KB4aU9mkY5qK8CqDYUO/story.html (accessed October 8, 2015).
40. Tucker, Anita and Steven Spear, "Operational failures and interruptions in hospital nursing," *Health Services Research* 2006, 41(3 Pt 1): 643–662.
41. Do, David, "Why EMR companies don't care about usability," KevinMD.com, http://www.kevinmd.com/blog/2013/06/emr-companies-dont-care-usability.html (accessed September 12, 2015).
42. Hendrich, Ann, Marilyn P. Chow, Boguslaw A. Skierczynski, and Zhenqiang Lu, A 36-hospital time and motion study: How do medical-surgical nurses spend their time? *The Permanente Journal* 2008, 12(3): 25–34.
43. Welton, John M., Maureen Decker, Julie Adam, and Laurie Zone-Smith, How far do nurses walk? *Medsurg Nursing* 2006, 15(4): 213–216.
44. Henrich, et al.
45. Herman, Bob, 10 Statistics on Hospital Labor Costs as a Percentage of Operating Revenue, http://www.beckershospitalreview.com/finance/10-statistics-on-hospital-labor-costs-as-a-percentage-of-operating-revenue.html (accessed September 12, 2015).
46. Bodek, Norman, *Kaikaku: The Power and Magic of Lean*, Vancouver, WA: PCS Press, 2004, p. 115.
47. Furnival, Joy and Jo B. Leece, Using Lean to Improve Handovers in Bolton, http://www.boltonft.nhs.uk/wp-content/uploads/2012/09/bics_using_lean_improve_handovers2011.pdf (accessed September 12, 2015).

Chapter 4

Observing the Process and Value Streams

Learning to See

The late Yogi Berra, a legendary New York Yankees catcher and member of the Baseball Hall of Fame once said, "You can observe a lot just by watching." That and other "Yogi-isms" draw a chuckle, but there is some truth in that statement. How often do managers, directors, vice presidents, and executives really know what happens on a daily basis in a health system? Do leaders really know what staff members and physicians are struggling with or frustrated with on a daily basis? Do leaders really know why waiting times or turnaround times are too long, or do they just review the same charts every month? Lean leaders help people solve problems by getting out of their offices and conference rooms. Going to see, to observe, or to watch is often the starting point for improvement.

How Do We Find Waste? Go and See

Waste is a very common word in Lean. Once we know the definitions of waste, we have to take action to improve. Before jumping to solutions, we have to understand the current situation or "go and see" (*genchi genbutsu*, in Japanese). Taiichi Ohno of Toyota was famous for training engineers and managers to look for waste by chalk drawing what came to be known as an "Ohno circle" on the floor.[1] The trainee was told to stand in the circle (just a few feet in diameter) and watch the process for hours, looking for waste. That might seem like an extreme method, but there are lessons to be drawn from it. First, you have to go and see with your own eyes, since that's more effective than just talking about a process in a conference room. Leaders at all levels have to go to the *gemba* (the place where work is actually done) to see what really happens.

In any organization, there are three forms of any process:

1. What the process *really* is
2. What we *think* the process is
3. What the process *should* be

Lean focuses on closing the gaps between these versions of the process. If there is a gap between what we think the process is and what it really is, it's important to learn to understand reality. That understanding is then necessary to close the gap between what the current process really is and what it should be (today) or will be (in the future).

Leaders cannot rely exclusively on reports, data, or metrics. You might ask, "How long are patients waiting in the emergency department before seeing a doctor?" The hospital might already have measures and reports in place, but the most effective way to actually improve the process is to go and see for yourself to identify waste. Instead of waiting for patient satisfaction surveys, go walk the units and talk to patients or waiting family members to see what praise, complaints, or ideas they have. This takes time, but that time will prove to be an extremely good investment for you and your team.

What Is a Value Stream?

As we see in many industries, hospitals and health systems are designed around specialized functions or departments. These departments or sites have their own physical space, their own budgets, their own employees, and their own management structures. Each department has its own job to do, but also plays a role in the overall patient experience and care. Problems and waste in hospitals are often found in the interactions or handoffs between those departments because of a lack of focus on patient pathways, or what are called "value streams" in the Lean methodology. A value stream generally represents and illustrates the end-to-end flow of a patient or a process, rather than just looking at the process in any one department.

For a hospital to provide waste-free patient care, it is not enough for each department to be great on its own. Dr. Paul Batalden, former president of the Institute for Healthcare Improvement, once said, "We have the very best pharmacy sitting right next to the very best laboratory, sitting right next to the very best X-ray department, sitting right next to the very best nursing department … and the hospital doesn't work."[2] A group of excellent departments does not lead to a system that performs at its best. We must also design and improve the value streams and our overall system.

> In *The Checklist Manifesto*, Dr. Atul Gawande cites Dr. Don Berwick's story that illustrates this point in a different way by saying if you try to build "the world's greatest car by assembling the world's greatest parts … the engine of a Ferrari, the brakes of a Porsche, the suspension of a BMW, and body of a Volvo … we get a pile of very expensive junk." Gawande adds, "In medicine, this is exactly what we've done."[3] This is also, perhaps, a cautionary tale about copying just a few parts of different organizations' Lean or quality improvement approaches. We need to think about both the health system and our Lean approach as systems instead of piles of tools and parts.

Womack and Jones defined the value stream as "the set of all the specific actions required to bring a specific product (whether a good, service, or increasingly a combination of the two) through the three critical management tasks of any business: the problem-solving task, the information management task, and the physical transformation task."[4]

For a hospital and a patient, the general value stream definition holds true. For example, when a patient arrives in the emergency department (ED), we have problem solving (finding what is wrong with the patient), information management (demographic or diagnostic information that guides or assists treatment), and the physical treatment path through the hospital. The value stream is that end-to-end patient journey from door to door, not just what happens in the ED. For scheduled appointments or procedures, a value stream can also encompass the time and steps that occur between the patient's referral for treatment and the hospital being paid for that care. Or, the value stream can include all of the time and activity that begins when the patient first feels pain or a symptom.

Value Stream Mapping

Value stream mapping has been a popular tool to help hospital leaders see the entire picture across departmental boundaries. A value stream map (VSM) is a structured diagram that originated with Toyota, as something they call material and information flow mapping.[5]

A VSM may seem similar to other quality improvement tools, such as the process mapping method that is also used in the total quality management and Six Sigma approaches. Both process maps and VSMs document the activities that take place, but VSMs tend to take a higher-level, less detailed view. A team might map the entire surgical value stream, showing the major steps or departments that a patient flows through. Once the team has identified where the biggest problems exist along that end-to-end value stream, they might take a deeper dive to do a more detailed process map for, say, the outpatient surgery arrival and intake process. VSMs are also unique in that they separate out the flow of the product or patient from the information flows that support that work being done.

Additionally, the process of creating a VSM also captures time elements and other data. VSMs identify how long each high-level process step typically takes to complete and, more importantly, the amount of waiting time between steps or departments. The maps typically reveal and illustrate that most of the time in the system, from a patient's perspective, is time spent waiting for the next process.

The books *Value Stream Mapping for Healthcare Made Easy* (Jimmerson) and *Value Stream Mapping* (Martin) are excellent resources for a more in-depth examination of this method.

Creating a Current-State Value Stream Map

Value stream maps are typically created by a cross-functional team of people who are dedicated to the mapping effort for anywhere from a day or two (for a smaller, limited-scope VSM) to a full week (for a full patient journey VSM). When mapping, it is important to have representatives (staff and leaders) from all departments and functions that work in that value stream. For example, the team for a patient discharge VSM (a subset of an end-to-end value stream) might include physicians, nurses, unit clerks, social workers, patient transporters, and others from multiple departments. It is important to have leaders and executives participate in the mapping, so they can better understand the broad system for which they are responsible. But, the frontline staff are generally the people who can tell you how things actually work today.

It might seem more efficient to do so, but don't assign a single process improvement specialist (or a team of them) to go create a VSM. The most important part of mapping is arguably the learning and the shared understanding that is created through the *process* of mapping. Usually, each department in a value stream just understands their work and maybe a little bit of the work that's immediately upstream and downstream. What's powerful about value stream mapping is the insights that come from those participants finally seeing and understanding the entire system.

Also avoid the temptation to create VSMs without leaving a conference room. If we only talk about the process rather than seeing it firsthand, we run the risk of capturing the "what we think it is" version of the process instead of "how it really is." Even the most knowledgeable employees will forget steps in the process or underestimate how often a step, such as rework, actually occurs. People also tend to underestimate or overestimate the process times or, more likely, the waiting times between process steps. The steps and times captured on a VSM must be verified through data collection and actual process observation to make sure we have an accurate current-state map that reflects how things work today.

Figure 4.1 shows a high-level value stream for a patient journey for outpatient surgery. Looking at the VSM, we see the information flows on top, showing what communication takes place among different people, departments, and information systems. The information flows, in this case, highlight the waste involved in three separate roles (registration, scheduling, and assessment), all contacting the patient, creating extra work for the hospital and confusion on the patient's part. Patients who were interviewed in the course of this mapping complained that they received multiple voice mails and did not always realize they needed to call all three people back. This often led to a patient arriving for a scheduled procedure without having completed needed lab work or preauthorizations.

In the bottom part of the VSM, we see the patient pathway, as the boxes represent the different departments or steps in the process. The black triangles represent the patient's waiting time between the process steps. This product or material flow might also represent the flow of a discharge order, a lab specimen, or supplies that have been ordered from a vendor.

When creating a current-state VSM, the team needs to identify problems that need fixing, such as a long waiting time between steps in the process or high amounts of rework. These are often drawn onto the map as "*kaizen* bursts." At this point, we should not jump to solutions. Rather,

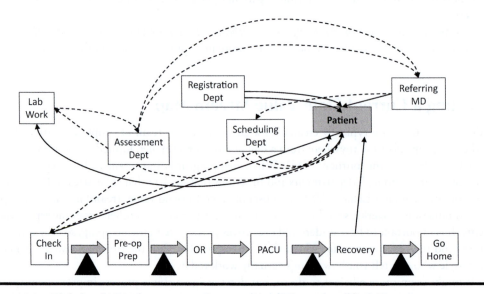

Figure 4.1   High-level VSM for an outpatient surgery patient, simplified view.

the team should start prioritizing problems based on the impact on patients or other stakeholders. Sometimes, problems can be solved quickly, right after the VSM is drawn. In other cases, specific follow-up on problems may need to be defined as formal improvement projects to be done later. It is important to recognize that some value stream problems cannot be fixed in the short term due to cost, timing, or technology constraints. But, those short-term constraints should not be used as excuses for not improving. As they say, don't let perfect be the enemy of better.

Dr. Jack Billi recalls, "I can't tell you how many times we've done a value stream map or an A3 with docs involved. They look at the mess on the walls when they're doing a map. They say, 'I can't believe what a mess this is. I can't believe a patient ever makes it through. Who designed this process?'"

"Of course, no one designed it. It's just the accretion of responses to regulatory requests and third party billing and some other customer service initiative. Before you know it, you've got an incredibly complex process to get work done."

"Once they have that 'ah ha' moment and they realize how complex and unnecessarily error-prone the process is, you start to see them become empowered and motivated. Instead of becoming victims of the process, they try to take it on and say, 'Why can't we do that? What about this? What about that?'"[6]

The Future-State Maps

Drawing the current-state VSM is just a starting point. The maps themselves are not terribly useful unless we, as an organization, use them to prioritize or drive improvements. A future-state map might not be helpful if we skip the important step of understanding and mapping the current state. In the example VSM, the hospital cross-trained the people who made patient contact calls so that everything could be handled in a single interaction—reducing the total number of calls, the duplicative information, and the missed calls that led to missing information.

After identifying improvements, the team also creates a future-state VSM that illustrates how the process should work or could work if redesigned. Typically, a future-state VSM shows a dramatically smaller number of process steps (as we simplify the process), less complexity in the information flows, and shorter waiting times between steps (as we improve flow).

Sometimes it is helpful to draw two future-state maps: one showing a long-term ideal future state and another showing a shorter-term practical future state. The ideal state allows a team to dream big and cast aside all constraints, working to envision a radically better process. For example, a cancer treatment VSM team might envision a future state where all care is provided under the same roof, reducing the non-value-added times of transportation and waiting. And, the ideal state might include the patients registering just once during their visits instead of a current state of registering twice, in oncology and in the infusion center. On the other hand, the practical state might be limited to processes that can be changed without major investments in facilities or technology.

Theresa Moore, a ThedaCare Improvement System consultant, says one downside of ideal state maps is that a team looks "five years out, then the world changes." Moore now has teams "focusing more on a six- to nine-month timeframe" for future-state maps.

Figure 4.2 A cross-functional team reviews and discusses a VSM they created.

It is tempting for value stream mapping facilitators to create electronic VSMs using standard office software or specialized software created specifically for VSM purposes. As with many things, just because you can draw a map electronically does not mean that you should. Many teams prefer to create maps in a very analog way, using sticky notes on large pieces of butcher paper, as shown in Figure 4.2. This allows a group to create a map in a far more collaborative way compared to one person controlling the mouse and keyboard. Instead of creating the waste of over-processing or redrawing the completed manual maps in software, consider the use of digital photos that can be easily shared with those who could not participate in the mapping. Even with a photo or digital map, insist that your leaders "go and see" by visiting the *gemba* instead of just staying at their computer.

Breaking Down Silos and Reducing Suboptimization

One Lean transformation challenge is to reconcile our vertical departmental organization structures with the horizontal flow of a patient's treatment, as shown in Figure 4.3. While this vertical organization structure makes sense for many reasons (such as the development of specialized skills and for employee career paths), this functional silo structure leads to many dysfunctions. Often, employees only know people or processes in their own department, which contributes to poor cooperation across departmental boundaries and delays for patients at the handoff points between departments. In one hospital, for example, key members of the laboratory staff had never visited the ED, a primary customer of lab results located only 50 feet down the corridor. Many hospitals suffer from poor communication between the lab and the ED, with most communication coming in the form of the ED calling the lab to ask (or sometimes yell) about delayed test results. This generally is not a collaborative, problem-solving form of communication. Through Lean efforts, we want to increase the collaboration and teamwork across departmental boundaries, as cross-functional VSM or project teams can help.

To treat patients more effectively, we need to start looking at end-to-end processes (the value streams) rather than just improving our isolated departments. Making isolated improvements

Figure 4.3 Illustration of vertical department silos and horizontal patient flow through a hospital.

within our own departmental boundaries runs the risk of suboptimization that helps the individual department but harms the overall system.

For example, a laboratory might decide, for the sake of cost and efficiency, to only run a certain specialized test two times per week, on Tuesdays and Thursdays. This local efficiency, however, might lead to delays in patient care or delays in discharging a patient, a delay that might cost the hospital far more (due to the increased length of stay) than was saved in lower laboratory staffing levels or the decreased cost of running larger test batches. Hospital leadership plays an important role in ensuring that the overall system is optimized and that individual departments are not punished, through their metrics and incentives, for actions or policies that help improve the overall system. The best solution for the hospital might be to increase lab staffing (or better yet, eliminate waste to free up time) so they can run the test more frequently.

Another hospital discovered, through the structured analysis of its own value stream, that the orthopedics department only performed trauma surgery two days a week. Considering that patients suffer trauma every day of the week, it was difficult for the hospital to justify how it was patient centered to perform two procedures on a patient—one to stabilize the patient until the second and final procedure could be done on one of the two scheduled days. When we ask, "Why is it done that way?" and the answer is "We've always done it that way!," we can challenge ourselves and make things better for everyone involved.

Observing the Process

In the course of value stream mapping, *kaizen* events, or other less structured Lean activities, an important fundamental skill is structured process observation. By *structured*, we mean more than just walking through a department or watching without a particular aim or goal.

To identify waste and improvements, firsthand observation is critical. There are two lenses through which we can observe the process and work. First is what we generically call the "activity of the product." Here, we ask what is happening (or, more often, not happening) to the product (or patient) at every step in the value stream. Second, we can view the process with the perspective of nurses, technologists, pharmacists, or others, something we generically call the "activity of the employee."

This direct observation can be extremely eye opening for employees and managers. Employees are often too mired in the details of their daily work to see waste, so stepping back and observing the process, watching different people do the work they normally do, can help. Managers, physicians, or other outsiders can gain firsthand visibility and appreciation of the problems that others struggle with every day, which can build teamwork and an appreciation for the need to improve the system instead of just trying harder. Observation can uncover opportunities for small *kaizen* improvements to the current process; the lessons from observation can also be used to influence the design and construction of new spaces that aim to better serve the needs of patients and staff, such as through "Lean design" initiatives, as described in Chapter 10.

In some cases, managers who were shown summaries of the waste their employees had directly observed responded by saying, "I don't believe you." Managers often do not want to believe that lab specimens sit for hours between batched steps or that employees are spending so much time on inspection and rework. We often have an idealized view of what we think is happening that does not line up with reality. Those skeptical managers saw reality when their own direct observation confirmed what had been reported to them. When we don't see problems, we can't help fix problems.

Activity of the Product

The product in a process can be a patient, an order, or a specimen, among other things. When we are observing through the lens of the product, we have to choose starting and ending points for the observation, which will vary based on the type of problem we are looking to solve. Depending on the value stream we are following, we might choose to start and end our observation at different points, as shown in Table 4.1. Observers will follow and directly observe the product through that part of the value stream.

The same methodology and tools can be applied when observing nonpatient products through a process. We also need to choose starting and stopping points, depending on what process we are observing and our improvement goals, as shown in Table 4.2.

We may limit the scope of an analysis because the total overall time frame might be too long to observe from beginning to end (or too hard to observe). If a patient is arriving for a scheduled procedure that will result in a planned inpatient stay, we might stop the observation at the point when the patient is physically in the hospital room. On the outbound side of the stay, we might do a different analysis, in this case examining the discharge process (with the same patient or a different set of patients). It is sometimes possible to piece together separate independent analyses to paint a picture of the entire door-to-door journey for a representative patient.

In any of these studies, we are looking for times when value-added work is being performed, times when non-value-added work is being performed, and times when the patient is just waiting (an example of non-value-added, pure waste). Some short waiting time might be required in even the best processes, where any waiting is consciously designed into the process for the sake of the overall value stream flow, but our goal is to minimize this waiting.

When observing, we track the start and stop times of new events. This can be facilitated with a range of tools, from simple to complex, including:

- Digital watch and notepad
- Digital camera with time/date stamp and notepad
- Video camera with time/date stamp

Table 4.1 Possible Start and End Points for Analysis of the Activity of the Product

Product/Value Stream	Possible Starting Points	Possible Ending Points
Laboratory testing	MD giving stat order	Arrival at laboratory
	Collection of specimen	Start of testing
	Arrival at laboratory	Release of test result
Pharmacy medications	Signal for replenishment is given	Medication sent to unit
	Order written by MD	Medication delivered to unit for storage
		Medication administered to patient
Pathology	First call to schedule biopsy procedure	Specimen delivered to histology
	Specimen taken from patient	Slide delivered to pathologist for reading
		Pathologist report sent to physician
Information systems (IS) call center support	Initial problem call to IS	Resolution of IS issue

- Specialized software for mobile devices, phones, or tablets
- Time study apps

Cameras, while a useful tool for capturing the context and timing of events, may make patients uncomfortable. Use your own judgment and consider hospital policies and legal releases that might be required. Video may be more appropriate for use in nonpatient areas. Having an observer scribbling notes down may lose some detail, compared to using video, but any method of direct observation will typically uncover many types of waste and opportunities for improvement.

A department or hospital might, but not always, have data on turnaround times or process flow times from start to finish. For example, what's often represented as "door-to-doc" time in the emergency department might actually be "triage-to-doc" time if patients are having to wait for their first official interaction that's trackable. That's a good reason to not just rely on data and reports—go and see and observe for yourself.

Data might be collected automatically through computer system event logs, bar code scans, or radio frequency identification (RFID) tags. For example, a lab might generate turnaround time data on every single test result by comparing the time when the patient's wristband bar code was scanned until the logged time when the result is released to the hospital's information system. These data do not give us direct insight into how that time breaks down into value-added and non-value-added components. We need direct observation to identify waste, waiting time, and other problems that can be fixed with Lean.

Activity of the product analysis is helpful because it helps us focus on the waste (the waiting time) in the process. Traditional process improvement often focuses on doing the value-added work in a faster or more efficient way. In the Lean approach, we first focus on the waste since

Table 4.2   Possible Start and End Points for Patient Flow Analysis

Patient Pathway/Value Stream	Possible Starting Points	Possible Ending Points
Emergency department	Patient is injured or feels pain	Discharge from ED
	Patient calling 911	Admission into hospital
	Ambulance arriving at home	Discharge from hospital
	Patient arrives at ED	
Immunization clinic	Caregiver and baby arrive	Caregiver and baby leave with correct immunization
Outpatient surgery	Arrival at door	Start of procedure
	First call for scheduling procedure	Start of postanesthesia care unit (PACU)
	First referral from general practitioner	Discharge
Outpatient cancer treatment	Arrival at door	Start of treatment
		Discharge
Primary care or specialist clinic	Patient requests appointment	Patient leaves office
	Patient arrives in office	Physician has discussed test results and plan of care with patient
Scheduled inpatient surgery	Arrival at door	Start of procedure
	First call for scheduling procedure	Start of PACU
	First referral from general practitioner	Movement into room
		Discharge
Patient discharge process	MD writing discharge order	Patient ready to leave
		Patient physically out door
		Room physically ready for next patient
Radiology	Order for procedure	Start of procedure
	Arrival at outpatient center	End of procedure
	Start of procedure	Report verified

there can be a greater, and more realistic, opportunity to reduce large portions of the waiting time instead of trying to reduce the value-added time. If 90% of the total value stream time is waiting, we are better off reducing that by half, as opposed to doing the value-added activity twice as quickly, if that were even possible.

Activity of the Product—Laboratory

The product flow in a value stream can be illustrated by a timeline that shows elapsed time and where the value-added and non-value-added time occurs. In the example in Figure 4.4, a team followed a tube of blood from the time the specimen was collected by a phlebotomist until the test result was released. The lab might have already had reports that would show average turnaround times, but this example shows one particular case for which the time was about 230 minutes, a fairly representative result for that lab.

After the phlebotomist drew the blood (the first value-added activity), the specimen was not put on the automated test instrument (the second value-added activity) until over an hour later. The final value-added activity was completed after about three hours (a technologist reading a slide for cell counts), and there was a further delay until the result was entered and verified in the information system (the final value-added activity). All of the other time was waste, including 87% of the time that was spent waiting—a tube of blood on the phlebotomist cart or sitting in a rack in the lab, or a printout sitting on a printer waiting to be verified.

Examples like those illustrate the potential for improving performance by eliminating the delays and "white space" in between the value-added steps. Finding faster ways to draw blood or purchasing faster test equipment would not yield the benefits of reducing waiting time, as we discuss more in Chapter 9 in our discussion on flow.

Activity of the Product—Patient

A patient can be followed through a clinic visit using similar analysis, asking when the patient is receiving value and when they are waiting or suffering through required waste. My primary care

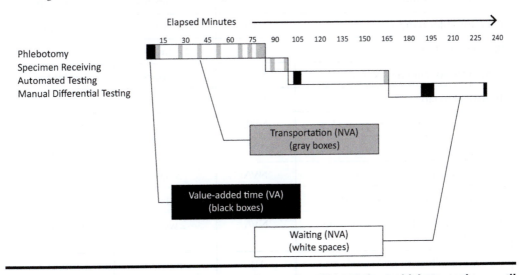

Figure 4.4 Product flow timeline illustration for a tube of blood; from phlebotomy draw until the result is ready for the ordering physician to view, most of the time is spent waiting.

visits are pretty typical, in that I make an appointment to see the doctor and then, during that visit, get told to get labs done, which requires a different visit on a different day. In a 2015 episode of care, 15 weeks elapsed between my initial appointment and having the opportunity to talk to my physician about the results. Some of that delay was due to my work travel, but the fastest I would have been able to have the discussion would have been a week or two if everything had gone perfectly in their process.

Dr. John Toussaint has shared his experience as a primary care patient at a ThedaCare clinic. In his clinic, they have a small-scale lab analyzer that can do basic blood work like a complete blood count (CBC) instead of having to send the specimen to an outside lab. Because the specimen was tested and lab results were received by Toussaint's physician within 20 minutes, they were able to discuss the results and his plan of care all within the same visit. The lab analyzer is an added cost to the clinic, but it has been paid for by reducing the number of follow-up calls about results that come into and go out of the clinic.

For my care, the physician's office did not send lab results to me after they were received from the outside lab. I had to call in to follow up (which costs them time). The only option was to receive the test results via fax or to pick up the paper report in person, which I could not do on the weekend. It then took about two weeks to be rescheduled once I requested the follow-up appointment, as my physician is not able to provide same-day access as some offices can. Thankfully, there was nothing life threatening about the slow value stream that I was a part of—it was just frustrating and far from ideal.

Table 4.3 shows a comparison of what the ideal time flow in my visit would have been compared to Toussaint's.

Table 4.3 A Comparison of Patient, Specimen, and Information Flows (Approximate and Best Case in the Design of Each System)

Step	VA or NVA	"Graban Care"	"Toussaint Care"
Wait in waiting room	NVA	20 minutes	0 minutes
Time in exam room	VA	10 minutes	25 minutes
Wait until blood drawn	NVA	24 hours	2 minutes
Blood collection	VA	2 minutes	2 minutes
Time until specimen was sent to lab	NVA	10 hours	0 minutes
Transport to lab	NVA	15 miles	50 feet
Time until specimen was on analyzer	NVA	1.5 days	0 minutes
Testing time	VA	5 minutes	5 minutes
Time until result sent to MD	NVA	3 days	10 minutes
Time until patient received results	NVA	2 days	0 minutes
Time until patient discusses results with MD	NVA	2 weeks	0 minutes
Discuss results with MD	VA	5 minutes	5 minutes
Total time		**3 weeks**	**25 minutes**

It's easier to identify the waste in my care journey than it is to solve it. One solution would be an electronic patient portal that would allow me to see test results more quickly and more easily online. Same-day or open access appointments for a follow-up visit would reduce the total time for care to a week. Giving the patient better warning that they should fast because blood might be taken could reduce a day from the journey. Even without buying the in-clinic lab analyzer, the value stream that treated me could be much better.

Activity of the Employee

The same direct observation method can be applied to the employees in a process. When working on a process or a value stream, we can choose a variety of roles to observe. Observers follow the employee as they perform normal work, looking for waste in the process and problems the employee encounters. Observers are usually staff from within the department, although some hospitals have found it helpful to have people trade off and observe in each other's departments. These "fresh eyes" bring an outside perspective and will notice things or ask questions that might not be brought up by those who are extremely familiar with that department and its work.

Video analysis is particularly helpful when observing employees; we might not have the same privacy restrictions or concerns we would have with patients, depending on the setting. With modern smartphones, it's easy to take videos that can be viewed later by observers or the people doing the work. You can buy specialized apps that take video with a running time and date stamp that can provide helpful time study data. Video can be helpful for a number of reasons:

- It accurately captures employee activities, movement, and timing.
- It captures walking patterns and distances to be documented.
- Observers can review and replay the video to capture detailed observations.
- An observed employee can watch the video to see the waste in the process and give suggestions for improvements.
- Time/date stamp data can help measure time spent on different activities.

Observing employees (and being observed) can be uncomfortable, even if handled with sensitivity and respect for people. Leaders must communicate to their employees, in advance, that observation is going to be done. Employees need to understand that observers are looking for waste and delays in the process and problems that interfere with employees doing their value-added work. The observation is not done to catch employees doing something wrong or to see who is the fastest employee. Employees will typically be on their best behavior, knowing they are being observed, but errors may occur as a result of nervousness. There is also the risk that observers see an ideal version of the process as opposed to seeing shortcuts or other problems with the way work is normally done. This risk usually goes away after a bit of time as those being observed get busy and forget that they are being shadowed.

In my role as a consultant, I recall a time when I was training nurses to do observation in their unit, and I shadowed them into a patient room. The nurse explained my role, and the elderly patient in the bed exclaimed, "I get it! He's the time study man!" In the early days of time and motion study (and even in relatively modern times when that patient may have been the subject of such studies), the practice was given a bad name because it was done disrespectfully. The original industrial engineering approach to study (with or without filming) was typically done by a specialist, such as an engineer or an outside consultant. The expert would observe and then tell people how to do their work better. A modern Lean approach to time and motion study is more respectful because it is based on employees helping each other improve in all dimensions instead of an expert pressuring them to work faster.[7]

Observers should strive to build rapport with the employee and allow them to concentrate on performing high-quality work. If the observer sees an error or mistake being made that would have an impact on a patient, the observer has a responsibility to help the employee (and patient) by saying something about the error. Employees who have done the actual work should conduct the employee observations, making it a peer-to-peer interaction. If outsiders or supervisors do the observation, employees might be more nervous about negative outcomes, or clinicians might be understandably upset if engineering interns are timing how long they are in the restroom, as has happened, unfortunately.[8] Staff members at any level deserve to be involved as a partner in this observation and improvement—to be a scientist, not merely a subject.[9]

In addition, having coworkers observe will lead to more accurate analysis and identification of waste. They are also more likely to know when observed employees are using methods that are inconsistent with others or standard practices. This realization serves as the first step in determining what the best work method should be. The observation and analysis can also uncover activities that those in certain roles should not be doing. For example, if a pharmacist is doing manual or lower-level work that a pharmacy technician could be doing at a lower cost, we might change the roles and responsibilities to better match tasks with skill levels.

Looking at walking patterns can help identify opportunities for layout improvements. Point-to-point diagrams (often called spaghetti diagrams because they look like you threw a handful of cooked spaghetti on the page) can help identify equipment and supplies that can be moved, based on how people actually work. Walking is not the only waste that can be identified through observation. Observers can see rework or workarounds that are normally hidden to supervisors and higher managers.

Spaghetti diagrams are typically drawn by hand, but some organizations are utilizing RFID technologies (chips placed on staff badges) to generate spaghetti diagrams in an automated way. It would not be very Lean, ranking very low in the respect for people scale, to track people without telling them. As with any workplace study, staff should be informed and fully involved in the entire process, including the analysis and discussion of any diagrams.

During many Lean projects, employees get an opportunity to watch video of themselves or their colleagues doing their daily work. Employees often say, "I never knew I did that!" In one example, three people from the same department, with seniority of one, seven, and 20 years, all watched video of someone else doing the work, and they each realized they did it different ways. They had been working together but until that moment had never realized how different their methods were. The team was also able to see the impact the variation had on the flow or the outcome of the process. Observation also allows professionals who are normally busy in their own silos of work to see and appreciate the work that others do as part of a team.

Activity of the Employee—Nursing

One hospital and its outpatient cancer treatment center undertook an assessment to identify opportunities for improvement. The staff knew they spent too much time walking and searching for supplies, but the formal activity of the employee analysis uncovered the full extent of the waste.

The chemotherapy area had nurses whose jobs and tasks included:

- Taking patients to their chair or bed and prepping them for treatment
- Getting medications and starting injections and drips
- Responding to patient requests for pain relief, comfort, or other needs
- Answering questions about the treatment and process for patients and families
- Stopping the treatment and preparing the patient to go home

One observed nurse walked 1,825 feet in 50 minutes, a pace of more than four miles per day. The spaghetti diagram of the walking is shown in Figure 4.5. For the observed time period, 32% of the nurse's time was spent walking. Only 30% of the time was spent on value-added activities, which were defined loosely as any time with direct patient contact.

Our first response should be to ask why—why does the nurse have to walk so far? Some of the walking is driven by the assignment of patients to chairs. Chemotherapy nurses would prefer that all of their patients be located together, but this is not always practical. When patients arrive, they tend to get whatever chair is available and any nurse who happens to be available.

Figure 4.5   Walking pattern of one nurse in a chemotherapy center, 50 minutes' time.

If a patient requests a certain nurse, the only available chair might be far away from that nurse's other patients.

More walking is caused by the location of other frequently visited areas, including supply closets and the tube station where medications are delivered from the pharmacy. This can all be challenged and questioned. Each patient chair and bed had a supply cart that was supposed to have standard supplies. The carts were not standardized, however, meaning nurses sometimes had to walk to the main supply room instead of using the closest cart. Some items on the carts were not restocked properly, so drawers or slots were empty, again necessitating a walk to a different supply cart or to the supply closet. When we directly observe a nurse walking from cart to cart, searching for hard-to-find supplies, that clearly identifies a problem that can be fixed.

Before Lean, the nurses might consider walking and searching to be part of their normal daily work rather than viewing it as non-value-added activity that can be fixed. Perhaps it's always been that way. One nurse was seen frequently walking to a storage cabinet to get blankets for patients, another sign that those blankets should be stored in more convenient locations throughout the department. Other walking leads to questions about what nurses should be doing and what assistants or technicians should do. Nurses might not be the best ones to walk around collecting supplies or medications, as this distracts them from the value-added work for which they have specialized training (and wastes their talent).

After identifying the waste, part of the department's Lean efforts were focused on standardization and improved organization, all in the name of reducing waste and freeing nurse time. This was in addition to separate attempts to reduce patient waiting times and delays. Note a point that will be repeated again in Chapter 5: The goal of standardization is not to standardize for standardization's sake, but rather to prevent waste and problems so we can accomplish our goals as a health system and providers.

Activity of the Employee—Primary Care

On four different days of the week, a young hardworking podiatrist worked at four rural clinics that were part of an integrated health system. One day, a patient was in his exam room for a quick minor toenail procedure. The doctor's work was interrupted, as he had to leave the exam room and the patient to gather his supplies and instruments, including a scalpel, freeze spray, gauze, and other material. Waste like this is often invisible to the office manager or the physician himself. Seeing this waste, one could question why he had to use his valuable time in such a non-value-adding way.

As illustrated in Figure 4.6, the doctor walked and searched—he hunted and gathered, as some would say. He walked back and forth across this clinic for a total of about 670 feet, delaying the patient's care for about 10 minutes (and delaying patients who were in the waiting room). He walked back and forth between the lab room and the minor procedures room, muttering a bit about forgetting which of the four clinics stored supplies in what location; there was a clear lack of standardization that hurt his productivity. He walked back to his office, back to the lab, and then finally to treat the patient, a procedure that had a value-adding time of about 30 seconds.

Keep in mind that while the podiatrist was terribly frustrated by what was taking place, he also felt it was normal. When he was shown the spaghetti diagram, he shrugged his shoulders and said calmly, "Well, that's how it has always been." The team in the clinic realized things could be better. Before the doctor arrived the next week, the staff took an empty unused crash cart and gathered all of the supplies that the podiatrist normally used (or their best first attempt at this). They created a checklist that could be used to restock the cart the evening before the doctor was in the clinic. The cart was rolled to the room where the physician worked that next time.

Figure 4.6 Walking pattern of a podiatrist prepping for one patient procedure.

When he saw it and first used it, the physician loved the cart, making just a few small suggestions to tweak what was in the cart and how it was organized. The waste in his daily work had been hidden because it was "normal," and the clinic was not accustomed to looking at their work as a process. "The way it has always been" turned into a new and improved process that made the physician very happy, wasted less of his time, and prevented delays for patients. The podiatrist's next question was to ask how quickly the other three clinics could put together the same standardized cart and checklist so he could be equally efficient all four days of the week.

In this same clinic, a physician assistant (PA) went into an exam room. She walked out of the room to go find a supply she needed for the exam. She then had to go in and out of the room five times within the span of a few minutes because other items had not been restocked properly, a problem that is addressed in Chapter 6. On each successive trip into the room, the PA had been putting on a fresh pair of gloves, anticipating being able to start the exam. After the last trip, she came out of the room and sighed, saying that she now had to go and get a new box of gloves for the room because she had used them all up with her trips in and out of the room. Rather than faulting the PA for not noticing everything that was missing all at once, a Lean clinic would have processes in place to ensure that she never had to leave to find anything, leaving more time to focus on patient care.

I often volunteer to take nursing students, residents, and healthcare administration students to visit and tour the Toyota truck assembly plant in San Antonio. One of the things they are all impressed with are the systems and support staff that Toyota has in place to ensure that the production team members on the assembly line always have the parts and properly working tools they need to do their jobs. Trucks are not as important as patients, but Toyota arguably puts far more effort into supporting their frontline staff than many hospitals do. Toyota allows the team members to focus on their work and the truck in front of them, leading to better results and satisfaction for all.

Activity of the Employee—Perioperative Services

In one hospital's perioperative services department, technicians and nurses built case carts that were later rolled into an operating room for surgery. These employees were observed by peers to identify waste and excess walking, identifying process improvements for building carts more efficiently. In two observed cases, a technician and a nurse walked more than 1,000 feet to build each of their carts. In the two cart builds, walking made up 44% of the technician's time and 36% of the nurse's time.

A spaghetti diagram representative of the case cart builds can be seen in Figure 4.7. Each star represents a location where the technician walked to get an item for the case cart.

In this case, some of the walking was caused by needed items not being stored in the case cart prep room. The technician had to walk to an operating room to get an item from a storage cabinet (an item that would then have to be transported back into an operating room). The Lean improvement team, made up of frontline staff, investigated and determined which supplies should be stored in the case cart area and which could be left off carts because they were part of the standard operating room inventory. They also observed frequent trips to the copier to copy the surgeon's case card, which specified what went on the cart. This walking could be reduced by putting a small copier in the case cart area (or totally eliminated by adopting a computerized case card system).

Within the case cart room itself, the layout and organization of supplies on the shelves led to excess walking. The team identified that high-volume supplies and items were scattered throughout

Figure 4.7 Walking pattern of one employee building one surgical case cart.

the case cart room. Because the cart room was congested with more than a dozen empty, partially, or fully completed carts, employees had little room to work and could not move the cart to the shelves. This was also a waste of overproduction issue, where the carts were sometimes built up to 24 hours before a planned procedure, partly to leave time for multiple cart inspections (the waste of defects). Carts were often broken down when the case was canceled, resulting in the waste of motion and underutilized employee talent. Also, when multiple carts were built in advance, staff often had to "raid" one cart to get something that was needed for another procedure, which often caused problems later when that raided cart was no longer ready for the other procedure.

The overproduction could have been reduced by building the carts closer to the time of the procedure, helping prevent the need to tear down carts after a procedure was canceled. But, reducing that buffer time of building carts in advance would have first required a number of quality and process improvements to ensure the proper instruments were always available and sterilized to be ready as needed.

Direct observation and study of the existing work can lead to process improvements that help a hospital avoid expensive capital improvements. Akron Children's Hospital spent $20,000 to overhaul their instrument sterilization process, allowing them to avoid a $3.5 million capital expansion project. Other patient flow improvements reduced the average time spent waiting for non-emergent magnetic resonance imaging exams from 25 days to less than 2 days.[10]

Conclusion

To improve our hospitals, there is no substitute for direct observation. We must first see problems before we can solve problems in a systematic way. Leaders need to see the waste that their employees and physicians have to deal with on a daily basis. Staff need to learn to identify waste that has become normal and accepted as part of the everyday work. We need to see what the patient experiences to help identify causes of delay, rework, and other waste. Data may show that product flows through the laboratory, pharmacy, or other support departments are on par with benchmarks, but direct observation will show the amount of waste and the opportunity for further improvement. With Lean, our goal is not to be better than our peers, but rather to be as good as we can be, aiming for the goal of a perfect, waste-free process.

Lean Lessons

- Managers have to go and see where the work is actually done, as observation can help identify waste.
- It is not enough for each department to be great; the pieces have to work together as a whole (the value stream and system).
- VSMs must be used to drive improvement; documenting the current state is not enough. Starting by designing a future state can cause other problems.
- Process maps are usually more detailed and limited in scope compared to a VSM.
- It is important to observe products (including patients) and employees as they move (or don't move) in the process.

- The observation and mapping should be done by those who do the work and their leaders, facilitated by an expert as needed, as opposed to being done by that expert. Outside eyes and a fresh perspective can be helpful as well.
- Walking and wasted motion are due to poor physical layouts and system design, not individuals being inefficient.

Points for Group Discussion

- How can we avoid having people take waste identification personally?
- Why must we observe processes firsthand to identify waste?
- Why are we sometimes surprised by what we see when observing the process?
- For a patient who arrives in the emergency department, how many different functions, departments, or silos are involved in their care?
- Can you think of an example where part of the entire value stream was suboptimized? Why did that happen? What can be done about that?
- Why do products and patients spend so much time waiting in the value stream?
- Pick a process you are accountable for. Could you sit down right now and diagram it for one of your customers? Would that match today's reality?
- What keeps nurses away from the bedside? What can be done to reduce that?
- What can we do to use freed up time instead of sending people home early?

Notes

1. May, Matthew, *The Elegant Solution: Toyota's Formula for Mastering Innovation* (New York: Free Press, 2006), 72.
2. CC-M Productions, Vol. 26—A study in continual improvement, part I, Video.
3. Gawande, Atul, *The Checklist Manifesto: How to Get Things Right* (New York: Picador, 2011), 185.
4. Womack, James P., and Daniel T. Jones, *Lean Thinking* (New York: Free Press, 2003), 19.
5. Rother, Mike, and John Shook, *Learning to See* (Brookline, MA: Lean Enterprise Institute, 2003), introduction.
6. Graban, Mark, Podcast #110, Dr. Jack Billi, Lean and Medicine, http://www.leanblog.org/110 (accessed September 12, 2015).
7. Graban, Mark, Time & Motion Studies Are Not "Discredited," Just How They Are Used, http://www.leanblog.org/2011/05/time-motion-studies-are-not-discredited-just-the-way-they-are-used/ (accessed September 12, 2015).
8. Kim, Christopher S., William Lovejoy, Michael Paulsen, Robert Chang, Scott A. Flanders, et al., "Hospitalist time usage and cyclicality: Opportunities to improve efficiency," *Journal of Hospital Medicine*, 2010, 5(6): 329–334.
9. Graban, Mark, and Amit Prachand, "Hospitalists: Lean leaders for hospitals," *Journal of Hospital Medicine*, 2010, 5(6): 317–319.
10. Weed, Julie, "Factory efficiency comes to the hospital," *New York Times*, July 10, 2010, http://www.nytimes.com/2010/07/11/business/11seattle.html (accessed March 26, 2011).

Chapter 5

Standardized Work as a Foundation of Lean

Helpful Standardization: From 171 Forms to Just Six

During a rapid improvement event at the University of Kansas Hospital, leaders were sent out to observe patients as they arrived at 5:00 a.m., not stopping until the patient was discharged later that day. In the course of the observation, the hospital learned that they had 171 different registration forms related to ambulatory care. They were able to reduce that to just six standardized forms. "A lot of executives sit in their offices all day and we think great thoughts and we analyze reports and have meetings and meetings, but one of the fundamental principles of this is get out of your office and go to where the work is," chief executive officer (CEO) Bob Page said. "This isn't new for us. [We've] done rounds and walked units forever but now we're looking at it differently."[1]

Why did they have 171 forms? They'd always done it that way. Or, if they had continued in their past ways, they might have soon had 183 forms. Standardizing on six forms undoubtedly saves the organization money and space and reduces confusion and the risk of the wrong forms or duplicate forms being given to a patient. Standardization is a not a primary goal in Lean; it is a helpful strategy that can solve or prevent certain problems and improve performance.

The Need for Standardized Work

In hospitals, even with all of the binders full of standard operating procedures (SOPs) and intranet sites full of policies, it is far too easy to find different people doing the same work in different ways, or not doing the work the best way, sometimes harming patients as a result. For example, one hospital initiated a Lean exercise with the assumption that nurses were not following protocols to prevent patient falls. After *gemba* visits and direct observation, a few things were learned. For one, many of the nurses thought they were following protocols, but they were actually following something incorrect or outdated. Other nurses knew what the protocols were but legitimately did not have time to complete all of the tasks they were expected to do in a given time span, so the protocol was skipped for some patients. Individuals should not be blamed for these conditions. Instead, the hospital and its leaders need to look at the environment that has been created and the culture that has allowed different work methods to be developed, not understood, and not followed.

Job instructions and policies are often communicated informally in hospital settings. Communication about process changes is ineffective when it happens through informal channels, including posted signs and verbal handoff communications. A typical nursing unit might have dozens of signs and postings, communicating new policies on hand hygiene, changes to the information system, and new practices involving medications. The visual noise can be overwhelming, as signs are posted on top of notices, in front of reminders. It is too easy for employees to miss or tune out the cacophony of signs. Hospitals are dynamic environments that operate with many people rotating in and out of jobs, 24 hours a day, seven days a week. We need a formalized method for managing and improving the way we do our work and how those methods are communicated. We can better support patient care and our employees with a standardized work system based on Lean practices.

When standardized work is not followed, risk is introduced for patients, and harm can occur. Problems with standardized work could be caused by work that is poorly designed, training that is ineffective, or supervision that is absent. At the University Hospital of Northern BC (British Columbia), about 10,000 patients over three years had procedures with endoscopes that were not properly cleaned. A hospital leader admitted that there was a "step incorrectly applied by our staff," where a channel was supposed to be cleaned for 30 seconds, but "some" staff didn't "normally" do so for the required time.[2] Problems with endoscope cleaning have been in the news around the world in recent years. Hospitals often blame staff or point to the need for retraining. Lean thinkers would ask why the initial training was not effective (if that was indeed the problem) or why supervisors did not notice that procedures were not being followed. These are systemic problems that require systemic solutions.

The Toyota House Metaphor

One common illustration of the Toyota Production System is the house model, adapted just slightly for hospitals. A house, like Lean, is an interconnected and mutually supporting system. A hospital leader looking to adopt Lean should realize that one would not "implement a house" by choosing just a kitchen and a bathroom while ignoring bedrooms and a front door. A house, like Lean, needs a solid foundation. Standardized work is one of those foundations.

As with other Lean illustrations, the house has people at its core, as shown in the Toyota version of the house in Figure 5.1. Figure 5.2 shows how the house is often customized for the particular needs of an organization, in this case Baylor Scott & White Health (Dallas, Texas).[3]

Overview of the Lean Foundations

The foundation of the Lean house consists of three core principles. Standardized work is the method for developing best practices and methods. *Heijunka* is a Japanese word for "level loading" workloads or demand for services, smoothing the workflow and patient flow, as discussed in Chapter 9. *Kaizen* is another Japanese word that can be translated as "continuous improvement," as discussed in Chapter 11 and in depth in the book *Healthcare Kaizen*.[4]

Figure 5.1   The TPS "House." (Image courtesy of Toyota, used with permission.)

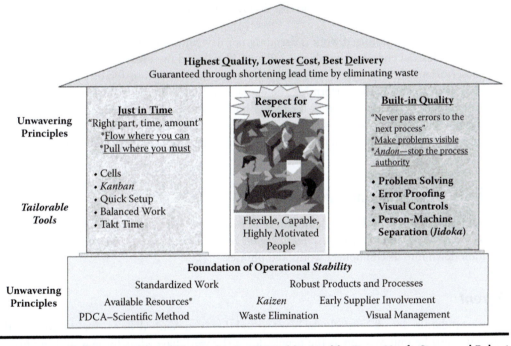

Figure 5.2   The house model used by Baylor Scott & White Health. (From Hoeft, Steve, and Robert M. Pryor, *The Power of Ideas to Transform Healthcare: Engaging Staff by Building Daily Lean Management Systems.* **New York: Productivity Press, 2015. With permission.)**

All three of these concepts are interconnected and necessary for a Lean system to thrive. Standardized work without *kaizen* would be a stagnant workplace that never improved. *Kaizen* without a basis of standardized work might be a chaotic environment where people randomly try new methods that do not necessarily improve the overall system. Standardized work without *heijunka* means employees will be stressed, and patients will suffer long waiting times.

Standardized work, *heijunka*, and *kaizen* all work together to support the concepts of eliminating waste and respecting people.

Lean Foundations: Standardized Work

Standardized work starts with a simple premise: People should analyze their work and define the way that best meets the needs of all stakeholders. Many of the problems in hospitals can be traced back to a root cause that involves the lack of standardization. For example, one commonly occurring preventable patient injury is pressure ulcers, or bedsores. To avoid these, one method requires staff to reposition at-risk patients every two hours. Many hospitals struggle with making sure this is done in the proper way and at the proper frequency. Instead of responding to this challenge by blaming our employees and exhorting them to do better (or by posting more signs), we need to instead look at a method for documenting standardized work and managing the work to ensure it is followed consistently. The bedsores example is revisited later in this chapter.

The idea of standardized work is not new. Henry Ford, whose words had a great influence on Toyota, wrote, "Our own attitude is that we are charged with discovering the best way of doing everything."[5] Toyota helped extend this discovery into more of an ongoing process, through *kaizen*.

The concept of standardized work is certainly not new within hospitals or medicine, tracing back to the industrial engineers Frank and Lillian Gilbreth and their research in the early 1900s. Their observations showed that a surgeon spent more time searching for instruments in the operating room than actually performing the operation. The Gilbreths recommended that trays be better organized and that a "surgical caddy" should hand the instruments to the surgeon as needed.[6] But, change often comes slowly in healthcare, as these new ideas were not accepted by the American Medical Association until 1930—having been proposed by the Gilbreths in 1914.

Definition of Standardized Work

So, what is *standardized work*? One definition is *the current one best way to safely complete an activity with the proper outcome and the highest quality, using the fewest possible resources*. We can break this definition down into its component words and phrases.

Current

Today's standardized work is merely the best method that is currently defined. Standardized work can (and must) be improved on as the people doing the work have ideas for new and improved methods.

Toyota called standardized work "the basis for *kaizen*."[7] Without a standard, you cannot have sustainable improvement. If employees do things in different ways, an improvement idea from one employee might either add to the variation in the current system or get lost because we do not have a standard method for transferring that new idea to other employees.

Do not confuse "current" as meaning that we simply need to document the way work is currently done. In the process of developing standardized work, employees must look for waste and challenge all aspects of how work is currently done. Far too often, traditional documentation just captures all of the waste in the current method, without stopping to make improvements, or *kaizen*.

Proper Outcome and the Highest Quality

A Toyota guidebook begins explaining standardized work by starting with the end goal in mind, saying, "Standardized Work is a tool for maintaining productivity, quality, and safety at high levels."[8] Hospitals must keep this in mind and not standardize for the sake of standardizing. There are countless numbers of tasks and procedures that our employees face every day. Trying to standardize all of our methods would seem like an overwhelming challenge. Hospitals must ensure that their standardized work benefits the patients, the employees, the physicians, and the hospital itself. We must prioritize our improvement and standardization activity so our initial efforts can have the largest impact on all of our stakeholders. We might ask, for example, "Does standardizing this method (and standardizing it to this extent) improve quality?"

Quality is continually emphasized as a core Lean principle, and our standardized work should reflect that. Standardized work is not an approach that emphasizes speed over quality. Our standardized work documentation must reflect the amount of time required to do the work in the proper way to avoid overburdening employees or inadvertently pressuring them to cut corners. This is one example of how standardized work can benefit employees and embodies the respect for the people aspect of Lean.

Standardizing methods that have an impact on patient safety is a great place to start. Areas in which hospitals have typically already made efforts at standardizing include

- Hand washing and hygiene
- Preparation steps for cardiac surgery
- Labeling of patient specimens
- Inserting and managing central lines
- Medication administration processes
- Communication with patient on outpatient or primary care appointment
- Proper cleaning and disinfection of patient rooms

Keep in mind that having a written procedure or policy in place does not mean that a standardized method is always going to be followed. Many hospital standards are, unfortunately, ignored or not followed consistently. Standardized work for hand hygiene would include deciding when to use sanitizing gel or soap and water and how that cleaning should be done. It is widely reported that hand-washing policy compliance is low in hospitals, with few studies or estimates showing at least 50% compliance.[9] Another study shows that healthcare professionals "who deal directly with patients" wash their hands less frequently as their workday progresses, with compliance rates falling 8.7 percentage points from the start to the end of a shift. The authors suggest the decline in hand hygiene is the result of depleted mental reserves and "accumulated work demands" and is "magnified" by workload intensity. This sounds like yet another reason to reduce waste and overburden in hospitals. The publication cites data that say every percentage point increase in hand hygiene rates reduces infections by 3.9 per 1,000 patients.[10] This illustrates the purpose behind standardizing hand hygiene practices and creating an environment where people are not exhausted or otherwise unable to follow them.

Standardization is meant to be a helpful countermeasure to problems that matter and deliver better outcomes. Standardizing the best method for cleaning an operating room can reduce rates of hospital-acquired infections, as one study found that employees overlooked more than half the objects that should have been disinfected.[11] The root cause of the problem could have been a poorly defined standard, or it could have been a case of managers not checking to see if the standard was being followed. The idea of a standardized work system and leadership's role in overseeing standards are discussed later in this chapter.

To Safely Complete

"To safely complete" further emphasizes the focus on outcomes and benefits from standardized work. As we discussed with quality, standardized work does not encourage speed or efficiency over safety. Safety practices, for both patients and employees, should be considered nonnegotiable aspects of our standardized work practices. Safety is very visibly a high priority when you visit a Toyota plant or any Lean factory. Every employee, leader, and visitor walks under a symbolic green safety arch that says, in part, "Safe work is the gate to all work." ThedaCare CEO Dean Gruner says, "If we can't do things safely, why should we be doing them in the first place?"[12] The ideas of "safety first" or "patient safety is always our top priority" need to be more than just slogans. They should be the daily reality in any Lean hospital.

One Best Way

For different types of work, is there truly "one best way"? Notice this is a question, not an assumption. It is important to ensure that the proper level of detail and specificity is documented in our standardized work. When medical technologists in the microbiology lab, for example, inoculate and streak patient specimens onto petri dish media, there might be variation in how that work is done. Certain details, such as the exact pattern of streaking the specimen across the plate, might make a big difference in how the culture grows and the resulting medical decisions. The book *Toyota Talent* refers to this as work of "critical importance"—the 20% of tasks for which work must be highly consistent.[13] The standardized work documentation might be detailed for this method, with pictures and examples used for initial training and continual refreshers on how the work should be done.

> "AIDET" is a common healthcare method that gives staff a standardized way to communicate more effectively with patients and families: **Acknowledge** the person by name, **Introduce** yourself, discuss the **Duration** of care or any delays, give an **Explanation** of what you are doing, and **Thank** them when done. Having a structured approach, and even some "scripting" of key phrases, should not prevent staff from having some flexibility, or even fun, in their interactions with people. Advocates of AIDET suggest that use of the practice can improve quality outcomes and patient satisfaction along with Hospital Consumer Assessment of Healthcare Providers and Systems (HCAHPS) scores, which can then result in financial rewards for the health system through value-based purchasing.

On the other hand, there might be details of the work that do not have an impact on safety, quality, or outcomes. Does it matter which hand a technologist uses to streak the plate? Probably not, so our standardized work documentation would not be that specific. Left-handed techs might disregard an overly specific standardized work method as an unjust standard. This creates an environment in which, unfortunately, individual employees feel like they are given choices over which standards to follow, contributing to inconsistent quality and outcomes. Standardized work methods cannot be considered optional by employees or managers if the methods truly have an impact on patient outcomes or other important results.

Other work tasks and methods might not require such detailed specification in the method. It would be a waste of resources to try to standardize every possible task. For some activities, there is room for some variation in the way the work is done (what *Toyota Talent* calls the "important tasks"), and there might be other activities (the "low-importance tasks") for which varying methods are not likely to have any impact on the quality or outcomes of the process.

At the outpatient clinic at one children's hospital, it was easy for staff to blame parents for their late arrival or for having children who violated orders for nothing by mouth (NPO) orders. When a team looked deeply into the process, they learned that each person in the scheduling office had a unique way of communicating to parents in the reminder call. Some explained that "no clear liquids" also meant that milk was forbidden, but others did not. Some staff were careful to explain that the hospital and the clinic were two different locations, to avoid mix-ups. The staff standardized their calls to parents, emphasizing certain key points in a consistent way, without having every single word scripted. Late patients and NPO violations dropped dramatically. It was not a matter of "bad parents"—it was "bad process."

Fewest Possible Resources

While safety and quality are nonnegotiable priorities in the Lean mindset, we are also concerned with making the best use of our resources: minimizing waste. "Resources" include our people and their time, supplies, equipment, physical space—anything that costs money. We should also consider resources that do not directly cost the hospital anything, such as the patient's time. Many attempts at productivity make minimizing resources the primary goal. Some managers have traditionally tried to limit resources, hoping that people will, of necessity, figure out a better way to do their work. The direct labor cost may drop in the short term, but quality becomes worse if people do not have enough time available to do high-quality work in that system. This often leads to a cycle of discouragement, making improvement even less likely to occur.

That is why in the Lean approach we first improve quality and productivity, only then considering any opportunity to reduce head count. Lean leaders keep in mind the idea that we respect people and retrain or redeploy them to do other work rather than laying them off. Therefore, health systems are able to increase the volume of care provided without adding people, ensuring quality remains high and that work is not too stressful for staff.

Standardized, Not Identical

It is often tempting to say *standard* instead of *standardized*, but there is a distinction between the two words and concepts. *Standard* can sound like an absolute, a method with zero variation or zero flexibility. It starts sounding like the word *identical*, which makes employees concerned that they are being turned into robots. Most employees—not just in healthcare—value their ability to use judgment to make decisions on the job. There is a balance to be struck somewhere between complete chaos, with everybody doing things differently, and mindless conformity. Employees who are constantly thinking through "How should I do this?" or "What do I do next?" may find themselves drained and worn out mentally by the end of the day (and, therefore, unable to follow hand hygiene guidelines). Standardized work is the plan that frees us from having to make hundreds of small decisions throughout our day, thus freeing brain capacity and reserving energy to deal with the smaller number of more important decisions that arise.

> Bill Marriott, CEO of Marriott Hotels, explained the company is not trying to turn employees into robots through the company's SOPs. Standardization has long been a part of the Marriott culture and management system. Marriott explained: "Mindless conformity and the thoughtful setting of standards should never be confused. What solid SOPs do is nip common problems in the bud so that staff can focus instead on solving uncommon problems."[14] These ideas are very compatible with the Lean philosophy.

If Toyota wanted its employees to be mindless robots, Toyota might have called its system "identical work" instead of standardized work. The *-ized* in *standardized* implies that some effort is made toward total standardization, but the effort often stops before 100% standardization is achieved. One might wonder if 100% standardization is even possible in any environment, let alone in complex hospital settings. There is almost always some necessary variation in customer needs and, therefore, in the way work must be done or care must be provided. Critics sometimes attack a straw man model that says Lean somehow forces the same care on every patient or that every patient has to be given the exact same discharge information. Those critics, unfortunately, don't understand what Lean is about.

Written by Those Who Do the Work

Standardized work is not a command-and-control approach that is dictated from managers or experts to their employees. A key difference with standardized work, compared to other process documentation models, is that Lean documents are written by the people who do the work. Toyota's Taiichi Ohno wrote, "Standards should not be forced down from above but rather set by the production workers themselves."[15] The assumption is that the employees know the work best and are in a better position to write accurate and effective documentation. Pascal Dennis, who worked at Toyota in Canada more recently, writes, "The people closest to the work develop standards and pull in specialists as required."[16] Yes, leaders and specialists should have some input, but standardized work is not embraced if staff members don't have significant input into what gets standardized and how (and for what purpose). Kathy Maass, director of process excellence for Avera McKennan (South Dakota), says, "The most successful [Lean] projects are the ones where the front-line staff gathers the data and develops the standard work."[17]

While the employees are the experts on the current methods, the process of writing standardized work must force a reevaluation of how things are done, rather than just documenting the current method. Before writing standardized work documents, teams spend time observing, videoing, and examining their current methods in detail, as described in Chapter 4. Having to talk through and write down methods with coworkers can lead to waste reduction, as Frank Gilbreth wrote about hospitals in 1914: "You will be surprised what improvements will suggest themselves to you as a result of seeing in cold ink exactly what you are doing now in your department."[18] Initial improvements will come from this documentation effort, with more improvements, or *kaizen*, to follow over time.

In a large department setting, it might not be practical to have everybody directly involved in the writing of the standardized work documents. A smaller group, such as a Lean project team made up of frontline staff, can write documents that are considered initial drafts. The entire department can review these drafts so that everybody has a chance to give input.

A major challenge with standardized work is getting everybody to agree on a standardized approach, particularly when people have been left to their own approaches in the past. It is not a cure-all, but employees are more likely to accept standardized work (and to follow it) if they have had the opportunity to provide input.

The radiology department at one hospital inadvertently learned the value of standardized work as they adopted Lean. Different people, including technicians, nurses, assistants, and radiologists, were formed into teams on different days, depending on the scheduling rotation. One particular combination had worked together, the exact same people every day, for about two weeks straight. "Things were working really well. We all knew exactly who was doing what and everything went smoothly," said one technician, showing pride in their efficiency (and their ability to get home on time).

Things worked well until the schedule changed, and the temporary team was broken up. Employees now complained that since "everybody does things differently," the new group was not as productive as that previous group. The employees started to ask why that had to be. With proper standardized work in place, the department expected to have that same productive and happy feeling every day, regardless of who was working on the team, since each team would not have to reinvent its own methods and team roles.

Considering How Long Tasks Take

Hospitals already have process documentation and SOPs, listing steps for completing many work tasks. Standardized work documents go beyond this by showing the expected duration for tasks or activities. On a Toyota assembly line, it would be unfair to employees, as well as being bad for flow and quality, to give employees more work than can be done in their repetitive job cycles.

Granted, most hospital jobs are not repetitive in nature, like assembly line jobs, but the same general principle should hold true. It should apply from the standpoint of not expecting 10 hours of work content to be done in an eight-hour shift. It should also apply within the day, such as not expecting employees to do two tasks at the same time or not overburdening an employee during a peak hour in the day. The hospital mentioned at the start of the chapter had nurses list every task they were expected to do in a given hour, including the fall protocols, along with an observed measure of how long each task usually took. They added up 80 minutes' worth of work to do in each hour—an impossibility. It's unfair to have nurses decide which work can be skipped, especially if they are blamed for any bad outcomes that result from, for example, skipping rounding on a patient because the nurse thought they were stable.

With the variability found in hospital work, determining precise workloads can be difficult. Departments should do their best to estimate workloads, trying to balance work evenly across employees and ensure that nobody is overloaded. Better yet, a department can draft standardized work that allows for employees to be cross-trained and to help each other as needed. A hospital department is unlikely to have a script that is followed as precisely as an assembly line job that repeats every 60 seconds. The standardized work document can be considered a guideline, more than a script. Again, standardized work should be as specific as is helpful in achieving our goals as a health system.

Staffing Based on Data

In many hospital settings, staffing levels are set by benchmarking data, rules of thumb, habit, or financial constraints. Ideally, staffing levels should be based on actual workloads, driven by patient demand, and the standardized work that suggests the pace at which people can work without jeopardizing quality or safety. It would also be ideal to ensure that employees are not always 100% busy, as some slack time is helpful to account for variations in workload and to allow time for continuous improvement.

Takt is a German word that should be familiar to readers who are musicians as it signifies a pace or tempo, as in a piece of music. *Takt* is a Lean term for expressing the pace of customer demand for a value stream or a process. An auto assembly factory might have a *takt* of 50 seconds, meaning a customer buys a car every 50 seconds during the hours the factory is running. *Takt* is calculated as the number of available working hours (or minutes or seconds) divided by the customer demand.

In healthcare settings, applications of *takt* can be difficult to find or can be more complex than in manufacturing. While a car factory can have a level-loaded production rate for a month, based on average *takt*, a hospital must do work in response to patient demand that varies each hour and each day, as hospitals cannot level their work and build a parking lot full of cars to sell later. That said, there are some cases for which *takt* is useful in understanding our workload to drive staffing decisions.

For example, a hospital laboratory might need to draw 360 patient specimens in a four-hour window each morning. *Takt* is then 14,400 seconds divided by 360 specimens, or 40 seconds per specimen. As we develop standardized work (having eliminated some waste from the process as we do so), we might learn that it takes a phlebotomist (at longest) eight minutes to properly draw a specimen and then walk to the next patient. One person drawing a specimen every 480 seconds cannot meet the patient demand of a specimen every 40 seconds.

Simple math tells us we would need a minimum of 480/40 or 12 phlebotomists to meet *takt*. Practically speaking, we would want 13 or 14 to account for variation in the time it takes to draw specimens. In this case, and in other settings, we would likely have different *takt* time and different staffing requirements throughout the day and throughout the week. We should do our best to use data to match staffing to demand, out of respect for our patients and for our employees.

It's sometimes misunderstood that the *takt* time for a process sets a time limit for work. For example, if the demand for a dentist says the *takt* time is 15 minutes, then the hygienist and the dentist each need to be able to complete a patient's work in about 15 minutes, otherwise the waiting room will be busy and everyone might have to stay late. Even if the planned appointment time is 15 minutes, if a particular patient requires more time, then you'd spend more time with that patient in a Lean environment. There is no buzzer that goes off to indicate the patient must leave because their time is up. If a patient encounter is running long and that is due to a process problem, that should lead to *kaizen* or improvement of the process, not rushing the patient out.

Types of Standardized Work Documents

So far, most of our focus has been on the concepts and philosophy of standardized work. What do these documents look like in practice? There is no single magic format; many types of standardized work documents can fit different situations. Some of the common formats are listed in Table 5.1, with examples of where those formats might be applied in a hospital.[19]

Table 5.1 Types of Standardized Work Documents

Tool or Document	Purpose	Healthcare Example
Standardized work chart	Primary document that shows job responsibilities, common work tasks, and how long they should take; often shows a diagram of where work is done	Daily routine for lab employees, nurses, pharmacy employees
Work combination sheet	Analyzes relationships between an operator and a machine to synchronize work and eliminate operator waiting time; used to determine how multiple people could divide that work	Clinical laboratory "core cell" automated area
Process capacity sheet	Analyze capacity of equipment, rooms, other resources; considers changeover or set time and other planned downtime	Analyzing operating room capacity and changeover time
Detailed work instructions or "job breakdown sheet"	Details important cyclical and noncyclical tasks; used as a reference or training document and is not posted in the work area; describes "key points" for quality and safety	Clinical laboratory core cell, pharmacy technician duties for responding to first-dose orders
Cycle balance chart	Used to balance work on an assembly line across workers, and matching up production rate with rate of customer demand	Nutrition services (sandwich production line)

In some instances, hospital departments have implemented the detailed work instructions as a posted document in the workplace. These documents spell out, in the appropriate level of detail, tasks, sequence, timing, and "key points" that are important for safety or quality.[20] The documents can be used for training or reference, or they can be used as checklists that help ensure that important steps are not forgotten or deviated from. The exact format of standardized work documents, as with other Lean practices, should be considered guidelines that can be adopted and adapted, depending on your situation.

Standardizing Daily Routines

While standardized work often looks at the details of specific tasks, we can also use the concepts to plan daily schedules. For example, a laboratory team might have certain activities (such as instrument maintenance or weekly inspections) that are routinely done. Departments often find benefits in determining the best time (or time frame) for certain activities to be done, with the goals of avoiding time conflicts and smoothing out workloads. Some labs, out of routine, have the first-shift technologist start machine maintenance when beginning his or her shift at 7:00 a.m., even if that is a peak busy period. Since the maintenance has to be done daily, the exact time does not matter, as long as it is consistent. Through the Lean process, teams quickly identify that tasks like machine maintenance can be done during slower periods, having less of an impact on testing turnaround time.

In another case, a radiology department had a team of three employees working at the front registration desk to sign in patients. Before Lean, two of the employees went to lunch together at 11:00 a.m. each day, even if large numbers of patients were arriving, leaving the remaining one clerk with a heavy workload. This clerk felt this was unfair, and it delayed patients (which also delayed imaging procedures). With Lean, the team started with a patient focus and instituted flexible lunchtimes. The employees would delay their lunch if patient volumes mandated it. The team also had to reconsider the staggering of lunch breaks, sending only one clerk at a time instead of two going together. This was not an easy change to make, but it was fairly applied to all employees and beneficial for the patients. The role of leadership was to emphasize why the changes were necessary and beneficial.

This approach of specifying when breaks are taken might seem to go against the idea that Lean is good for the employees. It is true that some employees may be asked to change their habits and schedules, but only if it is for the benefit of the patients. Nobody should ever hear a statement like, "Lean says you all have to take lunch at different times." The team should ask, "Is there a benefit to standardizing lunch and break times?" In some areas, employees might have more leeway in choosing their own break times. Managers need to explain why such standardization is necessary, rather than mandating it through their position of formal authority.

Avera Health realized that all respiratory therapy orders were due at just three times each day: 7:00 a.m., 3:00 p.m., and 11:00 p.m. "We really challenged the respiratory therapists and asked them why they were wedded to those times," said Kathy Maass, director, Process Excellence for Avera McKennan Hospital and University Health Center (Sioux Falls, South Dakota). Now, if an order comes in at 9:00 a.m., the timing for that patient's treatments starts at that time and, for example, every six hours afterward. "That level loads your flow," says Maass, "and you won't have 40 patients due at 7:00 a.m.," which is sure to improve patient care and reduce stress for staff.

Defining Roles and Responsibilities

Standardized work goes beyond the details of completing tasks and scheduling one's day. The writing of standardized work also gives hospitals an opportunity to reconsider which tasks are done by which employees. This is not a new question in hospitals, as a 1924 journal article highlighted, "I have seen competent nurses scrubbing floors, and doing other things which to the lay mind are functions of service not requiring the high skill and training so essential to the nursing profession."[21] This sounds like a point made in the discussion of not wasting employee talents in Chapter 3.

One example can be found in the laboratory. Since medical technologists are often in short supply and have specialized scientific education and skills, the hospital must use those skills wisely. We cannot afford to waste the time of technologists by having them do work that does not require their expertise or skills.

If technologists are performing manual tasks, such as replenishing supplies from the storeroom or moving specimens within the lab, we have to challenge that assignment of work. The fact that work "has always been done that way" should not be an excuse for not changing. Some labs have gone as far as to have laboratory assistants load specimens into automated instruments since the skill of the technologist is needed for interpreting results and troubleshooting the process. This can be controversial if the technologists have always loaded the analyzers. Loading a tube into an instrument is sometimes just a manual material-handling function that laboratory assistants can indeed do, given the proper training and having standardized work in place. The ability to shift this work may depend on legal or regulatory restrictions in a given state or country, so caution is advised.

Allowing technologists to focus on their skilled work fits with the philosophy of respect for people, as it values their special abilities. In one laboratory, prior to Lean adoption, a medical technologist with 25 years of experience complained that the work had become "robotic." This was due to new automated lab technology, for which all the technologist did was "move tubes, load them, and press a few buttons," compared to the manual methods used decades earlier. In a Lean environment, we can allow technologists to focus more on the work that requires their scientific training. In addition, as we engage employees in *kaizen* efforts, technologists and assistants can use their creativity to solve problems, a decidedly unrobotic activity.

Again, there may be instances, however, for which we have somebody working below his or her level in the name of teamwork or improved flow. For example, in some pharmacies, the pharmacist will load a medication into a tube system carrier immediately after verifying and inspecting the medication. Using the tube system does not require pharmacist training, but it requires only a few seconds and prevents a potential delay in waiting for a technician to send the medication to the patient.

The lab at Children's Health (Dallas, Texas) defined daily routines for different medical technologist or lab assistants and the role they each play on a given day. The responsibilities and daily plan for each role are posted on the wall for everyone to reference, and they are updated over time. A clearly visible whiteboard is updated each day, listing which person is in which role, to help improve communication and avoid any confusion that might occur as people rotate through their roles over time.

Quick Changeover as Standardized Work

One variation on standardized work is the methodology for quick changeover, also known as setup time reduction. Toyota's innovation, under the leadership of Shigeo Shingo, was to reduce stamping press changeover times from multiple hours to less than 10 minutes, via what was called single-minute exchange of dies (SMED). Setup times were often reduced by a factor of 40 in a 10-year period.[22] It's not uncommon for a factory, even today, to quickly reduce setup times from hours to minutes, even if they thought it wouldn't be possible. Challenging assumptions and being creative to change "the way we've always done it" can be very powerful. A hospital equivalent example would be significantly reducing the time required to change over an operating room between patients, including all of the cleanup, sterilization, and preparation for the next case.

Rather than accepting that changeover times inherently had to be long, Shingo taught a methodology that included analyzing the way work was done to find a better way. In manufacturing, a press can make different types of parts, but only after you change one "die" for another. At Toyota a worker walking to get the new "dies" would normally occur after the machine was shut down to stop production of the previous type of part. In the Lean system, tasks that could be done in advance of machine shutdown were "externalized," leaving only those "internal" tasks that absolutely had to be done while the machine was down.

Pit crews for professional auto racing are another inspiration for quick changeover work, with pit crews often teaching hospitals their methods.[23] Pit crews have highly orchestrated methods that are practiced frequently, with the goal of maximizing the time the driver is on the road, while also doing their work in the safest possible way. Hospitals can have a similar goal of maximizing the amount of time a surgeon and the surgical team can operate, thereby reducing the amount of time that surgeons or patients wait and increasing the number of cases that can be completed each day.

In the operating room setting, a hospital might have team members help stage everything that would be needed for the next case outside the room while the previous case was finishing, rather than doing that work during the downtime between cases. Roles and responsibilities for room cleaning and prep are highly specified, leading to faster room turns. Quality often improves as certain surfaces or sections of the room are no longer forgotten by previously hurried staff. In some circumstances, adding prep staff might increase cost in a way that is more than paid for by the increased operating room utilization and revenue (or a reduction in infections).

University of Michigan Health System (UMHS) reduced turnaround times between surgical cases by 20%, to 69 minutes. One improvement was to reduce some delays by starting to transport the incoming patient while some OR prep was still taking place, instead of waiting until prep was completed. Surgeon Carol Bradford, MD, chair of the UMHS Department of Otolaryngology, estimated that their methods could be extended to their 35 operating rooms to create 6,500 hours of new capacity each year. Dr. Bradford said that "staff from scrub nurses to anesthesiologists are more empowered and teamwork has risen to new heights."[24] Staff morale scores also improved by 20% and, Dr. Billi said, "This makes sense because Lean thinking abandons top-down thinking and emphasizes the perspectives of those closest to the work when rethinking and improving the workflow."

Presence Health's Sts. Mary and Elizabeth Medical Center (Illinois) formed a team to conduct a weeklong "rapid improvement event" that aimed to reduce operating room turnaround time from a baseline of 30.55 minutes. After the team analyzed their current-state process and tested new standardized methods, they were convinced their new process would get the turnaround time down to just 18.4 minutes, about a 40% reduction. The health system estimated that time to be worth about $1 million a year in additional revenue if they could utilize the capacity.[25]

Explaining Why through Standardized Work

"In healthcare, we're [normally] good about telling the what, but not the why," says Bill Schmidt, CEO of New London Family Medical Center (New London, Wisconsin), a part of the ThedaCare system. Another innovation of the Lean approach to standardized work is the extra effort taken to explain why certain steps are necessary or why things should be done a certain way. Instead of telling employees to perform a task a particular way because a manager said so, Lean shows respect for people by treating them like thinking adults. Detailed work instruction documents typically have two columns to the right of the list of steps and time durations. The first column highlights key points that are critical to safety or quality, and the second column explains why those key points should be followed.[26] Employees are more likely to follow the standardized work when they understand the reasoning behind the key point. If we rely on formal authority to enforce standardized work adherence, it is likely that employees will do things their own way when nobody is watching.

When managers are directive, they must explain why the policies, goals, or decisions are necessary. This shows respect for people. It is often said that people hate change. It might be more accurate to say people hate being told what to do. As Peter Senge says, "People don't resist change; they resist being changed." At any level in the organization, people dislike decisions that are forced on them, especially those that seem arbitrary or are just a change instead of an improvement. Signs or notices, when used, should not just be directive; they should explain why.

In one lab that was implementing Lean, a manager taped a sign to the centrifuge that read, "DO NOT CHANGE SPIN TIME. Should be 6 minutes." This was a command-and-control action; the employee was expected to follow the sign (an order) because of the manager's formal authority. Sure enough, a technologist soon walked by, saw the sign, and asked, "Why is that?" before moving on. The manager realized his error in not explaining why. A new sign was made that explained that the time was now six minutes rather than the old 10 minutes because they were using a new type of tube that required less centrifuge time. It was not, as the employee might have feared, an attempt to save time (at the expense of quality) by arbitrarily shortening the time.

The idea of explaining why can also apply to interactions with patients. In one hospital, instead of just telling patients, "You must wear masks," the signs were more informative and made it more likely that patients might follow the instructions. Signs explained that hematology-oncology patients must wear masks because of the construction of the new patient tower and how construction dust increased the risk of fungal infections if it was breathed. Another hospital changed its directive "no food or drink" signs in the waiting room to a slightly longer sign that explained that banning food was a courtesy to patients who were not allowed to eat before their procedures. The number of people who brought food into the waiting room dropped as a result. Treat people with respect, and good things will follow.

Standardized Work Documents and the Standardized Work System

All too often, health systems have focused on standardized work as a documentation exercise instead of viewing it as an ongoing management exercise. It is typical for organizations to go through waves and cycles of standardization and procedure writing, often corresponding with cycles of inspection and certification by outside bodies. We become excited about documenting our processes and devote employee time to the effort, but to what effect and results?

The standardized work documents themselves are an important starting point. Even if we have fully documented methods and procedures, leaders cannot guarantee that all employees will always perform the work in that consistent manner. Standardized work is a deceptively simple concept, but one that is difficult to implement and sustain. Managers have to do more than just assume that procedures or standardized work will be followed. We have to check, audit, or inspect that these are being followed consistently, with the right results.

There is a phrase that we use that attempts to capture the responsibility of leaders in overseeing standardized work: "You get what you expect and you deserve what you tolerate." As leaders, if you expect that employees will follow the standardized work, you have to take time to go and see, to verify that the standardized work is actually being followed. If you tolerate people not following the standardized work, you deserve the outcomes that result from the standardized work not being followed.

Coming back to our bedsores example, traditional management approaches might measure the number of bedsores in different wards or under each nurse's responsibility. There might be two different areas in which the employees are not following the standardized work of properly repositioning patients every two hours. Due to variation in our patients and, to some extent, pure luck, one area might have a patient who develops a bedsore, while the other area does not. Would it be right to praise the area where zero bedsores developed? Through the same actions (or inaction), that "zero bedsores" unit might have a patient develop a bedsore the next week. As leaders, we need to focus on the process and hold people accountable for doing the right things the right way, rather than just focusing on and reacting to bad outcomes. Lean leaders realize that the right process will lead to the right results.

Measuring and Observing for Standardized Work Adherence

Rather than waiting for measures or other reports, leaders should also spend time directly inspecting and observing the process to see if the standardized work is being followed. We can shadow employees on a regular basis. We can develop checklists or visual indicators that leaders can use throughout the day to see if routine or scheduled tasks are getting done.

For example, patients who are at risk for bedsores might have a checklist posted outside their room, where staff members who reposition the patient every two hours initial or mark the list. As part of their standardized work for leaders, charge nurses, team leaders, or other managers would, on a schedule, do rounds and verify that the standardized work is being followed at the right frequency. Managers would also occasionally directly observe to see if patients were being repositioned according to the standardized work.

Managers often have to dig beyond the superficial. In one hospital I visited, there was a daily check sheet that was supposed to be used to double-check that all of the required emergency supplies were present. The boxes were always checked. But, taking a few seconds to actually look for the supplies showed that many items were usually missing (and not because there had been an emergency earlier that day). When it appears that people are just checking the box, managers should ask "why?"

With checklists and other records, leaders have to be alert to employees going back and filling them out at the end of their shift. This could mean the standardized work was not getting done, and employees were fudging the checklist. Or, it could mean they are doing the work but not filling out the form until the end of the shift. Checklists and standardized work timing must be followed throughout the day.

Illustrating the need to "explain why," one hospital had a nursing assistant explain that she came by at the end of the shift and filled in any missing checkmarks on the tracking sheets. It seemed that managers wanted to see checked boxes more so than actual adherence to the standardized work.

In a non-Lean culture, this sort of oversight might be seen as hounding the employees or not trusting them. The key is how we react to the standardized work not being followed and how we engage with employees in a Lean setting. Leaders need to ensure that standardized work is being followed for the sake of the patients and the right outcomes, not because we like telling people what to do.

Frontline employees are not the only employees to have their standardized work audited. The first-level supervisors might have standardized work that indicates they audit their area once a day. That supervisor's manager will also conduct regular audits and check that the audits are getting done, as accountability does not stop with the first-level supervisor. More detail about this process is given in Chapter 11.

Leaders must have discipline to keep auditing standardized work. A case in point involves the experience of a radiology department with process audits before Lean. New rules from the Joint Commission required a radiologist to sign oral contrast orders before the contrast was administered to a patient. Managers and the director had been doing audits but stopped after about three months. Predictably enough, after the audits stopped, 100% compliance with the orders no longer occurred.

"Resistance" to Standardized Work?

While standardized work has clear benefits for the patients and the employees, it is common for some people in the organization to resist the idea. Some employees might resist, feeling insulted that they need to be told how to do their jobs. Of course, that is not the intent. Especially for many long-time employees, "We already know how to do our jobs" is a common complaint, but does everybody do their job the same way or with the best outcomes? Employees might also fear being unable to learn the new standardized work method. Employees should be reassured that they will be trained properly and given time to learn the new method, without being criticized.

It is often easier to gain acceptance of the general concept, to get people to agree that we should standardize. The real challenge often comes in the details of deciding whose standard or which combination of standardized methods is the best way. Building consensus can be time-consuming, but it is the best way to get agreement. If there is disagreement over which way is the one best way, we should rely on data rather than opinions. Teams can try different methods, measuring for the impact on safety, quality, time, or cost. Decisions on standardized work should be based on more than who is influential or who argues the loudest. If there are two equally good methods, a leader can help decide which method should be used.

Asking Why When Standardized Work Is Not Followed

When a leader sees that standardized work is not followed, the first question needs to be: "Why is the standard not being followed?" This question needs to be asked sincerely rather than in an accusatory manner. The question could be asked in a tone that really says, "You must follow the standard work," which might intimidate an employee into falling back in line (an approach that is neither sustainable nor morale building).

Asking why can also encourage *kaizen*. Some managers get focused on making sure employees are following the standard methods, no matter what. In this zeal to enforce standardized work, we might lose potential opportunities for *kaizen* if we are not careful. Again, standardized work is not meant to be permanent; it is to be improved on, over time, by the employees doing the work. If managers reacted negatively every time they saw someone not following the standardized work, *kaizen* and creativity would be stifled.

The lab at Children's Health (Dallas, Texas) has five questions displayed on a bulletin board, prompting people how to respond "if standard work is not being followed":

1. Is the standard work appropriate?
2. Are the right tools, equipment, and materials in place and of appropriate quality?
3. Is the person following the steps and sequence?
4. Has the person had adequate practice in the operation?
5. Does the system allow the person to meet the standard?

We ask why because there might be legitimate reasons the current standard is not being followed; there might be a problem in the process that necessitates changing the standardized work. As leaders, we need to encourage people to bring those problems to the surface so we can work on fixing them. If the employee is employing a workaround, we can encourage the individual to find and fix the root cause of the problem, as discussed in Chapter 7. When it looks like the standardized work isn't being followed, we might have found the employee trying a new method, a potential *kaizen* that could be incorporated into the new standardized work.

> In the example from Chapter 3, in which staff members were not using the proper lift assists, managers responded by hanging a sign on the wall that berated staff for not using that equipment. Again, the inconvenient storage location was a barrier to doing the right thing. A chastising "thou shalt" sign is more often the symptom of a problem than an effective root cause solution.

Most hospitals, for example, have portable computer carts for nurses and techs to use. The intent is to allow nurses to chart in the patient rooms. This would provide more patient access to the nurses, compared to the nurse going back to the nurses' station to chart at a fixed computer. The portable computer also should allow the nurse to chart throughout the day, rather than batching charting until the end of the day. These all sound like objectives everyone could agree on, but not all nurses use the portable computers. When we as managers introduce new technology, do we assume it will be used, or do we observe firsthand?

If we get reports that nurses are not using newly purchased portable computers (or better yet, when we observe it firsthand), we have to ask, "What prevents you from wanting to use the portable computers?" Some answers might be related to technology glitches, such as batteries that do not hold a charge or computers that reboot without warning. Nurses are busy enough, so the first time they have to repeat work or waste time because of a technology-related problem, it is understandable they might be leery of the tool. Some nurses question the assumption that they have time to chart as they go through their morning rounds. If a nurse is told, on the one hand, to see all their patients promptly, that may come into conflict with the objective of charting as they go. "If I charted as I went, there is a patient I wouldn't get to until a few hours into my shift. I don't have the time to chart as I go," a nurse may explain. Proper standardized work design for a nurse would include time estimates for how long daily routine tasks actually take, given technology tools, department layouts, and patient loads, among other factors. Employees are less likely to be able to follow standardized work if there is not enough time in their day to follow it as written.

Other times, healthcare professionals may question if the technology saves them any time. Principle 8 of the *Toyota Way* states: "Use only reliable, thoroughly tested technology that serves your people and processes." Effective technology would make things faster or easier, but many nurses and physicians report that charting in the computer system takes much longer than the old bedside paper charts; this is due to software design, screens that load slowly, or a system that requires many clicks to enter basic information. Resistance to computer systems is heightened by perceptions that the ultimate users were not consulted in the software selection process or that systems are not designed around how they work.

To a Lean thinker, those are all very understandable reasons for not being able to follow the process. Forcing people to follow a process, to force them to chart via computer at the bedside as they go, will most likely damage nurse morale if the system is not improved. Or, staff will get better at hiding or covering up the fact that they are not following standardized work.

This does not mean we can necessarily accept a suggestion to go back to paper charts. Leadership has a responsibility to articulate the many reasons why information systems and electronic charting are necessary and then make that as easy as possible. If leaders have to resort to telling nurses to follow the process because the bosses said so, they have an obligation to explain why in terms of benefit to the patients, physicians, and the hospital.

Employees might also be ignoring the standardized work as a way of testing new boundaries or management's commitment to the process. Supervisors and managers should be trained to coach employees and to assume, at least initially, that noncompliance is an issue of awareness or training. Only after multiple attempts to coach and train should we rely on formal disciplinary processes. Again, we should make sure it's not a legitimate issue of "can't follow" as opposed to "won't follow" the standardized work. If we start threatening to write people up at the first sign of noncompliance, we will likely get compliance—but only when we are watching. Since employees cannot be monitored 100% of the time, we have to build real support for standardized work to ensure that employees will follow the method all of the time through their intrinsic motivation.

Standardized Work Can Apply to Physicians

From the earliest days of the Gilbreths and their industrial engineering studies of hospitals in the early 1900s, the question has been asked: Does standardized work apply to physicians and surgeons?

Physicians would seem the most likely to resist the idea, countering that every patient is unique, and therefore their work cannot be standardized. Remember, though, that standardized does not mean identical, as in the feared "cookie-cutter" medicine. As in any Lean endeavor, we should standardize only those activities, tasks, and sequences that are proven to have an impact on safety, quality, waiting time, or other strategic factors. Physicians should not be forced to set aside their professional judgment in the case of a particular patient. Nor should standardization be forced on physicians from experts, outsiders, or managers. Physicians deserve the same respect that Lean principles demand for anyone in the system.

Dr. Billi, as a physician and Lean advocate, says he tries to "help clinicians see they're going to use that same standardized approach to try to solve the problems they face in work every day," such as research or diagnosis where the work is "really very standardized." He adds that they are not trying to turn this into "cookbook medicine" or "cookbook problem solving."

Emphasizing the scientific rigor of Lean with other physicians, he explains that they should "try to standardize whatever we can so that when we vary something, we get a different outcome, we actually can draw some conclusions. We can learn from that, and that informs the next experiment that we'll run."

"Physicians can gravitate to that. It's not the challenge of applying this method that I find most problematic for physicians. It's actually the fact that many of them consider themselves victims of the process. They don't believe they can change the process," he adds.[27]

Dr. Billi remembers a project where they wanted to reduce the length of stay in cardiac surgery. He says, "We tracked down some of the root causes, things related to problems with handoffs coming out of the operating room. So, we created standardized work around the handoffs."

"The people themselves, the anesthesiologists and the nurse receiving the patient in the ICU, developed a standardized handoff process with a form. They have a specific hand off exchange that can't be interrupted."

"As a result of that and some other interventions that arose out of that, we were able to cut two days off the simple cardiac surgery length of stay."

In many cases where standardized work has been successful in direct patient-physician interaction, the method has, again, been created by those who do the work. Geisinger Health System (Pennsylvania) recognized the need to decrease patient mortality after elective heart bypass surgery.[28] Rather than dictating standards of care, they enlisted cardiac surgeons to study their own methods and define their own standardized work, a system they call ProvenCare. Although this was not done using the Lean terminology (Geisinger does use formal Lean methods in other areas), the approach is strikingly familiar.

The cardiac surgeons discovered there were different protocols being followed by different surgeons before, during, and after surgery. "We realized there were seven ways to do something," said Dr. Alfred S. Casale, then director of cardiothoracic surgery and now associate chief medical officer at Geisinger. The surgeons, getting past their belief that they each had the best way, reviewed the literature and guidelines to document 40 steps that should always happen, including presurgical antibiotics and postsurgical beta-blockers.

The surgeons established the expectations that any of them could choose not to follow some aspect of the standardized work for a particular patient if circumstances demanded it, but they "rarely do so," said Dr. Casale. In any standardized work situation, employees deserve this right, but if people frequently deviate from the standardized work, we should take it as a sign that there may be a problem with the current documented method. The surgeons also follow the guideline that their standardized work can be improved if new research or evidence emerges.

The coronary artery bypass graft (CABG) standardization efforts at Geisinger led to improved patient outcomes, including

- Length-of-stay reduction from 6.2 to 5.7 days
- 44% reduction in readmission rates
- 21% reduction in patients with at least one complication
- 55% reduction in cases of reoperation due to bleeding
- 25% reduction in deep sternal wound infections[29]
- 17% increase in profit margin[30]

ProvenCare, "Geisinger's roadmap of safety and consistency" of care and "best practices," includes a goal of "getting care right the first time," which reduces readmissions and complications and has been expanded to 16 other service lines.[31,32] For example, Geisinger has realized a 50% reduction in readmissions and a 10% reduction in length of stay for hip replacement procedures. "By employing evidenced-based protocols for all hip and knee surgeries, we are able to ensure the same high quality care is delivered to every patient, every time," said Dr. Michael Suk, chairman of their Department of Orthopedic Surgery.

As healthcare shifts to pay for performance and value instead of fee for service, Geisinger offers a flat fee for ProvenCare procedures and 90 days of follow-up care, providing a warranty to patients and payers that means "if a patient suffers complications or has to come back to the hospital, Geisinger promises not to send the insurer another bill."[33] A more standardized approach to delivering care helps Geisinger feel confident they can deliver better quality at a lower cost, with a built-in incentive to avoid readmissions, complications, and warranty costs.

Dr. John B. Tebbetts, a cosmetic surgeon in Dallas, Texas, took it on himself to study and use Lean methods in the name of reducing patient recovery times.[34] His goals included minimizing the time the patient was under anesthesia not by working faster but by eliminating waste in motion and delays in the procedure itself. Dr. Tebbetts even experimented with his own surgical methods and instruments, finding methods that caused less trauma to the patient, thus reducing recovery time. Motivated by his patients' recovery time and comfort, the surgeon gained personal efficiency without sacrificing quality. Using the improved and standardized methods, 96% of patients were able to return to full normal activities within 24 hours, a goal deemed impossible by most.

Lean and Checklists

In recent years, an increasing number of hospitals are using checklists, as inspired by pilots in the aviation industry, to improve quality and patient safety. Books by Dr. Atul Gawande and Dr. Peter Pronovost explained the transference and applicability of these methods for reducing central-line-associated bloodstream infections (CLABIs), surgical errors, and other problems.[35,36] A group of 100 intensive care units in Michigan completely eliminated catheter-associated bloodstream infections within 18 months of using a simple five-item checklist to ensure the best-known care was given to every patient.[37] Similar efforts led to a 70% reduction of ventilator-associated pneumonia (VAP) cases in these same hospitals.[38] Dr. Richard Shannon has also been a leader of applying checklists and other Lean methods to reduce hospital-acquired infections in Pennsylvania, first at Allegheny General Hospital and then at the University of Pennsylvania Medical Center. At Allegheny in 2004, the hospital reduced CLABI occurrences by 87% and VAP by 83%.[39]

There are many direct parallels between the checklists methodology and Lean standardized work, including

- Checklists are written by the people who do the work.
- Clinicians have the ability to deviate from a checklist when necessary for a specific patient.
- Checklists are meant to be improved on over time, given new medical evidence.
- Checklists are not only documents, but are also about discipline, attention to detail, and organizational culture.

As a physician wrote to a newspaper in England, "The checklist in itself is not really the point. What is important is the quality of its implementation."[40] This includes factors such as communication and having a proper team environment in which everybody is allowed to speak up if they see a problem.

Standardized Work for Raising Concerns

The use of checklists is part of the broader approach to aviation reliability and safety called crew resource management, or TeamSTEPPS. Operating rooms are typically very hierarchical environments, where nurses or techs are often afraid to question a surgeon or speak up about a potential error or safety risk. TeamSTEPPS training doesn't just lecture lower-ranking staff that they *should* speak up; it teaches them how to speak up in a way that is more likely to be effective.

Steve Harden, chairman and CEO of LifeWings, a team that includes former NASA astronauts, pilots and flight crew, and medical professionals, said, "TeamSTEPPS, done well, is standard work for communications and collaboration."[41]

Any employee in a Toyota factory or any Lean culture is empowered to point out any perceived risk to safety or quality, using an "andon" process to stop the line if needed, as explained in Chapter 8. This requires that leaders, physicians, and surgeons be willing to listen and respectfully consider those who express concern.

The author attended TeamSTEPPS conducted by LifeWings. In the training, hospital staff were taught a four-step method for raising concerns. The steps can be summarized as[42]

1. Get attention, calling the person by name in a respectful way
2. Express concern, saying "I am concerned" or "I need clarity"
3. State the problem, real or perceived, being clear and objective in less than 10 seconds
4. Propose a solution or restate the problem

If a nurse says, "Dr. Jones, I am concerned that we don't have enough units of blood on hand for this patient, so I think we shouldn't start the procedure until we do," it is a statement of fact; it's a fact that the nurse has a concern. It might turn out there are enough units of blood on hand. But, as in any Lean culture, the nurse should not be punished for speaking up about a potential concern.

If the assertive statement is ignored, TeamSTEPPS guidelines say to repeat the statement and, if there is no response, to address the situation through leadership chain, even up to the executive level.[43] Virginia Mason Medical Center has a similar escalation process through their "patient safety alert system," as described in Chapter 8. As with any standardized work, leaders must verify, through rounding or audits, that the proper behaviors and expectations are being followed by all involved.

Standardized Work Can Apply to Leaders

Increasingly, healthcare managers at all levels are realizing that standardized work does not just apply to frontline staff. Frontline supervisors might have up to 80% of their day driven by standardized work, including their plan for the day and the checklists they use to help manage their team.[44] As we move higher in the organization chart, less time is typically spent in a standardized work mode, with relatively more time being unstructured.

Baylor Scott & White (Texas) has introduced "leader standard work" up through levels including the hospital CEOs. Leader standard work "documents what leaders do to ensure their processes run as designed, and then improve them."[45] Standardized work doesn't mean a minute-by-minute script for executives any more than a nurse would have a detailed script for their entire day. "A top leader may only have a quarter of his or her typical week defined in leader standard work," but vice presidents and directors might have "half" of their time covered by standardized work, and frontline supervisors "really need to have most of their day and week scripted."[46] The system explains, "After following leader standard work for a few weeks, a subtle shift will occur. You will get your day back … you will have time to lead continuous improvement in your areas … the most important job of a leader."[47]

Some organizations, including ThedaCare (Appleton, Wisconsin), are instituting "no meeting zones" for the first two hours of the day, creating time for leaders to do structured rounding or *gemba* walks.[48] Supervisors and leaders at ThedaCare have checklists and standardized work documents that prompt how they spend their time and which questions they ask at the *gemba*. Even vice presidents have a standardized "stat sheet" (short for status sheet) that they carry with them to remind them to start all team discussions with a discussion about employee and patient safety, among other standard topics.[49] Leaders might also carry with them guidelines for effective problem solving, as discussed in Chapter 7.

As with other roles, standardized work for managers is not meant to be restrictive or to limit people to simple check-the-box thinking. Standardized work provides helpful structure, planning those management tasks that can be standardized while freeing mental bandwidth for times when creativity is necessary.

Training through Standardized Work

Standardized work documents can be used to support effective training of new employees, compared to informal, verbal training that's generally ineffective. In one hospital microbiology lab, before Lean, students were given unstructured, verbal training that forced the student to scribble notes to serve as individual process documentation. Verbal training brings many risks, including miscommunications and inconsistency among employees.

In another example, a new pharmacy technician was given the responsibility of delivering medications to multiple units, being told, "figure out your own best route." This approach slows the learning curve for the employee, as he or she experiments with different routes. It is fine to ask the employee to find the best way, but only after starting with a standardized work plan for what the current one best route has already been determined to be. Each new employee should be able to build on the accumulated knowledge of previous employees. A new employee who discovers a better route needs to share it with the rest of the team through the *kaizen* process.

Some hospitals have once again started utilizing the training approach from the Training Within Industry (TWI) program that was so influential at Toyota.[50] Following a standardized approach to training can help ensure practices that are more consistent and will lead to quality that is more consistent. The job instruction training approach follows four steps.

Step 1: Prepare the employee. Start by discussing the need for standardized work and by talking through the formal documents. This is best done offline when the employee does not also have to do his or her regular work and so can focus on learning the method. The expectation should be set that the employee can challenge the standardized work and improve it if he or she finds a better method.

Step 2: Demonstrate the job. Have the trainer demonstrate the standardized work, allowing the employee to observe and follow along in the documentation. The trainer should emphasize the key points in the standardized work to highlight quality and safety considerations.

Step 3: Observe the job being done. Trainers must observe the employee trying the new job, coaching and providing guidance or clarification as they go. It is the trainer's job to confirm that the employee understands and can perform the standardized work. In the TWI approach, a frequently used phrase is, "If the worker hasn't learned, the instructor hasn't taught."[51]

Step 4: Follow-up. The trainer (and supervisors) must follow up periodically to ensure that the standardized work is followed. After the new employee has some experience with the job, the trainer can follow up to see what *kaizen* ideas they might have, for the sake of improving the standardized work.

Having a formal training approach brings much better results than haphazard methods. A department should consider training supervisors and other senior employees in how to train others, as it is a bad assumption to think that the best employees would necessarily make good instructors. Often, the opposite is true, when experienced employees have little patience for those who are new to a role.

The book *Getting to Standard Work in Health Care* (Graupp and Purrier) tells the story of Virginia Mason Medical Center's Lean approach to training and standardized work and is a great reference for deeper study.

The histopathology lab at Yuma Regional Hospital (Yuma, Arizona) struggled with finding a person to effectively perform an order entry role, having "chewed up" six people over the course of three years.[52] Each new person made order entry mistakes, so the lab blamed the individuals or the inability of the lab to attract a careful person. Through their early Lean efforts, they were introduced to the TWI method for training, and they started looking at the system. The disciplined use of the job instruction approach of TWI to train the next new person led to a reduction of errors from 33.5% to 2.5%. The lab learned that the problem was not the person; it was the system.

Conclusion

Standardized work is a method that can benefit all hospital stakeholders. Consistent methods can lead to improved quality and reduced delays for patients, while being fair and respectful to employees. Part of being fair and respectful is that we do not force inflexible standardized work methods on people; rather, we let them develop and refine their own standardized work. That is the only way to ensure that staff want to follow the standardized work, based on their own intrinsic motivation to provide the best care for their patients. The goal is not to standardize. The goal is improvement and the best possible results for the organization. Standardized work is just a means to that end.

Lean Lessons

- The foundations of Lean are standardized work, *heijunka*, and *kaizen*.
- Practices that are more consistent lead to quality that is more consistent.
- Standardized work should reflect an emphasis on quality and safety, not speed.
- Standardized work is written by those who do the work.
- Do not standardize for the sake of standardizing.
- Standardized work frees people to be creative problem solvers, rather than turning them into robots.
- Explaining why shows respect for people.
- Standardized work is not just a one-time documentation exercise.
- Managers must directly observe and audit to see if standardized work is being followed.
- Standardized work is not permanent; it must be improved over time.

Points for Group Discussion

- How is patient safety impacted by standardizing our work?
- How do irregular or unexpected circumstances fit into standardized work?
- Why is it important that the people who do the work author standardized work documentation?
- How does standardized work apply to physicians and surgeons?
- How can standardized work be helpful for your supervisors and leaders?

- How can we gain acceptance of standardized work?
- In your workplace, what might be some examples of critical tasks, important tasks, and nonimportant tasks?
- What methods do you currently have in place to verify if work methods are being followed?
- What would be an example of overly specified work in your area? What problems does this cause?

Notes

1. Jost, Ashley, KU Hospital Channels Toyota's Method at Cutting Waste, http://www.bizjournals.com/kansascity/news/2015/08/14/ku-hospital-toyota-lean-management.html (accessed October 8, 2015).
2. CBC News, Improperly Cleaned Endoscopes Used in 10,000 Procedures, Says Northern Health, http://www.cbc.ca/news/canada/british-columbia/improperly-cleaned-endoscopes-used-in-10-000-procedures-says-northern-health-1.2901895 (accessed October 27, 2015).
3. Hoeft, Steve, and Robert M. Pryor, *The Power of Ideas to Transform Healthcare: Engaging Staff by Building Daily Lean Management Systems* (New York: Productivity Press, 2015), 311.
4. Graban, Mark, and Joseph E. Swartz, *Healthcare Kaizen* (New York: Productivity Press, 2012), 4.
5. Ford, Henry, *Today and Tomorrow* (Garden City, NY: Garden City Publishing, 1926), 51.
6. Baumgart, André S., and D. Neuhauser, "Frank and Lillian Gilbreth: Scientific management in the operating room," *Quality and Safety in Health Care*, 2009, 18: 413–415, doi:10.1136/qshc.2009.032409.
7. Public Affairs Division and Operations Management Consulting Division, *The Toyota Production System, Leaner Manufacturing for a Greener Planet* (Toyota City, Japan: Toyota Motor Corporation, 1998), 32.
8. Ibid.
9. Pittet, Didier, "Improving compliance with hand hygiene in hospitals," *Infection Control and Hospital Epidemiology*, 2000, 21: 381–386.
10. American Psychological Association, Hospital Workers Wash Hands Less Frequently Toward End of Shift, Study Finds, http://www.apa.org/news/press/releases/2014/11/wash-hands.aspx (Accessed October 8, 2015).
11. Carling, P., N. Church, and J. Jefferson, "Operating room environmental cleaning—An evaluation using a new targeting method," *American Journal of Infection Control*, June 2007, 35: E26–27.
12. ThedaCare Center for Healthcare Value, Lean Thinking at ThedaCare DVD Preview, https://www.youtube.com/watch?v=5uaRI2IUxRE (accessed October 8, 2015).
13. Liker, Jeffrey K., and David P. Meier, *Toyota Talent* (New York: McGraw-Hill, 2007), 143.
14. Marriott, Willard J., and Adrian Zackheim, *The Spirit to Serve Marriott's Way* (New York: HarperCollins, 2001), 17.
15. Ohno, Taiichi, *Toyota Production System: Beyond Large-Scale Production* (New York: Productivity Press, 1988), 98.
16. Dennis, Pascal, *Lean Production Simplified*, 2nd edn, (New York: Productivity Press), 17.
17. Maass, Kathy, email correspondence, 2009.
18. Gilbreth, Frank B., "Scientific management in the hospital," *The Modern Hospital*, 1914, 2: 87–88.
19. Liker, Jeffrey K., and David P. Meier, *Toyota Talent*, 119.
20. Dinero, Donald A., *Training within Industry: The Foundation of Lean* (New York: Productivity Press, 2005), 175.
21. Brown, Percy S., "A few facts about scientific management in industry," *American Journal of Nursing*, 1927, 27: 828–832.
22. Shingo, Shigeo, *A Revolution in Manufacturing: The SMED System* (New York: Productivity Press, 1985), 113.
23. American Society for Quality, "Ferrari's Formula One handovers and handovers from surgery to intensive care," *Quality in Healthcare*, http://asq.org/healthcare-use/why-quality/great-ormond-street-hospital.html (accessed March 26, 2015).

24. University of Michigan Health System, Auto Industry Lean Techniques Boost Morale and Teamwork in the Operating Room, http://www.uofmhealth.org/news/lean-techniques-in-surgery-0529 (accessed October 8, 2015).
25. Rice, Sabriya, "Learning to be Lean," *Modern Healthcare*, http://www.modernhealthcare.com/section/learning-to-be-lean (accessed October 8, 2015).
26. Liker, Jeffrey K., and David P. Meier, *Toyota Talent*, 173.
27. Graban, Mark, Podcast #110, Dr. Jack Billi, Lean and Medicine, http://www.leanblog.org/110 (accessed October 8, 2015).
28. Abelson, Reed, In Bid for Better Care, Surgery with a Warranty, *New York Times*, May 17, 2007, http://www.nytimes.com/2007/05/17/business/17quality.html?_r=2&ref=policy&oref=slogin& (accessed March 26, 2015).
29. Geisinger Health System, 2009 System Report, http://www.geisinger.org/pages/newsroom/includes/pdf/ar09-111714.pdf (accessed October 8, 2015).
30. Geisinger Health System, Geisinger's Renowned ProvenCare® Program Launches Three New Orthopaedic Offerings: Total Hip, Total Knee and Hip Fracture, http://www.prnewswire.com/news-releases/geisingers-renowned-provencare-program-launches-three-new-orthopaedic-offerings-total-hip-total-knee-and-hip-fracture-274334131.html (accessed October 8, 2015).
31. Geisinger Health System, ProvenCare® by Geisinger Ensures Quality Care Comes Standard, http://www.geisinger.org/sites/provencare/index.html (accessed October 8, 2015).
32. http://www.geisinger.org/sites/provencare/pages/provencare-frequently-asked-questions.html (accessed October 8, 2015).
33. Abelson.
34. Tebbetts, John B., "Achieving a predictable 24-hour return to normal activities after breast augmentation. Part I. Refining practices by using motion and time study principles," *Plastic and Reconstructive Surgery*, 2002, 273–290.
35. Gawande, Atul, *The Checklist Manifesto: How to Get Things Right* (New York: Metropolitan Books, 2009), 136.
36. Pronovost, Peter, and Eric Vohr, *Safe Patients, Smart Hospitals: How One Doctor's Checklist Can Help Us Change Health Care from the Inside Out* (New York: Hudson Street Press, 2010), 1.
37. Brody, Jane E., "A basic hospital to-do list saves lives," *New York Times*, January 22, 2008, http://www.nytimes.com/2008/01/22/health/22brod.html (accessed March 26, 2015).
38. Henry, Tanya Albert, "Hospital checklist helps pneumonia rates tumble by 70%," *American Medical News*, March 11, 2011, http://www.amednews.com/article/20110311/profession/303119992/8/ (accessed March 26, 2015).
39. Institute for Healthcare Improvement, Allegheny General Hospital: Lower Infection Rates Have Lowered Costs, Institute for Healthcare Improvement, January 20, 2006, http://www.ihi.org/resources/Pages/ImprovementStories/AlleghenyGeneralHospitalLowerInfectionRatesHaveLoweredCosts.aspx (accessed September 9, 2015).
40. Bleakley, Alan, "Letter to the editor," *The Independent*, July 2, 2008, http://www.independent.co.uk/opinion/letters/letters-interfering-state-858284.html (accessed March 26, 2015).
41. Montague, Steve, personal communication, 2015.
42. LifeWings, Stop-the-Line Assertiveness Training, http://www.saferpatients.com/Newsletter/Stop%20the%20Line%20Assertive%20Statements%20Training.pdf (accessed October 8, 2015).
43. AHRQ, Pocket Guide: TeamSTEPPS, http://www.ahrq.gov/professionals/education/curriculum-tools/teamstepps/instructor/essentials/pocketguide.html (accessed October 8, 2015).
44. Mann, David, *Creating a Lean Culture* (New York: Productivity Press, 2005), 33.
45. Hoeft and Pryor, 192.
46. Hoeft and Pryor, 247.
47. Hoeft and Pryor, 248.
48. Toussaint, John, and Roger Gerard, *On the Mend: Revolutionizing Healthcare to Save Lives and Transform the Industry* (Cambridge, MA: Lean Enterprise Institute, 2010), 174.
49. Barnas, Kim, *Beyond Heroes: A Lean Management System for Healthcare* (Appleton, WI: ThedaCare Center for Healthcare Value, 2014), 35.

50. Liker, Jeffrey K., and David P. Meier, *Toyota Talent*, 40.
51. United States, *Hospital Adaptation for the Job Instruction Manual*, August 1944, Subgroup 211.22.3 General Records of the Training Within Industry Service, Records of the War Manpower Commission (WMC), Record Group 211, National Archives Building, Washington, DC, http://chapters.sme.org/204/TWI_Materials/National_Archives_March_2006/Job_Instruction/Hospitals/Materials-Hospitals.pdf (accessed March 26, 2015).
52. Chuy, Jesus, and Peter P. Patterson, A Breakthrough in Training—Call It Near-TWI, Lean Blog, June 30, 2009, http://leanblog.org/2009/06/breakthrough-in-training-call-it-near/ (accessed March 26, 2015).

Chapter 6

Lean Methods: Visual Management, 5S, and *Kanban*

Lean Is More Than Tools, but Tools Can Help

Looking back to the Toyota Triangle from Chapter 2, technical tools are just one component of the integrated system of Lean. Rather than documenting all of the details of how to implement these methods, this chapter focuses on some of the healthcare-specific examples of the use of visual management, 5S, and *kanban*. We also focus on the management methods and philosophical concepts that are embedded in the effective use of these methods. This chapter is by no means an all-inclusive list of tools, but these are some more commonly used in the early stages of health system implementations, methods that remain helpful over time when practiced with discipline and continuous improvement. Many of the existing guidebooks or manuals for these methods, published for manufacturing, can be adapted for a hospital setting. In addition, healthcare-specific books are now being published on some of these methods, including 5S and *kanban*.[1,2]

Reducing Waste through Visual Management

Another form of standardized work is the method of visual management. The goal of visual management is to make waste, problems, and abnormal conditions readily apparent to employees and managers. As Fujio Cho, honorary chairman of Toyota, says, "One of the worst situations … is not being able to tell whether things are standard or out of standard (normal or abnormal)."[3] Our aim should be to expose problems so they can be fixed, as opposed to the old approach of hiding problems to make things look good. Toyota's Bonini says, "The ideal, the basic principle behind *jidoka*, is to be notified of any abnormality and solve problems immediately, one by one, as they occur, while the situation is still fresh."[4]

Many organizations have old habits of ignoring, hiding, or covering up problems. As an alternative approach, visual management is a mindset, more than a specific technology. Our goal, as leaders, should be to ask how we can make our process more visual and our problems more apparent, as the first step in improvement. As previously noted, the famed Taiichi Ohno of Toyota once said, "Having no problems is the biggest problem of all."[5]

Gwendolyn Galsworth wrote that the purpose of visual management is to reduce "information deficits" in the workplace.[6] She wrote that, "In an information-scarce workplace, people ask lots of questions and lots of the same questions, repeatedly—or they make stuff up."[7] These questions about missing information waste time and cause delays. This happens throughout health systems. Listen to the questions employees ask, such as

- Does this patient have any more tests, or can he go home?
- Have these medications been double-checked?
- Which patient should be brought back next?
- Are these tubes ready to load into the test instrument?
- Is this pump clean?
- Who is the physician for this patient?
- Which patients are assigned to that nurse?
- Have these papers been signed?

These questions are rooted in a lack of information, information that either does not exist or is not readily apparent—thus the need for visual management. Visual management should also, ideally, be used for real-time decision-making. Visual management has two main tenets: first, make problems or status visible; and, second, manage those situations, reacting as needed in the short term and solving root causes of those problems over the longer term. Even before Lean, hospitals and clinics often have multi-colored plastic "flags" in the hallway outside each patient room or exam room door. These flags, if used consistently by staff, can provide a clear visual indicator that answer questions such as, "Is there a patient in that room yet?" or "Which patient is waiting on test results?"

In some hospitals, nurses have a set of colored flags that they display on their portable computer carts that indicates their current status, with red meaning they could use help from others, yellow meaning things are normal, and green meaning they currently have some extra time to help others. The organizational culture has to allow nurses to speak up, making it acceptable to admit that they are currently overloaded with tasks instead of keeping their heads down and being tough. But, if nurses are allowed to be honest about their current status, leveling workloads and providing help to each other can be a self-managing process that helps reduce stress and improve patient care.

Some mistakenly understand visual management to be primarily the posting of performance measures or signs throughout the workplace. Yes, performance metrics are important, as discussed more in Chapter 11. But, a chart on the wall is not necessarily visual management. Is it just a visual or does the chart drive the right discussions and improvement? Real-time visual management is much more effective than waiting for monthly, or even daily, reports and metrics to gauge the performance of a process.

Hospitals and clinics have many visuals that are essentially just signs that warn employees against making errors. For example, a piece of pharmacy automation has a label that says, "Warning! Risk of injury. Do not reach inside until motion stops." Labels or signs posted by managers, such as "Check drawers for home medications before discharge!" are not visual management and are a poor substitute for root cause analysis and error proofing (see Chapters 7 and 8). In the case of the pharmacy automation, it would be better if the machine stopped automatically when the door opened, or if the door could only be opened once the machine had already stopped.

Examples of Visual Management for Patient Flow

In the radiology department of one children's hospital, some of the children are scheduled for multiple imaging appointments, such as a sonogram and magnetic resonance imaging (MRI). Because most patients just have one modality to visit, and employees can only see the schedule for their modality, it is common for a technologist or nurse to say, "You're done now" after the first procedure. Because many young children do not know what they are in for, and some parents might not fully understand the plan for their child's care, some leave without having the second imaging completed. This leads to idle equipment (which was in high demand), rework for the scheduling staff, wasted transportation and time for the patient and parents, and delays in care.

The front desk staff in the radiology department came up with a simple visual management tool to prevent this waste from occurring. When a child has two modalities to visit, the desk staff clips together two color-coded laminated cards and attaches them to the patient's shirt. This gives a clear indicator to the staff of the first modality that the patient has to move to a second procedure. This is also a form of error proofing, as discussed in Chapter 8. Rather than managers browbeating employees to be careful (or hanging signs), the team took a more effective, simple, and visual approach to solving that information deficit.

Hospitals often use visual management to identify the status of patients or their needs, facilitating real-time decision-making. Tracking boards (either low-tech whiteboards or high-tech plasma screens) are used to identify which rooms are open or to let families know where patients are currently located in the value stream. One outpatient orthopedic clinic used to just stack patient charts on a desk. They now place charts in wall holders that create a clear visual of how many patients are waiting for each physician. In addition, there are clear visual signals that indicate if the patient is ready or is still getting an X-ray. The registration desk staff can easily look down the hallway and use this visual information to prioritize the registration of patients who might arrive at the same time. Instead of the old first in, first out approach, which seems reasonable, they decided it was better for patient flow to first register a patient whose physician is currently available rather than the patient who will be just be waiting until their physician has seen their already waiting patients. These visuals are all used to close information gaps or to make decisions, hence visual management.

Many hospitals have used software systems that display patient status on large flat-panel televisions. It is a common Lean principle to use technology and automation only after the process has been piloted in a manual way. Principle 8 of *The Toyota Way* says to "use only reliable, thoroughly tested technology that serves your people and processes."[8] Lean thinkers are not against technology or software, but they tend not to jump immediately to technology solutions. One large children's hospital created a large whiteboard with color-coded magnets laid over a drawing of the inpatient unit layout. While the board was intended to be a prototype to help them choose an electronic system, the hospital decided the whiteboard worked just fine and was flexible enough to be changed quickly as their needs evolved. Another hospital built a prototype of a patient tracker in a shared network spreadsheet that could be displayed on screens throughout the hospital. They were surprised to conclude that their inexpensive homegrown solution also eliminated the need to buy the commercial system. Homegrown visual systems (analog or digital) have the advantage of being completely customized to your own situation.

New London Family Medical Center built a "Real-Time Monitor System" (RTMS) that is displayed on digital screens throughout the hospital. Major areas of the hospital self-report their workload status and "staff control the color," says chief executive officer (CEO) Bill Schmidt. Like a modified traffic light, green means they have enough capacity, yellow means there is a concern, and red means immediate help is required. Again, it's visual management because managers respond and help. The RTMS traffic light is unusual in that each area has a fourth color, blue, that indicates they are "overstaffed." In many hospitals, a department's staff would be afraid to admit they were overstaffed because that would mean being sent home early. Their staff are cross-trained and could be shifted to departments that are in yellow or red status, helping level workloads throughout the hospital.

Examples of Visual Management to Prevent Process Problems

Visual management can also be used to create awareness or prevent problems. In one hospital laboratory, simple visual management methods were used to prevent specimen testing delays. Certain specimens were transported from the main lab site to microbiology through a pass-through box built into the wall that divided the departments. Once used by microbiology, the specimen was placed back in the box for the main laboratory to continue testing. Often, the specimen would sit up to one hour in the pass-through box, waiting to be taken back out by the main lab. The delay was caused partly by the ambiguous signal (or information deficit) of a specimen being seen in the box. The main lab employees could easily, and incorrectly, assume the specimen was still waiting to be taken into microbiology when it was actually done and waiting to be brought into the main lab. Laboratory technologies came up with a simple visual control—a laminated sheet that microbiology could place in the lab side of the pass-through window when a specimen was coming back in that direction. When the main lab took the specimen back, they could take the sign down until it was needed the next time. The visual wasn't a perfect system (it only worked if microbiology actually put the sign up), but things worked better with the sign than without. There were still opportunities for continued *kaizen* or mistake proofing.

Care must be taken that visual controls or indicators are standardized across units or even across hospitals. Patients' color-coded wristbands help identify special needs or do not resuscitate (DNR) requests. Unfortunately, wristbands are not always standardized among different hospitals in the same community, leading to opportunities for confusion when nurses or physicians work at different sites. A yellow wristband that indicates "do not draw blood from this arm" in one hospital might indicate DNR in another, creating an opportunity for catastrophic errors.[9]

The practice of "hourly rounding" has become popular in hospitals, with the aim of ensuring each patient is checked on in a standardized way at least once per hour. Benefits of this practice include 12% higher patient satisfaction rates, 52% fewer falls, 14% fewer skin breakdowns, and 20% less walking for nurses.[10] But, if nurses and techs are overburdened with work, hourly rounding might not always occur, meaning we lose those benefits. One hospital installed an inexpensive visual 60-minute countdown timer outside each patient room, indicating when 60 minutes has elapsed without rounding. Instead of relying on reports, managers can see, in real time, if hourly rounding is occurring. As mentioned in Chapter 5, if it appears that hourly rounding is not happening, managers should ask "why?" and proceed from there, working to reduce waste and fix the system so that hourly rounding can occur more consistently. Again, the visual (the clock) is not useful without the management of that system.

Avera McKennan has used visual management to improve the consistency of patient care in a number of ways. The hospital added "electronic status boards" in the electronic medical record (EMR) system that alerts nurses to the need to remove Foley catheters within 48 hours, if possible. Beyond the visual, the standardized work was changed for this decision to be "nurse directed" and carried out by nurses. The hospital is "monitoring the process, not the outcome," but ensuring the right process is being followed lead to better outcomes. Avera McKennan has also added a status board showing which patients need immunizations. Since "people always have their face in a computer," it made sense to them to put the visual alert in the EMR, since it was more likely to be seen. The "individual status board for each patient drives [the nurses'] day."[11]

5S: Sort, Store, Shine, Standardize, and Sustain

Another example of workplace waste might be evident when questions such as these are asked:

- Where are the blankets?
- Why did we run out of syringes?
- Where did those medications go?
- Why are we walking so far within the department?
- Why do we spend so much time looking for things we need?

The 5S (sort, store, shine, standardize, and sustain) methodology reduces waste through improved workplace organization and visual management. Implementing 5S is not about looking neat and orderly, and it should not be confused with a one-time or annual "spring cleaning" exercise. The primary goal of 5S is to prevent problems and to create a work environment that allows people to provide the best patient care in the most effective way. For example, John Toussaint, MD, former CEO of ThedaCare (Appleton, Wisconsin), estimated that 5S improvements had helped reduce the amount of wasted time in an average nurse's eight-hour shift from 3.5 hours a day to just one hour per day.[12] 5S is often used as an early Lean method as a way to start engaging staff in small improvements as a precursor to addressing bigger challenges, leading to the "revitalization of the workplace."[13]

> The surest way to alienate medical professionals is to push the 5S methods in a top-down way that does not seem to be solving any meaningful problems. 5S (and Lean) might become dirty words if your first efforts involve a Lean facilitator or a single staff member moving around other people's stuff and putting tape around things. Nurses at one hospital were trying to engage leadership on patient safety issues, yet they rightfully complained about "being told to reduce the number of pens and pencils" at the nurses' station.[14] 5S needs to engage everybody and needs to focus on important problems, rather than the trivial.

The term *5S* comes from the origins of the method in five Japanese words, as shown in Table 6.1. Rather than forcing more Japanese words on employees, most hospitals refer to some variations of English translations, but the principles behind the 5Ss are the important thing. Health systems in other countries often translate the words into their own local language.

First S: Sort

The first 5S activity is to go through the department or area, looking for items or equipment that are no longer needed, items that are just taking up space. In one laboratory, for example, the team conducting the initial 5S sorting activity found things such as

- Old, yellowed stationery and forms with a 1970s hospital logo
- Expired reagents or slides dating back decades
- Broken computers and keyboards
- Specimen collection tubes that expired months ago in the bottom of drawers

Items that can be clearly thrown away without controversy or the risk of someone later saying "I needed that" can be immediately disposed of, recycled, or donated. When unneeded items take up valuable workspace, the department ends up being larger than it needs to be, which results in excess construction and maintenance costs. These larger departments and workspaces lead to excess employee walking and other types of waste. Broken equipment and expired supplies take up space that could otherwise be used for supplies and tools that are used more frequently or for value-adding activities.[15] Before 5S, Seattle Children's Hospital (Washington) had an operating room that served as a cluttered storage room or "boneyard." Thanks to 5S, they were able to convert that room back into usable, revenue-generating clinical space in just three days.[16]

One medical laboratory found a box of slides that, to the employees' best estimates, dated to the 1960s. The slides were found in the new building, opened in the 1990s, meaning they had been moved from the old building to the new building, just to clutter up the new space. Any new construction, major renovation, or department move should be preceded by a major 5S activity.

If there is some question about items that *might* be needed, a buffer zone—a 5S sort area—is set up somewhere in the department. Since not all employees can be present during the sort activity, holding items for a week allows everyone to review what the team is planning to throw away. This prevents rash decision-making and the waste of disposing of items that would have to be repurchased. At the same time, we have to prevent people from reclaiming all items just because they think they might need the item someday. If there is disagreement over what is needed, a supervisor can facilitate or intervene. Items that might possibly be needed could be kept in a central supply or off-site storage location (with good records kept about what is being stored off-site).

5S should not be viewed as only being about throwing items away. As part of this initial sort process, a team should also identify needed items that are not readily available in their workplace.

Table 6.1   5S Term Translation

Japanese word	Translation 1	Translation 2	Description
Seiri	Sort	Sort	Sort out unneeded items, keep items based on frequency of use
Seiton	Store	Straighten	Organize for the reduction of waste
Seiso	Shine	Shine	Keeping the workplace clean, daily
Seiketsu	Standardize	Systemize	Developing a consistently organized workplace
Shitsuke	Sustain	Sustain	A system for ongoing support of the first four Ss

Second S: Store

Some organizations make the error of stopping after the first S, sort. While it is beneficial to get unneeded items out of the way, the most ongoing waste elimination will come from properly organizing the material and equipment that remain and "new" items that had been previously missing or unavailable, leading to the store phase.

In the store phase, employees identify how frequently each item is used. Items used most often should be stored closest to the point of use. If items are used by multiple people in an area, such as latex gloves in an emergency department (ED) or laboratory, consider having multiple storage points. There is a trade-off between reducing the waste of motion (keeping supplies close by) and the increase in inventory that might result with additional storage points. If supplies are inexpensive and take up little space, it is better to err on the side of more locations to avoid employee walking and wasted time.

The guidelines in Table 6.2 are only a suggestion. Common sense should prevail over hard-set rules. If an item is used infrequently but takes up little space, or if it is needed urgently (such as a crash cart or maintenance items for an instrument), it should be kept closer to where it is needed.

Items that are used most frequently should be kept in good ergonomic zones, on benchtops or shelves that are not too high or low. Employees waste motion, and can get hurt, by bending to get commonly used supplies out of low drawers. They also exert unnecessary motion opening doors to reach for supplies.

In one Japanese hospital, the nurses all wore a standardized bag around their waist that kept frequently used items with them at all times. The bag included hand sanitizer (to prevent having to walk to a dispenser), pens, alcohol swabs, and other potentially helpful items. A key decision for a nursing team about adopting an idea like this would be how standardized the bags need to be. In other words, can staff personalize the bag, or should they be identical, so anybody can grab any bag at the start of a shift?

Before Lean, most supplies are kept in closed cabinets or drawers, which create waste as employees search for items and cannot see what is located where. With improved organization, employees will no longer waste time opening multiple cabinets or drawers, searching for what they need. When determining storage locations, Lean leaders challenge the need to store items in closed cabinets or drawers. Well-organized departments are not afraid to keep supplies visible and in the open since there no longer are the piles of disorganized supplies that used to be hidden, as pictured in Figure 6.1. Figure 6.2 shows how the organization was improved with 5S. Hiding the old mess in a drawer or behind closed doors was often a workaround to the problem of not keeping things organized.

Table 6.2   5S Guidelines for Storing Items Based on Frequency of Use

Frequency of use	Storage proximity
Hourly	Within arm's reach
Every shift	Within a short walk
Daily	A bit further away
Monthly	Department storage
Annually	Hospital storage

Figure 6.1 Drawers that are unorganized and cluttered before 5S.

Figure 6.2 Drawers that have been organized through 5S, with supplies in divided bins.

Figures 6.3 and 6.4 show a comparison of OR supply storage, before and after 5S. With effective 5S, it's not just a matter of looking better, but making it easier to find the right supplies more quickly and to ensure that needed items are available.

Figure 6.5 shows, in their "*kaizen* report" format, the before and after situation in a biomed storage room at Franciscan St. James Health (Illinois). As with all *kaizen* style improvements (see more in Chapter 11), Joe Walkowiak was self-motivated to 5S the room, creating a less cluttered and more enjoyable working environment, saving some money for the health system in the process.

In the case, from Chapter 5, of the hospital unit where the lift assist was not being used, it was stored upstairs on a different floor. The room in the unit with equipment and supplies was overcrowded with broken walkers and way too many old commodes. The 5S process then became an effective way to make it easier for people to use the correct equipment. Freeing space allowed the unit to bring its lift assist to the second floor, where it was much more convenient and became used much more regularly. This countermeasure was more effective than hanging signs.

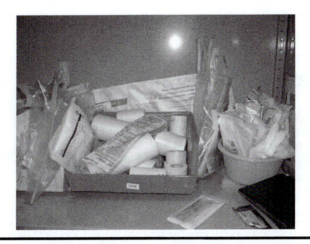

Figure 6.3 Disorganized operating room supplies before 5S.

Figure 6.4 An operating cabinet that has been better organized through 5S.

Third S: Shine

After removing unneeded items and determining the best storage location for those that remain, the 5S focus turns to cleanliness. Hospital departments often rely on the centralized housekeeping department, a group that often only does major cleaning, such as floors and trash cans. Dust often accumulates on top of instruments and behind equipment in the pharmacy or laboratory. In the 5S approach, people who work in the area take responsibility for their own light cleaning (areas not cleaned by housekeeping) and the overall cleanliness of the department.

In manufacturing settings, the focus on shine was typically related to oil that might leak from machines. Floors that are always oily not only would be unsafe but also make it hard to determine if machines were leaking at the moment (remember visual management means to make problems visible immediately). Clean floors are safer and let you immediately detect problems with equipment. In healthcare settings, the focus on shine is more correctly oriented toward infection control.

Cleanliness, or the lack thereof, can affect the patients' experience and their perception of the hospital. Dr. Toby Cosgrove, CEO and president of Cleveland Clinic, wrote about a surprise

Figure 6.5 A *"kaizen"* improvement summary showing the before and after pictures of a biomed room.

he saw when visiting a postsurgical inpatient unit, saying, "The operation had been a great success, but the family was unhappy. When I asked why, they suggested that I have a look under the bed. I looked, and to my everlasting humiliation, saw litter and dustballs. The patient and family felt neglected and disrespected—and they were right to be offended … As the dustball incident proves, no detail is too small to spoil a patient's perception of your care."[17]

Cleaning should not be considered a "make-work" activity but rather an opportunity for the team to show pride in their workplace by keeping it clean at all times. A side benefit is an opportunity to inspect the equipment and benches that are being wiped down. If problems such as frayed wires are seen, they can be reported immediately.

Fourth S: Standardize

The fourth stage of 5S is often the most visible when you visit a Lean hospital or a department. Once staff have determined the best locations for needed items, it is time to ensure that items are always kept in the defined locations. We can standardize in a department, or we can standardize across departments, bringing benefits to employees or physicians who work in multiple units. At one hospital, the automated supply cabinets in different inpatient units were each organized differently, with no attempt made to standardize. This frustrated nurses who worked in different units, as they wasted time reorienting themselves when in a different unit. Standardized cabinets might have 80% of items that are the same across units, with customized space based on the needs of a particular unit. Again, standardized does not have to mean completely identical.

We often standardize through visual methods, the marking of "home locations" with vinyl tape, shadow outlines, as shown in Figures 6.6 and 6.7. In situations where tape cannot be used on floors or work surfaces because of infection control concerns, there are alternatives for marking locations, such as hanging signs from ceilings or putting signs on walls.

Figure 6.6 A laboratory bench shows clearly marked locations for specimen drop-off and supply storage.

Figure 6.7 A different lab's workbench with 5S labeling and visual controls.

Marking the locations of items brings many benefits, including

■ Being able to see instantly when an item is missing or out of place
■ Less wasted time looking for items
■ Subtle psychological incentives for employees to return items to their home locations

In a workplace, we often find an item is missing just when it is most urgently needed. This can be true for tools (such as pipettes in a lab or wheelchairs in an ED) and information (such as maintenance manuals or a patient's plan of care). By using 5S and visual methods to mark standard locations, it is obvious when something is missing. Instead of just seeing a blank space, we see an outline labeled with what is supposed to be in that space. This allows for more proactive problem solving.

In one hospital lab, a collection of binders contained important maintenance and troubleshooting information for a test instrument. Over a weekend, the instrument malfunctioned, and the employees could not find the binder. This led to delays in getting the instrument back in working order, extra work for the team, and increased stress. It turned out that an employee with good intentions had taken the binder home to study it. A clear expectation had not been set that the binder needed to stay in place. The group responded by putting a diagonal tape stripe across their binders, so it became apparent when one was missing, as shown in Figure 6.8. In the future, a supervisor might be able to find the missing binder proactively before it is desperately needed.

In addition to using inexpensive vinyl tape, the practice of "shadowing" the location of items can be helpful. A shadow is a physical outline or photo of an item that is supposed to be in a location. These can be created with digital pictures or by tracing the outline of the item. A laminated plastic shadow can be attached to the location. Some orthopedic surgical trays already use this approach, using photos on the bottom of the tray to indicate which tool goes where. The photos are so realistic that it can be, at times, difficult to tell from a distance if the tool is actually there or not. In cases like that, a solid shadow showing the shape might be more useful than a realistic image.

In a Japanese hospital, the drawers of desks and cabinets had home positions that were cut out of foam board, as shown in Figure 6.9. An advantage of this approach is that it's not only clear if

Figure 6.8 Laboratory documentation binders set up so that a missing binder would be visually apparent.

Figure 6.9 Japanese medication cart drawer that is organized with foam cutouts indicating where items are to be kept.

something is missing, but it's also easier to see if staff are loading the drawers with more supplies than are really necessary. This 5S foam board is relatively inexpensive, but it is harder to change than tape outlines when standard items or quantities need to be changed.

Standardize Things That Matter

As with other methods, we need to take care that we are not using the tool (5S) without thinking about the problem that is being solved or the waste that is being prevented. In some health systems, people go overboard by labeling or outlining everything they can. If an item is heavy and not likely to move, such as a large desktop printer, there is no value in putting a tape outline around it and no problem being solved. We are, in fact, wasting tape. Likewise, putting printed labels on obvious items, such as a label that says "Printer" on the machine, adds no value and does not prevent a problem; however, a label may be helpful to identify the specific name or use of a printer to prevent clinicians from having to run around to different machines to find their printout.

Asking people to do 5S for an individual office desk that is not a shared workspace might also bring little benefit to patients or the organization. Banning personal items or family photos from a finance analyst's desk probably doesn't do anything other than irritate people. Common sense should drive the use of this method. If people start questioning the benefit of the approach, it might be a sign that we have gone overboard with the tool. Again, 5S is a method that is meant to engage the staff, not impose top-down mandates on them.

Standardizing Airway Carts

At Avera Health, a group of emergency physicians decided it was important to standardize the airway carts used at their various hospitals. "When we looked across the service line, we could tell that every single one of our regional centers has a different way of using their airway equipment," said Kelly Rhone, MD. Some centers had equipment on a wall or in a bag, and some centers did not have mobile equipment, meaning "you could only do an airway in certain rooms."

Their goal, and their need, was to have "the right equipment in the right room at the right time," eliminating the situation where "it was a real scramble ... with a nurse going one direction and me going another" to get the equipment they needed, according to Jared Friedman, MD, the clinical vice president for the emergency medicine service line.

The system created a standardized airway cart, which "works out very well for the patient and the staff," said Friedman. Rhone says, "It benefits the patient because they can get all of their airway care in the emergency department and we don't have to call down for equipment for the operating room." This reduces delays, saving time for staff and improving care. Physicians now know that, no matter where they are working, they have all of the equipment they need in a standardized, organized cart. "Now we have drawers that are clearly marked and they are the same throughout the system," said Rhone.

The airway cart was the first example of other mobile carts that will be created, allowing them to bring the equipment to the patient. Friedman said, "I think the greatest thing is that it's really created a dialogue for all of the regions and all of the staff, both physicians and nurses, to start talking about who has best practices ideas that can be spread around, to create a greater quality experience for our patients."[18]

Fifth S: Sustain

To prevent 5S from becoming a one-time event (or a repeated annual event), we need a plan for sustaining and continually improving our workplace organization. The department needs a formal audit plan so supervisors and leaders can see if the new standards are being followed. As with standardized work audits, this can be done on a scheduled basis. The visual management methods also make it possible for leaders to scan the department as they are walking through. If something seems out of place or missing, a leader can ask a few questions and coach employees about maintaining the proper setup. If an item is out of place, it might be because an employee has found a better or more convenient location. For situations like this, the 5S tools (outlining tape and label makers) should be kept available so employees can update their own workplace organization.

Safety as a Sixth S?

Some organizations add a sixth S to the methodology—safety. Detractors point out that safety should be an underlying philosophy of the organization, not something to be tacked on to 5S just because it also starts with the letter *s*. Attention to safety should be the focus of all 5S stages as it should be a focus on any regular day. For example, removing unneeded equipment can reduce tripping hazards that might result from cluttered spaces. Having the right supplies and equipment in nearby locations can help improve patient safety, as well, as the case study at the end of this chapter illustrates. Excluding safety as a formal *S* does not mean that safety is not important; instead, it signifies that safety is not something that can be delegated only to those implementing Lean. A culture of safety is owned by executive-level administrators and all other leaders in the organization.

A 5S Case Study: Saving Time for Respiratory Therapists

5S is not just a matter of labeling items on shelves. The following case study illustrates how deciding *where* to store items in a supply room can reduce waste and free up time for caregivers.

Maggie Reed was a supply coordinator in charge of the respiratory supply room at one of the hospitals within Franciscan St. Francis Health (Indianapolis, Indiana). In her role and with her view of the hospital, it made sense to organize her supply items alphabetically. For a respiratory therapist to quickly find something in her supply room, they had to reference a detailed wall chart that listed each item, alphabetically, along with its precise shelf location.

Joe Swartz, the director of business transformation for the system, visited Maggie's supply room to see recent improvements she had made. For example, Maggie had made supplies more visual by placing sample supplies on the outside of the glass cabinet doors.

During his visit, Maggie was pulled away for a few minutes and Joe began observing the respiratory therapists retrieve items, asking about their work. They mentioned things like needing to set up a patient on a vent in the ICU or needing a bilevel positive airway pressure (BIPAP) for a patient in the medical/surgical unit. Joe noticed a pattern—her customers, the therapists, seemed to be coming to get systems rather than random, individual parts. But, he didn't want to jump to conclusions or tell Maggie what to do.

If the pattern he observed was true, then Joe also needed to get Maggie to see this pattern, because she felt a strong sense of ownership of the area. Joe asked Maggie if she would do him a favor, saying, "Could you ask therapists periodically throughout the week what they are here for, and could you group them into two categories: here primarily for parts, or here primarily for systems like a vent or a continuous positive airway pressure (CPAP)?" Joe said he'd stop back by in a week. Maggie agreed.

A week later, Joe asked what Maggie had observed. She said, "It's interesting, about 80% of the time, they are here primarily to get a system." "That's really interesting," Joe said, raising his eyebrows and asking, "Does that influence your thinking about how the supply room should be organized?" "Yes," Maggie said, "I've been thinking—I might reorganize it by systems. What do you think?" "Wow, that's a great idea," Joe replied.

Maggie reorganized items, so that all vent, airway, and tracheotomy supplies were in one area. This made work easier and reduced waste, as therapists could stand and reach all those items without moving their feet. She also placed all BIPAP items in another area, and so on. The resulting layout enabled the therapists to get what they needed in half the time, increasing the time available for patient care.

Maggie was motivated to put in the effort to reorganize her supply area because she felt like it was her idea, and she took ownership. The only thing Joe did was to help her see her world from her customer's point of view and to discover what was needed for her internal customers. Because she was able to see things from a new perspective and took action, Maggie became a hero to the therapists she serves.

Kanban: A Lean Approach to Managing Materials

Kanban is a method that builds on the concepts of standardized work, 5S, and visual management to give health systems a simple yet effective method for managing supplies and inventory. *Kanban* is a Japanese word that can be translated as "signal," "card," or "sign."[19] A *kanban* is most often a physical signal, such as a paper card or a plastic bin, that indicates when it is time to order more, from whom, and in what quantity; it can also be an electronic signal that is sent by an automated cabinet or computer system. See Figures 6.10 (Children's Health, Dallas) and 6.11 (Rouge Valley Health System, Ontario) for examples of a laboratory *kanban* card and a pharmacy shelf that has been nicely organized and set up with *kanban* cards.

Creating *kanban* cards can require a significant time investment just to get the system up and running. One hospital pharmacy created 1,600 laminated cards to manage medication inventory. After a few months, inventory levels had fallen from $600,000 to $350,000 by preventing the accidental overordering that occurred under the old method—not a bad return on that time investment! The time spent in the initial set up of the cards and the *kanban* system is also offset by effort saved over time through the simplicity of the approach.

The *kanban* approach is sometimes mistakenly thought of as a system that just focuses on low inventory levels when its goals are actually to support the patients and the employees by ensuring needed supplies are in the right place, in the right quantity, and at the right time and to ensure the availability of material with the lowest required inventory levels. *Kanban* systems typically have fewer stockouts and better availability of materials than traditional materials management methods.

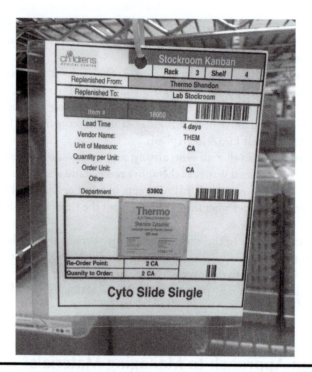

Figure 6.10 A *kanban* card from the core laboratory at Children's Health.

Figure 6.11 A hospital pharmacy's shelves with *kanban* cards indicating when to order more of each medication.

Problems with Traditional Materials Systems

Before Lean implementation, inventory management in hospital departments is often an informal process with a lot of waste. Responsibility for ordering supplies for a department might fall on a single person. When that key person is on vacation, or in the hypothetical case of that person winning the lottery and quitting, the system often falls apart, leading to stockouts on key supplies or other employees mistakenly ordering large amounts of inventory. Even with capable people managing supplies, if there is not a standardized, quantitative methodology for managing materials, there is a risk that the hospital is not optimizing its total inventory management costs.

Problems with Standing Orders

One traditional materials management method that is problematic is the standing order; a vendor sends a predetermined amount each period (weekly, monthly, or quarterly). Standing orders are indeed easy to manage (the material arrives automatically), but it is a "push" system that is not responsive to variation in material usage. Since hospitals and departments have demand that changes for many reasons (seasonality, population changes, broader health trends), the standing order method sets us up for holding excess inventory (when usage of an item drops) or stockouts (when usage increases). Reactions to inventory levels tend to be late and overreactive. When an item is out of stock, the department spends money unnecessarily to expedite the order. This wastes employee time, and the expedited shipment costs more. We might see the same reactive approach every time an item runs out instead of using the situation to drive a systemic change to the ordering method or order quantities.

Problems with Par Levels

The common practice of "par levels" is generally an advance over standing orders; par levels create a "pull" system, as items are replenished only in the quantities in which they are being used. Par-level systems are, unfortunately, full of wasted motion as each individual item must be counted every time restocking occurs—which means a lot of extra motion, time, and cost. If the par level of an item is 15, a physical count must be done each time. If there are four items remaining, then 11 are restocked. This number is likely to vary, and restocking 11 items might require breaking open a box of 20, which requires additional time and motion.

At organizations like St. Clair Hospital (Pittsburgh, Pennsylvania), the reality might be that material handlers are short on time, so they would sometimes do a visual scan, restocking only the items that seemed to be very low in supply. As a staff member said, "A seasoned material handler could be very effective with this [par level] method, thanks to years of service. For a new employee, however, there's a lengthy learning curve." By comparison, a *kanban* system is simpler and does not rely on the same level of judgment and experience to be successful.

Creating the *kanban* system at St. Clair meant converting 28 stock areas in 21 units over the course of 10 months. Now, instead of counting, a material handler only needs to scan the bar code on each empty bin, which automatically sends a replenishment signal. Wendy Luppino, an ICU nurse, says, "Since [*kanban*] has been implemented, we do not run out of things. There's much less frustration about having to wait on things from materials management. Things are here at our fingertips … it just helps your flow of care."[20] With the par system, the ICU sent down 73 urgent requisitions in a month, a number reduced to zero with *kanban*.

Problems with Electronic Inventory Cabinets

A more modern hospital practice is the electronic or automated inventory supply cabinet. These cabinets promise easy restocking if staff members press a button each time they remove an item. While this is a pull system that works in theory, people often forget to press buttons in the haste of their waste-filled days, or buttons do not properly register each time. When the buttons are not pressed, the computer system thinks inventory levels are higher than in reality, so items run out, and staff are left to scramble to find supplies elsewhere. Because staff have to log in to the system, each encounter with the machine consumes precious time; furthermore, only one person can use the cabinet at a time, leading to a queue of nurses waiting to access the cabinet during peak times.

In one hospital pharmacy, the automated medication cabinets in the nursing units were set, in the computer system, to send a restocking signal when inventory reached zero. This was too late, as nurses and patients would not have medications available for many hours, requiring an expedited "missing med" order that generated more work for the pharmacy. In a Lean process, the restocking signals have to be sent before inventory is completely depleted to allow for the time it takes for more material to arrive.

Seattle Children's Hospital (Washington) realized a *kanban* system with open wire shelves could work better while allowing more than one person to take items at a time. They went from 100 of these cabinets to just six, reducing their maintenance costs. Since items were unfortunately at "zero inventory" 40% of the time with the automated cabinet, the *kanban* system provided higher service levels by not letting inventory get to zero. In addition, the hospital found that a vast majority of "chargeable" items were not actually charged to patients, eliminating another common justification for the cabinets. The only items left in these locked automated cabinets are expensive items that are actually charged to a specific patient or items for which there is a safety concern.

Trade-Offs with Inventory

In any system, there are trade-offs between high availability of materials and increased inventory costs, especially when the use of supplies is not perfectly predictable or steady. This is certainly the case in hospitals.

Generally speaking, the cost of inventory rises as we want to be more certain that we never run out. Industrial engineering and supply chain management principles teach us that inventory levels must unfortunately increase exponentially if we are to approach a guarantee of 100% availability for an item.

While our primary goal is to keep patient care flowing and ensure staff have the supplies they need, we sometimes have to look at the trade-offs and costs involved. This trade-off can be seen with expired or obsolete inventory. We cannot expect constant availability yet also insist there be zero wasted inventory. For example, if a hospital's blood bank needs to ensure that it never runs out of O-negative blood, it is inevitable that some waste (expired blood that has to be destroyed) will occur since it might be difficult to perfectly predict blood usage. Other industries, such as manufacturing, might not want to run out of a particular item because the cost of shutting down an automotive assembly line for an hour is very high. That, however, does not compare to the cost of a life lost because a critical blood component, medication, or supply was not available. When the cost of stockouts is high, we have to err on the side of excess inventory. For items that are less critical, or have a close substitute, we can more easily allow some risk of stockouts.

Another trade-off to consider is the frequency of ordering from outside vendors. If we order less often, we can order in larger quantities. This often leads to volume discounts from vendors, or we can spread out fixed ordering costs (such as the labor cost of cutting a purchase order and the often fixed shipping cost from the vendor) across more material. The downside with ordering less frequently is that we have higher inventory management costs, which include

- Cash tied up in inventory
- Space required for storage
- Labor required to move, count, and maintain inventory
- Risk of damage, obsolescence, or expiration

> Keeping inventory low by ordering more frequently is not always the approach that minimizes the total system cost. For example, the laboratory at Henry Ford Hospital (Detroit, Michigan) had been ordering some reagents and quality control materials in six-month batches. Rather than moving to an extreme of ordering weekly or monthly, they found the optimal point was to order somewhere between every three and six months. This was because each time they ordered reagents, technologists had to do time-consuming calibration, time and cost that could be considered part of the cost of ordering. So, the lowest inventory (ordering monthly) would not have led to the lowest total cost.[21]

Ordering more frequently also reduces the overall risk of stockouts because we can reevaluate actual usage and respond more quickly if we are ordering small amounts weekly instead of large amounts quarterly.

The *kanban* method allows us to quantify an optimal reorder point for supplies. This formula considers a number of factors, including

- Average usage or demand for an item
- How frequently we consider reordering (often daily or weekly)
- The vendor's lead time for replenishing items
- Safety stock, considering the variation of usage and variation in replenishment time and the cost of stocking out

The amount of safety stock required will depend on the amount of variation involved with a given part. If an item is critically important, has highly variable usage, and comes from an unreliable vendor who might deliver more in two days or two weeks, the hospital would hold a relatively high amount of safety stock.

Using *Kanban* to Replenish Supplies

Kanban can be used to pull materials from a central hospital supply room or a departmental stockroom to the point of use. Or, we can have a series of pulls, each with its own *kanban* signal and reorder points, as shown in Figure 6.12. The *kanban* pull signal is meant to be simple and visual, such as an empty bin, a card, or a message sent by a bar code scanner.

Charles Hodge, formerly the vice president of support services at Seattle Children's Hospital, has helped design and implement *kanban* systems at more than 20 organizations. One more

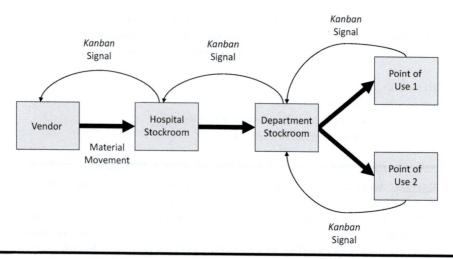

Figure 6.12 Illustration of the flow of supplies through a multi-stage *kanban* system, where each downstream area (to the right) pulls material from an upstream location or vendor.

specific goal he expressed for these health systems is to "get the clinicians out of the supply chain." The goal for supplies is that "when you need it, it's there ... reach for it, it's there," says Hodge. One health system he worked with saw "a 7% bottom line cost savings on medical supplies" as a result of adopting *kanban*.[22]

Park Nicollet Health Services has implemented *kanban* across 68 hospital departments and 33 clinic departments since 2004. They have created and maintained over 60,000 *kanban* cards that are used to signal replenishment of their supplies. Between 800 and 1,000 items are replenished via *kanban* on any given day.[23] The central materials department works with departments to setup *kanban*, with the central materials specialists placing orders and restocks from the main storeroom. Park Nicollet estimates it has saved $1.1 million in the past three years with this method.

One visual way of managing inventory is a style of *kanban* called a two-bin system. This method uses two plastic bins at the point of use, bins that can stack together or sit in front of or behind each other on a shelf, as pictured in Figure 6.13. For an employee who uses the items, the system is simple. Anyone can take items for use, but when the first bin is empty, that empty bin becomes a visual signal to order more. With the two-bin system, when one bin is empty, we still have enough with which to continue working. This system does not require the manual counting of a par-level system. The empty bin, which is labeled with information such as the item name, number, and source of more material, can be set in a designated area (properly labeled in a 5S and visual management manner). Some electronic two-bin systems combine the visual simplicity and open access of *kanban* shelves with the ability to charge specific items to patients and automatic ordering based on an RFID chip that's placed on each bin.

At Seattle Children's Hospital, 95% of supplies are replenished using bins, with anything too large to fit in bins being triggered by *kanban* cards.[24] The *kanban* system, combined with working

Figure 6.13 Laboratory bench with supplies set up with two-bin *kanban* replenishment.

with suppliers to deliver items more frequently and in smaller lot sizes, helped the hospital reduce on-site inventory from $1.5 million to less than $500,000.[25] Again, the goal of *kanban* is not only less spending; an effective *kanban* system also helps ensure the rotation of stock to ensure the oldest supplies are used first. For the first three years after the initial *kanban* adoption, the Joint Commission found "zero expired items."[26]

The *kanban* bins or cards are collected by a single person on a regular basis (typically every shift or every day). Instead of multiple unplanned trips to the stockroom, one person makes one trip. Having good standardized work for a *kanban* process is critically important. As Hodge says, "You can't just buy two bins and call it a *kanban* system. You need the daily management system and standardized work around that."[27] This includes properly training everybody about their role in the system and properly supervising, auditing, and improving the approach over time, as discussed more in Chapter 11.

As discussed in Chapter 5, one aspect of standardized work is deciding who should do what work based on their skills and abilities. Hospitals, generally, should not pay highly skilled and highly trained individuals, including technologists, nurses, and pharmacists, to do manual material-handling work. The goal of the *kanban* system and the materials management department should be to properly support the highly skilled employees who do the value-added work in an area. Martin Health System (Martin, Florida) freed up the equivalent of nine clinical full-time equivalents (FTEs) as the result of their *kanban* system.[28] One staff member said, "The coolest thing is that I can go in, get my item, and get back to the patient and I don't have to waste time away from the bedside."[29]

At Seattle Children's, time was also freed up for more patient care, as unplanned calls for materials were reduced by 85%, and the time nurses spent searching for materials was cut in half, saving 80,000 hours each year.[30] In keeping with 5S principles, more supplies are kept at the point of use in patient rooms, with the most common supplies, like saline, being delivered twice a day.

In one hospital's operating room project, implementing *kanban* helped reduce the time required to restock the rooms. Before Lean, nurses in each room would spend 10 minutes at the end of each day counting inventory and replenishing each item in its proper location. With the *kanban* process, the Lean implementation manager highlighted the ease and time savings, saying, "Now, the nurses just throw empty bins into a basket, and people refill them during their downtime. It doesn't seem like a big deal until you add it up and realize that we're saving 600 nursing hours over the course of a year."

One benefit of a *kanban* approach is that we no longer wait until we are very low on (or completely out of) an item to order more, as might commonly happen before *kanban*. This minimizes the number of interruptions to employees and the flow of work, whether it is testing specimens, processing medication orders, or caring for patients. In traditional materials systems, an employee, such as a medical technologist, sees that the supply of an item is dangerously low. Because inventory levels have gotten so low, the technologist might interrupt work to immediately run to a stock area or immediately stop to get an expedited purchase order issued. This time away delays the primary workflow in the area, and the reactive nature of the interruptions causes stress and frustration, especially when conditions like this are the norm.

The systematic *kanban* method not only minimizes stockouts, but also prevents an accumulation of excess inventory. Often, when we run out of a needed item, the natural reaction is an overreaction to order more inventory to protect against running out again. In a *kanban* system, any stockout needs to be investigated to identify the root cause. Was this a one-time event or a consistent shift in the usage of an item? Instead of just reacting by ordering more, the person responsible for the *kanban* system needs to determine if the reorder point needs to be changed. This systematic analysis prevents an emotional reaction to what might have been an unforeseen one-time event. At Seattle Children's, supplies that are ordered more or less frequently than expected have their *kanban* bin sizes adjusted to account for this demand change.[31]

Before *kanban* is put in place, we often find that employees hide or hoard needed supplies, often in response to a materials replenishment system they cannot trust. A nurse at another hospital admitted to the author that she hid supplies above ceiling tiles to ensure her own supply. One laboratory found there were eight different storage locations for a particular type of blood tube, all right within the phlebotomy department. Different drawers and shelves were full, with tubes tucked away in many hidden places. This took up excess space and increased the risk that tubes in the bottom of drawers would expire before getting used.

By installing an effective *kanban* system, the department better organized its supplies into a single stock location on exposed shelves for all to see. Because the *kanban* system was reliable, employees no longer felt the need to hoard supplies. Instead of just mandating that employees quit hoarding supplies (a mandate that would force the practice further underground), the need to hoard was eliminated. Making the proper supplies available with high reliability also creates conditions that make it easier for staff to properly use gloves and other protective equipment.

In a very advanced case, Seattle Children's has essentially eliminated its central supply room by restocking directly from vendors to departments, in most cases, leading to lower inventory and better response to the units or departments that pull materials.[32]

The New York Health and Hospital Corporation (HHC) is using "just in time" ordering to replenish materials, as part of their Lean program called Breakthrough. As many organizations do in conjunction with their supply chain redesign efforts, HHC rationalized the variety of rubber gloves that are available. Instead of 20 different colors and thicknesses, there are now just two options available (in different sizes, of course). This saves HHC $4 million a year on gloves alone.[33] In keeping with the principle of respect for people, changes like this should be made with significant staff and clinician participation, rather than being mandated from the top.

A Kanban *Case Study*

Northampton General Hospital NHS Trust (Northampton, England) is a 695-bed acute hospital that can trace its history to an infirmary that was built in 1743. The pathology department struggled with inventory management prior to their use of Lean methods, starting in 2008. "We were under increasing pressure from Hospital Management to improve our level of service," says then pathology directorate manager Peter Martin.[34] The environment was often stressful, with high absenteeism due to illness. Lean was a method aimed at improving the service provided to physicians and patients, while also being a way to reduce stress and overtime for staff.

One cause of stress and interruptions during the day was the waste caused by problems with the existing materials management system. Some supply storage points would run empty, and some items were replenished from a somewhat inconvenient location, a lower level called the "undercroft." In other cases, the newest supply of specimen collection tubes would be poured on top of the old supply, causing some tubes at the bottom of the bin to expire. This represented either wasted money or the risk that an old tube would be used to collect a patient specimen, causing problems with test results.

Describing the old process, Samantha Martin, a biomedical support worker, said, "We had several storerooms, some on the other side of the hospital," adding, "You'd look at what you had and think, 'I need a bit more of this, some more of that.' We'd end up with loads of things we don't use and not enough of the things we do use." It wasn't always clear, from a visual management or process perspective, when items should be restocked, so staff often overordered on a "just-in-case basis."[35]

Pathology staff members worked to implement a *kanban* system, first auditing the quantity used of each item in a year, and then calculating daily and monthly usage rates. The team created and utilized laminated *kanban* cards, as pictured in Figure 6.14, that display the full product information, stock level, and required ordering volumes for an item. The cards then visually marked the reorder point for items, as shown in Figure 6.15. When it was time to restock items, pathology staff would place the appropriate card in a pocket, as pictured in Figure 6.16. In some cases, the two-bin *kanban* approach was used for small items that could be kept in plastic bins. For items that ran the risk of expiration, the two-bin system ensured that stock could be properly rotated, so the oldest supply was always used before the new.

Figure 6.14 A *kanban* **card from Northampton General Hospital's pathology department.**

Figure 6.15 Shelves with laboratory supplies and *kanban* cards for each item.

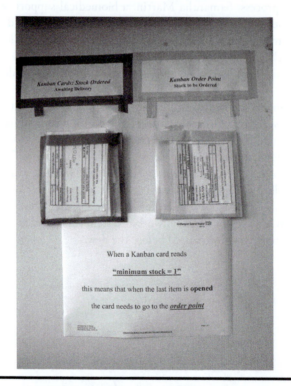

Figure 6.16 *Kanban* card collection point for items that need to be ordered or have already been ordered.

New standardized work was created to help ensure that the processes for using the *kanban* system were clear and that staff were well-trained in their role in using or maintaining the *kanban* system.

After the initial implementation in the blood sciences area, the *kanban* system was also put in place in histopathology. Now, 80% to 90% of their stock is managing using *kanban*, says Clare

Wood, biomedical scientist. Wood adds, "We have definitely improved the tidiness of our stock and we have had a reduction of stockouts for some items. People like *kanban* in histology, so much so, that I have just had a look in the pocket and we have a post-it note for a rare item of stock, something that doesn't have a *kanban* card. So, people like them enough to make their own!" Wood says the only difficulties with *kanban* are managing items that don't stack neatly, cards going missing, or cards not being returned to shelves when new stock arrives, but these problems happen rarely.

With all of their initial Lean improvements, the pathology department avoided a total of £158,000 in labor, storage, and inventory costs with the *kanban* system, as well as improvements to the physical layout and standardized work. *Kanban*, specifically, enabled them to save money by maintaining a smaller standing inventory. More importantly, staff had what they needed to perform their vital work for patients, and fewer people are involved in the management of stock. "We've had no stockouts in a year," says Samantha Martin.[36]

Reflecting on the overall improvements to the layout and workflow, including the *kanban* system, Peter Martin reflected, "Thanks to Lean, we can absorb the added work. We are finishing on time now and on good days, slightly early. We've taken the stress out of the process."[37]

Case Example: The Use of Lean Methods to Prevent Patient Harm

At a large children's hospital, a young patient, having been sedated, started vomiting while secured inside the machine for head and neck MRI. The MRI tech detected this situation and interrupted the scan to go care for the patient, an action that might be considered first-order problem solving: make sure the patient's airway is clear.

In her attempt to rescue the patient, the tech looked to the MRI-safe clips that were on the wall inside the room—but there were no suction tubes available as there should have been. This created a second-order problem to solve: the lack of needed equipment to solve the first-order problem.

The MRI tech, in a rush, walked back to the control room to get suction tubes from the high-tech inventory cabinet—except that the cabinet also had zero stock, another problem. The tech then ran and interrupted another MRI procedure, taking suction tubes from the other room back to her patient. The child was, ultimately, unharmed, and the first-order problem was solved: The patient's airway was cleared, without injury.

Problems in this case include:

- First order: Patient in distress
- Second order: No suction tubes available
- Third order: No reliable, consistent process to ensure needed supplies are available in the cabinet or the MRI rooms
- Fourth order: Lack of a robust management system to more quickly react to or prevent problems like this

What happened next? When asked about this the next day (after she volunteered the story), the MRI tech answered, "We completed the scan." There was no immediate problem solving around the second-order problem—the absence of suction tubes. After the scan was completed, the team brought in the next patient (since they were now behind schedule). Even without working on the third-order problem (fixing the system that led to missing supplies), one might have expected that somebody would have simply gone and gotten more tubes (via the proper channels, not robbing them from another room), just in case that patient (or the next one) also started vomiting.

We should not blame the individual MRI tech for her reaction or lack of immediate problem solving, as she was working within the culture and management systems of the radiology department and the hospital. She had no "support chain" to ask for help to resolve even the second-order problem: Why was there no help to immediately restock the needed supplies?

If the MRI suite had been a Lean setting, such as an outstanding Lean factory, the MRI tech would have been able to pull a physical "andon cord," which would have immediately drawn a helpful response from a supervisor to assist with the recovery of the patient or to get more suction tubes so the MRI tech could focus on her work and the patients.

In this case, the MRI tech also did not have a process or a mechanism for getting a response about the third-order problem: the lack of a reliable, consistent system. She said nothing to her supervisor and did not escalate the issue until the next day, when she discussed it with the outside consultant who was in the area (as opposed to the supervisor, who was usually in meetings). The team almost missed the opportunity to investigate, to learn, and to improve.

In a Lean setting, a group would be quickly convened from the natural work team, including representatives of roles such as MRI techs, respiratory therapists, anesthesiologists, nurses, and managers. This team might come together during a gap in the schedule for the day or at the end of the cases scheduled that day. In the most serious patient safety situations, the manager and team might consider fully stopping procedures until the underlying root causes and risks had been eliminated.

In this case, we could ask why suction tubes were missing from the room. It turned out that there was no clear responsibility or consistent standardized work regarding who restocked the MRI rooms and at what interval. This showed an opportunity to define the standardized work for restocking the rooms, including clear responsibility for who would restock the room after an item was used and what escalation process could be used if that could not occur—to prevent putting another patient in harm's way.

Looking at the supposedly "automated" inventory cabinet that had no suction tubes, the team discussed some of the limitations of that technology. If staff did not press the proper button when taking supplies, the right restocking signals were not sent electronically to materials management. The closed cabinet did not lend itself to easy visual management of the inventory levels; if inventory were low or zero, it was hard to see behind the glass doors. The team started to discuss a simple, visual, two-bin *kanban* system for inexpensive items that were not charged to patients—a process that might work better, and at a lower cost, than the cabinet.

In addition, the team, having learned about 5S and visual management, realized that there were not enough wall clips for all needed items, including suction tubes. Some items were stuffed into plastic drawers, making it difficult to determine, at a glance, if any items were missing. The manager responded by ordering more MRI-safe clips in place of the drawers, an improvement that would also reduce the time required to rescue a patient in distress.

While the team consistently performed a pre-MRI checklist to help ensure, for example, that the patient did not have metal on or inside his or her body, the team did not have a similar checklist to ensure, with a visual scan, that all needed safety supplies were stocked and in place before each procedure started, a clear opportunity for improvement to the system.

Finally, this situation provided an opportunity for managers, directors, and senior leaders to talk about their culture and management system. Why did employees feel uncomfortable asking for help or raising concerns about patient care? Why were supervisors and managers unavailable to provide help as problems occurred? Why did the culture emphasize and tolerate immediate first-order "firefighting" without also focusing on identifying root causes and improving systems? What could senior leadership do to create an environment for continuous quality improvement?

This scenario was used in ongoing Lean efforts in the department to emphasize the importance of 5S, visual management, *kanban* replenishment, and standardized work and how these methods could solve real problems that previously affected patient care and created unnecessary stress for staff members. The MRI tech who told the story to an outside consultant (not her supervisor) 24 hours after it occurred was upset for two reasons: The patient could have been harmed, and the technician was afraid that these problems could easily happen again, with unfortunate results, without improvements to the process. It is in this way that Lean improvements and waste reduction serve patients and employees in a respectful way.

Conclusion

As with any Lean tools or methods, hospitals should not implement visual management, 5S, or *kanban* because a book says so or to be part of a trend. The point of any of these tools is to create a culture for solving problems in the workplace, reducing or preventing waste from interfering with our work and patient care. Any of these methods should not be a one-time event; they should be part of an ongoing management system that helps sustain the methods and drives continuous improvement out of respect for patients and workers. Implementing these methods not only can reduce waste, but also can get employees engaged in improving the workplace instead of just complaining about problems.

Lean Lessons

- Visual management helps expose problems and avoid miscommunications and waste.
- 5S reduces waste through improved organization and visual methods.
- 5S is not a one-time event—it is a plan to be sustained to maintain and improve workplace organization.
- Supplies and items that are used most frequently should be kept closest to the point of use.
- Hiding the mess behind cabinet doors does not fix the root cause of the disorganization problem.
- *Kanban* can be implemented using cards, plastic bins, or electronic signals.
- *Kanban* requires much less counting and time than par levels.
- With materials, we need to view trade-offs between the cost of inventory and the cost of running out. Hospitals might need to err on the side of not running out.
- When we have more variation in the system, we need more safety stock to protect us.

Points for Group Discussion

- What is an example of an information deficit in our area? What waste does that cause? Can we use visual management to eliminate that waste?
- How much time is wasted each day due to disorganization? What could we better use that time for?
- How can we free up time to work on Lean methods?

- What are some problems we face with our existing materials management systems? What drives people to hoard supplies?
- Is it possible to calculate the cost (financial or human) of a patient being harmed or dying because of an inventory shortage or stockout?

Notes

1. Takahara, Akio, and Collin McLoughlin, *Clinical 5S For Healthcare* (Bellingham, WA: Enna, 2010), 1.
2. Leone, Gerard, and Richard D. Rahn, *Supplies Management in the OR* (Boulder, CO: Flow, 2011), 1.
3. Harada, Takehiko, *Management Lessons from Taiichi Ohno: What Every Leader Can Learn from the Man who Invented the Toyota Production System* (New York: McGraw-Hill, 2015), 45.
4. Bonini, Jamie, presentation at 2014 Lean Healthcare Transformation Summit.
5. Toyota, Ask "Why" Five Times about Every Matter, http://www.toyota-global.com/company/toyota_traditions/quality/mar_apr_2006.html (accessed October 8, 2015).
6. Galsworth, Gwendolyn, *Visual Workplace, Visual Thinking* (Portland, OR: Visual-Lean Enterprise Press, 2005), 13.
7. Ibid., 15.
8. Liker, Jeffrey K., *The Toyota Way* (New York: McGraw-Hill, 2003), 159.
9. Tennessee Hospital Association, Color-coded patient alert wristband standardization implementation toolkit, http://www.tha.com/files/wristbands/toolkit/9-1-2009/complete-toolkit.pdf (accessed September 20, 2015).
10. Stanford Health Care, Purposeful Rounding, https://stanfordhealthcare.org/health-care-professionals/nursing/quality-safety/purposeful-rounding.html (accessed September 20, 2015).
11. Maass, Kathy, personal interview, September 2015.
12. Touissant, John, presentation, First Global Lean Healthcare Summit, June 25, 2007.
13. Takahara and McLoughlin, *Clinical 5S*, 11.
14. Yee, Chen May, Hard times curtail Park Nicollet's ambition, *StarTribune.com*, May 23, 2009, http://www.startribune.com/business/45871162.html?elr=KArks:DCiU1OiP:DiiUiD3aPc:_Yyc:aULPQL7PQLanchO7DiUr (accessed March 26, 2015).
15. Productivity Press Development Team, *5S for Operators* (New York: Productivity Press, 1996), 12.
16. Wellman, Joan, Howard Jeffries, and Pat Hagan, *Leading the Lean Healthcare Journey* (New York: Productivity Press, 2010), 88.
17. Cosgove, Toby, Patient Experience: Time for Hospitals to Look under the Bed, https://www.linkedin.com/pulse/20130528135038-205372152-titlepatient-experience-time-for-hospitals-to-look-under-the-bed (accessed September 20, 2015).
18. Avera Health, unpublished video, used with permission.
19. Productivity Press Development Team, *Kanban for the Shopfloor* (New York: Productivity Press, 2002), 1.
20. Lyon, Tania, Two Bin Supply System at St. Clair Hospital, https://www.youtube.com/watch?v=yjSwwPF5BUU (accessed October 22, 2015).
21. Lusky, Karen, "Laying Lean on the line, one change at a time," *CAP Today*, July 2009, http://www.cap.org/apps/cap.portal?_nfpb=true&cntvwrPtlt_actionOverride=%2Fportlets%2FcontentViewer%2Fshow&_windowLabel=cntvwrPtlt&cntvwrPtlt%7BactionForm.contentReference%7D=cap_today%2F0709%2F0709h_laying_lean.html&_state=maximized&_pageLabel=cntvwr (accessed March 26, 2015).
22. Hodge, Charles, personal interview, August 2015.
23. Brook, Andy, presentation at Park Nicollet Health Services, August 2010.
24. Wellman, *Leading the Lean*, 91.
25. Moody, Patricia E., Lean Factor: Seattle Children's Hospital, http://www.ame.org/target/articles/2014/lean-factor-seattle-children%E2%80%99s-hospital (accessed September 20, 2015).
26. BlueBin, Seattle Children's Hospital (accessed September 20, 2015).

27. Hodge.
28. Hodge.
29. Martin Health System, Blue Bin Demand Flow Process, https://www.youtube.com/watch?v=A5Y_3NuN5Ng (accessed October 22, 2015).
30. Moody.
31. Wellman, 91.
32. Wellman, 91.
33. Jones, Del, "Hospital CEOs manage staff time, inventory to cut costs," *USA Today*, September 10, 2009, http://usatoday30.usatoday.com/money/industries/health/2009-09-09-saving-money-hospitals_N.htm (accessed August 9, 2015).
34. ValuMetrix Services.
35. ValuMetrix Services.
36. ValuMetrix Services.
37. ValuMetrix Services, Northampton General Hospital Uses Lean to Cut Turnaround Time by 40%, Avoids £158,000/Year in Labour, Storage, and Inventory Costs, http://markgraban.com/wp-content/uploads/2011/04/NGH-summary.pdf (accessed August 9, 2015).

Chapter 7

Proactive Root Cause Problem Solving

The Tragic and Preventable Mary McClinton Story

Mary McClinton's death at Virginia Mason Medical Center (VMMC) (Seattle, Washington) is a well-known patient safety incident. McClinton died in 2004 after being injected with chlorhexidine, an antiseptic solution, instead of a contrast dye. During her procedure, there were three clear liquids that were kept in stainless steel bowls on a tray: the antiseptic, the dye, and a saline solution. Anticipating the interventional radiologist's need, an experienced technician prelabeled an empty syringe as "contrast dye." However, he later allegedly filled the syringe with the antiseptic, not the dye.[1] A Lean thinker would recognize the potential for systemic error in a situation like this and would not be satisfied with asking or expecting well-trained people to be careful. The error that caused McClinton's death was an accident waiting to happen.

Before the fateful day, the hospital had switched from a brown iodine solution to the clear antiseptic. Some versions of the story said the hospital had "recently" switched, but another report said the clear antiseptic had been in place for two years before McClinton's death.[2,3] It is hindsight, but one might ask how a risk like that could have gone ignored. The technician involved, Carl Dorsey, knew of the change and mentioned this "setup" for error to his supervisor two months before the incident. This error was not the result of an unforeseen risk. The technician knew, the supervisor knew—yet the risky situation persisted.

McClinton, a 69-year-old social worker, and her family suffered from this preventable error, but so did the technician. Before the incident, Dorsey had an "unblemished" 34-year career, with 17 of those years at VMMC. He was "fined by the state, accepted blame, and resigned from the hospital," although he was "not certain" whether he or the doctor actually filled the syringe.[4] As Dorsey reflected on what happened, he said, "Mistakes will happen, we are exceptionally human."

The Toyota philosophy was originally called the "respect for humanity" system. This means that we not only respect each individual but also respect our own humanity—our human nature. Humans are not perfect. As much as we try to be careful, mistakes can happen. Again, as Sir Liam

Donaldson, former chief medical officer for the British National Health Service, said, "Human error is inevitable. We can never eliminate it. We can eliminate problems in the system that make it more likely to happen."[5]

After McClinton's death, the antiseptic was replaced with a gel on a swab, eliminating the risk of mistaking chlorhexidine for the dye with future patients. That's an improvement to the system. We can only hope that this same systemic risk has been addressed at every other hospital instead of waiting to react after another tragedy occurs.

Improving Quality and Patient Safety

As we saw in the house diagram in Chapter 5, quality is one of the two pillars of Lean. Of all the motivations for implementing Lean in healthcare, there is likely no higher purpose than that of improving the quality of care delivery and improving patient safety. Certainly, hospitals and advances in medical care are saving many lives, thanks to clinical excellence and new technologies, but the complexity of modern hospitals makes processes and value streams hard to manage. Dr. Atul Gawande said, "As individualistic as we want to be [in medicine], complexity requires group success."[6] While it is a testament to the extraordinary efforts of many healthcare workers that there are not more errors, hospital leaders must work to create an environment in which errors and harm can be significantly reduced.

How many patients are injured, suffer infections, or die as the result of preventable errors in hospitals? Statistics from various sources use different estimates and methodologies, all trying to determine numbers that cannot be known precisely. Some studies rely on the review of medical records, for which the true nature of errors may be underreported. While there are some mechanisms for voluntary reporting, it is hard to argue that all hospitals or people report all errors equally.[7] Many errors may go undiscovered since it is often difficult to tell if an error caused a death or just contributed to it, leading to further problems with the data.

There is, however, widespread agreement that the relative scale of this problem is unacceptable—whatever the numbers, too many patients are being harmed, and much of it is preventable. This is a global problem, not isolated to certain countries or certain payer structures. We also have proof that Lean methods for quality improvement can reduce the number of preventable injuries, infections, and deaths, while also improving clinical outcomes even when harm is not an issue.

Lean is not a "silver bullet" approach that will instantly eliminate all errors, but the tools and the mindsets can help our hospitals and employees reduce preventable errors.

Cultural Obstacles to Quality Improvement

Hospitals have some long-standing cultural obstacles to overcome before Lean quality improvement methods can be effective. For one, we have to shift from "naming, blaming, and shaming" employees to an environment in which we learn from errors, near misses, and identified risks, using knowledge gained to prevent future errors.[8] Hospitals need to be more proactive in preventing errors, anticipating possible or likely errors or responding to near misses, rather than responding only after injury or death has occurred. Improving quality relies more on leadership, culture, and creative thinking than on any specific technology or tool.

McLeod Regional Medical Center (Florence, South Carolina) changed its culture from one of blame to one of problem solving and prevention. While the national average for adverse drug events is two to eight per 1,000 doses, McLeod's own rate was reduced from four per 1,000 in 2002 to less than one per 1,000 in 2004.[9] Donna Isgett, RN, MSN, vice president of Clinical Effectiveness, said, "We are very oriented toward problem solving. We don't deny problems; we focus on them and work to solve them. And we are very team-oriented; we never try to fix things alone. We work together."[10]

Another obstacle is incorrect perceptions about medical errors, in the general public and the medical community. One study showed that patients and physicians thought published estimates of avoidable death numbers were "much too high."[11] This is despite the fact that some estimates are based on errors that were actually reported, which makes those conservative estimates, given underreporting. Surgeons and the general public often blame individual surgeons, rather than the system, for errors. This perception was confirmed in *To Err Is Human*, as the general public viewed medical mistakes as an "individual provider issue" instead of a systems failure.[12]

The tendency to blame individuals leads to responses that focus on punishing or removing bad people instead of improving the system. Look at almost any news report on high-profile medical errors, and you will likely see reports of individuals being punished, fired, or even jailed. Senior leaders often publicly criticize their own organizations, after the fact, for not following policies and procedures, saying that there is "no excuse" for such errors.[13] Instead of retrospective lambasting, we all need to work together as a team toward proactive prevention. Leaders play an important role in ensuring that policies and procedures are followed on a regular and ongoing basis.

Why Do Errors Occur?

If adverse events are not always caused by individual negligence, why do errors occur? Where traditional management is quick to blame individuals for errors, the Lean mindset understands Dr. W. Edwards Deming's teaching that 94% of errors "belong to the system."[14] *To Err Is Human* concluded, "The majority of medical errors do not result from individual recklessness or the actions of a particular group—this is not a 'bad apple' problem. More commonly, errors are caused by faulty systems, processes, and conditions that lead people to make mistakes or fail to prevent them."[15]

Accountability and personal responsibility are important and cannot be minimized. Unfortunately, in many organizations the word "accountability" is just a synonym for "blame." One might say that responsible individuals are necessary, but not sufficient, to ensure quality in a highly complex system. The Lean philosophy does not encourage us to make excuses for individuals who knowingly do the wrong thing and take wild risks. Leading patient safety experts, including Dr. Robert Wachter, concurred that we must find the proper balance between "no blame" and "no accountability."[16]

Filling a syringe with the wrong unlabeled clear liquid seems like a systemic error. Arguably, prelabeling a syringe before it is filled is a risky practice and somebody's intentional choice. That might seem like a time to "hold somebody accountable." But, if the physician on the case is known to become extremely upset about delays, such as waiting for a syringe to be filled, that might lead an individual to do something they know is a risky or bad choice, to avoid that situation, although there are no indications that was the case with Dorsey. People making bad choices in an environment of fear and stress might well be a systemic cause.

Violations and Errors, Lapses, and Slips

Violations are intentional actions that go against accepted practices and are, by definition, avoidable; however, not all violations are motivated by bad intentions. A violation might be necessary and defendable in certain conditions for the sake of the patient. For example, an anesthesiologist might not take the time to keep all normal records for an emergency surgery.[17] Harmful and willful violations, such as an addicted anesthesiologist skimming some of the drugs intended for surgical patients, fall more squarely on individuals, making traditional punishment approaches more appropriate (although we could ask if the hospital had been previously aware of an ongoing problem without taking action, making it a systemic issue). One study concluded that only 27.6% of adverse events were caused by negligence, including willful violations of policies.[18] Prelabeling a syringe might be considered a violation.

Errors, on the other hand, include events when things go wrong even if every party involved had the best intentions and was performing properly. Errors can be further broken down into skill-based errors that result in an unintended action. These include *lapses* (mental errors, such as forgetting a step in a procedure) and *slips* (physical errors, such as turning the wrong knob on a piece of equipment).[19] Unintentionally filling a syringe with the wrong clear liquid would be considered a slip. The fact that something is described as human error is not an excuse for tolerating the error or thinking it is inevitable. Lean thinkers work to create an environment where lapses and slips are less likely.

Many errors can often be traced to a lack of training or awareness, a problem that is the responsibility of managers and the system. Lapses can be prevented through the use of checklists and standardized work, while slips and errors can be prevented through error-proofing methods, as discussed in Chapter 8.

There are some simple questions that leaders can ask to help determine if a problem was the result of a systemic error or a willful violation.

Was this an error that has happened before, in some other place, involving some other person?

Would another caregiver or employee likely have done the same thing in the same situation?

Should administration have anticipated that this type of error could have happened?

If an answer to any of these questions is yes, then we probably have a systemic error that cannot be prevented in the future by merely removing a particular "bad apple" from the process. Without Virginia Mason making the systemic change from a clear liquid antiseptic to a gel and swab, the same error might have occurred again with a different technician on a different day.

Just Culture

Instead of assuming that an individual is to blame, unless proven otherwise, a Lean thinker starts by assuming the problem is with the process or the system, unless proven otherwise. Lean has much in common, philosophically, with an approached called "just culture."

James Reason defines a "just culture" as "an atmosphere of trust in which people are encouraged (even rewarded) for providing essential safety-related information, but in which they are also clear about where the line must be drawn between acceptable and unacceptable behavior."[20] A "just culture" "recognizes that individual practitioners should not be held accountable for system failings over which they have no control."[21] It is "just" to protect patients from harm, but it's also "just" to not destroy a healthcare professional's career over understandable human error.

David Marx, JD, quotes Dr. Lucian Leape as saying, "the single greatest impediment to error prevention is that 'we punish people for making mistakes.'"[22] Marx defines four "evils" that lead to patient safety problems:

- Human error: "Should have done other than what they did."
- Negligence: "Failure to exercise expected care. Should have been aware of substantial and unjustifiable risk."
- Recklessness: "Conscious disregard of substantial and unjustifiable risk."
- Intentional rule violation: "Knowingly violated a rule or procedure."[23]

There might sometimes be good reasons why a person intentionally violates a rule. For example, standardized work might say to wear gloves when examining or treating a patient. But, there might be emergent situations where a small delay to put on gloves might not best serve the patient, even if that creates some risk for the patient and the caregiver.

Just culture algorithms help guide people to decide if there was intentional harm or bad intent (which should be punished because the individual is "culpable") or a systemic error (where punishment could be counterproductive when a person is "blameless" in the circumstances). An error is considered systematic in situations where[24]

- Procedures were not available, workable, intelligible, correct, and routinely used
- There are deficiencies in training, selection, or experience
- A person did not knowingly violate a safe procedure

The book *Managing the Risks of Organizational Accidents*, by James Reason, is a great resource for further study.

Examples of Quality Improvement

It is not all bad news in healthcare. Many hospitals are using Lean methods to improve quality and patient safety. VMMC was named a "Top Hospital of the Decade" by Leapfrog Group for their impressive improvement work.[25] With Lean, a better process leads to better results. For example, VMMC has seen 100% compliance with venous thromboembolism (VTE) prophylaxis in the intensive care unit (ICU) for 20 months[26] and reduced pressure ulcers from 8% to 2%, or 838 patients.[27] As a result, VMMC has seen their professional liability insurance premiums fall by 76% since 2004[28] and a 75% reduction in litigation claims.[29]

ThedaCare (Wisconsin) is widely known as one of the leaders in applying Lean to healthcare.[30] Former chief executive officer (CEO) John Touissant, MD, set an ambitious goal of reducing defects by 50% each year.[31] This is not a case of cautious, incremental improvement goal setting—it is a very aggressive goal that seemed likely to drive serious action.

ThedaCare began measuring defects per million opportunities (DPMO) in 2005 and estimated that their processes had 100,000 DPMO in areas, including not always providing consistent protocol-driven care for Code STEMI (segment elevation myocardial infarction) patients. A defect might include an instance when a step in the protocol was not followed, introducing risk to the patient. This corresponded with a Six Sigma-style quality level of 2.78 sigma, where the goal of Six Sigma quality corresponds with 3.4 DPMO. In 2006 and 2007, ThedaCare estimated its defect rates had fallen to 60,000 DPMO (3.05 sigma) and 20,000 DPMO (3.55 sigma), respectively. Overall, they were ahead of the 50% annual goal and continue to improve, aiming for perfection instead of just being better than they were before.

In examples with more specific data, ThedaCare has also

- Reduced lab specimen collection errors from 941 DPMO to just 100[32]
- Improved pneumonia bundle compliance rates from 38% to 95%[33]
- Reduced "early-term" induced births from 35% to zero, shortening neonatal ICU length of stay from 30 days to 16[34,35]
- Reduced medical reconciliation errors on admission from 1.25 per chart to zero, when done by a pharmacist[36]
- Reduced the percentage of warfarin patients with lab readings outside of the safe zone from 40% to 0.3%[37]

As a type of error, specimen collection errors are pretty straightforward. But, in the third example given, ThedaCare started viewing an early-term induction, often done for the convenience of the mother or physician, as a "defect," although it was considered normal beforehand. Medical evidence pointed them not to perform delivery before 39 weeks if at all possible.

Hospitals can take steps, including standardized work, to prevent hospital-acquired infections. Hospitals that have successfully cut infection rates have analyzed work methods to identify the best way to insert lines and catheters. Allegheny General Hospital (Pittsburgh, Pennsylvania) first set zero infections as a goal, an important strategic direction. Second, a team of clinicians standardized the methods for determining the proper line placement location, as well as the methods and tools for inserting the line itself and methods for maintaining the line. Improved communication methods were also put in place when anybody needed help with lines. The results after the first year were dramatic. The rate of line infection was reduced from one in 22 to just one in every 185. They still had not reached the goal of zero infections, but they had made significant progress.[38] Similar results have been achieved throughout the world; in a World Health Organization study on the use of checklists, hospitals in Michigan nearly eliminated catheter-related bloodstream infections and reduced ICU mortality rates by 10%.[39]

Allegheny General also learned that quality improvement freed time for staff to solve problems, to utilize known infection control procedures, and to spend more time on direct patient care. Some hospitals now understand that reducing infections reduces the average length of stay, which essentially frees beds and creates additional capacity, doing so in a far less expensive way than building a new patient tower. These central-line-associated bloodstream infection reductions are clearly good for the patients, the employees, the physicians, and the hospital.

Such infection reduction efforts require leadership, not just the right process. Dr. Richard Shannon, who led the efforts at Allegheny, repeated these results when he moved to the University of Pennsylvania Health System. Using Lean methods and principles, bloodstream infections were reduced by 86%, reducing mortality by 29% and saving $5.1 million over a two-year period.[40]

Finding Root Causes and Preventing Errors

Errors and near misses in hospitals need to be turned into learning opportunities with the goal of preventing future occurrences. When errors are discovered, the best response, in the Lean approach, is to ask two straightforward questions:

1. What allowed that error to occur?
2. What can we do so the error never occurs again?

The Lean response is different from traditional responses to errors, which usually ask, "Whose fault is it?" Managers often look to assign blame and rely on punishment to show they are addressing the problem, asking those employees who remain to "be careful" as an attempt at prevention. Placing blame is often unfair to employees, resulting in frustration, resentment, and the hiding of problems. Telling caregivers to be careful and hanging cautionary signs do not prevent errors from harming other patients.[41] On the contrary, Lean managers start with the assumption that people are trying to do a good job (Douglas McGregor's theory Y)[42] and ask the question "How could this have happened despite the best of intentions?"

To teach problem solving, Toyota offers a two- to three-hour workshop that first covers the basics in about 30 minutes, with the remaining time spent applying these principles and "learning by doing." In application, one goal should be 100% of the right medications given, in the right dose, at the right time, with the other "rights" of medication administration also being correct. Any time that does not happen, there needs to be a signal and immediate problem solving, says Bonini.[43]

Workarounds and the Need for Fixing Root Causes

Before Lean, we often find hospital employees inventing and using workarounds in their daily work. A workaround is a short-term response to an immediate problem that does nothing to prevent the problem from occurring again. For example, a thermometer is missing from an exam room, so the nurse runs to another room to take its thermometer—helping her patient, but creating a new problem for the next patient and nurse in that other room. Although they seem to help in the short term, workarounds ultimately harm both quality and productivity as they doom us to wasting more time in the future responding to that same problem or error. The creativity that goes into workarounds should be redirected into root cause problem solving and continuous improvement.

Time pressures on employees and managers often prevent us from doing deeper analysis and problem solving. At a hospital pharmacy that had not yet implemented Lean, pharmacists spent a good deal of time inspecting physician medication orders and patient charts, looking for errors or process defects. They often found a number of preventable process defects, including

- Orders that did not match what was in the patient's chart
- Doses that were not appropriate for the patient's age, weight, or condition
- Medications that conflicted with recorded patient allergies

When an error was spotted, the pharmacist just corrected it. It was difficult for the pharmacist to give feedback to the person who might have been the original source of the error, be it a physician (who might have written an order incorrectly) or a unit clerk (who might have incorrectly recorded or entered a physician's verbal orders). Rather than blaming individuals (since many people may make the same errors), we should investigate to see if the design of the computer system makes it more likely for an error to occur. The pharmacist felt like there was not the time to call, page, or track down the person who entered the order, or did not want to be in the position of trying to give constructive feedback to a physician, fearing a negative response.

If people are unaware that errors are occurring, they cannot begin a problem-solving process that could help prevent future errors. Pharmacists reported finding the same errors every day, causing frustration from the wasted time and the perceived inability to work with others to fix the root of the problem. When errors occur, people often assume that others do not care or that others are "bad employees." Instead of blaming individuals, we need to shift to a constructive problem-solving mindset. Table 7.1 shows some examples of errors and the reaction of workarounds and blaming versus the problem-solving reaction.

When an error is found, the immediate reaction should still include fixing the problem in the short term. In the case where a pharmacy technician finds a pill in the wrong bin, the pharmacy technician should still put the pill back in the correct bin. This might be called a short-term countermeasure or a containment of the problem, aimed at protecting the customer. As soon as possible, problem-solving measures should be used to identify the root cause so we can prevent reoccurrence of that particular problem through a long-term countermeasure.

Table 7.1 Workarounds and Blaming versus Problem-Solving Mindsets

Problem	Workaround	Blame Mindset	Problem-Solving Mindset
Medications are missing or not available in the cabinet	Nurse walks to other cabinets or units to find the medications	"The pharmacy doesn't help us"	"Why are meds often not available? How can we work together to fix this?"
Labels are crooked on laboratory tubes	Technologist relabels the tube properly	"That assistant never gets this right"	"Is the assistant aware of proper labeling practices and their impact on the process?"
Medical record does not have a diagnosis code that will get the system paid for a home nebulizer	Billing clerk searches through the record to find a way to recode the diagnosis	"The doctor's office doesn't know how to code properly"	"Why do multiple offices make the same error? What is the systemic cause?"
EMR system is too hard to use, information is in too many screens	Nurse creates a hand written single page summary for all patients and key information	"IS and the vendor doesn't care about how we work"	"Can we work with the vendor to create a report or a single screen that matches the way we work?"
Medication is found in the wrong bin	Pharmacy technician puts medication back in the right place	"Other people aren't careful"	"Why could that pill fall into the adjacent bin?"

In some cases, employees take pride in their ability to work around common problems. Heroic measures are often rewarded as a sign of a can-do attitude or a willingness to go above and beyond job expectations. An employee may become known as an expert in working around problems and is often called on to work around problems for others. These employees who define their work as being a hero or frequently working around problems may feel a sense of loss as the system is stabilized and improved with Lean methods.

Adopting these mindsets can create a leadership challenge, as one hospital chief operating officer (COO) realized he puzzled his employees by talking about the newly discovered need to eliminate workarounds. The COO had worked his way up through the organization, starting as an entry-level nurse, and employees knew he had risen through the ranks by being "the best fire-fighter." His pronouncements were counter to his 30 years of demonstrated behaviors, which was difficult to overcome, even as he worked on changing his approach away from being a firefighting senior leader.

Managers and executives sometimes employ ineffective workarounds. For example, an executive might complain that nurses and techs are "wasting time" using websites like Facebook or YouTube at their computers. Instead of asking why staff are doing this, executives often ask the information technology department to block certain websites, causing other problems. For one, blocking websites can have the unintended side effect of preventing staff from accessing valid learning videos. Secondly, the management workaround leads to an obvious staff workaround, where they start accessing such material more discreetly via a smartphone.

Signs do not work. Hospitals have to find better ways to solve this problem other than hanging up clever signs (or wearing buttons) that admonish or encourage people to wash. One hospital had a yellowed hand-washing sign with a 1984 copyright hanging along other signs that featured cute kittens, cartoon germs, or a warning that struck fear in parents. If signs actually worked, hand hygiene compliance problems would have been solved decades ago. Our problems are often more complex, so we need an approach that involves more than the print shop. Organizations are well-intentioned, using signs because they are assumed to be effective (or they don't know what else to do). Instead, we can apply plan-do-study-adjust (PDSA) thinking to these signs: Do they really work, and if not, can we find a better way?

Asking Why Instead of Who

When staff appear to be "goofing off," Lean leaders would ask why employees are not fully engaged in improvement. If there is no direct patient care or value-adding work to do, employees can use free time to work on small *kaizen* improvements or help in other ways. Whatever the solution, asking why is more effective than blaming individuals or jumping to conclusions.

Additionally, when errors occur, the Lean approach prompts us not to ask who, as in "Whose fault is it?" Again, this is the Deming influence in the Lean culture and management system. Recalling Sir Liam Donaldson's quote about needing to eliminate problems in the system, we see similar wording from Gary Convis, former chairman of Toyota Motor Manufacturing Kentucky, who taught "You respect people … you don't blame them. Maybe the process was not set up so well, so it was easy to make a mistake."[44]

Many errors cannot be simply traced to a single individual. We often blame the person who was physically present when the error occurred, but many errors are caused by upstream departments or other processes. When a nurse administers an incorrect medication to a patient, we have to look beyond that nurse to the value stream and different points at which errors could have been introduced into the system. When a pharmacist does catch a medication error, we have to look upstream to the point at which the error was created (without simply blaming the pharmacy tech).

Our first line of questioning ("What could have allowed that to occur?") leads us to systemic root cause problem solving. A *root cause* is an underlying condition or an aspect of the system that led to the error. As the term implies, thinking of the roots of a tree, we have to look beyond the surface symptoms of the problem. If a problem we think is "fixed" reoccurs, it is a sign that we have not discovered or fixed the root cause. This is one reason Lean hospitals must use the plan-do-check-act (PDCA) or PDSA cycle. Any time we put a countermeasure in place for a problem, we have to measure (through observation or metrics), or check, to see that the problem truly has been solved.

Some behavioral experts caution people against asking employees questions that begin with the word *why*, as it can often cause defensiveness.[45] This might be especially true at the start of your Lean journey if a blame-and-shame culture still exists. Be sensitive about this and realize that understanding why a problem occurred can be understood using less blaming phrases such as "What allowed that wrong medication to reach the patient's bedside?" instead of "Why did you send the wrong medication?" Another approach would be to focus on the event and the facts instead of the person, asking questions such as "Why did the wrong medication arrive at the unit?"

Start at the *Gemba*

When an employee comes to report a problem to a manager, the first step for a Lean leader should be to take the discussion and problem solving to the place where the problem occurred, the *gemba*. Lean teaches that problems are more effectively solved at the *gemba* instead of in meeting rooms. Going to the *gemba* allows us to see with our own eyes and to talk with other people who are directly involved in that process. When we are at the *gemba*, we can start asking why in our attempt to discover what could have allowed that problem to occur.

Summary of Lean Problem Solving

- Go to the *gemba*.
- Talk to the people working in the process or area in question.
- Go beyond surface problems to the root cause (use the five whys).
- Look across departmental boundaries, across the value stream.
- Improve processes before spending money on capital or expansion.

Dr. John Toussaint shared a story in his book, *On the Mend*, that illustrates these principles and mindsets.[46] While on a *gemba* walk, Toussaint asked a nurse in a unit about their remarkably low medication error rate. The nurse told Toussaint, bluntly, they were simply not recording the errors. This admission might be a fireable offense in some organizations.

Instead of yelling or telling the nurse to follow the process, the first question was an honest and sincere "Why?" Why were they not recording the errors? The nurse responded that there was not enough time, and that the reporting method in the computer system was too complex. The nurse showed Toussaint how she had to go through different screens in the computer system and it took almost four minutes to submit an error. In addition, there was fear that reporting an error would bring punishment instead of improvement. These systemic and cultural issues are the responsibility of management.

The fact that the nurse felt comfortable raising the issue without fear of blame or punishment was a positive sign of a maturing Lean culture. Another positive sign was that Toussaint thanked the nurse for bringing up the issue so openly. Toussaint immediately contacted the information systems department and requested that they improve the system to make it easier to report medication errors, an excellent example of servant leadership.

Find Root Causes Using Simple Methods

One powerful, yet simple, method for getting to a root cause of a problem is the five whys method, developed at Toyota. In this method, we ask a sequential series of why questions until we get an answer that seems like a correctable root cause. There is no particular magic in the number five. Sometimes, the root cause is found after three whys, and sometimes it might take ten. The point is to get beyond more commonplace problem solving that might only ask why once, leading to a surface symptom instead of the root cause. The five whys method is particularly effective in a group setting, where people can build off each other's ideas and gain shared understanding across department boundaries. For this to work well, we need an open environment in which people are less defensive and less fearful about being honest.

The five whys can be used in response to a specific process defect, for example, "Why did that specimen arrive at the lab unlabeled?" or "Why did that nurse walk back to the station instead of using the portable computer?" The five whys can also be used to ask general questions, such as "Why are patients being boarded in the ED?" When we have multiple contributing causes, we can use other basic quality tools like a "fishbone" diagram, otherwise known as an Ishikawa diagram.[47]

A fishbone diagram can be helpful in breaking down a large, complex problem. For example, a hospital in Ontario, Canada, identified that the length of stay was too long for many patients, as measured by what they called "conservable days." One conservable day would be a patient staying overnight in the hospital for four nights when they were medically ready to go home after three. When the hospital asked, "Why are there too many conservable days?" there was a single, simple root cause. A fishbone diagram allowed a rapid improvement event team to brainstorm different contributing causes, as shown in Figure 7.1.

A few of those causes were then identified as the greatest contributors to the problem, such as "inpatient care delayed" and "waiting on long-term care [LTC] beds." Additional whys were asked to drill down toward root cause or causes that would ideally be addressed through various countermeasures. Various causes become smaller bones on the fishbone diagram. The team thought the LTC bed capacity was out of their scope (requiring process improvement in the LTC facility or an increased government budget). But they continued to ask why inpatient care was delayed, and

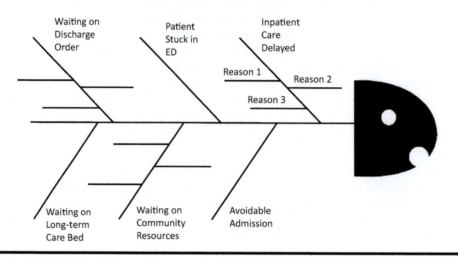

Why are patients in the hospital longer than necessary?

Figure 7.1   A fishbone diagram.

reasons included "patients not being mobilized enough." Another branch of the causal tree went as follows:

1. Why are there delays in inpatient care?
   a. The plan of care (POC) is unclear
2. Why is the POC unclear?
   a. Responsibility for the POC is unclear (this was one of many answers)
3. Why is responsibility unclear?
   a. There is poor role definition for RNs and MDs
4. Why?
   a. Unclear who the most responsible physician (MRP) is
5. Why?
   a. The "bullet round board" is not updated
6. Why?

The big broad problem of conservable days was seemingly unsolvable. But, the team was energized by the ability to solve some of the smaller problems that contributed to the larger problem, such as improving the consistency of updating the bullet round board. Doing so required additional whys that could not be answered by that team, leading them to work with unit teams to better understand the problem in the *gemba* and asking them for solutions to that problem (and others).

Bill Schmidt, CEO of New London Family Medical Center, says, "One thing we've learned is the power of grass-roots problem solving." In one example, staff reacted to a patient fall with a 10-minute "mini root cause analysis" discussion. The brief discussion was followed immediately by testing ideas through rapid PDSA cycles, instead of "having a six-hour discussion" as many organizations might do.

A3 Problem Solving

An increasingly popular problem-solving methodology in the world's hospitals is the "A3." An A3 gets its name from the international paper size that is roughly 11 inches by 17 inches. The method began in the 1960s as part of the Japanese "quality circles" movement but evolved at Toyota to become their standard format for problem solving, planning, and status reports. More important than the size of paper or any given template is the structured problem analysis (left side of the A3) and further PDCA/PDSA (right side of the A3) thinking and scientific method that is embedded in the document.

A problem-solving A3 should be embedded with Lean thinking and practices. An example A3 is shown in Figure 7.2.[48] In writing the issue and background statements, authors of an A3 must take care not to jump to a solution. An A3 titled "Get All Patients to the OR Prep Room by 7:00 a.m." might be jumping to a solution for the broader problem of cases not starting on time. A better issue or title might be "First Case On-Time Starts" or "Improving OR Flow."

ISSUE   *Patients complain that meals are not hot in the Rehab Unit.*

BACKGROUND

Patient satisfaction survey results are less than 80% for hot meals. Meals are on large carts and often travel to other floors before arriving at the Rehab Unit.

CURRENT CONDITION

PROBLEM ANALYSIS

1. *Coffee arrives cool at the patients' bedside*
     Why? The coffee is not coming out of the coffee maker at the specified temperature (180 degrees)
          Why? The thermostat in the coffee maker is faulty
     Why? The coffee sits in cups for a long period of time while the trays are being assembled
          Why? Cups are poured in advance and arranged with other beverages to be added to the tray as prescribed
2. *Food spends too much time in transit*
     Why? Trays travel from kitchen to the 3rd floor before being delivered to Rehab
          Why? Delivery carts are large and trays for more than one unit are loaded together on one cart
               Why? Delivery carts are designed for more trays than there are patients in Rehab

(a)

Figure 7.2   (a,b) An example of problem-solving A3. (Jimmerson, Cindy, *A3 Problem Solving for Healthcare: A Practical Method for Eliminating Waste.* New York: Productivity Press, 2007.)

TARGET CONDITION   Title: Hot Food in Rehab Unit

TO	Tim
BY	Jane
DATE	March 5, 2007

COUNTERMEASURES

1. Repair thermostat in coffeemaker.
2. Rearrange order of filling coffee cups to fill one by one at the end of tray assembly.
3. Deliver trays to patients in order of assembly.

IMPLEMENTATION PLAN

What	Who	When	Outcome
Replace thermostat in coffee maker	Jane	March 12	Coffee will come out at 180 degrees
Re-order the assembly of trays so that coffee is poured and put on trays just before they leave the kitchen	Jane	March 20	Coffee will spend less time on the tray before arriving to patient
Use smaller transport carts so they carry only one unit's trays	Jane/ Tim	April 1	Less travel time from kitchen to Rehab
Educate staffre: delivering trays from top of cart to bottom to avoid 1st loaded tray spending most time on cart	Tim	April 5	Trays will all be warm when delivered

COST/BENEFIT

Cost	$$$
Thermostat for coffee maker	$8.50
Benefit	$$$
Patients are satisfied with the temperature of the food they receive	Patient Satisfaction

FOLLOW UP

May 30, 2007 – Patient satisfaction scores for hot food: 100%

(b)

Figure 7.2 (Continued)

Instead of relying on opinions or feelings, the current condition combines fact-based data that are gathered by going to the *gemba* and observing the process in a detailed way. The emphasis in this early stage is to "grasp the situation."[49] The current condition might include a value stream map or other drawings and visuals.

Before moving to the right-hand side of the A3 to talk about possible "countermeasures" (the word *solution* sounds too definitive for continuous improvement), we have to make sure we understand the root cause or causes of the problem. To solve a problem, we must properly define and understand that problem.

John Shook from the Lean Enterprise Institute says the three most common problems in problem solving involve not properly grasping the situation:

- Assuming you know what the problem is without seeing what is actually happening
- Assuming you know how to fix a problem without finding out what is causing it
- Assuming the action you have taken to fix a problem is working without checking to see if it is actually doing what you expected[50]

The target condition (similar to a future-state map), the countermeasures (what we plan on trying), and the detailed implementation plan comprise the "do" of the PDSA cycle. An A3 also prompts us to plan for the check and the adjust, or act, phases. The author of an A3 anticipates which qualitative and quantitative factors will be used to evaluate success in the problem-solving process. In the PDSA mindset, we do not assume that our countermeasures will work. If our honest assessment shows that improvement did not occur, we can go back and try again in a blame-free manner, capturing and reflecting on what we learned about the situation and our problem-solving efforts.

Writing an A3 is not meant to be a solitary exercise. A3s are usually written as part of a group improvement exercise, and even solo A3 authors do their best when coached by an experienced A3 mentor. As John Shook said, "It takes two to A3," meaning the author and coach.[51] The best A3s are iterative documents, continually refined and adjusted as the author and team better grasp the situation and root causes, frontline workers provide additional feedback, and the mentor asks challenging questions and provides constructive feedback.

A3s are also used to gather feedback and input from a larger group, laying the groundwork (*nemawashi* in Japanese) for consensus that ensures the problem and root cause are understood, and that the team is in agreement regarding how to move forward. The A3, as presented to others, is the basis for discussions and further refinement of the ideas on the paper.[52] The Lean facilitator at one hospital commented, "When I coach A3 authors, I always know they are on track when they have to rewrite something on either side when they share progress with people."

Effective use of the A3 methodology leads to people development in addition to tactical problem solving. John Toussaint, MD, said:

> A3 thinking was critical in my development as a Lean leader. It made me understand that getting the problem clearly defined is the most important aspect of improvement work. Thinking about it in a medical model, the hard part of what a doctor does is to make the diagnosis. This occurs when all background information (history), the patients' current state (physical examination) and core data (lab analysis) are completed. The treatment is fairly straightforward, once you understand the problem. This is basic scientific method thinking. It's simple but it changes the way you manage."[53]

Example of the Five Whys: Hand Hygiene

Hospitals often struggle with getting caregivers and employees to follow proper hand hygiene practices. Different studies place hand hygiene adherence rates as anywhere from 30% to 70%. It is common knowledge that unclean hands can spread germs that cause hospital-acquired infections (HAIs), harming patients, increasing length of stay, and increasing costs. Hospitals have policies that say, for example, that people must clean their hands on the way in and out of any patient room or patient encounter. Managers cannot audit this by following people 100% of the time. Employees often resent being spied on by managers or high-tech monitoring and fear being written up. They would likely prefer to have their leaders be partners in improvement instead of having them serve a policing role.

Solving this problem should start with the question "Why?" The focus must be on eliminating barriers to hand hygiene—not making excuses for people, but finding legitimate problems that can be solved.

One hospital had a team of nurses and other employees go through a five whys exercise. Their first attempt at answers can be seen in Figure 7.3. You can see there was not a single answer to the question, and that the team probed certain responses more deeply—this initial brainstorming could have also been done as a fishbone diagram.

Many of the root causes focused on training, resources, and senior leadership, rather than blaming the individual employees. The group found a few practical changes that could be made to further encourage hand hygiene, such as making carts more readily available to help keep people's hands free. More training could educate people about using only hand gel instead of alternating between gel and soap and water. Gel dispensers had already been placed in every patient room and many other locations, but putting them on the portable computers was another small step that could be taken. Doing more to make carts available was another action, utilizing the 5S method to properly locate and organize carts.

The question of time and general overwork was also raised as a barrier to hand hygiene. Employees and physicians complained that they were too busy or that they had too many patients to see in a short time. This is an instance when, instead of taking this overwork as a given, waste reduction can free time that can be used for proper hygiene. Additionally, level loading (*heijunka*) and standardized work methods can be used to make sure that workloads are properly balanced and that staff members are not pressured into cutting corners to get their work done.

Many of the practical items, as well as the more difficult cultural issues, can be traced to the responsibility of top leadership. We are more likely to find effective solutions when we quit blaming or assuming that problems are the fault of individuals. Blaming others is often a hard habit to break, as this is deeply engrained behavior in humans from early childhood through our experience working in organizations.

Was this five whys exercise a cure-all? No, but it helped shift the mindset from one of thinking nothing could be done about the problem to a belief that actions could be taken that would help increase hand hygiene compliance.

If you look at the problem slightly differently, one could ask, "Why do we have to wash our hands?" One answer might be, "Because we touch the patients." Some have suggested that one real root cause solution would be to avoid touching patients unless absolutely necessary.[54] A more complete solution to hand hygiene would include training and a leadership commitment to responding appropriately when unsafe behaviors are seen.

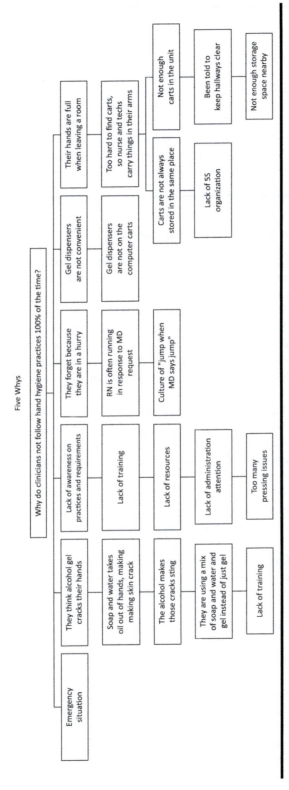

Figure 7.3 An illustration of a "five whys" problem-solving method, showing multiple branches and root causes.

At one Pittsburgh veterans' hospital, an effort was made to solve problems that prevented employees from washing properly, issues raised in response to the why question. Supplies and tools (such as stethoscopes) were properly located in each room. The unit started testing all patients for methicillin-resistant *Staphylococcus aureus* (MRSA) to properly isolate carriers. With the new methods, MRSA infection rates fell 90% in a short time. The approach, unfortunately, spread to only one other unit in the hospital and fell apart when the main driver of the program left to work on another project. That illustrates the need for having a true systematic standardized work system, as opposed to relying on a single change agent.[55]

Example of the Five Whys: Lost Specimens

A few years into their Lean journey, a hospital lab realized that they were still fighting their hospital's predominant shame-and-blame culture, even with the local improvements they had made in methods and departmental culture.

On a single day, the histology lab lost three separate patient specimens. This delayed testing and results and meant that two of the patients had to undergo a second biopsy—adding pain for the patient and consuming additional time and resources, increasing cost due to the waste. Because this was a serious sentinel event, the quality department at the hospital did what they called a root cause analysis, with the conclusion being that the histology technologist simply needed to be retrained.

The lab director realized that the analysis was flawed. A truly actionable root cause had not been identified. He wondered how retraining could be the answer if the original training had not prevented a lost specimen. So, he started his own analysis—going to the *gemba* and talking to all of the histology techs to understand what had happened. The analysis looked like this:

> Why were the specimens lost?
> *The one technologist was overworked that morning.*
> Why?
> *Because one technologist was sick, and one was late due to traffic.*
> Why was the technologist rushing and trying to do the work of three people?
> *He was trying to hit the "first slides by 8:00 a.m." deadline.*
> Why?
> *He wanted to please the pathologist.*
> Why?
> *That is the traditional hospital culture.*

This view led the director to see the problem as the local management system, not as "that technologist." The team agreed that "first slides by 8:00 a.m." should be more of a general goal than a hard deadline that had to be hit no matter what. In talking with the pathologists who receive slides from histology, nobody had ever yelled at the lab for being late or being slow (a fact confirmed by the technologists). Part of the director's response was to emphasize that nobody should ever cut corners to hit that, or any, target.

The director also realized that there had been no standardized work for how to respond when one or two people were off. With a short staff situation, work would obviously be done more slowly than with all three technologists. In addition, there had been no communication plan for letting the pathologists know that slides would be late and why (working more slowly due to short staffing). The pathologists, sharing everybody's concern for quality and patient safety (not wanting mixed-up specimens), were happy to have communication in place of rushing and cutting corners.

So, what had started with an exercise in blaming the individual turned, instead, into an exercise in improving standardized work, communication, and the management system. The lab director, managers, pathologists, and team members looked deeply into their problems, finding proactive ways to prevent reoccurrence of the same situation and errors.

Toyota's Practical Problem Solving

Lean problem-solving methods can range from the simple (just do it) to the extremely rigorous, such as an A3. Whether a problem and the analysis method are simple or more complex, the common thread should be the PDSA discipline.

One more rigorous method that incorporates previous themes of going to the *gemba*, not jumping to solutions, and root cause analysis is sometimes described as "practical problem solving" (PPS) or the "eight-step problem-solving method." Some even call this "eight-step A3 problem solving," as the steps are very similar to the thought process that would be seen in an effective A3.[56] PPS lays out a multi-step approach similar to structured analysis methods used under the banner of Total Quality Management (TQM), as TQM "quality circles" often have 10 similar steps.[57]

The steps of PPS are shown in Table 7.2, as mapped to the PDSA cycle.

In keeping with the "don't jump to solutions" theme, steps one through five are focused on understanding the problem and the current situation. For steps seven and eight, we would not assume that every problem-solving attempt or countermeasure is going to be successful, initially. If we do not see the results we expected, if we are not hitting our target, or if a side effect has been created, we would loop back to an earlier step in the PPS process and try again. PPS is rarely a

Table 7.2   Steps in the Practical Problem-Solving Process

Step #	Step	PDSA Phase
1	Clarify the problem	Plan
2	Break down the problem	
3	Target setting	
4	Root cause analysis	
5	Develop countermeasures	
6	See countermeasures through	Do
7	Monitor the results and processes	Study
8	Standardize successful processes	Adjust

simple linear path. More often, we iterate and cycle back to an earlier step as we discover more about the problem.

Clarifying the Problem

Before clarifying a problem, we might start with what some call a "big vague concern," such as "nobody's scanning the patient paperwork upon check-in." To clarify the problem, we would try to state the problem in a more specific, fact-based way. This might require *gemba* observation and discussion or some data collection. It's important to understand the scenario, answering questions of what, when, who (not whose fault, but who is involved), where, and how. A precise problem statement is a measurable gap between actual performance and desired performance.

There are two types of gaps: caused and created. A caused gap is seen in a situation where our performance is not meeting a goal or target. For example, a department has a goal of reaching the 90th percentile in patient satisfaction surveys, but the current performance is in the 40th percentile. This gap between 40th and 90th percentiles has multiple causes that we could investigate in the name of improving patient satisfaction. A created gap is a situation where a current goal or target is being met, but leaders decide to "raise the bar" on performance. For example, once the department has reached the target of 90th percentile, a gap no longer exists. Leaders might choose to increase the goal to the 95th percentile, thereby creating a gap to be closed through additional problem-solving efforts.

Breaking Down the Problem

Breaking down the problem can include narrowing the scope to something that is more accurate, more understandable, or more easily solvable. A reported problem might actually only be occurring in one department in one hospital within our system. Or, we might choose to solve a subset of a broad problem, as we saw earlier in the conservable days example. Working to solve that smaller problem (or at least make things a little better) would contribute to reducing length of stay, at least somewhat. A team working to close a created gap in patient satisfaction might identify meals and food to be the largest remaining cause of dissatisfaction, giving some focus on their efforts. There might be a gap between 85% patient satisfaction regarding food, with a goal set at 95%. That helps focus our efforts.

When data are available, Pareto charts can be helpful statistical tools to focus problem-solving efforts. For example, if the big vague concern is "patients are unhappy with their meals," a Pareto chart can help us understand and prioritize the different reasons patients are unhappy, including food tasting bad, being the wrong temperature, or not having enough variety. The "Pareto principle" often means that 80% of complaints or problems are caused by 20% of the causes, meaning focused improvement efforts can sometimes drive meaningful results. Without data, teams are often forced to guess about likely causes until they are able to prove or disprove their hypothesis by testing countermeasures.

Target Setting

In the paper scanning example, a team defined a more formal problem statement, saying, "Only 35% of records brought in by patients to outpatient surgery are scanned into the [electronic medical record] EMR system, instead of 100% as desired." Note the problem statement does not blame, it does not propose causes, and there is no solution stated. As the team started to understand why paper was not being scanned 65% of the time, somebody walked to talk to a downstream customer—the surgical department.

In this situation, 100% is their target. In some situations, a team might state that the ideal situation, say for patient falls, is zero, but the short-term goal for a particular effort might be to reduce falls by 50%. That improvement would be followed by additional efforts to further reduce falls.

Problem Solving Is Iterative

Problem-solving teams quickly learn that the PPS approach is often neither straightforward nor linear. In the process of breaking down the problem or setting a target, what the team learns by going to the *gemba*, gathering data, or talking to others may cause them to go back and make a change.

As they talked to internal customers, the paper scanning team was stunned to hear the surgical department ask, "Why are they scanning any of the printouts the patient brings in? Those are just printouts from the EMR to begin with." Given this new knowledge, the team circled back to redefine their problem statement so that instead of going from 35% to 100% scanning, the goal was to go from 35% to zero. Had the team not gotten out of their silo to talk to the customer, they might have wasted a lot of time or might have actually made things worse by solving a problem that was not really a problem.

Countermeasures Help Verify or Disprove Root Causes

In steps four through seven, the team would start with tools mentioned earlier, including fishbone diagrams and five whys analysis. It can be easy to think one has discovered a root cause through such discussions. However, talking about a root cause can only lead to a *suspected* root cause. Developing and testing countermeasures allows us to prove or disprove the effect of that cause, allowing us to answer, in practice, the question, "Have we found the root cause?" Implementing countermeasures is not just a matter of getting things done; it's about better understanding our problem and situation.

In the patient meals scenario, Pareto and root cause analysis might suggest that the main cause of patient dissatisfaction is the wrong temperature being caused by "charger plates" not being used properly. Asking "why?" again might uncover that training was ineffective or that one piece of equipment was faulty. Until a countermeasure is tested, all we have is a theory. If a countermeasure is proposed to improve food temperatures, it has to be tested in practice. If fixing the faulty machine, a countermeasure, results in better food temperatures and higher patient satisfaction, we have proven our understanding of the root cause. If we could turn off the countermeasure (assuming it was safe to do so), and the problem reappeared, that would give us further evidence that our root cause analysis was accurate and helpful.

Standardize Successful Improvements

After step seven, the team might realize they have not made a measurable improvement, which suggests they have not really found a root cause. That means they need to go back and better understand the system or try other countermeasures to address newly suspected root cause(s). If a change was deemed successful, step eight says to standardize the new methods. As discussed in Chapter 5, updating our standardized work documents and methods helps us manage that system to ensure sustainment and continued improvement, along with the spread of newly discovered practices to other units or hospitals in our system.

Be Proactive and Use Failure Modes and Effects Analysis

A methodology called failure modes and effects analysis (FMEA) is a helpful tool for identifying and prioritizing errors that could occur in a process, rather than just reacting after an incident has occurred. FMEA was originally developed by the U.S. military in 1949 to proactively anticipate potential failures and became more widely used in the automotive industry in the 1970s. FMEA is already commonly used in hospital transfusion medicine and pharmacies but can be used to improve any process.[58]

An FMEA document is typically built in a spreadsheet and is based on team brainstorming about what could go wrong in their process. As with standardized work and *kaizen*, FMEA is most effectively done by the people who actually do the work, although the FMEA process could be facilitated by someone experienced with that methodology. An FMEA could have helped antici- pate the error that caused the death of Mary McClinton, along with other risks in the interven- tional radiology setting.

To create an FMEA, we brainstorm all of the different errors that could occur in an area or a process. For each failure mode, the team ranks each of three categories:

What is the severity of the error when it occurs?
What is the likelihood of occurrence?
How difficult is it to detect the error?

Each category gets a score on a 1–10 scale (low to high), and the scores are multiplied together to give a risk priority number (RPN) for each failure mode. To help prioritize our improvements (assuming we cannot fix everything at once), we sort the failure modes by their RPN score. The failure modes with the highest scores should receive our initial attention. If a failure mode is very likely to occur (score of 10), is very hard to detect (score of 10), and would cause a patient death (score of 10), the RPN score would be 1,000.

Using an FMEA is in keeping with the Lean concept that we have to be open in talking about problems (and potential problems) in our workplace. FMEA is just a tool. If participants in an FMEA feel somehow pressured to understate the likelihood or severity of an error or overstate their ability to detect the error, our problem prevention might not be as effective. Leadership must take the responsibility for creating an environment of openness in the name of patient safety and error prevention. Again, no problems is a problem.

Proactive Resolution of Near-Miss Problems

In addition to using FMEA to anticipate problems, hospitals must react appropriately to near misses, turning each occurrence into an opportunity to drive process improvements that prevent that same near miss (or actual harm) from happening again.

One foreseeable hospital process defect is administering an incorrect intravenous drip to a patient. Potential risks include giving the wrong dose or the wrong medication. One study estimated a clinical error was made in 69.7% of intravenous preparations and administrations, and 25.5% of those were "serious."[59] While there are numerous checks and rechecks of intravenous bags during the intravenous production process in the pharmacy, errors still get through to the point at which a nurse is poised potentially to administer the wrong drug. The fact that all errors are not caught in the pharmacy is evidence of how 100% inspection is not 100% effective, even with multiple successive inspections. Some problems, such as a drug incompatibility, can be difficult to find through inspection, while other errors are caused in the nursing units, including incorrectly setting a rate on a pump.

Think about a case in which a nurse properly inspects the medication and finds an error at that last stage of the value stream. In a perfectly error-proofed process, an error should never get that far. The nurse's reaction—and the reaction of the organization—to such a near miss are crucial. A non-Lean organization might consider the nurse catching the error by the pharmacy as proof that "the system worked." People might ask, "What is the problem? The patient was not harmed." Catching the error before the patient was harmed is certainly a positive event, but that's a containment step, not a long-term root cause solution. It should be considered the sign of a weak process that the error got as far as it did. The next time, the nurse might not catch the error in time or at all, leading to harm.

A common workaround would be for the nurse to correct the immediate problem, for example, by going and getting the right dose. The real problem is not solved, however, as the error is likely to be repeated if the root cause of the underlying error is not solved. The nurse might say, "We were lucky. Let's hope that doesn't happen again." There might be a temptation not to report the problem or to cover up the near miss. Employees, including the nurse, might not have the time to follow up properly or conduct root cause problem-solving analysis because of overwork and the need to move on to caring for other patients. The error will certainly happen again, at some point, because of the same systemic cause.

In the McClinton case, let us assume that the syringe was being filled with the wrong solution (or almost being filled), but another person in the room saw the error and called it out. This would-be "near miss" (or a "good catch" as some call it[60]) would have been as much of an opportunity to improve the process and to prevent any harm to patients.

In a Lean culture, we need a number of conditions to ensure that the root cause is solved, including

An environment in which employees are encouraged to stop and contain problems when they are found (or as soon as possible)

Available time for root cause problem solving (freed up through earlier waste reduction)

A blame-free environment in which employees are not punished for pointing out problems, near misses, or risks

Managers who take the time to help resolve issues with or for employees as they are raised

Cross-functional cooperation to work together on problems that are generated upstream but create waste for a downstream function or department

The Heinrich Safety Pyramid

The Alcoa Corporation has built an impressive track record for improving employee safety in what was traditionally considered a dangerous industry. Rather than being resigned to employee injuries and deaths, the company, under the leadership of CEO Paul O'Neill, set out on a quest to become the safest company to work for in the world. Although many in the company felt it was unrealistic, O'Neill set a goal of zero lost workdays as the only acceptable goal—a goal that was set to break the complacency and the idea that accidents were bound to happen. The company reduced its lost work per day rate from 1.87 in 1987 to 0.42 in 1997[61] and then down to 0.07 in 2013 (compared to an American manufacturing average of 1.0).[62] Alcoa posts updated data on its public website and states, "This accomplishment requires the commitment of not only our leaders but also our employees, who are empowered to take personal responsibility for ensuring their safety and that of their coworkers—even if that means stopping work when they feel unsafe or unsure."[63] O'Neill has, in recent years, focused on spreading these mindsets and results throughout healthcare, including his work with the Pittsburgh Regional Health Initiative and Dr. Shannon.

A key to the safety improvement at Alcoa was the use of the safety triangle or pyramid, created by H. W. Heinrich, as shown in Figure 7.4. Regardless of the exact ratios, the triangle shows that we have many more opportunities to react to minor incidents, solving the underlying problems that might have otherwise later caused a major injury or fatality. Rather than only reacting to employee fatalities or severe injuries, O'Neill and Alcoa management focused on learning from near misses, minor injuries, and unsafe behaviors. Unsafe behaviors might include rushing through one's work, acceptance that risk is part of the job, being distracted, or being fatigued.

This same idea can apply to hospitals, for both patient care and employee safety. For example, it is estimated that for every drug mistake there are 100 near misses.[64] ThedaCare's Theresa Moore, formerly a plant manager at Alcoa, recalls that "there was a high sense of urgency around near misses and, if there was an injury in your plant, there was an executive review of your analysis within 24 hours." ThedaCare is now "working lower on the pyramid," says Moore, looking for true root causes of injuries in the name of preventing future occurrences.

For every case in which a patient died because a central line was flushed with insulin instead of heparin, there are many more instances when insulin and heparin vials are sitting next to each other in bins at a nurses' station. For every intravenous administration error, there might have been many instances when intravenous solutions, stored next to each other in overflow bins, fell into the wrong location. Each time a wrong-site brain surgery was performed, there may have been many cases when the "time-out" or "universal protocol" process was not followed. Reacting

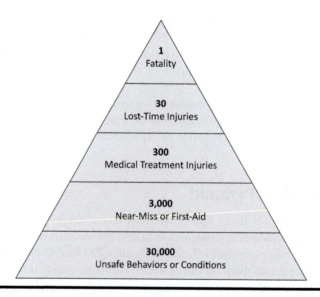

Figure 7.4 The Alcoa "Safety Pyramid." (Adapted from Woletz and Alcoa.)

with root cause problem solving and prevention when unsafe conditions are found can help avoid patient harm and catastrophic situations.

In a Lean culture, leaders have to create an environment in which employees are encouraged or obligated to speak up when they identify unsafe conditions or see a near miss. We must change the culture of workarounds that leads employees to "fix" problems without telling anybody, a culture in which we consider fixing problems as part of our job instead of viewing the problems as waste or process defects that must be prevented.

Conclusion

Improving quality, through Lean methods, relies on philosophy and mindset in addition to specific tools, like fishbone diagrams and FMEAs. It can take time for individual leaders, or an entire organization, to unlearn old habits of blaming individuals, hiding problems, and employing workarounds. Leadership can set expectations, such as a goal of zero infections, that emphasize that patient safety incidents should not be considered a given or necessary part of providing care. Beyond just setting goals, however, leaders also have a responsibility to set an example for the daily behaviors and structured methodologies that will lead to meaningful and sustainable improvement. Training in tools can help, but establishing a culture of safety, quality, and root cause problem solving is critical.

Lean Lessons

- Hospitals need to shift from naming, blaming, and shaming to a more productive systemic improvement method.
- Most errors are caused by the system rather than by individual negligence.
- Look at the process rather than blaming individuals.
- Start your problem solving by going to the *gemba*.
- Keep asking why to identify the root cause of a problem.
- Use the simplest problem-solving method that you can for a particular problem, but realize it's always based on PDSA.
- Lean provides structured problem-solving methods, but does not create a simple cookbook method of analysis and improvement.
- Use proactive methods for identifying problems before they occur.
- Use near misses as opportunities to prevent future problems that would cause harm.

Points for Group Discussion

- What are the lessons from the Mary McClinton case? Is it fair that Carl Dorsey lost his job? Was that "just?"
- Why do we tend to blame individuals when errors occur? What can we do to reduce our tendency to blame?
- If workarounds prevent identification of root causes, why are they so tempting?
- Is leadership taking responsibility for creating an environment of openness in the name of patient safety and error prevention?

- What can we do to encourage people to report errors, near misses, and unsafe conditions?
- How can we free time for proper root cause problem solving?
- How do you turn errors into learning opportunities?
- How do we find a balance between blaming the system and making excuses for people?
- What prevents hospitals, employees, or physicians from being open about problems, errors, or near misses?
- Is a goal of "zero infections" inspiring or demotivating? Why is that? What can you do to change the culture that makes it OK to aim for zero?

Notes

1. Kenney, Charles, *Transforming Healthcare: Virginia Mason Medical Center's Pursuit of the Perfect Patient Experience* (New York: Productivity Press, 2010), 58.
2. Ibid., 59.
3. Nalder, Eric, and Cathleen Crowley, "When few hospitals report, honest ones look bad," *Hearst Newspapers*, July 30, 2009, http://www.chron.com/news/article/When-few-hospitals-report-honest-ones-look-bad-1721173.php (accessed March 26, 2015).
4. Ibid.
5. Szabo, Liz, "Global goal: Reduce medical errors," *USA Today*, August 23, 2005, http://usatoday.com/news/health/2005-08-23-medical-errors_x.htm (accessed March 26, 2015).
6. Lillie, Ben, How Do We Fix Medicine? Atul Gawande at TED2012, http://blog.ted.com/atul-gawande-at-ted2012-2/ (accessed October 8, 2015).
7. Woolcock, Nicola, and Mark Henderson, Blundering hospitals "kill 40,000 a year," *The Times Online*, August 13, 2004, http://www.thetimes.co.uk/tto/news/uk/article1927712.ece (accessed August 9, 2015).
8. Black, Nick, "Management mistakes in healthcare: Identification, correction and prevention," *Journal of the Royal Society of Medicine*, 2005, 98: 432–433.
9. Bodinson, Glenn W., "Change healthcare organizations from good to great," *Quality Progress*, 2005, 22–29.
10. Institute for Healthcare Improvement, Pursuing Perfection: Report from McLeod Regional Medical Center on Leadership Patient Rounds, http://www.ihi.org/resources/Pages/ImprovementStories/PursuingPerfection ReportfromMcLeodRegionalMedicalCenteronLeadershipPatientRounds.aspx (accessed October 8, 2015).
11. Testimony on Patient Safety: Supporting a Culture of Continuous Quality Improvement Hospitals and Other Health Care Organizations, testimony of Carolyn M. Clancy, MD, before the Senate Permanent Subcommittee on Investigations Committee on Governmental Affairs, June 11, 2003, Agency for Healthcare Research and Quality, Rockville, MD, http://www.hsgac.senate.gov/download/clancy-testimony (accessed August 9, 2015).
12. Committee on Quality of Healthcare in America and Institute of Medicine, *To Err Is Human* (Washington, DC: National Academies Press, 2000), 43.
13. Breuer, Howard, "Dennis Quaid's newborn twins hospitalized," *People*, 2007, http://www.people.com/people/article/0,,20161769,00.html (accessed March 26, 2015).
14. Deming, W. Edwards, *The New Economics*, 2nd edn (Cambridge, MA: MIT CAES, 1994), 33.
15. Committee on Quality, *To Err Is Human*, 19.
16. Wachter, Robert, and Peter Pronovost, "Balancing 'no blame' with accountability in patient safety," *New England Journal of Medicine*, 2009, 361: 1401–6.
17. Committee on Quality, *To Err Is Human*, 110.
18. Merry, Allan, and Alexander McCall Smith, *Errors, Medicine, and the Law* (Cambridge: Cambridge University Press, 2001), 32.
19. Committee on Quality, *To Err Is Human*, 54–55.

20. Reason, James, *Managing the Risks of Organizational Accidents* (Surrey: Ashgate Publishing, 1997), 195.
21. Brunt, Barbara, Developing a Just Culture, http://healthleadersmedia.com/page-1/NRS-251182/Developing-a-Just-Culture (accessed October 8, 2015).
22. Marx, David, Patient Safety and the Just Culture: A Primer For Health Care Executives, http://www.safer.healthcare.ucla.edu/safer/archive/ahrq/FinalPrimerDoc.pdf (accessed October 8, 2015).
23. Marx.
24. Frankel, Allan, Decision Tree for Unsafe Acts Culpability, http://www.ihi.org/resources/pages/tools/decisiontreeforunsafeactsculpability.aspx (accessed October 16, 2015).
25. Leapfrog Group, The Leapfrog Group Announces Top Hospitals of the Decade, http://www.leapfrog-group.org/news/leapfrog_news/4784721 (accessed October 8, 2015).
26. Virginia Mason Medical Center, Virginia Mason to Receive 2015 Washington Quality Award for Improving Patient Safety, https://www.virginiamason.org/body.cfm?id=158&action=detail&ref=3939 (accessed October 8, 2015).
27. Minich-Pourshadi, Karen, Systemwide Process Improvement, http://www.healthleadersmedia.com/print/MAG-264905/Systemwide-Process-Improvement (accessed October 8, 2015).
28. Virginia Mason Medical Center, Fast Facts, Virginia Mason Production System, https://www.virginiamason.org/workfiles/pdfdocs/press/vmps_fastfacts.pdf.
29. Minich-Pourshadi.
30. Mamberto, Carola, "What factory managers can teach hospital wards," *Wall Street Journal*, 2007, B3.
31. Toussaint, John, presentation, First Global Lean Healthcare Summit, June 25, 2007.
32. Toussaint, John, and Roger Gerard, *On the Mend: Revolutionizing Healthcare to Save Lives and Transform the Industry* (Cambridge, MA: Lean Enterprise Institute, 2010), 69.
33. Ibid., 29.
34. Toussaint, John, "Writing the new playbook for U.S. health care: Lessons from Wisconsin," *Health Affairs*, 2009, 28: 1347.
35. Toussaint and Gerard, *On the Mend*, 106.
36. Ibid., 24.
37. Ibid., 120.
38. Hollenbeak, Christopher S., Dispelling the myths: The true cost of healthcare-associated infections, *Healthcare Financial Management*, 2007, http://www.highbeam.com/doc/1G1-160927074.html (accessed August 9, 2015).
39. Pronovost, Peter, et al., "Sustaining reductions in catheter related bloodstream infections in Michigan intensive care units: Observational study," *British Medical Journal*, 2010, 340: c309, http://www.bmj.com/content/340/bmj.c309.full (accessed March 26, 2015).
40. Shannon, Richard P. "Eliminating hospital acquired infections: Is it possible? Is it sustainable? Is it worth it?" *Transactions of the American Clinical and Climatological Association*, 2011, 122: 103–114. Print.
41. Agnew, Judy, and Aubrey Daniels, *Safe by Accident?* (Atlanta, GA: Performance Management Publications, 2010), 57.
42. Kopelman, Richard E., David J. Prottas, and Anne L. Davis, "Douglas McGregor's theory X and Y: Toward a construct-valid measure," *Journal of Managerial Issues*, 2008, http://www.jstor.org/stable/40604607?seq=1#page_scan_tab_contents (accessed August 9, 2015).
43. Bonini, presentation at 2014 Lean Healthcare Transformation Summit.
44. Rode, Jenny, "Breaking the Rice ceiling," *Battle Creek Enquirer*, 2006, http://www.battlecreeken-quirer.com/apps/pbcs.dll/article?AID=/20060212/NEWS01/602120304/1002 (accessed August 9, 2015).
45. McSween, Terry E., *The Values-Based Safety Process: Improving Your Safety Culture with Behavior-Based Safety* (New York: Wiley, 2003), 90.
46. Toussaint and Gerard, *On the Mend*, 115.
47. Ishikawa, Kaoru, *Introduction to Quality Control* (New York: Productivity Press, 1990), 448.
48. Jimmerson, Cindy, *A3 Problem Solving for Healthcare* (New York: Productivity Press, 2007), 102.
49. Shook, John, *Managing to Learn* (Cambridge, MA: Lean Enterprise Institute, 2008), 13.

50. Shook, John, Managing to Learn, workshop, January 19, 2010.
51. Shook, Managing to Learn, 113.
52. Sobek, Durward K., II, and Art Smalley, *Understanding A3 Thinking: A Critical Component of Toyota's PDCA Management System* (New York: Productivity Press, 2008), 82.
53. Toussaint, John, personal correspondence, April 7, 2011.
54. Gawande, Atul, *Better* (New York: Metropolitan Books, 2007), 21.
55. Ibid., 24.
56. Goldsmith, Robert H., *Toyota's 8-Steps to Problem Solving* (Charleston, SC: Create Space, 2014), 22.
57. Graban, Mark, "Quality Circles" Are Alive and Well in Japanese Organizations; We Might Call It A3 Problem Solving, http://www.leanblog.org/2014/11/quality-circles-are-alive-wed-probably-call-it-a3-problem-solving/ (accessed October 8, 2015).
58. Institute for Healthcare Improvement, All FMEA Tools, http://app.ihi.org/Workspace/tools/fmea/AllTools.aspx (accessed August 9, 2015).
59. Westbrook, Johanna I. et al., "Errors in the administration of intravenous medications in hospital and the role of correct procedures and nurse experience," *BMJ Quality & Safety*, 2011, 20: 1027–34. *PMC.*, Web, October 9, 2015.
60. Kearns, Sarah, Good Catch Program Encourages Reporting Near-Miss Medical Errors, http://healthleadersmedia.com/page-1/QUA-248568/Good-Catch-Program-Encourages-Reporting-NearMiss-Medical-Errors (accessed October 8, 2015).
61. Committee on Quality, *To Err Is Human*, 160.
62. Alcoa, Creating a Safety Culture Where Zero Is Possible, http://www.alcoa.com/sustainability/en/info_page/safety.asp (accessed October 8, 2015).
63. Ibid.
64. Bates, D. W., D. L. Boyle, M. B. Vander Vilet, J. Schneider, and L. Leape, "Relationship between medication errors and adverse drug events," *Journal of General Internal Medicine*, 1995, 10: 199–205.

Chapter 8

Preventing Errors and Harm

A Serious Problem with Large, Unknowable Numbers

It is hard to know exactly how many patients are harmed by preventable errors or how many die as a result. Different studies use various methods to estimate the scale of the problem in different countries. A landmark 1999 Institute of Medicine (IOM) study said medical mistakes cause as many as 98,000 deaths a year in the United States.[1] In 2014, Ashish Jha, MD, professor of health policy and management at Harvard School of Public Health, testified to a U.S. Senate subcommittee, saying, "The IOM probably got it wrong. It was clearly an underestimate of the toll of human suffering that goes on from preventable medical errors."[2]

In 2013, the Journal of Patient Safety published that an estimated between 200,000 and 400,000 deaths per year occur due to preventable harm, which would make medical error the third leading cause of death in the United States.[3,4] Another study estimated that 18% of patients were harmed, and more than 60% of those injuries were considered preventable. Data in a 2011 study in the journal *Health Affairs* showed that medical errors and adverse events occur in one of three admissions, and that errors may occur 10 times more frequently than the IOM study indicated.[5]

Medical harm is not a uniquely American problem, as per-capita death rates are very similar in Canada and in other developed countries.[6] Regardless of the exact numbers or the methodologies used to reach them, it is easy to agree that too many patients are harmed and that much of that harm is preventable through Lean methods and mindsets.

Moving beyond Blaming Individuals

The late management professor Peter Scholtes said, "Your purpose is to identify where in the process things go wrong, not who messed up. Look for systemic causes, not culprits."[7]

In recent years, a number of high-profile medical errors have made the news, in addition to the untold suffering that occurs on a daily basis. Josie King, an 18-month-old girl, died at Johns Hopkins after being given an additional dose of morphine by a visiting nurse after a physician had already changed her orders. The error worsened her dehydration as she should have been on the path to recovery.[8] Josie's tragedy has inspired her mother, Sorrel,[9] and clinical leaders such as

179

Dr. Peter Pronovost to work tirelessly to educate healthcare professionals and patients about the need to improve processes, systems, and communication in healthcare.[10]

The twin babies of the actor Dennis Quaid were harmed after multiple nurses mistakenly gave them adult doses of the blood thinner heparin while in the care of the neonatal intensive care unit (NICU) at Cedars-Sinai Hospital in California. This was the result of a number of process errors that should not have occurred.[11] Nurses did not think to check for an adult dose, as the pharmacy should have never delivered an adult dose to a neonatal unit. Even if nurses had been on guard for that mix-up, the packaging of heparin and Hep-Lock were too similar: two shades of light blue that could be hard to distinguish in the proverbial dark room at 2:00 a.m. Sadly, Cedars-Sinai could not prevent this medical harm after the same set of circumstances had led to the deaths of three babies at an Indianapolis, Indiana, hospital.[12]

After the incident, Dr. Michael L. Langberg, the chief medical officer for Cedars-Sinai, said, "This was a preventable error, involving a failure to follow our standard policies and procedures, and there is no excuse for that to occur at Cedars-Sinai."[13] Situations like this illustrate the need for leaders to oversee and manage standardized work (as discussed in Chapter 5). Failures to follow standardized work must be detected proactively, rather than reacting after harm has occurred. Leaders must work with staff to make sure it is possible to follow policies and procedures, improving training and reducing waste to make sure enough time is available to do work the correct way.

The Darrie Eason Case

In another case that made the news, Darrie Eason, a woman from New York, was the victim of an unnecessary radical double mastectomy after another patient's laboratory specimen was mislabeled with her information.[14] Not only was Eason misdiagnosed with cancer, but another patient had her cancer diagnosis delayed because of the mix-up. As is common in such cases, news reports included quotations that blamed an individual, as the chief executive officer (CEO) of the private pathology lab that handled her case said, "The technician responsible for the mix-up also no longer works there."[15]

Another news report contained the detail that the "technician who handled Eason's test admitted to his supervisors that he 'occasionally cut corners by batching,' or handling more than one tissue specimen at a time, and did not always verify patients' initials when labeling them."[16] That sounds like a situation in which standardized work was not being followed. If not, why?

One could ask if "occasionally" cutting corners was actually a common practice in the lab. Given that working on more than one specimen at a time greatly increases the risk for errors, why would this take place, especially given that observation shows there is minimal time savings from labeling multiple patients' slides at once? Lean thinkers might suspect that the technicians had too great a workload or they were pressured, explicitly or implicitly, into working faster than they should have been.

If supervisors knew that corners were being cut, what is their responsibility in this case? The supervisors should have been ensuring that standardized work (one specimen at a time) was followed, and that the environment and workload allowed people to work at the correct pace for high quality. The CEO said the technician no longer worked there, but what about the supervisors? What about the CEO's responsibility? As Dr. W. Edwards Deming wrote, quality starts with top management.

The Eason case is not an isolated error, as other cases are regularly reported, even highlighting "batching" and working on multiple cases at the same time as a cause.[17] I have seen the practice

Figure 8.1 Three stacks of slides representing three different patients, creating risk of error.

of "batching" histology specimens in a number of hospital laboratories, as shown in Figure 8.1. The three stacks of slides are all sitting in the field of work, each having been labeled for a different patient. When the laboratory manager was asked about this opportunity for error (thinking in terms of failure modes and effects analysis [FMEA], as described in Chapter 7), the manager said, "It's OK. My people are very careful." Careful people are a good starting point, but that is, unfortunately, not enough to ensure perfect quality and patient safety. To ensure the best quality, we need Lean methods, such as error proofing, and Lean mindsets, such as looking at systems instead of blaming individuals.

Creating Quality at the Source through Error Proofing

Ensuring quality at the source (the Japanese word *jidoka*), through detecting and preventing errors, is one of the pillars of the Toyota Production System.[18] The history of *jidoka* dates to the time before the company even built cars. Sakichi Toyoda invented a weaving loom that automatically stopped when the thread broke; this invention saved time, increased productivity, and reduced the waste of defective fabric.[19] The automatic weaving loom and that level of built-in quality have served as an inspiration throughout Toyota and among adopters of the Lean approach.

Thinking back to the Quaid case, even if we have not had a death at our own hospital from a mix-up of heparin doses, the opportunity for error and the unsafe conditions might be present. Preventing that same error from occurring in our own hospital is good for the patients (protecting their safety), good for the employees (preventing the risk that they will participate in a systemic error), and good for the hospital (avoiding lawsuits and financial loss, while protecting our reputation as a high-quality facility).

Being Careful Is Not Enough

When managers blame individuals for errors, there is an underlying—but unrealistic—assumption that errors could be prevented if people would just be more careful. Errors are often viewed as the result of careless or inattentive employees. Warning, caution, or "be careful" signs throughout our hospitals are evidence of this mindset. If signs or memos were enough, we would have already solved our quality and safety problems, not only in hospitals but also in the world around us.

A good exercise is to go on a "*gemba* walk" through a department looking for signs that remind or tell employees to be careful. Each sign is an indicator of a process problem and evidence that the root cause of the problem has not been properly addressed through error proofing. A good metric for the "Leanness" of a hospital might be the number of warning signs—fewer warning signs indicate that problems have been solved and prevented, eliminating the need for less-effective signs and warnings.

For example, we might see a sign in the pharmacy that reads: "Please remember fridge items for cart delivery." This suggests that this process error was made at least once. We need to ask why it was possible to forget the refrigerated items. Does the department not have a standard checklist that is used before going out to make a delivery? Is the refrigerator in an inconvenient location, making it easy to forget about when employees are in a rush?

One hospital laboratory had two analyzers that performed similar testing. For one analyzer, five specimen tubes would get loaded into a plastic rack, which was then inserted into the analyzer. The newer analyzer had a warning from the manufacturer printed on the loading chute that stated "CAUTION: When setting the stat sample rack, confirm the direction of the rack." When asked how often a rack was inserted incorrectly, facing the wrong way, the lab supervisor said it happened quite frequently, causing the rack to jam and not load properly, delaying test results and taking up time. The older analyzer, used as a backup, was physically error proofed, making it impossible to load the rack in a backward orientation; it was a far more effective approach than the warning sign on the other.

Nurses' stations might be full of signs, such as "Avoid overtightening syringes in microbore tubing." In this case, a new type of tubing was being purchased by the hospital, tubing for which the connector had "wings" that made it too easy for nurses to get too much leverage into the twisting motion. Instead of asking nurses to be careful, a root cause might point more to the design of the tubing or the purchasing decision of the hospital. Too many signs can, in and of themselves, present a safety hazard. If each bears a truly important admonition, the worker can develop what pilots call "alarm fatigue," with too much confusing dialogue going on around them.

Of course, we would not want just to go around taking down signs without first preventing the problem. Signs may be, at best, a short-term response (or a symptom of a problem) that can eventually be replaced with a root cause fix.

Why 100% Inspection Is Not 100% Effective

Healthcare organizations tend to rely on inspection and double-checks, for which the focus is on finding problems before they reach the patient. Error prevention is preferable to inspection for a number of reasons. First, if we rely on people to inspect their own work or work done by others, we introduce the risk of human error into the process. At the end of a long day, a person might forget to do a particular inspection or check, a problem that we could address by rotating jobs frequently to keep people mentally alert. Or, we can rely on checklists, similar to what an airline pilot uses before every flight, as mentioned in Chapter 5. Asking people to not get fatigued is unrealistic and violates Lean's core "respect for people" principle.

Adding extra inspections is not guaranteed to prevent surgical errors, as evidenced by Rhode Island Hospital, which was in the news for having performed four wrong-site brain surgeries over six years.[20] After an incident in July 2007, the hospital was ordered to add a second physician to review the proper site before surgery (a form of inspection). Even so, another wrong-site surgery occurred in August 2007, leading to yet another review. The hospital is now requiring an attending physician be present for brain surgery procedures since the last error was committed by a resident. The hospital appears to be blaming residents, saying they are incapable of working unsupervised. The added attending physician is serving partly as an inspector of the resident's work. It is possible that this inspection may also suffer from the same sort of human error that failed to prevent previous errors that occurred when the first extra inspection was in place. Residents may very well be capable on their own, without errors, if better error-proofing methods and standardized work were in place. Lean thinkers would ask why those errors occurred, looking for the systemic problem that allowed the same error to occur so many times. As further evidence of a systemic problem that was not being solved, the same hospital had a wrong-side surgery on a cleft palate patient in 2009.[21]

Eric Cropp, a pharmacist in Ohio, was convicted and jailed in 2009 for his role in a medication error that killed a two-year-old girl, Emily Jerry.[22] Cropp was blamed for not finding an error created upstream by a pharmacy technician who was admittedly distracted and violated a standardized work practice. Michael Cohen for the Institution of Safe Medication Practices was among those who spoke out and called Cropp an easy target, saying that healthcare quality and patient safety are better served by focusing on process issues that allow tragedies like this to occur.[23] Emily's father, Chris Jerry, has appeared with Cropp at conferences, publicly forgiving him and speaking out about the injustice of jailing an individual for a systemic error.[24] Dr. Lucian Leape, a world-renowned patient safety expert, said, "I think criminalization is a terrible thing. In every case, there were obvious explanations for why a mistake happened and those explanations have to do with the systems they were working in and the institutions that were responsible for those situations."[25]

When multiple people, in parallel or sequentially, have responsibility for inspecting for a defect, a normal human reaction is to get complacent, to think that the other person will catch an error if you miss it. Or, it is easy to "see" what we expect to see (the lack of an error) instead of what is actually in front of us. At one health system's billing department, up to five different employees inspected charts to make sure details, such as the ordering physician's name, were correct. In this case, even with all of the inspections, errors were frequently found at the final inspection step and sometimes got out as erroneous payment submissions.

Types of Error Proofing

Error proofing can be defined as the creation of devices or methods that either prevent defects or inexpensively and automatically inspect the outcomes of a process each and every time to determine if quality is acceptable or defective. Error proofing is not a specific technology. Rather, it is a mindset and an approach that requires creativity among those who design equipment, design processes, or manage processes.

Make It Impossible to Create the Error

Ideally, error proofing should be 100% effective in physically preventing an error from occurring. In everyday life, think about gasoline pump nozzles. Diesel nozzles are larger and do not fit into an unleaded gas vehicle. It is impossible to make that error. The error proofing is more effective than if we only relied on signs or warning labels that said "Be careful; do not use diesel fuel in this vehicle." This error-proofing method does not, however, prevent the opposite error of using unleaded fuel in a diesel vehicle (an error that, while harmful to a diesel engine, is less harmful than putting diesel into a regular car).

In a hospital, we can find examples of 100% error proofing. One possible hospital error, similar to the gas pumps, is connecting a gas line to the wrong connector on the wall. Many regulators and gas lines have pins and indexing that prevent a user from connecting to the wrong line, medical air instead of oxygen, as shown in Figure 8.2. The different pins are more effective than color coding alone would have been. The connectors will not fit, and there is no way to circumvent the system to make them fit.[26]

One type of preventable error is the injection of the wrong solution into the wrong IV line, an error that has been reported at least 1,200 times over a five-year period, meaning it has likely occurred far more that, given the common underreporting of errors.[27] Instead of telling clinicians just to be careful, some hospitals have switched to IV tubing that physically cannot be connected to feeding syringes—a strong form of error proofing, similar to the gas line error proofing. Again, a physical device that prevents an incorrect connection is more effective than simply color coding the lines, as some hospitals have done.

In 2006, a Wisconsin nurse, Julie Thao, was convicted and imprisoned after mistakenly injecting an epidural, instead of an antibiotic, into the bloodstream of a 16-year-old expectant mother. The patient's death "might have been avoided if containers, tubing and connectors for epidural medications were vastly different from intravenous medications," said a newsletter from the Institute for Safe Medication Practices. In fact, the Joint Commission had put out a bulletin in early 2006 warning of such line risks, yet a patient died, and an experienced nurse ended up in jail.[28]

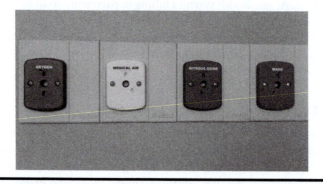

Figure 8.2 Error-proofed connectors for medical gases.

Make It Harder to Create the Error

It is not always possible to fully error proof a process, so we can also aim to make it harder for errors to occur. Think about the software we use every day to create word-processing documents (or e-mail). One possible error is that the user accidentally clicks on the "close" button, which would lose the work. Most software requires a confirmation step, a box that pops up and asks, "Are you sure?" It is still possible for a user to accidentally click "yes," but the error is less likely to occur. A better, more complete error proofing is software that continuously saves your work as a draft, preventing or severely minimizing data loss. Another type of error is forgetting to attach a file to an e-mail before hitting the send button. There are software options that look for the word "attached" or "attachment," creating a warning message for the user if one tries to hit send without a file being attached.

In hospitals, a certain type of infusion pump has a known issue that makes it too easy for a data entry error to occur—it even has its own name, the double-key bounce. The keypad often mistakenly registers a double digit, so if a nurse enters 36, it might be taken as 366 and could lead to an overdose.[29] Some hospitals have posted signs asking employees to be careful. A better approach might be a change to the software that asks "Are you sure?" and requires an active response when double numbers are found or when a dose above a certain value is inadvertently entered. This approach would still not be as effective as a redesign or an approach that absolutely prevents that error from occurring. Such a change also would not prevent the mistaken entry of 90 instead of 9.0, highlighting the need for multiple countermeasures to address complex problems.

Hospitals have already made some efforts to error proof medication administration, as medication errors are a common cause of harm to patients; yet some experts estimate there is still, on average, one medication error per day for each hospital patient.[30] Automated storage cabinets are one error-proofing method that many hospitals have implemented to help ensure that nurses take the correct medications for their patients. With these cabinets, nurses must scan a bar code or enter a code to indicate the patient for whom they are taking medications. The computer-controlled cabinet opens just the drawer (and sometimes just the individual bin) that contains the correct medication. This makes it harder to take the wrong drug, but there are still errors that can occur:

The nurse can reach into the wrong bin in the correct drawer (with some systems).
The pharmacy tech might have loaded the wrong medication into the bin.
The wrong medication might be in the correct package that the pharmacy tech loaded into the correct bin.
The correct medication might still be given to the wrong patient after being taken from the cabinet.

When error proofing, we have to take care that we do not create complacency and overreliance on a particular device. Properly error proofing the entire process requires wider analysis and error-proofing methods at each step along the way.

Often, the workplace can be retrofitted with simple, inexpensive error-proofing devices if we have the mindset of prevention. One laboratory implemented two simple error-proofing devices in a short time. In one area, a centrifuge had knobs that controlled timing and speed—knobs that were too easily bumped by a person walking by the machine. Instead of hanging a "be careful" sign, a technologist took a piece of clear plastic packaging material that would have otherwise been thrown away and put it over the knobs, as shown in Figure 8.3. The prevention method was

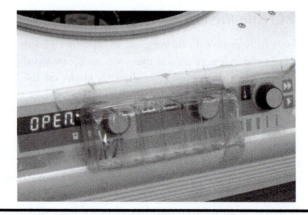

Figure 8.3 Simple error-proofing device that protects against accidental bumping of two centrifuge knobs.

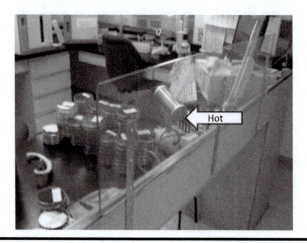

Figure 8.4 Plexiglass shield prevents burns and specimens from being dropped off in the wrong location.

effective, cost nothing, and was probably faster than making a sign. The mindset was in place to figure out how that error could be prevented.

In the microbiology area, visitors dropped off specimens on a counter and were often tempted to reach across the counter rather than walking to the end, where the official drop-off spot was located. The problem with reaching across the counter is that a person, unfamiliar with the area, could have easily burned himself or herself on a small incinerator that sat on the counter, without an indication that it was hot. Instead of posting warning signs, a manager had maintenance install a flexiglass shield that prevented people from reaching across the bench, as shown in Figure 8.4. It was a small investment but helped prevent injury better than a sign.

Pharmacies often have signs warning personnel about high-risk medications, for which similar names or different doses can cause harm to patients. Many pharmacies are rethinking the practice of placing medications in alphabetical order on shelves in an effort to prevent some errors. In one case, UPMC St. Margaret reduced readmission rates for chronic obstructive pulmonary disease (COPD) by 48% by moving different doses of a drug that is commonly used with these patients. Instead of the 0.63- and 1.25-milligram doses being side by side, they were placed in different drawers with distinctive labels.[31]

Make It Obvious the Error Has Occurred

Another error-proofing approach is to make it obvious when errors have occurred, through automated checks or simple inspection steps. The early Toyota weaving loom did not prevent thread from breaking, but it quickly detected the problem, stopping the machine and preventing bad fabric from being produced.

One possible error in instrument sterilization is that equipment malfunctions or misuse result in an instrument pack not being properly sterilized. There might be multiple methods for error proofing the equipment or its use, but common practice also uses special tape wraps or inserts that change colors or form black stripes to indicate proper sterilization. The absence of these visual indicators makes it obvious an error has occurred, helping protect the patient.

In a hospital setting, there is a risk that intubation tubes are inserted into the esophagus instead of the trachea, which would cause harm by preventing air from getting to the patient's lungs. A 1998 study indicated this happens in 5.4% of intubations.[32] Another study suggested that "unrecognized esophageal intubations" occurred in 2% of cases, meaning the error was not detected or reversed quickly. Warning signs posted on the device or in the emergency department would not be an effective error-proofing strategy. If we cannot engineer the device to ensure the tube only goes into the airway, we can perform a simple test after each insertion. Plastic aspiration bulbs can be provided so the caregiver can see if air from the patient's lungs will reinflate a squeezed bulb within five seconds.[33] If not, we can suspect that the tube is in the esophagus, and look to correct the error before the patient is harmed. This form of error proofing is not 100% reliable because it relies on people to adhere to the standardized work that they should check for proper placement.

Other error proofing might include monitors and sensors that can automatically detect and signal the anesthesiologist that the patient was intubated incorrectly, although there are limitations to the effectiveness of monitoring oxygen saturation levels as an inspection step for this error. A chest X-ray might also be used as an inspection method, but studies show that is an ineffective method.[34] "Commonly used" clinical inspection methods in this case are often inaccurate, so medical evidence should drive the standardized work for how clinicians check for intubation errors.

Make the System Robust So It Tolerates the Error

At gas stations, there is a risk that a customer could drive away without detaching the pump nozzle from the car. They have been able to error proof this not by physically preventing the error or by hanging signs; instead, gas stations have anticipated that the error could occur and designed the system to be robust and allow for this. If a driver does drive off, the pump has a quick-release valve that snaps away and cuts off the flow of gasoline, preventing a spill or possible explosion (although you might look silly driving down the road with the nozzle and hose dragging from your vehicle).

In a laboratory, one hospital found a test instrument that was not designed to these error-proofing standards as the instrument was not robust against spills of patient specimens. The lab had responded by posting two separate signs on the instrument that told employees: "Do Not Spill; Wipe Spills Immediately." The signs did nothing to prevent the error as employees generally tried not spilling patient specimens. The root cause of the situation was that a circuit board in the instrument was exposed underneath the place where specimens were loaded. A different hospital, using that same equipment, posted a memo notifying staff that they had "blown three electronic boards in just a few weeks," which cost $1,000 each. The memo emphasized that people should not pour off specimens or handle liquids above the equipment as part of their standardized work. As a better root cause preventive measure, the designer of the instrument should have anticipated that patient specimen spills were likely to occur at some point in the instrument's use and taken steps to protect the sensitive board.

One lesson for hospitals is to consider design and error proofing, even going through an FMEA exercise, when buying new equipment. Hospitals can pressure manufacturers and suppliers to build error-proofing devices into equipment, using their market power to reward suppliers who make equipment that is more robust against foreseeable errors.

Error Proofing, Not Dummy Proofing

Error proofing has a Japanese equivalent term, *poka yoke*, which is sometimes used in Lean circles. With this phrase, the focus is on the error itself, and our problem-solving response is to understand and prevent the error. The phrase *mistake proofing* is sometimes used interchangeably with *error proofing*, but that phrase seems to steer focus toward who made the mistake and blame. Errors occur, often as the result of a system, in which a *mistake* is defined as "a wrong action attributable to bad judgment or ignorance or inattention."[35] Not all errors are necessarily caused by bad judgment, ignorance, or inattention.

Everyday use of the English language features phrases such as "idiot proofing" or "dummy proofing." Terminology like this should not be used, as it does not demonstrate respect for people. Errors, particularly in hospital settings, are not caused because people are stupid. Errors are caused by smart people who mean well but are forced to work in complex and often broken systems.

There is another Japanese phrase, *baka yoke*, which translates to "fool proofing." Shigeo Shingo told a story about using the *baka yoke* phrase in a factory in 1963. Shingo wrote, "One of the company's part-time employees burst into tears when the department head explained that a 'fool-proofing' mechanism had been installed because workers sometimes mixed up left- and right-hand parts. 'Have I really been such a fool?' the employee sobbed."[36]

As much as some of us might not want to admit it, we are all human, even in a medical environment, and we are prone to committing errors and mistakes. Systems need to be designed and error proofed accordingly.

Examples of Error Proofing in Hospitals

There are many examples of error-proofing methods that already exist in hospitals, with varying degrees of effectiveness. Many of the examples we see are error proofing through standardized work, a method that is more likely to reduce errors than to prevent them altogether.

Banned Abbreviations as Error Proofing

Many hospitals have implemented lists of banned handwritten abbreviations that have the potential to be confusing or misinterpreted. For example, micrograms and milligrams can be confused when micrograms is written by hand and abbreviated with the Greek letter for *micro*, leading to an incorrect dose being given to a patient. Rather than telling doctors and employees to be careful, hospitals have recognized there is a risk from using the old abbreviations. The preferred abbreviation is to designate micrograms as "mcg," which is much harder to confuse with milligrams ("mg") when written by hand. In addition, the use of the letter U for units can be mistaken for a zero, leading to a dosing error.

The challenge with this form of error proofing is that we are relying on individuals to follow the new standardized work. It is not enough to say, "We have a policy in place, so the problem is solved." Leaders must check constantly for adherence to the standardized work and need to encourage employees to monitor each other for, in this case, the proper use of abbreviations.

In a Lean hospital, when the old abbreviation is found, we cannot just work around the problem by fixing the abbreviation (as might be done by a nurse or a unit clerk). Employees must feel obligated to address the process defect (somebody using the banned abbreviation) with the physician, or report the practice to managers, using something like the "patient safety alert" process at Virginia Mason Medical Center (Seattle, Washington).[37] Unfortunately, a survey by the American Association of Critical-Care Nurses showed that fewer than 10% of physicians, nurses, and other critical care providers directly confronted their colleagues, and 20% of physicians had seen patient harm as a result. Leaders have to create an environment in which raising a patient safety concern does not lead to punishment or retribution, which is one reason caregivers would avoid confronting each other. Hospitals might also want to consider providing training in constructive confrontation and communication skills to help employees work together more effectively. Teaching healthcare workers the most effective way to speak up is one aspect of the increasingly popular "crew resource management" (CRM) training that brings aviation and cockpit safety practices into healthcare.[38]

In the CRM approach, workers are not "encouraged" or "empowered" to speak up: They are expected to speak up. At Allegheny General Hospital in Pennsylvania, where central-line insertion and care were being 100% standardized, the chief of medicine, Dr. Richard Shannon, instructed the nurses to stop a nonstandard procedure. Until this time, this was not part of the hospital culture. Ultimately, the nurses did stop procedures that were being done incorrectly, and Dr. Shannon backed them up. The result was a change in culture, more respect for nurses as team members, and drastically reduced central-line infections.[39]

Leaders must follow up with physicians and remind them of the importance of using the approved abbreviations, emphasizing the impact on patient safety (focusing on the customer) and, secondarily, the risk to the hospital if an error were to occur. It can be a difficult dynamic when we are reliant on keeping physicians happy to drive new patient revenue to the hospital. In cases like this, hospitals in a community should reach common agreements that they are going to hold all physicians accountable, equally, to standardized work and patient safety guidelines, reducing the risk that a physician takes his or her patients to a competing hospital.

Computer Systems as Error Proofing

One technological method for reducing handwriting errors, for pharmacy prescriptions, laboratory test orders, or other communications, is electronic systems, such as computerized physician order entry (CPOE) or other electronic medical record (EMR) systems. The Leapfrog Group estimates that if CPOE were implemented at all urban hospitals in the United States, as many as three million serious medication errors could be avoided each year.[40] By 2010, only 14% of hospitals had at least 10% CPOE use, the minimum required for so-called meaningful use standards.[41] But, as the result of federal stimulus efforts, 72% of hospitals had CPOE by 2012.[42] A study at Brigham and Women's Hospital (Boston, Massachusetts) showed that CPOE adoption reduced error rates by 55%, and serious errors fell by 88%.[43]

Even at hospitals with CPOE, physician resistance is often high, particularly when systems are not designed effectively around physician workflow. As with nurses not wanting to use mobile computer carts, physicians might resist using CPOE or EMR systems if the technology slows them down. The situation is complicated by dynamics between physicians and hospitals, where most physicians are not direct employees. This eliminates the ability of management to mandate use of the system through traditional supervisor control. Of course, as discussed in Chapter 5, the Lean management style relies more on explaining why and convincing people of the benefits of a tool or method instead of relying on formal positional authority. When physicians, or others, resist standardized work or new tools, we should first ask why.

The former Toyota executive Gary Convis is often quoted as being told by Japanese Toyota leaders to "lead the organization as if I had no power."[44] Although Convis had much formal power (with thousands of employees reporting to him), relying on mandates was a last resort, after first using coaching, setting an example, and understanding others to help them achieve their goals. This leadership style should be particularly transferable to a hospital environment in which senior leaders have little or no formal control over physicians.

In a further connection between quality and efficiency, CPOE and other hospital information systems provide automated checks of pharmacy prescriptions, inspecting for interactions and patient allergies, among other process defects. This reduces the amount of time required of pharmacists for manual order review and inspection, freeing them to serve more of a clinical advisory role to physicians and patients.

Alerts sound like a good solution, but some studies show "alerts are only modestly effective at best."[45] EMR and CPOE systems also introduce the risk of alarm fatigue if systems present too many warnings deemed to be incorrect or unimportant by clinicians. Experts recommend improvements such as ensuring that inconsequential alerts are eliminated, that alerts are tailored to patient characteristics, and that only severe alerts interrupt workflows.[46]

Dr. Bob Wachter of UCSF Medical Center (San Francisco, California) wrote about how new residents were told by senior residents to "ignore the alerts" by just clicking through them.[47] This, among other problems, led to a pediatric patient mistakenly receiving 38 times the normal dose of a medication. Pharmacists and nurses along the way either ignored warnings or were too trusting of automation and technology that gave the appearance of being error proofed. Scanning the bar codes on 38 times too many pills only ensures that the wrong dose is being given to the right patient. Technology can help but must be part of a holistic system design.

Case Example: Best Practices versus PDSA

While Lean emphasizes a structured, controlled, and experimental method for solving problems and testing new methods (plan-do-study-adjust or PDSA), some question if all that's needed is for hospitals to find and adopt proven "best practices" that are recommended by other health systems, clinical associations, or government bodies.

A hospital had a patient fall that, sadly, resulted in a fatal injury. One of the nurses involved reviewed three years' worth of charts of patients who had fallen. She looked for commonality in the patients and their conditions and developed a scale and a paper form that could be used to evaluate patients for the risk of falling, allowing caregivers to better prevent falls. When presented with that option, senior leaders told staff to implement and use the Hendrich II fall risk scale instead, as that is considered to be a best practice.

What happened? The number of falls actually increased, even with that protocol being used. Senior leaders were frustrated with the results, but staff pushed back and reminded them they chose the scale. Staff were allowed to try their own form, which was actually more prescriptive and more standardized. What happened then? Falls were reduced significantly. The team continued to improve their scale and protocol, adding checks with certified nursing assistants (CNAs), leading to even better results.

Then, there was a patient fall. The hospital CEO came and personally ran a 10-hour root cause analysis meeting. The chief nursing officer said that "started the healing process," as "everything the CEO said gave them confidence they had done everything they could," and that the protocol had been followed. However, there had been an unseen possibility, which gave them an opportunity to update the scale for future use.

Preventing Surgery Errors through Error Proofing

Wrong-site surgeries, while not the most frequently occurring medical mistake, can have a severe impact on patients, creating high-profile cases in the news. One study estimated that a typical large hospital would have a serious surgical incident every five to 10 years.[48] Mistakes like these can be error proofed through standardized work (including checklists) and visual management methods, as they are often caused by poor communication, time pressures, and organizational dynamics that prevent people from speaking up.

In July 2003, the Joint Commission released its "Universal Protocol for Preventing Wrong Site, Wrong Procedure, and Wrong Person Surgery," aimed at putting standardized work methods in place for accredited hospitals. The three major components of the protocol are

A formal process for presurgical verification
Marking the operative site
A time-out process done immediately before the procedure

Since this is a standardized work approach to error proofing, the success of the method mainly depends on consistently following the standard. The Joint Commission stated that time-out compliance is only at 78% to 80%,[49] a slight increase from the 2007 report of 74.2%.[50] Nurses and other employees are often afraid to speak up with certain surgeons, so leaders have an important role in creating an environment in which fear does not prevent the time-out from taking place.

Guidelines include the person performing the procedure marking the site in an unambiguous way (such as "YES") and making sure the mark remains visible after skin prep. An "X" (a commonly used mark) might be interpreted as "cut here" or "wrong spot," an ambiguity that could lead to an error. Compliance with this protocol is higher, at 93.4%. Leaders need to ensure that surgeons are not just following the letter of the law, as one news account suggested some surgeons make what one surgical chief called "passive-aggressive marks," tiny marks that cannot be seen and cannot be helpful.[51]

As with any example of standardized work, leaders have an obligation to look for signs that methods like the universal protocol are not being followed. We need to do so proactively, rather than assuming the standardized work is being followed and just reacting after an error occurs. Inspections and audits can be done respectfully, but send a message that patient safety must always be the top priority. Leaders can also continually emphasize the importance of taking time for quality when employees are concerned about moving patients through operating rooms as quickly as possible.

Stopping the Line (*Andon*)

A method frequently associated with Toyota is the *andon*, cords or buttons near the assembly line that are activated when any worker sees a problem. Lights blink and chimes sound. Within seconds, a team leader appears to help the production associate. The line will stop if additional time is needed to solve the problem before the car moves on to the next station. In more than 99% of cases, the problem is solved quickly without stopping production.[52] Problems are generally fixed at the source (the concept of *jidoka*) instead of being passed along to be fixed at the end of the line.

In a hospital setting, we can teach the *andon* concept, the idea that any process should be stopped at the sign of a problem (or problems should be solved immediately if possible). The time-out process is one example, but ThedaCare (Wisconsin) took the idea of stopping the line even further, in the name of patient safety.

In 2004, ThedaCare had gone nine years without a wrong-site surgery before one occurred. Then, they soon had three more, for a total of four errors in eight weeks. When she learned about the errors, hospital president Kathryn Correia decided that the operating rooms would be shut down until the root cause of the problem had been found—stopping "the line." ThedaCare's error, according to former CEO Dr. John Toussaint, was that they had not been able to stop the line immediately after the first error, taking time to find the root cause right then. Being early in their Lean journey, there were "no metrics defined" and errors "slipped under the radar" and were not brought to the attention of leaders.[53] As ThedaCare investigated the errors, it was discovered that surgical teams had stopped doing the time-out procedure, another warning that we cannot let success (good results) lead to complacency (falling back to bad processes). As a temporary fix, the hospital added an independent auditor to be present at each presurgical time-out, with random audits taking place long term.

Understanding Lean is one thing; implementing it in the face of an existing culture can be another story altogether. For example, Ford Motor Company's new truck plant (Dearborn, Michigan) copied a tool, installing *andon* cords. Workers, though, were afraid to pull them, expecting a negative response from their supervisors instead of a supportive or helpful one.

Why do Toyota employees pull the cord 2,000 times per week, while Ford employees only do so twice a week at this one plant?[54] It is not because Toyota has 1,000 times the problems. Toyota has created a culture in which it is acceptable, even encouraged, to report problems instead of covering them up. At the Ford plant, the infrequent use of the *andon* cords was attributed to "the legacy of generations of mistrust between shop-floor workers and managers."[55]

The equivalent of *andon* cord pulls or line stoppages in a hospital setting should be immediate and direct communications. At some hospitals, the mechanisms for identifying problems include an e-mail account and a phone line (that sometimes might go to voice mail). While it is good to have avenues for employees to report safety concerns, a true *andon* system requires people to stop and address the problem (or at least ask a question) immediately, so that patient harm can be prevented. Again, leaders have a responsibility for building a culture in which employees are not afraid to speak up without retribution from colleagues.

One hospital described a "potential incident" that resulted from a physician ordering Coumadin for a patient who had a very low hemoglobin count. A nurse noticed that potentially unsafe condition and asked, "Are you aware of the bleeding time test result?" so the physician said "hold off" on the medication. In a Lean culture, staff need to feel free to speak up, even if it turns out they are incorrect about a potential risk. If the physician had not responded appropriately, the nurse would need to have a way to escalate the concern.

Virginia Mason Medical Center has been a leader in the use of the *andon* philosophy, calling them "patient safety alerts," or PSAs.[56] PSAs are reviewed by a specialist and categorized as

- Red (1%): Life-threatening situations, a "never event," or anything that could pose serious harm to a patient
- Orange (8%): Less severe situations
- Yellow: Slips or latent errors (situations that carry the potential for patient harm)

Beyond the mechanisms for reporting problems, the leadership team at Virginia Mason has emphasized that they have "got your back" if you are a staff member who raises a concern, reducing the fear of retribution. By 2004, an estimated one-third of employees had reported a PSA, and the hospital generally sees 800 to 1,000 reports each month. Jamie Leviton, manager of patient safety, says "More PSAs are not an indication that we are less safe but that our teams feel safer to report—which is the ultimate goal."[57]

The hospital attributed staff acceptance of this system to the fast response that people received when calling an alert and the cultural changes that have surrounded this system. At Virginia Mason, problems, falls, and near misses lead to systemic improvement, not punishment.

As a result of their safety improvement efforts, the professional liability costs at Virginia Mason fell by 26% from 2007 to 2008, and they declined another 12% the next year.[58] As a result of their quality and safety improvement, Virginia Mason was named one of two "Hospitals of the Decade" by the Leapfrog Group.[59]

Error Proofing the Error Proofing

When implementing error-proofing methods, we have to take care that employees do not have easy ways of working around the new system. One example of this, from outside the hospital, was shared by an employee who had observed a neighbor who used an electric lawn mower with an error-proofing device. The user had to press a lever together to keep the engine running. As a safety measure, releasing that lever stopped the mower engine and blade. But, in an effort to save motion, the neighbor had circumvented the protection by wrapping the electric cord around the lever so it would stay engaged without having to hold the lever, creating a safety problem and risk of injury.

We should keep that example in mind when looking at error-proofing methods, particularly when the method creates extra work for employees. If employees are overburdened and already have too much other waste in their day, they may resist having the extra work or look for ways to cut corners to save time. We need to anticipate how employees might circumvent the error proofing by applying the same thought process that went into the original error proofing itself:

- How can we prevent the circumvention of the error proofing?
- Why do people feel the need to circumvent error proofing?
- How can we make it harder to circumvent the error proofing?
- How can we make it obvious or apparent that the error proofing has been circumvented?

Leaders need to watch for the proper use of error-proofing methods and must hold people accountable for following the correct standardized work. At the same time, we should first ask why, as in "Why would that employee want to circumvent the error proofing?" We have to look for the root cause of why that person might do so, either because there is not enough time in his or her day (a need to reduce waste) or because the error-proofing method is too hard to use.

In some hospitals, nurses are required to scan bar codes on patient wristbands to ensure the proper match of patient to medication. If nurses call in sick and a unit is understaffed, the nurses on duty might feel pressured to cut corners to save time. Nurses sometimes create surrogate patient wristband labels to scan all of the medications at once (in a batch) instead of doing it at the bedside. This corner cutting is a workaround to the problem of being understaffed. Lean hospitals would hold nurses accountable but would also look to solve the root cause of the problem—the pressure and the need to cut corners. A five whys analysis could be performed to identify weaknesses in staffing policies and reaction plans for when nurses call in sick.

Many anatomic pathology labs now utilize bar code labels on "blocks" with processed patient tissue. As technologists cut blocks to create slides to be read by pathologists, scanning the labels on the block and the slide can flag mismatches and errors of the type that caused the Darrie Eason case from Chapter 7. But, as with nurses, the error-proofing technology can be circumvented if technologists are not disciplined about only keeping one patient's specimen and slides in their field of work at any given time.

Conclusion

It's easy for a hospital to say "patient safety is always our top priority," but is that really the case every day? Hospitals are full of smart, conscientious employees, yet errors and patient harm still occur. If telling people to be careful were effective, we would have already eliminated quality and patient safety problems in our hospitals. Error proofing is a mindset that we have to adopt, always asking why an error could have occurred and what we can do to prevent that error from occurring the next time. In keeping with the principle of respect for people, Lean thinkers assume that people want to do safe, high-quality work; we just have to design a culture with systems and processes that allows that to happen.

Lean Lessons

■ Being careful and hanging warning signs is not enough to prevent errors.
■ A 100% inspection is not 100% effective.
■ Adding more inspection steps will not ensure quality outcomes.
■ Error proofing (*poka yoke*) physically prevents errors from occurring or makes them less likely to occur.
■ Avoid phrases like "dummy proofing" to keep with the principle of respect for people.
■ Do not forget to error proof the error proofing.

Points for Group Discussion

■ Are the caution and warning signs in your hospital anything more than a short-term response to quality problems?
■ Can you find a sign that can be replaced with better standardized work or with error proofing?
■ How would you evaluate your equipment and tools differently, keeping error proofing in mind?
■ How should leaders react if presurgical time-outs are not taking place?
■ What are frequently occurring errors and mistakes in our area?
■ What ideas for simple error proofing do our team members have?
■ How do we ensure that methods like banned abbreviations are followed all of the time?
■ How can hospitals better learn from mistakes made at other facilities?
■ In what circumstances would it be appropriate for society to jail individuals who are involved in errors that harm patients?
■ Can you recall a time when patient safety was made a top priority, even if that wasn't a popular decision or if it cost more in the short term? How can you celebrate stories like that in the organization?

Notes

1. Grady, Denise, "Study finds no progress in safety at hospitals," *New York Times*, November 24, 2010, http://www.nytimes.com/2010/11/25/health/research/25patient.html (accessed October 16, 2015).
2. McCann, Erin, Deaths by Medical Mistakes Hit Records, http://www.healthcareitnews.com/news/deaths-by-medical-mistakes-hit-records (accessed October 16, 2015).
3. James, John T., PhD, "A new, evidence-based estimate of patient harms associated with hospital care," *Journal of Patient Safety*, 2013, 9(3): 122–28.
4. Allen, Marshall, How Many Die from Medical Mistakes in U.S. Hospitals? http://www.propublica.org/article/how-many-die-from-medical-mistakes-in-us-hospitals (accessed October 16, 2015).
5. Classen, David C., Roger Resar, et al., "'Global trigger tool' shows that adverse events in hospitals may be ten times greater than previously measured," *Health Affairs*, 2011, 30(4): 581–89.
6. Graban, Mark, Statistics on Healthcare Quality and Patient Safety Problems—Errors & Harm, http://www.leanblog.org/2009/08/statistics-on-healthcare-quality-and/ (accessed October 16, 2015).
7. Scholtes, Peter, *The Leader's Handbook* (New York: McGraw-Hill Education, 1997), 92.
8. Josie King Foundation, What Happened, http://www.josieking.org/page.cfm?pageID=10 (accessed March 26, 2015).
9. Graban, Mark, LeanBlog podcast #78: Sorrel King, Improving Patient Safety, http://www.leanblog.org/78 (accessed October 16, 2015).

10. Pronovost, Peter J., *Safe Patients, Smart Hospitals: How One Doctor's Checklist Can Help Us Change Health Care from the Inside Out* (New York: Hudson Street Press, 2010), 1.

11. Kroft, Steve, "Dennis Quaid recounts twins' drug ordeal," *60 Minutes*, March 16, 2008, http://www.cbsnews.com/news/dennis-quaid-recounts-twins-drug-ordeal/ (accessed April 6, 2015).

12. Davies, Tom, "Fatal drug mix-up exposes hospital flaws," *Washington Post*, September 22, 2006, http://www.washingtonpost.com/wp-dyn/content/article/2006/09/22/AR2006092200815.html?nav=hcmodule (accessed March 26, 2015).

13. Ornstein, Charles, and Anna Gorman, Possible Medical Mix-Up for Twins, http://articles.latimes.com/2007/nov/21/local/me-twins21 (accessed October 16, 2015).

14. Celizic, Mike, "I don't want this to happen to anyone else," *Today*, October 4, 2007, http://today.msnbc.msn.com/id/21127917/ns/today-today_health/ (accessed March 26, 2015).

15. CBS News, Woman Has Needless Double Mastectomy, Sues, http://www.cbsnews.com/news/woman-has-needless-double-mastectomy-sues/ (accessed October 16, 2015).

16. Epstein, Reid J., "Medical blunder," *Newsday*, October 2, 2007, http://www.newsday.com/news/medical-blunder-1.664691?firstfree=yes (accessed March 26, 2015).

17. Graban, Mark, Pathology Mistakes (Again) on Oprah and in the News, http://www.leanblog.org/2009/06/pathology-mistakes-again-on-oprah-and/ (accessed October 16, 2015).

18. Toyota Motor Corporation, Toyota Production System, http://www.toyota-global.com/company/vision_philosophy/toyota_production_system/ (accessed March 26, 2015).

19. Ibid.

20. Kowalczyk, Liz, "R.I. raps hospital for errors in surgery," *Boston Globe*, November 27, 2007, http://www.boston.com/news/local/articles/2007/11/27/ri_raps_hospital_for_errors_in_surgery/ (accessed March 26, 2015).

21. Brownstein, Joseph, Rhode Island Hospital Fined for Fifth Surgery Error in Two Years, http://abcnews.go.com/Health/rhode-island-hospital-fined-surgery-error-years/story?id=8988619 (accessed October 16, 2015).

22. Atassi, Leila, Former Pharmacist Eric Cropp Gets 6 Months in Jail in Emily Jerry's Death from Wrong Chemotherapy Solution, http://blog.cleveland.com/metro/2009/08/_former_pharmacist_eric_cropp.html (accessed April 6, 2015).

23. Institute for Safe Medication Practices, An Injustice Has Been Done: Jail Time Given to Pharmacist Who Made an Error, http://www.ismp.org/pressroom/injustice-jailtime-for-pharmacist.asp (accessed October 16, 2015).

24. Emily Jerry Foundation, Surfing the Healthcare Tsunami: Chris Jerry & Eric Cropp Unseen Footage, https://www.youtube.com/watch?v=MseId9FcVOI (accessed October 16, 2015).

25. Emily Jerry Foundation.

26. Grout, John, *Mistake-Proofing the Design of Healthcare Care Processes*, AHRQ Publication 07-0020 (Rockville, MD: Agency for Healthcare Research and Quality, 2007), 41, 76.

27. Wahlberg, David, "Day 1: Medical tubing mistakes can be deadly," *Wisconsin State Journal*, http://host.madison.com/news/local/health_med_fit/day-medical-tubing-mistakes-can-be-deadly/article_bc888491-1f7d-5008-be21-31009a4b253a.html (accessed April 6, 2015).

28. Joint Commission, Tubing Misconnections—A Persistent and Potentially Deadly Occurrence, http://www.jointcommission.org/sentinel_event_alert_issue_36_tubing_misconnections%E2%80%94a_persistent_and_potentially_deadly_occurrence/(accessed April 6, 2015).

29. Institute for Safe Medication Practices, Double Key Bounce and Double Keying Errors, January 12, 2006, http://www.ismp.org/Newsletters/acutecare/articles/20060112.asp?ptr=y (accessed March 26, 2015).

30. Anderson, Pamela, and Terri Townsend, Medication Errors: Don't Let Them Happen to You, http://www.americannursetoday.com/assets/0/434/436/440/6276/6334/6350/6356/8b8dac76-6061-4521-8b43-d0928ef8de07.pdf (accessed October 16, 2015).

31. California Healthcare Advocates, Creative Interventions Reduce Hospital Readmissions for Medicare Beneficiaries, October 7, 2010, http://www.cahealthadvocates.org/news/basics/2010/creative.html (accessed March 26, 2015).

32. Sakles, J. C., E. G. Laurin, A. A. Rantapaa, and E. Panacek, "Airway management in the emergency department: A one-year study of 610 tracheal intubations," *Annals of Emergency Medicine*, 1998, 31: 325–32.

33. Grout, *Mistake-Proofing*, 78.
34. Dittrich, Kenneth C., "Delayed recognition of esophageal intubation," *CJEM Canadian Journal of Emergency Medical Care*, 2002, 4(1): 41–44. http://www.cjem-online.ca/v4/n1/p41 (accessed April 9, 2011).
35. Vocabulary.com, Mistake, http://www.vocabulary.com/dictionary/mistake (accessed October 16, 2015).
36. Shingo, Shigeo, *Zero Quality Control: Source Inspection and the Poka-Yoke System* (New York: Productivity Press, 1986), 45.
37. Kenney, Charles, *Transforming Healthcare: Virginia Mason Medical Center's Pursuit of the Perfect Patient Experience* (New York: Productivity Press, 2010), 50.
38. Gaffney, F. Andrew, Stephen W. Harden, and Rhea Seddon, *Crew Resource Management: The Flight Plan for Lasting Change in Patient Safety* (Marblehead, MA: HCPro, 2005), 1.
39. Grunden, Naida, *The Pittsburgh Way to Efficient Healthcare: Improving Patient Care Using Toyota Based Methods* (New York: Productivity Press, 2007), 53.
40. Leapfrog Group, Computerized Physician Order Entry, http://www.leapfroggroup.org/for_hospitals/leapfrog_safety_practices/cpoe (accessed October 16, 2015).
41. Monegain, Bernie, "CPOE: Stumbling block on way to meaningful use," *Healthcare IT News*, June 17, 2010, http://www.healthcareitnews.com/news/cpoe-stumbling-block-way-meaningful-use (accessed March 26, 2015).
42. Wood, Debra, EHR Adoption Report: The Latest Trends, http://www.amnhealthcare.com/latest-healthcare-news/ehr-adoption-report-latest-trends/ (accessed October 16, 2015).
43. Leapfrog Group.
44. Convis, Gary, Role of Management in a Lean Manufacturing Environment, Society of Automotive Engineers, http://www.sae.org/manufacturing/lean/column/leanjul01.htm (accessed March 26, 2015).
45. PSNet, Alarm Fatigue, http://psnet.ahrq.gov/primer.aspx?primerID=28 (accessed October 16, 2015).
46. PSNet.
47. Wacher, Robert, *The Digital Doctor* (New York: McGraw-Hill Education, 2015), 135.
48. Kwann, Mary, David Studdert, Michael J. Zinner, and Atul A. Gawande, "Incidence, patterns, and prevention of wrong-site surgery," *Archives of Surgery*, 2006, 141: 353–58.
49. ISHN, Time-Out Designed to Avoid Surgical Mistakes Being Largely Ignored, http://www.ishn.com/articles/95150-time-out-designed-to-avoid-surgical-mistakes-being-largely-ignored (accessed October 16, 2015).
50. Joint Commission, Improving America's Hospitals—The Joint Commission's Annual Report on Quality and Safety—2007, http://www.jointcommission.org/Improving_Americas_Hospitals_The_Joint_Commissions_Annual_Report_on_Quality_and_Safety_-_2007/ (accessed April 6, 2015).
51. Davis, Robert, "'Wrong site' surgeries on the rise," *USA Today*, April 17, 2006, http://usatoday30.usatoday.com/news/health/2006-04-17-wrong-surgery_x.htm (accessed April 6, 2015).
52. Meier, David, personal interview, January 2, 2008.
53. Toussaint, John, and Roger Gerard, *On the Mend: Revolutionizing Healthcare to Save Lives and Transform the Industry* (Cambridge, MA: Lean Enterprise Institute, 2010), 88.
54. Schifferes, Steve, "The triumph of Lean production," *BBC News Online*, February 27, 2007, http://news.bbc.co.uk/2/hi/business/6346315.stm (accessed March 26, 2015).
55. Ibid.
56. Kenney, *Transforming Healthcare*, 52.
57. National Patient Safety Foundation, Environmental Factors that Contribute to Falls, http://www.npsf.org/blogpost/1158873/Patient-Safety0-Blog?tag=&DGPCrSrt=&DGPCrPg=2 (accessed October 16, 2015).
58. Kenney, 65.
59. The Leapfrog Group, The Leapfrog Group Announces Top Hospitals of the Decade, November 30, 2010, http://www.leapfroggroup.org/news/leapfrog_news/4784721 (accessed March 26, 2015).

Chapter 9

Improving Flow

Lean Is Both Quality and Flow

As introduced earlier in the book, the core pillars of the Toyota Production System are *jidoka*, or quality at the source, and "just in time." Just in time refers to the concept of always providing the right product or service as needed by the customer in the right quantity, at the right place, and at the right time. Quality and flow go hand in hand; one supports the other. For example, reducing defects in the discharge process means fewer delays and better patient flow. Improving flow by reducing delays leads to better quality and outcomes. For example, faster lab results means better and more timely medical decision-making and outcomes. Reducing delays in the emergency department means faster treatment, less pain, and better outcomes.

Waiting: A Worldwide Problem

Go online and look up waiting times for your state or country and compare them to those for your own organization. Waiting times don't get reduced as the result of people working harder or working longer hours. Rather, waiting times and flow are improved by reducing or eliminating delays and interruptions by reconfiguring and improving the way work is done. Lean is a methodology that reduces waiting times by improving flow.

Around the world, patients often wait far too long for their medical care. In Ontario, Canada, the government maintains a website that shows the expected delay for different types of surgery. As of August 2015, patients near Toronto could expect to wait up to 177 days (up from 118 days in 2011) for cataract surgery and 89 days (down from 114 days in 2011) for magnetic resonance imaging (MRI), much longer than their target of 28 days.[1] In England, the National Health Service (NHS) often misses their target that says 90% of patients will wait no longer than 126 days (18 weeks) between referral and the start of treatment after sometimes waiting for "years" back in the 1990s.[2] Care delays in different countries are typically attributed to a lack of capacity or budget constraints, but Lean can help increase capacity while reducing cost at the same time.

In the United States, waiting times for primary care appointments have increased in recent years, with waiting times for new patient appointments ranging from five days to 66 days, depending on the city.[3] Many blame a shortage of physicians, but another way to ensure access is by improving flow and productivity. Increased throughput, or seeing more patients per day, is an alternative to adding more physicians. Cleveland Clinic has used a "value-based care" model in primary care, utilizing a physician and two medical assistants working together to increase "the number of patient encounters per day" by 16.4%, while reducing the "direct cost per patient encounter" by 7.5%.[4] In a different type of clinic setting, ThedaCare (Wisconsin), for example, has reduced the waiting time between referral to the first CyberKnife cancer treatment from 26 days to just six days.[5] Reducing waste and redesigning workflows is more cost-effective and more sustainable than working harder or longer hours.

Lean success stories are becoming more common in emergency care around the world, including Mary Washington Hospital (Virginia), which reduced length of stay from four hours to three, reducing "left without being seen" rates from over 6% to 2%, while seeing a 25% higher patient volume.[6] Hôtel Dieu Grace Hospital (Windsor, Ontario) reduced the average length of stay for discharged patients from 3.6 to 2.8 hours, also reducing the number of patients who left without being seen from 7.1% to 4.3%.[7]

In outpatient settings, one survey showed that excessive waiting room time was the primary complaint of 72% of U.S. dental patients.[8] Sami Bahri, DDS, is an example of a dentist who has used Lean to eliminate waiting room time for patients while increasing patient volumes. Traditionally, patients who required care beyond a basic cleaning would be diagnosed and then scheduled for a follow-up appointment. The Bahri Dental Group (Jacksonville, Florida) rethought this and changed the flow to be able to treat most patients in a single visit if the patient wishes. The time required for a complex patient's complete treatment fell from 99 days in 2005 to 10 days in 2008.[9]

Traditionally, access and cost are seen as trade-offs. The oft-proposed solutions for reducing delays typically mean spending money to increase capacity, meaning constructing or expanding new facilities, purchasing new equipment, and hiring additional staff. Lean is helping organizations improve patient flow in far less expensive ways. One major children's hospital reduced waiting times for outpatient MRIs from more than 12 weeks to just 2.5 weeks through setup reduction, waste elimination, and a change in anesthesiologist staffing patterns. MRI utilization levels during working hours were increased from 40% to about 65% through an initial Lean project, a far more cost-effective approach than buying another MRI machine. The hospital has sustained its success, keeping waiting times down for seven years by monitoring their waiting time metrics and continuously improving their workflows.

Targets without a Means for Improvement Might Lead to Improvement or Dysfunction

While measuring flow and delays is an important part of the improvement process, be careful to not put undue pressure on organizations about hitting specific targets. There are many cases around the world where people end up "gaming," as some say, or distorting the system instead of improving it.

For example, the British NHS established a target that said 98% of patients needed to be seen, treated, and then admitted or discharged within four hours. The target was later reduced to 95%, as hospitals struggled to perform at the 98% level. A number of distortions occurred, including 40% of units that said "patients were discharged from A&E before they had been properly assessed or stabilised."[10] Another example of gaming would be keeping patients in an ambulance after it arrives to the hospital because the four-hour clock does not start until the patient is brought inside.[11] In 2015, NHS hospitals, on the whole, had missed the 95% target for 90 consecutive weeks, with roughly 30 to 40 hospitals out of 140 reaching the target.[12]

Focusing on Flow

Traditional organizations often focus more on cost and the efficiency of individuals or departments. One way in which Lean is different from traditional thinking is the focus on flow. Instead of asking people to work faster, Lean organizations focus on reducing delays and systemic barriers to flow. By focusing on flow, we can often increase capacity (which often leads to revenue increases) and reduce costs as an end result of these improvements.

It is often said that there are seven types of flow in healthcare, as shown in Table 9.1. These seven flows are considered in space and process design exercises called "3P" or the production preparation process. Seattle Children's Hospital is among those using 3P as part of an "integrated facility design" approach, as discussed later in this chapter.[13]

Using this approach to build their outpatient surgery center in Bellevue, Washington, led to not just a beautiful, environmentally certified building, but the following results when compared to a similar facility they had completed six years earlier:

- Completed 3.5 months faster (20%)
- Built 34,000 square feet smaller (20%)
- Cost $6.7 million less (17%)[14]

The real innovation came from rethinking typical designs and layouts to be better for the patients and their families. The new space was created to minimize distances and improve flow from the parking garage to the front desk of the surgical floor, where people are greeted immediately after stepping out of the elevator. Instead of assuming that patients had to be transported down long hallways, two pre-surgical prep rooms connect directly to each operating room (OR). This allows the patient to be induced with their family by their side, before being brought through a door for their procedure. The patients are then brought directly into the recovery

Table 9.1 The Seven Flows of Healthcare

Type of Flow	Example
Patients	Movement of patients through acute care; high-level care process, including handoff from primary to specialty care
Clinicians and staff	Physical movement within or between departments
Medications	Physical flow from pharmacy to floor stock or patient rooms
Supplies	Processes, movement, and storage of consumables
Equipment	Processes, movement, and storage of pumps, beds, wheelchairs, etc.
Information	Discharge information passing from clinician to clinician
Process engineering	Flow of equipment through the biomed department or the repair process

room, through a door on the other side of the OR, where they can wake up with their family with them again. Reducing those distances improves communication and flow between what might otherwise be silos in the value stream, with the added benefit of improving patient and family satisfaction.

Value Streams Should Flow Like a River

Smooth, steady flow through a value stream should be a primary goal of a health system. That might mean the smooth flow of support products (such as test specimens, medications, or surgical instruments), or it might mean the smooth flow of patients through the hospital and their continuum of care. There are many causes of delays—some just occur, while others are imposed by our own decisions and policies. Flow improvements do not come from doing the value-adding work faster; improvements generally come from reducing and eliminating waiting, interruptions, and delays from the value stream.

Lean literature often includes references to "one-piece flow" or "single-piece flow." In a perfect flow environment, the product (or patient) would move in batches of one, as this minimizes delays that occur when a batch accumulates. Think of an escalator, which allows people to move between floors in a continuous single-piece flow, as opposed to an elevator, which accomplishes the same thing by batching passengers. One-piece flow is more of a directional goal than an absolute, however, as we might not be able to move to batches of one due to short-term constraints in the system. But, teams can work to reduce batch sizes as much as they can and then work to reduce these constraints, rather than letting the barriers become an easy excuse for not having good flow.

For example, the anatomic pathology lab at Children's Health (Dallas, Texas) improved the physical layout of various steps, including specimen receiving, grossing, processing, cutting, slide making, and staining. As flow improved with smaller batches (not "one-piece flow") throughout the process, medical transcriptionists began receiving work in smaller batches. This meant changing their standardized work and daily routines, but for the benefits of patients and physicians who had ordered tests.

Lean instructors often use visualization from Toyota, viewing flow as a river or stream. In a river, rocks stick up through the surface of the water, impeding the smooth flow of water or boats. In the analogy, we view those rocks as problems that need to be solved so flow can be improved (as opposed to speeding up the stream in some artificial way).

In making improvements, we should first identify the "rocks," asking why we cannot have predictable schedules that are followed like clockwork. Rocks in the surgery department system might include the following:

- Patients sometimes show up late.
- Lab results are not always back in time for the surgery.
- Order sets were not completed properly.
- Supplies, blood, or instruments needed to start surgery are missing.
- Surgery lengths are unpredictable.

We may be able to find effective countermeasures for some of those problems. Improvements in the laboratory could reduce turnaround times, preventing some surgery or discharge delays. We can also ask why patients are late, viewing the process through their experience. Reasons could be a confusing hospital layout and a lack of clear signage to direct first-time visitors, or a proper reminder call not being placed. One hospital had an ongoing problem with patients showing up at the wrong building. After years of blaming the patients, a team realized that paperwork sent to the patients was confusing, leading someone to arrive at the outpatient services building instead of the main hospital or vice versa.

In some hospitals, surgery patients wait for hours because they are all instructed to arrive first thing in the morning. This is typically done because there is uncertainty (real or perceived) about how long procedures might actually take, and surgical teams set up the system to ensure that they are never waiting, maximizing their own utilization. The trade-off in this approach is long patient waiting times. Some hospitals are starting to give patients actual surgery times throughout the day, a more patient-centered approach. Initially, patients are asked to arrive 90 or 120 minutes before their case, but we might gradually reduce the patients' early arrival time from 90 to 60 minutes as we make improvements.

Uneven Workloads as a Barrier to Flow

Many delays, for patients and products, are caused by uneven workloads. As introduced in Chapter 5, *heijunka* is one of the three foundations of the Toyota house. Having level demand for processes leads to lower resource requirements, in both staffing and equipment. Some unevenness in our demand occurs naturally, but a large amount is due to our own policies and choices. Lean teaches us to identify sources of *mura* (uneven workloads) so we can work on leveling the load instead of taking the unevenness for granted.

Naturally Occurring Unevenness

Hospitals have many examples of workloads that are not level. This unevenness is often beyond our immediate control, such as when patient volumes increase during the winter months because certain illnesses are more prevalent. The heavier seasonal illness volume leads to increased costs for the hospital, as emergency departments (EDs), the number of inpatient rooms, and support departments must be sized to account for the busy periods. Otherwise, patients will suffer longer delays when demand is high. Even though we can often vary staffing levels by hiring seasonal employees, physical resources go to waste when volumes are lower. Hospitals cannot control all of the seasonality, even with improved preventive care and community safety initiatives.

Lean hospitals might view slow periods during the year as opportunities to more actively market elective procedures in an attempt to level out the overall load on the hospital and its resources, shifting cross-trained personnel between the ED and the OR as demand shifts. Slow periods can also be used as opportunities for staff training and process improvement efforts, as Toyota does during slow sales periods.[15] This training and improvement activity has a cost, but it is considered an investment that will pay off for the long-term good of the organization.

Mura *Caused by Morning Rounds*

The traditional practice of morning rounds by physicians leads to *mura* for support departments, such as the laboratory. Since physicians want daily lab results on patients' charts before their morning rounds, laboratories have to get a large volume of work done by 7:00 a.m. In one very typical lab, 34% of the daily volume arrived in a three-hour time frame from 3:00 a.m. to 6:00 a.m. Figure 9.1 shows the hourly test volumes for that typical clinical laboratory.

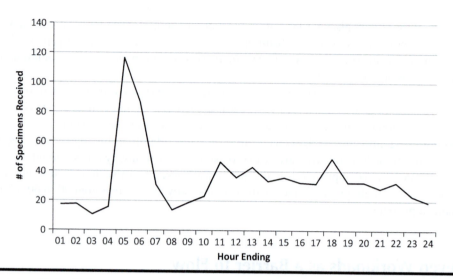

Figure 9.1   Clinical laboratory: # of specimens received each hour during an average day.

Since we cannot schedule medical technologists (or other lab employees) for short shifts just to cover the busy time, we end up with excess staffing and equipment during the slower periods that follow the morning spike. To meet this demand, hospitals typically send out large numbers of phlebotomists to draw patients' blood early in the morning, resources we continue to pay for after the rush is over.

Morning physician rounds also lead to a spike in inpatient discharge activity. This bolus of discharge orders passes through the system, creating *mura* in support roles ranging from social work (preparing to get patients discharged into nursing homes) to patient transport (trying to move many patients at the same time) to housekeeping (trying to clean many empty rooms at the same time).

In hospitals where physicians are not employed, it might not seem practical to level-load physician rounds, even with the benefits for patients and some departments. On the other hand, some hospitals with employed physicians have some afternoon rounds, including Saint Göran Hospital (Stockholm, Sweden). The physicians must initiate or agree to changes like this rather than having this forced on them, not that Lean thinkers should make a habit of forcing new processes on anyone.

Level Loading Physician Charting

The norm for many physicians in clinic settings is to see all of their patients and then chart at the end of the day, as a batch. With a busy patient schedule, this often means staying late to complete charting, which can hurt the quality and accuracy of the information that gets entered into the chart. And, getting home late for dinner is a frequent cause of physician frustration and dissatisfaction.

Dr. Luis Rojas, a physician in the gynecologic oncology clinic at Avera Health, often had to stay until 7:30 p.m. to enter orders and complete his charting. "We were stressed, always running late, patients had to wait a long time, and I was always behind on documentation," says Dr. Rojas. When the physician is running behind, "that means the thing that's going to wait is not patient care, but dictation," says clinic manager Jamie Arens. When progress notes are sometimes being dictated days later, that means the billing coder has to wait, and the clinic gets paid more slowly.

Arens attended a 90-minute introductory Lean class and had a discussion with the internal process excellence consultant, Doreen Hardy, about challenges they faced. The consultant observed for a full day in the clinic, noticing a lot of interruptions to patient care, asking questions with an outsider's perspective.

Dr. Rojas was challenged by the consultant to stay in the room with each patient until the charting is complete. "I was very skeptical about Lean, but it works," says Dr. Rojas. He is now spending 10 more minutes with each patient, dictating and entering orders in front of them. "If a physician dictates something that's incorrect, the patient can correct them," says Arens. Hearing the physician explain their situation and care a second time is helpful to patients when care can be complicated. Dr. Rojas is able to go home two hours earlier each day, immediately after seeing his last patient, and "feels sharper and more effective" according to Kathy Maass, director of process excellence. She adds, "You can't put a value or return on investment (ROI) on that."

"When you have people willing to change and willing to help lead those changes [through Lean], you're going to get those types of phenomenal outcomes," says Hardy. "When the team is happy because of changes they made, they're going to stick to those changes," says Arens.[16]

Mura *Caused by Suboptimizing Courier Routes*

In many situations, uneven workloads are caused by decisions made by a single department looking to minimize its own cost, often at the expense of the overall system. Labs that receive specimens from outside sources, such as off-site clinics or private physician offices, often find that courier deliveries are not level loaded throughout the day.

Kaiser Permanente of the Mid-Atlantic States (Rockville, Maryland) made changes in its regional laboratory to level the flow of specimens to test instruments. Before Lean, specimens arrived infrequently, said laboratory operations manager Jane Price Lewis. "At three in the afternoon, we would get a giant 'fish cooler' full of specimens from all 29 medical centers," said Lewis. "At 7:30 p.m. we received another one, and then at 10:30, and then again at 1 a.m. Each time we had a huge spurt of activity while the staff struggled with this bolus of work." The lab had wasted and unused capacity during the late morning and early afternoon, so the lab arranged for the courier service to deliver smaller batches of orders starting in the morning. While this added courier expense, the lab was able to reduce overtime within the lab, as work was more easily completed during the afternoon shift. Similar effects are often seen inside the hospital, where adding additional phlebotomists (one of the lower pay rates in the hospital) can help reduce overall laboratory costs or costs for the entire hospital.

Leveling also improved service. When Kaiser's couriers delivered the fish coolers at 10:30 p.m., the large batches often contained samples from the morning or early afternoon. "Many times, doctors would be waiting for follow-ups on highly abnormal results," said Lewis. "But we might not call them until three or four o'clock in the morning." After adopting an approach that calls for smaller, more frequent batches, the lab now calls with those results by 5:00 or 6:00 p.m. "The doctor can get the patient back into the medical center for additional testing or get them on therapy more quickly," said Lewis. "We're actually having an impact on our patients by providing more timely results to our providers."[17]

At one large reference laboratory, trained Lean team members went to the *gemba* and rode along with couriers on their routes. In many instances, couriers drove right past the entrance to the lab as their route brought them to additional offices to pick up specimens. When asked why they did this, the couriers responded that they were measured on the number of specimens they collected each hour—stopping to drop off specimens they had already collected would hurt this measure. The lab realized that this suboptimization (caused by their own policies) was to the detriment of overall lab flow and unnecessarily delayed patient care.

Mura *Created by Clinic Scheduling*

In another example of self-imposed *mura*, an outpatient chemotherapy center struggled with a midday peak of patients, with a typical daily schedule shown in Figure 9.2. This led to delays, as more patients arrived than could be seated for treatment, as chair or nurse availability became a constraint. Before looking at the problem with a Lean perspective, the treatment center, looking only within its own silo, was convinced it needed more people and more space.

After some initial training, the department started looking at the entire value stream from the patient's perspective. The typical patient pathway included an appointment with an oncologist at one of the clinics in another part of the building before walking to receive chemotherapy. While observing in the oncology clinic, the treatment center discovered that the oncologists built their schedules so that chemotherapy patients were clustered together (or batched) first thing in the morning. This left other patients, such as those receiving a consultation or radiation therapy, for later in the day.

When the treatment center asked the oncologists why they created this kind of schedule, the oncologists replied they thought the schedule helped the patients. From the limited visibility oncologists had within their department silo, they thought that scheduling the chemotherapy patients first thing in the morning helped get them through treatment so they could get home earlier. This would have been true for a single patient but was not true for the full patient schedule. Clustering chemotherapy patients caused the artificially high number of patients who arrived for treatment in the middle of the day. This, ironically, led to longer patient delays and increased stress for the staff.

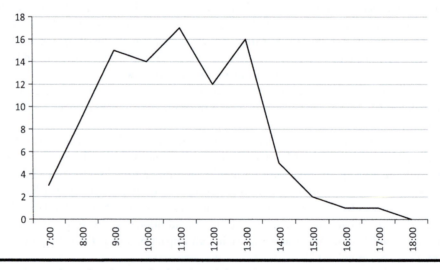

Figure 9.2   Number of patients scheduled each hour in an outpatient chemotherapy treatment center.

The clinic and the treatment center put together a plan for leveling the load of chemotherapy patients throughout the day (taking care to schedule those with longer, five-hour chemotherapy treatment early enough in the day). Changing the schedule did not have an impact on the oncologists, but leveling the workload made a big difference for the chemotherapy center, as the department had less of a busy time in the middle of the day. The chemotherapy center was able to increase its capacity while shortening patient delays, eliminating the need to expand the physical space or increase staffing.

Mura *in the Patient Discharge Process*

A common impediment to patient flow is the discharge process. Delayed discharges can hamper the flow of patients through the ED and postanesthesia recovery units, as patients cannot be admitted or moved to inpatient rooms until discharges have occurred. In extreme cases, these delays can lead to EDs going on diversion or canceled surgical procedures.

When a hospital has a high percentage of Medicare or Medicaid patients, this delay and increased length of stay have a direct impact on the bottom line for the hospital, as costs increase without additional revenue coming in. One hospital estimated that, in the course of analyzing its existing discharge process, a length-of-stay reduction of just half a day, created by reducing discharge delays, would represent a $6 million saving.

There can be, of course, *muda* or waste in the discharge process itself once it is initiated. The University of Michigan Medical Center was able to reduce the elapsed time in the discharge process by 54%, from 195 minutes to 89. Process improvements included doing more discharge work in parallel, instead of serially from physician to clerk to nurse. Improving the discharge process had a positive impact on the emergency care value stream, as patients could be admitted more promptly.[18] This illustrates a case for which the discharge process maybe a bottleneck to overall patient flow.

Discharge delays also cause frustration for patients and their families when an expectation has been set that a patient will be discharged soon, yet process problems or miscommunications prevent that from happening. Even if the patient gets out that same day, a family member might have been waiting many hours at the hospital to transport that patient home.

Discharge processes are complex, involving many different functions, roles, and departments. Multiple handoffs increase the risk of miscommunications that can push a planned discharge into the next day. A value stream map (VSM) of a discharge process tends to be complex, with process steps and communication taking place among more than a dozen different roles. At one hospital, not a single person could accurately describe the entire discharge process; each only knew his or her own work and, in some cases, the work of a few people with whom he or she directly interacted. The VSM activity created greater awareness and understanding of the interactions between roles and highlighted some opportunities to improve coordination and reduce waste.

It is common for hospitals to discharge the bulk of their patients in the afternoon hours. That timing often does not match with the need for beds, particularly planned admissions and postoperative admissions. Figure 9.3 illustrates how that mismatch between bed demand (admissions) and bed supply (discharges) might appear during the day.

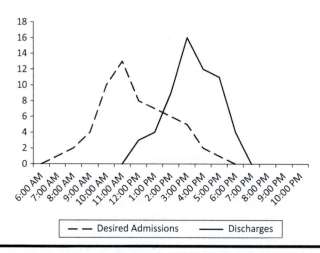

Figure 9.3 Actual pattern of discharges and admissions during a day, showing how beds are needed (admission) earlier than discharges are occurring; neither is leveled over the day.

Figure 9.4 Improved pattern of discharges and admissions, where discharges occur just before an admission; both are leveled out over the day.

Since discharges are time-consuming for nurses and other inpatient unit staff, the spike in workload might overburden and distract them from other patient care needs. The hospital might also find a conflict between a desire to get patients discharged by the end of the day and the end of nurses' shifts. When nurses change shifts at 5:00 p.m., they might avoid or delay discharges in an attempt to get home.

When the hospital has a spike of discharge activity in just a few afternoon hours, it creates an artificially high load on other hospital resources, including housekeeping, patient transport, and the laboratory. Goals for improvements would include matching bed supply with demand, as well as applying *heijunka*, as shown in Figure 9.4.

A just-in-time discharge would occur right before the bed is needed by the next patient (allowing time for proper room cleaning and changeover activities). Of course, a patient should be discharged as soon as medically ready, rather than waiting until the bed is needed. A Lean discharge process would also bring a fast resolution to the discharge order once written. At one hospital, improvement efforts for the entire discharge process were initiated after it was found that while 46% of discharge orders were written before 11:00 a.m., only 5% of patients left before 11:00 a.m.[19]

Many hospitals now measure the percentage of patients who are discharged by a certain time in the late morning, such as 10:00 or 11:00 a.m. The idea is that discharging more patients early helps improve patient flow and helps level load discharges. One hospital patient told a story about a hospital that would not discharge his wife and baby, once medically ready, in the late evening because it would hurt the unit's "discharged by 10:00 a.m." metric. Be careful that performance measures are not interfering with staff doing what's right for a given patient.

Discharges are also often not levelly loaded throughout the week. In many cases, significantly fewer discharges are done on weekends, which can be due to physicians not having rounds, social workers not working on weekends, or nursing homes not accepting new patients on weekends. This increases length of stay and leads to another spike of discharge activity on Mondays. A Lean approach would look for ways to increase weekend discharges, finding the root causes of what prevents them from happening.

While it's important to prevent discharge delays, it should be noted that a Lean health system would not push patients out the door before they are medically ready. A Lean hospital needs to make the quality of patient care a priority. In addition to being the right thing for the patient, sending patients home too soon would lead to higher readmission rates and, for American health systems, financial penalties if readmission rates are too high.

Addressing *Mura* by Matching Staffing to Workloads

If workloads cannot be leveled, the next best alternative is to make sure staffing levels vary with demand. As basic as it might seem, staffing levels and workloads are not always synchronized. Staffing levels might be based on historical guidelines, benchmarks, or arbitrary financial targets more so than the workload.

Figure 9.5 shows a lab's staffing and hourly testing volume, before Lean; phlebotomist and technologist staffing increased after the morning run period.

By analyzing workloads, the lab was able to bring phlebotomists in earlier and reduce afternoon overstaffing. New staffing levels are shown in Figure 9.6.

The adjusted staffing schedules, combined with waste reduction and productivity improvements, allowed the lab to reduce total phlebotomy staffing (through attrition) by 21% and technologist staffing by 14%.

Looking again at the chemotherapy example, typical nurse staffing for a day is shown in Figure 9.7. As the scheduled workload increased in the middle of the day, staffing levels decreased due to scheduled lunch breaks. This disparity between workloads and staffing caused a number of problems, including longer patient waiting times or nurses feeling pressured into not taking lunch breaks. With Lean, the level-loaded schedule helped solve the midday spike, but the nurses also

Figure 9.5 Clinical laboratory hourly test volumes, shown with phlebotomy and "core lab" technologist staffing, before Lean.

Figure 9.6 Clinical laboratory hourly test volumes, shown with phlebotomy and "core lab" technologist staffing, after Lean.

had to reconsider when they took their lunch breaks and how many could go at the same time to ensure there were no interruptions in patient care.

EDs often complain that their workloads are unpredictable because they do not know who is going to arrive and when. Data consistently show that patient arrival patterns are actually quite consistent and predictable on given days of the week and given hours, as shown in Figure 9.8.[20] Looking at a pattern like this can help a department determine when to increase capacity, either

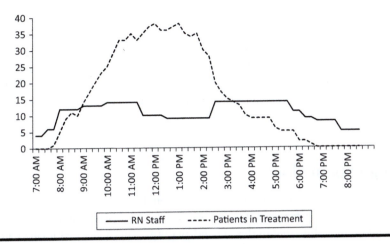

Figure 9.7 **Number of chemotherapy treatment center patients in chairs or beds plotted with nurse staffing levels; a one-day snapshot prior to Lean efforts.**

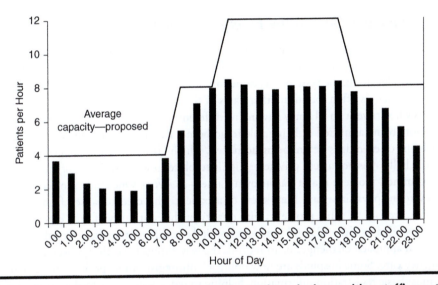

Figure 9.8 **Expected emergency department patient volume by hour with a staffing pattern to match. (From Crane, Jody, and Chuck Noon,** *The Definitive Guide to Emergency Department Operational Improvement: Employing Lean Principles with Current ED Best Practices to Create the "No Wait" Department.* **New York: Productivity Press, 2011, 195. With permission.)**

by opening more groups of rooms in the department or by adding staff. An old staffing pattern of 12-hour shifts all running from 7:00 to 7:00 might not best match demand. More EDs are moving to staggered scheduling; physicians and staff start at varying times of day to create the right total staffing levels.

The idea of matching staff to workloads sometimes gets interpreted, unfortunately, as meaning that a hospital needs to send staff home any time patient census drops, a practice sometimes called "flexing." While it might make financial sense not to be habitually overstaffed, sending nurses home early with a few hours left in their shift is a personal loss and disruption that might not rank highly in the scale of "respect for people." This practice is a known dissatisfier for nurses, if they're not volunteering to leave early, as one nursing journal reported that some nurses left their hospital because flexing made them feel not valued.[21] When census is low and there are a few hours left in the day, alternatives to sending nurses home early include training and education or following Toyota's lead by participating in process and quality improvement efforts. A visual idea board or a *kaizen* process, as discussed in Chapter 11, provides a ready queue of small projects for nurses and other staff to work on when time is available.

Improving Patient Flow

Problems with patient flow are a major issue that hospitals can address using Lean concepts and methods. In this section, a few examples are shown to demonstrate some of the problems that interfere with flow, including that in the ED and an outpatient cancer treatment center. Hospitals are using Lean to improve patient flow in other areas, including outpatient surgery, radiology, and physician clinics.

Improving Patient Flow in the Emergency Department

When EDs become congested, a number of problems have an impact on patients and employees. The congestion and stress have an impact on ED employees, as they face patient complaints and often feel powerless to fix the system. Headlines often incorrectly point blame at the ED, when the root of the problem is often found in other parts of the value stream.

Patients who arrive at an ED may have many different waits, between different steps in the value stream, before being admitted or being able to go home. Patients also might wait in the ED hallways for hours or even days before being admitted, which creates physical congestion and mental stress as the hallway is not a very private or dignified place to wait. Waiting for an inpatient room is such a common problem that it has its own name—*boarding*. One study showed that 200 U.S. emergency room physicians said they knew of a patient who died because of boarding in their hospital.[22] Boarding can cause problems with quality or the continuity of care, especially when the ED is understaffed or if the ED and inpatient hospital use different medical record systems.

The Lean approach challenges us to rethink the way things have always been done, including in emergency care. Some hospitals are now doing a "miniregistration" prior to triage that includes just the most basic registration information, helping to reduce the "door-to-doc" time. The department then uses what would otherwise be time spent waiting for test results (or some other natural delay) as an opportunity to do the full registration. The Kaiser Permanente South Sacramento Medical Center used Lean to create a "rapid triage and treatment" (RTT), leading to the following results:

- Average length of stay reduced from 4.2 to 3.6 hours,
- ED arrival to physician time reduced from 62 to 42 minutes, and
- Left without being seen rates reduced from 4.5% to 1.5%.[23]

In addition, it is becoming more common for hospitals to question the value and effectiveness of traditional triage processes and sequential care, realizing that triage often leads to the patient telling his or her story to multiple people—a cause of complaints. While triage was intended to expedite treatment for highest-acuity patients, more experts are taking the view that triage can actually delay treatment in the acutely ill.[24] Newly rethought triage models often involve a physician or a team consisting of a physician, nurse, and paramedic performing that initial triage.[25]

An increasing number of hospitals are also creating, under the banner of Lean, "split flow" departments that triage patients into two separate value streams based on their acuity and condition. Often, the split is based on patients being "horizontal," meaning they have to remain lying down, versus those who are "vertical" and walk or sit upright. With a split flow, the ED can continue to give the highest priority to the most sick or injured, while also creating a "fast track" for patients who need more of an urgent care style of treatment. At Denver Health, Scott Nimmo, a clinical nurse educator, reported that their fast track, implemented through a "rapid improvement event," or RIE, improved flow and satisfaction. Nimmo added, "Patients were excited. They expected to wait six hours, and they were out in an hour. And they were delighted to see a physician out front [performing triage]."[26]

The Penn State Hershey Medical Center used Lean concepts to help design what they call a "no-wait ED." The physical layout and the care model both changed, as triage is now done by a physician.[27] As a result of their changes, the average length of stay was reduced 23%, rates of those who left without being seen fell from 5.6% to 0.4%, door-to-physician time was reduced to an average of just 18 minutes, and patient satisfaction increased from the 17th to the 75th percentile.[28]

When emergency rooms are backed up, hospitals may place themselves "on diversion"; a hospital requests that ambulances take patients to other hospitals unless the patient would be harmed by a delay or additional transportation. Notice two of the types of waste in that example, waiting and transportation. Being on diversion might negatively impact patients and their care, and it also can have an impact on the hospital in terms of lost revenue in some countries, since that diverted patient is likely to be admitted to the hospital to which they are ultimately taken.[29] Most would probably recognize that the practice of diversion is hardly fixing the root cause of ED overcrowding. It is, at best, a stopgap measure.

EDs have incredible demands placed on them, as the number of ED beds in the United States has declined while visits have increased. For patients in many countries, the ED is their best or only option for what should be addressed in primary care settings, causing further congestion. Between 1995 and 2005, ED visits in the United States increased by 20%, while the number of beds decreased by 38%.[30] ED visits increased another 18.5% between 2005 and 2011.[31] EDs face some serious systemic challenges that cannot be fixed by asking people to work faster. Many hospitals around the world are using Lean methods to improve patient flow in the face of enormous challenges and resource constraints.

When directly observing patient flow, hospitals find waiting times that can be eliminated through process improvements. At Avera McKennan (Sioux Falls, South Dakota), a team observed ED patients, looking for value-added time (the times they were being examined) and waiting time. While the average length of stay was 140 minutes, two-thirds of that time was spent waiting. Part of this delay was caused by lab tests not being ordered until 45 minutes into the patient visit. The department reconfigured its triage process, ensuring each patient would be initially seen within 20 minutes of arrival. If that does not happen, protocols are triggered (a form of standardized work), which include the automatic ordering of lab tests, reducing testing and patient delays. As mentioned in Chapter 1, Avera McKennan was able to use flow improvements to reduce a planned ED expansion from 24 rooms to just 20, saving $1.25 million in construction costs.

If a hospital does not get to the root causes of poor ED flow, it risks spending large amounts of money on mere symptoms of the problem. Many solutions to ED overcrowding focus on expanding the ED itself, spending millions to add rooms and bays to the physical space, often not reducing length of stay. We can use a five whys exercise for this problem:

- Why are we having to divert ambulances?
  We don't have any open ED rooms.
- Why don't we have any open ED rooms?
  We can't get patients admitted into inpatient beds fast enough.
- Why can't we get patients into beds faster?
  Patients are physically out of the rooms but do not show as discharged in the system.
- Why are they not discharged in the system?
  The nurse did not notify the unit clerk to enter the discharge into the system.
- Why is the process dependent on the nurse notifying the unit clerk?
  It has always worked that way.

Instead of only looking at expensive capital spending, we now have a root cause (and other root causes) that can be fixed through other improvement efforts, illustrating that it is a value stream problem, not a departmental one. In other situations, such as one Ontario hospital visited by the author, one answer to "why are they not discharged?" was that there were not enough long-term care beds available in the community, due to government budget constraints. Yet, the hospital was blamed and put under pressure to fix what some described as an "ED problem." In 2015, an estimated 14% of Ontario hospital inpatients were ready to discharge, but could not be due to a shortage of non-hospital beds, including long-term care facilities.[32]

Reducing "Door-to-Balloon" Time

Patients arriving at the ED with chest pain could be suffering from a type of heart attack called a STEMI (segment elevation myocardial infarction). A core measure of flow is often referred to as "door-to-balloon time," measuring the time that elapses from the patient's arrival to the point when their heart blockage is cleared in the cath lab. As in many cases, improving flow by reducing delays leads to better patient outcomes since less damage occurs to the heart if the arterial blockage is cleared more quickly.

Over a number of years, ThedaCare used Lean methods to reduce its average door-to-balloon time from 92 minutes to 37 minutes, leading to measurably better care. As they say, "time is muscle," since mortality increases when the time exceeds 90 minutes.[33] When ThedaCare first

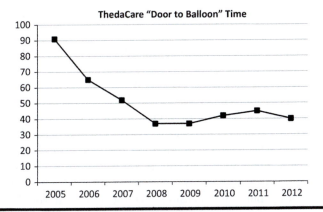

Figure 9.9   ThedaCare "door-to-balloon" time.

looked at this value stream in 2006, they were hitting the national 120-minute target 70% of the time.[34] Benchmarks aside, there was a clear opportunity for improvement.

ThedaCare continued to improve, decreasing the average time for each of the next three years, as shown in Figure 9.9. Clinicians standardized the process for evaluating patients, hanging a sign in each ED bay reminding everyone of the standardized work sequence that best minimized time, to complete an electrocardiogram (EKG) most quickly. Cardiologists ceded control of reading the EKGs to emergency physicians, ensuring everybody was properly trained to do the highest-quality work. This change eliminated a possible delay that would occur when cardiologists would be called at home during the middle of the night. With the new process, there were only two "false-alarm" diagnoses in the first 2,000 patients with heart attack.[35]

Even now, ThedaCare strives to further reduce variation and the average door-to-balloon time. Any time an individual patient exceeds 90 minutes, which happens rarely, the team takes the opportunity to investigate, looking for a root cause and process changes that can be implemented to prevent delays for future patients. In keeping with the Lean thinking mindset of always pursuing perfection, ThedaCare would now like to have ambulance drivers performing the EKG, transmitting the readout electronically to be read before the patient even arrives at the hospital.[36]

The average door-to-balloon time for ThedaCare's outlying hospitals has been reduced from 212 minutes, in 2005, to 91 minutes in 2013.[37] ThedaCare's rural access hospitals, such as New London Medical Center, now strive to always get patients from their door to "balloon" in the cath lab at Appleton Medical Center within 90 minutes, even though it is a 20-mile drive (or a flight by helicopter). System-wide average door-to-balloon times have increased to 56 minutes in 2014 and 50 minutes in 2015, but those data include the outlying hospitals and their transport time. ThedaCare sets a great example by being committed to providing the best possible care to all patients, regardless of where they arrive.[38]

Improving Patient Flow in Outpatient Cancer Treatment

Back to the case of the cancer center, the scheduling of appointments and physician schedules created many of the patient delays in the oncology clinics. One general challenge with patient scheduling is that it is not known exactly how long different appointments will take. Physicians value their time—and it is indeed valuable time—so everyone has an incentive to avoid the waste of waiting for physicians; however, many of the steps taken to avoid this physician waiting impose significant waiting time on the patients.

As discovered during the direct observation of patient flow, many morning patients saw their oncologist 30 to 60 minutes late, even the first patient of the morning. One particular oncologist arrived 40 minutes late during the observation, and the nurse assistant commented, "That doctor is always 45 minutes late." By purposely creating a backlog of three patients to start the day, the oncologist was helping ensure there was no waiting time in case some appointments went faster than expected. A different oncologist was said to always schedule a two-hour block of patient appointments when he was scheduled for rounds at the hospital. A third oncologist intentionally scheduled 14 patients in a single hour, knowing this was unrealistic. The nurse assistant commented, "The nine o'clock patient probably won't be seen until 10:30." This behavior created patient backlogs and waiting, but again, it ensured that the oncologist would have a steady stream of patients to see.

A Lean process would do more to balance the objectives of preventing physician and patient waiting times. Some amount of patient waiting time might have to be tolerated, but a hospital should decide which scheduling policies are acceptable for consistency and to avoid upsetting patients. Getting physicians to cooperate with scheduling changes might be difficult, as they might justify their methods as ensuring the effective use of their time. Attempts to change these practices should involve the physicians, with leadership helping to establish the case for minimizing patient delays, asking physicians to help come up with solutions.

If the delays to see the oncologist were long, patients might have already missed their treatment appointment at the chemotherapy center. Treatment appointment slots were scheduled based on the expected time for getting through the oncologist appointment, but these times were not perfectly predictable. Disrupted chemotherapy schedules created additional rework and motion for the charge nurse, who had to prioritize patients, constantly juggling and readjusting the schedule throughout the day.

Once they were ready for the chemotherapy session, patients often waited due to defects in the process. This included the physician's office not properly sending the treatment order, a problem that consistently occurred 20% of the time. This created more rework for employees, more adjustments to the schedule, and more delays for the patients. When that process defect occurred, the chemotherapy staff fixed the short-term problem—they called or faxed the physician's office to get the orders, and the problem was considered solved. Certain offices were known to frequently create the same process defects, but the chemotherapy center had neither the time nor the political pull to give feedback to the physician's office in an attempt to solve the root cause. This lack of root cause problem solving made it unlikely that the defects would be prevented in the future.

Even getting a treatment chair did not guarantee that the patient's waiting time was over. For treatment to begin, many factors had to line up. Missing any one of these would cause a delay in treatment:

- Treatment chair
- Nurse
- Lab results
- Chemotherapy intravenous bag

One of the required factors was often missing. A patient might get seated in a chair, only to be delayed because the nurses were busy with other patients. The treatment center had standard patient-to-nurse ratios, but if too many patients were starting or finishing treatment at the same time, there was a short-term spike in the workload that could not be handled without causing treatment delays. The lab results were often delayed, sometimes because the wrong orders had been sent, leading to more rework and delays. The chemotherapy intravenous bag was often delayed because there had been a question with the order, and they were waiting for the physician to call back. In other cases, the intravenous bags had been sent to the treatment center but were misplaced because of poor organization. This led to the nurse walking and searching for the bag, which delayed that patient and other patients who were waiting for that chair.

The hospital realized that to reduce or minimize patient delays, it had to make a number of systemic improvements. It started with first identifying the root causes of process errors and defects over which it had control, including ensuring that nurse schedules lined up with patient demand and that charge nurses had standardized methods for prioritizing and rescheduling patients. After fixing problems in its control, the treatment center planned on working with the oncology clinics to help prevent delays due to errors that were created there, related to orders for chemotherapy, the lab, and the pharmacy.

Improving Flow for Ancillary Support Departments

Beyond patient flow, hospitals have successfully used Lean methods to improve the flow in many ancillary or support functions, including laboratories, pharmacies, perioperative services, and nutritional services. In these settings, the product is not the patient, but an item that is required for decision-making or continued care.

Improving Flow in Clinical Laboratories

Many hospitals have applied Lean methods to multiple areas of the laboratory, including the clinical lab, transfusion services (or blood bank), microbiology, and anatomic pathology. Many Lean efforts begin in the clinical lab area because testing volumes are highest, and the turnaround time expectations are often the fastest and most critical. Clinical lab specimens may be delayed in multiple stages of the value stream: during specimen collection, specimen receiving, or testing areas.

Reducing Delays in Specimen Collection

To understand the causes of long delays that keep specimens from getting to the lab, we need to observe the process to identify waste and delays in the complete testing value stream. During initial assessment activities, labs often find that up to 90% of the total turnaround time from specimen collection to lab result is spent waiting. To improve turnaround times, labs should reduce those delays instead of getting faster equipment or asking employees to work faster.

In this chapter, we discussed that labs typically have a busy morning spike due to physician rounds. In many cases, the lab might not start receiving specimens until 4:00 a.m., even though phlebotomy draws started at 3:00 a.m. This delay is due to intentional batching, either directed by managers or initiated by the phlebotomists themselves.

What might seem inefficient from the perspective of the lab, or the patient, is completely rational and efficient for the phlebotomist. The individual phlebotomist is maximizing productivity, which is often measured in terms of patient draws per hour. To minimize the waste of motion, the phlebotomist reduces the number of walking trips to the lab or to the tube system station. Tube systems that automate the transportation of specimens to the lab are often located in nurses' stations, which are sometimes inconveniently located at the end of long hallways.

In the Lean philosophy, we have to understand the root cause of the batching. Just mandating that phlebotomists send smaller batches to the lab might lead to unfortunate corner cutting, such as rushing through their work. If phlebotomists are pressured, they might take a single larger batch from their cart, dividing it up and sending small batches in succession to the lab. That workaround, creating the appearance of small batches, is not a true system improvement, as individual turnaround times would still be as slow as before.

By defining standardized work for phlebotomists and understanding the trade-offs with smaller batches, laboratory managers can make a decision that helps optimize the entire value stream. The exact balance point will vary based on the physical layout of the department and the inpatient units, but moving phlebotomy toward single-piece flow often means that phlebotomists make trips to the tube station after every two or three patients, a planned and consistent delay of 10–15 minutes, which is better than longer and less consistent delays. If the layout allows, phlebotomists might travel to the tube station after each and every individual patient, minimizing delays.

Managers must take care that phlebotomists are treated fairly in this process, that they are not given an unfair faster standard to which they are held accountable. Standardized work will help employees and managers understand how long the work takes to complete—drawing specimens and transporting them to the lab in a timely manner. Some hospitals have even taken the step of increasing the number of phlebotomists, recognizing that the trade-off between adding phlebotomist labor (which is relatively inexpensive) and time and reducing turnaround time is worthwhile. The trade-offs between larger and smaller batches are summarized in Table 9.2.

Reducing Delays in the Receiving Areas of the Lab

When observing the flow of specimens through the laboratory, we are likely to see more batching and more delays, including those in the preanalytical phase of the process.

Typically, specimens first arrive at a dedicated receiving area. This area might be further divided into an accessioning area (where specimens are received into the computer system by an assistant) and a processing area (where specimens are centrifuged or receive further preparation for testing). In many labs, the processing department is located out of the main flow, as specimens go into a separate room and then backtrack to testing. The physical separation of the processing area leads to poor communication and teamwork between assistants and medical technologists in the main laboratory testing area.

The distance and separation also lead to another understandable result—more batching. When the preanalytical work is further divided across two separate subdepartments, two different employees do the work with a handoff in between, as shown in Figure 9.10. When faced with the prospect of carrying a tube of blood 20 feet to the processing area, the assistant who did the accessioning work will naturally want to accumulate a batch (a tray or a bin) before moving specimens.

Table 9.2   Batch Size Trade-Offs

Larger Batches	Smaller Batches
Less phlebotomist walking	More phlebotomist walking
Longer turnaround time	Faster turnaround time
Fewer phlebotomists required	More phlebotomists required

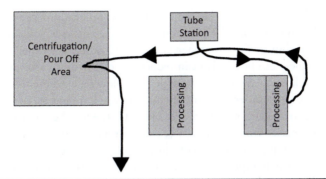

Figure 9.10   Functional silo layout encouraged batching and delay.

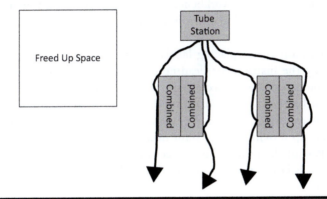

Figure 9.11   Combined flow benches allowed specimens to flow without batch delays.

Again, to be locally efficient, the assistant (like the phlebotomist) figures it is better to wait and carry 10 specimens instead of just one.

Children's Medical Center (Dallas, Texas) took the step of combining its accessioning and processing departments into a single area. Flow benches were created that had all of the tools required for accessioning and then immediately processing or centrifuging each specimen, without batching or delay. Employees were cross-trained, and responsibilities were reconfigured into the single area, as illustrated in Figure 9.11. Specimens that previously took up to 30 minutes to get through accessioning and processing flowed through in five to 10 minutes. Employees were not working faster; instead, the underlying system and layout had been improved. The new layout made the waste of walking (transportation for the specimen and motion for the assistant) that had been "required" under the old process unnecessary. Reconfiguring the benches in the lab was quick and inexpensive. The biggest expense was purchasing a few centrifuges for a few hundred dollars each, well worth the improvement of testing turnaround time.

Improving Flow Also Improves Quality and Teamwork

Other benefits of changing the layout and improving the flow include improved quality and teamwork. When batches are created, it is possible that the same process defect is created for each and every specimen. With single-piece flow, a defect can be caught immediately, preventing the accumulation of defects. Before Lean improvements, one lab director explained, "We would have

12 patient labels curled in a strip on the floor. So the first order didn't get processed until all 12 had been labeled. When you took all 12 of those over to the analyzer, you could only do four at a time. Think of the possibilities for error when you label 12 orders at a time."

By moving to single-piece flow, a lab can reduce the opportunities for mislabeled specimens. As the lab director explained, "Switching to single-piece flow reduced the risk of errors due to mislabeling. You have one set of orders in front of you, and you have one set of labels in front of you. It's almost impossible to mislabel somebody else's blood." The number of mislabeled specimens, as tracked by the lab, decreased from an average of eight per month to an average of four per month, leaving some opportunity for additional root cause problem solving.

Poor layouts can also hamper communication, teamwork, and problem solving. In one hospital lab, the old layout had receiving separated from the testing area. A new bench was created where specimens were processed and centrifuged by a lab assistant, who then handed specimens directly across a shared workbench to a technologist. Working directly across from each other improves communication and allows for immediate feedback and quick corrective actions.

If a new lab assistant is not placing labels on the specimen tubes just right, the labels might be misread by the instruments, leading to delayed test results. With the new layout, the technologist could provide immediate coaching and feedback. Before, the technologist would typically just fix the label (a workaround) instead of communicating with the person who created the process defect. In a Lean environment, having the opportunity to give direct feedback often ends up proving the assistant meant to do a good job but had not been fully trained properly. Part of the principle of respect for people is that we assume people want to do a good job, and it is fair to them to give feedback about their errors so they can do quality work the next time.

This new layout also helped improve specimen flow by building flexibility into the standardized work. Since the centrifuges were in the middle of the workbench, they were accessible by both the technologist and the assistant. While it was ideal for the assistant to unload the centrifuge for the technologist, the technologist could also unload specimens if time allowed.

Reducing Delays inside the Testing Areas of the Lab

Clinical laboratories tend to have very departmentalized, fragmented layouts that hamper efficient specimen flow in the testing areas. This is partially due to history, where testing specialties, such as chemistry and hematology, were their own academic departments. When hospitals created unified labs, the habit of maintaining separate subdepartments, often separated by walls or tall cabinets, remained. The overly functional layout does not correspond with the skills of medical technologists, who are often cross-trained and could do different types of testing work without harming the quality of results.

On night shifts, when volumes and staffing are low, a traditional lab might have just one medical technologist assigned to hematology and urinalysis, with work areas that might be more than 100 feet apart. Given that distance, the technologist is not likely to constantly walk back and forth between departments. Specimens tend to accumulate (or "batch up") in hematology when the technologist is in the urinalysis area and vice versa. One lab observed employees and measured that one night shift technologist walked more than four miles per shift between the distant urinalysis and microbiology departments. This added up to more than one hour per day of walking waste. This distance and walking slows turnaround, since many overnight test requests need to be done quickly for the sake of patient care. Employees feel pressured to be in two places at once, which is not realistic or fair to them, especially given the poor layout.

In some labs, this departmentalization might translate into higher staffing levels than would be needed in an improved layout. Before Lean, medical technologists are stationed in each area for the work that comes into the subdepartment. "We had several people who worked one instrument only," said a director in one hospital. "So someone might be sitting in microbiology, waiting for work, while people in hematology or urinalysis were flooded with orders." With long distances between departments, we cannot easily take advantage of efficiencies that would come from having a combined department that has all of the high-volume test instruments located close together.

Instead of two people each in the four subdepartments, we might be able to get the same amount of work done with just six people in a combined department. This conclusion would come from a detailed study of the work content and workloads in both subdepartments, not from a gut feeling. Labs might reassign any extra employees to test development work, do more cross-training with the freed time, or dedicate time to further improvements. When an employee leaves voluntarily, we might choose not to fill that position again. But, the remaining employees will not be overworked, stressed out, or fear future head count reductions.

Improving Flow in Anatomic Pathology

Before Lean was introduced at St. Paul's Hospital (Vancouver, British Columbia), part of Providence Health Care, the anatomic pathology lab's turnaround times for pathology reports were slower than desired. Less than 7% of reports were completed within one day, and only about 33% were completed within two days. Another challenge the lab faced was an increasing workload in a time of technologist shortages and fiscal constraints. After analyzing the existing process, the lab realized there were opportunities for improving turnaround times and handling the increasing work volume without pressuring employees to work faster or sacrificing quality. The lab rearranged the physical layout, created standardized work methods and schedules (as discussed in Chapter 5), and made other systemic changes that improved flow and reduced delays.

After improvements were made, the average turnaround time was reduced by one day, from four days to three, meaning that physicians had information earlier, allowing them to make key decisions about patient care, including those who had cancer, in a more timely manner. With a Lean process in place, the lab was now completing more than 30% of reports in one day and almost 60% in two days. The average turnaround times include all pathology reports, even highly complex cases that require in-depth analysis and therefore inherently longer testing and analysis times.

Lean improvements helped the patients through the faster turnaround time. The changes also helped improve the workflow for pathologists who review slides and dictate reports that are sent on to the patient's physician. Before Lean, work was done in large batches, resulting in slides not being delivered to the pathologists for reading until 11:00 a.m. This created a spike of work and increased pressure to finish reports quickly before the end of the day, to avoid extending the workday into the evening. As the lab improved its flow by reducing batching and other forms of delay, slides began arriving to the pathologists earlier in the morning, spreading out their workload and increasing their satisfaction.

Improvements to the layout and the overall design of the laboratory also reduced wasted time and motion for the employees. Reduced batching helped minimize the risk for errors and mislabeled specimens, reducing some stress on the employees (who feared making errors) and improving quality for the patients. After the pathologists examined slides, transcriptionists received dictated tapes from the pathologists that contained single cases, instead of lengthy tapes with multiple cases. This smoothed out the workload for the transcriptionists and further reduced waiting time for the final reports to be sent to the ordering physicians.

Employee satisfaction surveys, taken before and after the improvements, show how Lean did not lead anyone to sacrifice quality or employee morale in the name of productivity. When asked if "quality is a top priority in my area," the average score was 4.5 on a 5.0 scale after Lean was started (where 5.0 indicated employees agreed strongly), compared to a 3.5 score pre-Lean. Employees also agreed they were "satisfied with the department as a place to work," with a 4.0 score compared to an average score of 3.5 before Lean. These results and attitudes are common in effective Lean implementations.

All of the above benefits are good for the hospital: improved patient outcomes through faster turnaround time and improved quality, improved physician satisfaction, and improved employee satisfaction. Additionally, the hospital recognized direct financial savings from the Lean efforts. The department was able to phase out $60,000 worth of pathology equipment that was no longer needed as a result of improved flow. More importantly, the technologists were able to safely absorb a 9% increase in workload with existing staff.

Jane Crosby, the laboratory services director, commented, "St. Paul's Laboratory has always had a reputation for high quality. Sometimes this made our processes very complex as we tried to cover every possible contingency. With Lean we were able to further improve quality while simplifying our processes, and it has been very rewarding for the staff who feel less stressed while handling a higher work volume."

Improving Flow in Pharmacies

Unlike the lab, where faster results are better (unless results sit and wait before being read by the ordering physician), pharmacies have a different set of time and flow requirements. Speed in response time is important for some medication orders. In many cases, though, one of the general objectives is not delivering medications too early since medications delivered early are more likely to be returned to the pharmacy, creating more work for nurses and pharmacy employees.

Medication orders (such as first doses or missing medications) that do need a fast response might be delayed for a number of reasons before reaching the pharmacy. The flow of the order from the physician's thought of "I need to prescribe this medication" until the pharmacy receives the order could have delays due to miscommunication or bad processes. Unit clerks or nurses might literally not see an order due to disorganization or being busy with other tasks. Physician order entry can help reduce these missed handoffs and delays.

Inside the pharmacy, medication orders might be delayed in numerous ways. One delay may come from an overall mismatch in workloads and pharmacy staffing. If the overall workload is not level loaded, delays may occur at certain peak periods. At one pharmacy, before Lean, there was one "cart fill" run per day, when medications were gathered in the pharmacy to be sent to the inpatient units, and a single large daily batch of work was done for all units. Unfortunately, this cart fill was done during the morning, when doctors wrote new prescriptions (first doses) that had to be filled as soon as possible. This lack of *heijunka* led to delayed medications and frustrated employees, as one pharmacist recounted, "Somebody in here was crying just about every day because of the stress." With a Lean implementation, the pharmacy started doing four cart fills per day, which spread out the workload more evenly and avoided the morning conflict.

The response time of the pharmacy may also suffer from badly designed physical layouts and processes. Technicians might be walking many miles per day because the tools they use (such as label printers, computers, and the tube system station) are not located near each other. High-use medications may be scattered throughout the lab, which increases technician walking and delays medications. Poor layouts may, again, encourage employees to batch up work to suboptimize their own walking at the expense of medication flow.

Once medications have been picked, the layout and process may cause delays and batching of the pharmacist verifications. If pharmacists sit in their own area, outside the flow and separated from the pharmacy technicians, a single-piece flow verification might not be possible, meaning verifications will be batched. If technicians drop off medications to be verified, there might be a delay before the technician comes back to pick up verified medications, further delaying transportation to the patient.

Other medications are not sent individually. Many medications are stored, as general nonpatient-specific inventory, in the ED or inpatient units, so nurses can easily take them from a cabinet, as needed, although these are usually not made available until a pharmacist has reviewed the order and released the medication. Medications are also stored in units to allow the batching of replenishment from the pharmacy. Instead of sending commonly used medications one at a time all day long (which requires additional labor, packaging materials, and delivery time), larger quantities are restocked in a batched trip.

Before Lean, this is often done just once a day or a few times per week. As with many situations, there are trade-offs that need to be considered. Delivering every other day minimizes the walking involved in technicians delivering medications throughout the hospital. On the other hand, more frequent replenishment, while requiring more walking, leads to higher availability of medications in the units and fewer instances of unplanned (when meds are not available) "as needed" orders coming down to the pharmacy throughout the day. It may seem unintuitive to pharmacy employees at the start of their Lean journey, but delivering more frequently (hourly or every few hours) can reduce the total workload as the reactive trips to the inpatient units are reduced.

For medications that are stored in the nursing unit for a patient, the goal for the pharmacy is just-in-time delivery. If a physician writes a prescription for a medication to be given three times every eight hours, it is not in the best interest of the pharmacy to deliver three doses at once. Delivering a large batch would reduce walking, but it increases the chances that some of those doses will not be needed because of a change in the orders or the patient being moved or discharged. Often, when a patient is moved, meds are sent down to the pharmacy to be reissued to the new unit instead of being moved with the patient (creating the waste of transportation and the waste of motion).

Memorial Health (Savannah, Georgia) is one example of a hospital pharmacy that has improved using Lean. A team of department employees started by analyzing their own process, directly observing and measuring waste in the value stream and wasted motion by employees. The team made a number of systemic improvements over a 17-week period that reduced waste and improved response times and the availability of medications where they were needed.

The layout of the pharmacy was redesigned, reducing walking times and distances for the technicians by more than 50%. This led to faster response time for the typical first-dose order. In the new layout, one pharmacist was incorporated into the flow, as technicians could hand medications to the pharmacist for verification in a single-piece flow manner. This redesign impacted not only the layout but also the standardized work for the pharmacists. Before Lean, all three pharmacists did everything and anything. The overlap in responsibilities often led to confusion and delays when medications were waiting to be verified. Each pharmacist might have thought another was going to review a particular medication, or, more often, all three of the pharmacists were busy with phone calls or other consultative duties. The standardized work dedicated each pharmacist to one of three roles (fills, ordering checking, and phone consultations), although they could help each other out if time allowed and it did not hamper the flow in their area of responsibility.

At the end of the Memorial Health project, the pharmacy was providing better service for the patients and nurses. In an internal survey, nurses agreed with the following statements (as measured on a scale for which "strongly agree" scores a 1 and "strongly disagree" scores a 5):

- Medications seem to be more available when they are needed than they were six months ago. (Score = 2.04)
- I am pleased with the main pharmacy's improvements and attempt to provide better service to the floors and the patients. (Score = 1.75)

At Memorial, and other hospitals, improvements to pharmacy processes have helped make sure the right medications in the right doses are available in the right places as needed at the right time. This improves patient care while making work easier for the employees and reducing costs for the hospital. Lean also moves the emphasis away from process problems, such as missing doses and the resulting phone calls that come in, to letting the pharmacists focus on their true role of optimizing a patient's medication use.[39]

Conclusion

Many of the root causes of poor flow illustrated here can be seen in other departments, such as poor layouts, a lack of *heijunka*, and poorly designed value streams. If you work in a department not mentioned in this chapter, try to see how the general concepts fit your processes. If you do work for a department mentioned here, you still do not just copy what others have done. Make sure the Lean principles are being used to solve your particular problems. To improve flow, go to the *gemba* and observe the process firsthand. Look for value-added and non-value-added time and identify the root causes of delays. Rather than accepting delays or the causes of delays as given, go and make changes that will improve flow.

Lean Lessons

- Make improvements that remove rocks instead of covering the problems with more water (workarounds or waiting queues).
- Single-piece flow is a direction more than an absolute mandate.
- Flow improvements apply to patients, both waiting for appointments and waiting for care on arrival; similar ideas can apply to the flow of any material or information.
- Unevenness in flow can be the result of natural occurrences or our own policies.
- Lean teaches us to not accept *mura* as a given.
- When flow is interrupted, ask why, and fix the systemic causes of batching or other delays.
- Improving flow often improves quality and teamwork and reduces cost.
- Faster is not always better, depending on the customer needs.

Points for Group Discussion

■ How would hospital processes or your department be different if physician rounds were level loaded?

■ How can you better balance staff levels with workloads?

■ Why might nurses feel disrespected or not valued by being sent home early when census is low?

■ What improvements would the hospital see if we could discharge patients evenly across all seven days of the week? Is this possible?

■ How might the hospital level load elective surgeries throughout the year? What departments or functions might need to get involved?

■ How might improved flow help improve the quality of care for patients?

■ What are the longest waiting times for appointments or care that we might want to address with Lean?

■ What is the proper balance between patient waiting time and physician waiting time?

Notes

1. Ontario Ministry of Health and Long-Term Care, Ontario Wait Times, http://www.health.gov.on.ca/en/public/programs/waittimes/surgery/default.aspx (accessed March 26, 2015).

2. Chorley, Matt, Waiting Times Target to Receive Treatment within 18 Weeks Which Kept Being Missed Will Instead Be SCRAPPED, http://www.dailymail.co.uk/news/article-3111227/Waiting-times-target-receive-treatment-18-weeks-kept-missed-instead-SCRAPPED.html (accessed October 16, 2015).

3. Neergaard, Laura, The Difference in Doctor Wait Times from State to State Will Astound You, http://www.huffingtonpost.com/2014/06/13/doctor-wait-times_n_5493445.html (accessed October 16, 2015).

4. Barlow, Linda, Cleveland Clinic's Value-Based Care Team Improves Patient Wait Times, Saves Costs, http://www.realworldhealthcare.org/2013/08/cleveland-clinics-value-based-care-team-improves-patient-wait-times-saves-costs/(accessed October 16, 2015).

5. Toussaint, John, and Roger Gerard, *On the Mend: Revolutionizing Healthcare to Save Lives and Transform the Industry* (Cambridge, MA: Lean Enterprise Institute, 2010), 95.

6. Crane, Jody, and Chuck Noon, *The Definitive Guide to Emergency Department Operational Improvement: Employing Lean Principles with Current ED Best Practices to Create the "No Wait" Department* (New York: Productivity Press, 2011), 195.

7. Ng, David, Gord Vail, et al., "Applying the Lean principles of the Toyota Production System to reduce wait times in the emergency department," *CJEM Canadian Journal of Emergency Medical Care*, 2010, 12(1): 50–57.

8. NPress, NPress Reveals Patient Pet Peeves Survey Results, February 13, 2010, http://www.prlog.org/10529537-npress-reveals-patients-pet-peeves-survey-results.html (accessed August 29, 2015).

9. Bahri, Sami, *Follow the Learner* (Cambridge, MA: Lean Enterprise Institute, 2009), 29.

10. BBC News, Target "Putting A&E Care at Risk," http://news.bbc.co.uk/2/hi/health/4339653.stm (accessed October 16, 2015).

11. *The Guardian*, "Patients forced to wait in ambulances outside "too full" A&Es, says Labour," http://www.theguardian.com/society/2014/aug/10/patients-forced-wait-ambulances-accident-emergency-hospitals-nhs (accessed October 16, 2015).

12. Siddique, Haroon, Hospital A&E Waiting Time Target Missed for 90th Week in a Row, http://www.theguardian.com/society/2015/apr/13/hospital-waiting-time-target-missed (accessed October 16, 2015).

13. Wellman, Joan, Howard Jeffries, and Pat Hagan, *Leading the Lean Healthcare Journey* (New York: Productivity Press, 2010), 216.

14. Ibid., 227.

15. Graban, Mark, Toyota's Commitment to People, LeanBlog.org, September 1, 2008, http://www.lean-blog.org/2008/09/toyotas-committment-to-people/(accessed March 26, 2015).

16. Avera Health, unpublished video, 2015.

17. ValuMetrix Services, Kaiser Permanente Case Study, http://www.valumetrixservices.com/sites/default/files/client_results_pdf/CS_KaiserEast_Lab_OC10113.pdf (accessed August 29, 2015).

18. Berczuk, Carol, "The Lean hospital," *The Hospitalist*, June 2008, http://www.the-hospitalist.org/details/article/186537/The_Lean_Hospital.html (accessed March 26, 2015).

19. Korner, Kimberly T., and Nicole M. Hartman, "Lean tools and concepts reduce waste, improve efficiency," *American Nurse Today*, March 2011, http://www.americannursetoday.com/lean-tools-and-concepts-reduce-waste-improve-efficiency/(accessed March 26, 2015).

20. Crane and Noon, *Definitive Guide*, 133.

21. Nelson, Roxanne, and Maureen S. Kennedy, "The other side of mandatory overtime," *American Journal of Nursing*, April 2008, 108(4): 23–24.

22. American College of Emergency Physicians, Emergency Department Waiting Times, http://www.acep.org/content.aspx?id=25908 (accessed March 26, 2015).

23. Murrell, Karen L., Steven R. Offerman, and Mark B. Kauffman. "Applying Lean: Implementation of a rapid triage and treatment system," *Western Journal of Emergency Medicine*, 2011, 12(2): 184–91.

24. Otto, M. Alexander, "ED triage may delay treatment in acutely ill," *ACEP News*, http://www.acep.org/Content.aspx?id=49469 (accessed March 26, 2015).

25. AHRQ Innovations Exchange, Team Triage Reduces Emergency Department Walkouts, Improves Patient Care, http://www.innovations.ahrq.gov/content.aspx?id=1735&tab=1#a3 (accessed March 26, 2015).

26. Meyer, Harris, "Life in the 'Lean' lane: Performance improvement at Denver Health," *Health Affairs*, November 2010, 29(11): 2054–60 http://content.healthaffairs.org/content/29/11/2054.full (accessed October 16, 2015).

27. Hafen, Mark, "A case for getting rid of waiting rooms," *Veterinary Hospital Design*, January 4, 2011, http://veterinaryhospitaldesign.dvm360.com/hanging-with-hafen-case-getting-rid-waiting-rooms (accessed March 26, 2015).

28. Przybylowski, Ted, Jr., and Mary Frazier, "No waiting," *Healthcare Design*, November 2010, http://www.healthcaredesignmagazine.com/article/no-waiting (accessed March 26, 2015).

29. McConnell, K. J., et al., "Ambulance diversion and lost hospital revenues," *Annals of Emergency Medicine*, 2006, 48: 702–10.

30. Ibid.

31. Centers for Disease Control, "Emergency Department Visits," http://www.cdc.gov/nchs/fastats/emergency-department.htm (accessed February 18, 2016).

32. Boyle, Theresa, Ontario Health Budget Rises, but by Much Less Than Last Year, http://www.thestar.com/news/gta/2015/04/23/ontario-health-budget-rises-but-by-much-less-than-last-year.html (accessed October 16, 2015).

33. Toussaint and Gerard, *On the Mend*, 34.

34. Toussaint, John, "Writing the new playbook for U.S. health care: Lessons from Wisconsin," *Health Affairs*, September 2009, 28(5): 1343–50.

35. Ibid.

36. Toussaint, John, presentation to Healthcare Value Network, March 2011.

37. ThedaCare, Teamwork Speeds Up Heart Attack Response Time, https://www.thedacare.org/about-us/ThedaCares-Improvement-Journey/Code-STEMI-Case-Study.aspx (accessed October 13, 2015).

38. Moore, Theresa, personal correspondence, September 2015.

39. ValuMetrix Services, Pharmacy at Memorial Health University Medical Center Case Study, http://www.valumetrixservices.com/sites/default/files/client_results_pdf/CS_MemorialHealth_Savannah_Pharmacy_OC10134.pdf (accessed August 29, 2015).

Chapter 10

Lean Design

Better, Faster, and Cheaper

In recent years, health systems have partnered with their architects and construction builders to embrace "Lean design" principles and practices. It is possible to build, renovate, or finish out spaces in a way that breaks traditional trade-offs. Spaces and buildings can work better (for patients and staff), faster (completed before estimated dates), and cheaper (coming in under budget or less expensive than similar projects). As with anything Lean, these benefits come from engaging people and improving processes, not by cutting corners or somehow limiting the value that is being created.

What problems are being solved with Lean design? For one, traditional design processes don't involve frontline staff in the process enough, either getting no input or superficial input, until the new space is handed over to staff. Or, input is received only from a select few, making it more difficult for others to accept the design.

Secondly, traditional design focuses too much on the space or layout, often focused on making it larger or look better, without considering workflows—fitting the space to the workflows or simultaneously improving workflows and space to get the fit that works best in practice.

Thirdly, design and construction is often a batch process, with major stages of work being "thrown over the wall" without many opportunities to iteratively improve a design throughout the process. Instead of a hospital asking the architect to design a building for them, the Lean design process means that everybody works together to design and build more effective spaces and buildings.

Bernita Biekmann, AIA, EDAC, LSSBB, an architect and director of Lean strategy for architecture firm HKS, says, "The traditional approach was more of a 'Band Aid' approach, trying to fix immediate problems instead of looking out beyond today for how to be a hospital of the future or to create an ideal state of working."[1] Space design must consider future ways of working, and vice versa. A hospital that expects nurses to spend more time at the bedside might build smaller nurses' stations, while providing technology and workflow improvements that help make that work effectively.

"We no longer rely on experts or architects to tell us how to design the building," says Dr. David Munch, former chief clinical and quality officer at Exempla Lutheran Medical Center (Colorado). Instead, Munch continues, "We deeply engage the frontline in codifying their ideal work flows.

Architects are design team participants who take the process information and transform it into a design. They are not the project leads. They are team members."[2]

Understanding the Current State before Designing the Future

In many hospitals, staff members often ask for new spaces that are similar to what they already have, but larger. Or, a health system will spend time and money sending leaders to benchmark other organizations. The risk with benchmarking or copying is that a design that worked well in one situation and with one set of workflows might not work well in another setting. An alternative to investing in travel is to invest in staff and leaders better understanding their own current space and workflows from a Lean perspective.

It's difficult for staff to have a vision and to truly understand their needs (and patient needs) until they have participated in workplace observation activities or value stream mapping, as discussed in Chapter 4. When the people who actually do the work observe each other and draw spaghetti diagrams, they can identify ways in which the existing layout leads to wasted motion for staff or patients. A future-state design can help address many of those problems more effectively, instead of just building a larger department (which can create new types of waste, such as more walking).

"When done properly, observation is a way to honor the person whose work is being observed," say Naida Grunden and Charles Hagood, authors of the book *Lean-Led Hospital Design*, an excellent reference that takes a much deeper look at this topic. They add, "Observation is the only way to understand the complexity, waste, and cost of processes, as well as how those things may be frustrating workers while impeding on the flow to the patient."[3]

Array Architects worked with a health system to redesign a dialysis unit. Jon Sell, an architect, writes, "Understanding how the client operates is an important first step that healthcare designers need to accomplish prior to designing a space that can support their workflow and processes. In many cases, the results are eye opening for both the designer and client and the insights gained will inform the design and possibly the way clinicians do their work."[4] Shadowing a nurse through a patient's treatment uncovered issues and opportunities, including supply storage being "scattered around the unit," leading to excessive walking. Drawing spaghetti diagrams led to insights including

- "The existing unit does not have proper space clearances around Treatment Bay 3 and it became a bottleneck on the unit as staff needed to access a computer on wheels.
- A utility room is located off the Unit and added excessive footsteps.
- There is not a patient nourishment station, so the clinician needed to go to the staff lounge for necessary items.
- Necessary supplies are not at the patient's bedside, two main supply cabinets are centrally located, however the location is not always convenient to the staff.
- There is one charting station per two patients (aligns with the RN-to-patient ratio), however these workstations are not at the bedside, which results in unnecessary transcription on paper to entering the information into the computer."

The observations and spaghetti diagrams helped influence their future-state design of space and process. The nurses will spend more time greeting the patients and discussing their treatment, in part, because "dialysis tubing and necessary supplies are prepped and ready on a tray at patient

Figure 10.1   Spaghetti diagram showing nurse walking patterns in a heart center.

bedside." Beds with built-in scales help reduce the waste of patient transport, and each treatment bay has bedside charting computers, which reduces waiting and reduces some risk of error.

Figure 10.1 shows a spaghetti diagram that traces a nurse through Riley Hospital's existing heart center, which then influenced design of the new space and improved workflows.

Better Care at a Lower Cost through Better Design

Teams at organizations like Seattle Children's are able to deliver less expensive spaces that work better for patients and staff. The lower cost doesn't come from cutting corners or "being cheap," but rather making sure spaces are built to be the right size—not too large and not too small in a way that leads to immediate expansion or additional construction expense.

Another way that cost is reduced is through the improved collaboration between the hospital team, the architects, and the construction company. As needs are better understood early in the process, there are fewer change orders and other requests that tend to add cost and delays to a construction project. A project the size of the Bellevue surgery center might normally lead to 600 "requests for information" or RFIs, but their project had only 30, which was a contributor to the project being completed early and under budget.[5]

Designed to be Staff Centered and Patient Centered

Since Lean design is meant to create spaces that work better for everybody involved, input from those stakeholders at every stage of the process is invaluable. Understanding the need for staff to spend less time walking to gather supplies aligns with a patient's need to have staff with them at the bedside. Adding additional inventory points, in each patient room or for each set of rooms, is a Lean design decision that supports staff and patient needs.

In the Lean spirit of rethinking "the way it's always been done," one hospital was inspired to make sure that all exterior space in the building was dedicated to patient care or staff break rooms. Managers gave up windows and took offices in interior parts of the building, giving higher priority for the best locations to others. Plus, in a Lean culture, managers realized they would spend less time in their offices anyway, reducing the need for windows.

Designed for Uncertainty of Volumes or Workflows

Lean factories are typically designed to be flexible, since it's difficult to perfectly predict future demand for different types of products. As much as possible, flexible assembly lines or cells are created to allow multiple products or variations to be built together, reducing the risk of inaccurate forecasts. Lean factories are also designed to consider different growth and expansion scenarios, creating possible answers for the question of "what happens if demand increases by 50%?"

Key decisions, such as the number of beds needed in a new emergency department, are dependent not just on volume assumptions and scenarios (such as the impact of standalone urgent care centers being built). The number of beds required also depends on Lean improvements taking place in other departments, such as laboratory and radiology. If planned reductions in turnaround times do not materialize, the emergency department (ED) might open with complaints that it was underbuilt. Building layouts based on a shift to team-based care or *kanban* replenishment might be risky if those new process models and workflows are not successful.

With all of the uncertainly facing healthcare in 2015, health systems are smart to build spaces that are flexible for different scenarios. What happens if hospital admissions drop dramatically, or if more intensive care unit (ICU) beds are needed because the patients who do get admitted are much sicker? Biekmann says, "No one can predict the future, but we can prepare for the future."[6] Hospitals that build flexible rooms might spend a bit more on casework, but those rooms can be converted more easily from a heart room to an ICU room, says Biekmann.

Designed Using Mockups and Iterations

Lean design efforts include the construction of full-scale mockups built from cardboard, wood, or other temporary materials. Mockups are often constructed in rented warehouse space, empty shell space, or parking garages. Mockups include everything from a single patient room to an entire unit, based on the time and resources available, among other factors.

While it takes effort and expense to create the mockups, tweaking the design by simulating the work is easier and far more effective than looking at architectural drawings. Although architects and engineers can typically visualize a space based on two-dimensional plans, it can sometimes be hard for hospital staff to see the architect's vision from paper. Full-scale mockups allow staff to see the physical space, touch it, evaluate it, and modify it as needed.

It's generally less expensive (and definitely less frustrating) to make changes earlier rather than later. Relatively major changes can be made before physical construction, such as moving walls or adjusting hallway corners to allow easier, bump-free patient transport. Or, minor details get discovered, such as the need to add a wall hook for a patient's IV bag in each room's bathroom. In the design and construction of the Seattle Children's Hospital Bellevue facility, mockups meant that "participants often made their spaces smaller, changed traditional adjacencies, or completely changed their design thinking after seeing and using" their paper design brought to life.[7]

Greater Baltimore Medical Center built a mockup of an entire pharmacy unit in a parking garage, allowing staff to simulate different tasks and workflows. In doing so, the team identified waste and improved both their work processes and the layout design. Through these efforts, their architecture firm, Hord Coplan Macht, estimated that the medical center would reduce pharmacist hours by 19% and pharmacy tech hours by 11%.

Riley Hospital for Children (Indianapolis) worked with their architecture firm, HKS, in the Lean design process for finishing out various floors and units in an inpatient tower. The author provided assistance from a Lean perspective, teaching staff members how to conduct analysis of their current workflows in their current spaces. This structure observation, typically conducted over two or three full days, influenced a discussion about future layouts and workflows, along with ideas for short-term *kaizen* improvements in their current space. Staff and managers were able to have constructive discussions with the architects about what they absolutely needed and what was a "nice to have" desire, based on their shared goals of improving patient care. Direct input from the parents of former burn unit patients helped everybody better understand the specific needs and concerns of that type of patient and how and why the space needed to be different from a typical medical/surgical space.

About Riley, Biekmann wrote, "Portions of the design were constructed simply on the shell floors to do day-in-the-life testing to validate the design. The affectionately called 'plastic hospital' enabled the users to see what they could not see on paper, and that is how they would work in the new design, before the new design was complete. Each department ran 6–8 scenarios from changing of shift to code blue tests on the design to make sure the design supported the operational plan *before* construction."[8]

Mockups were valuable as the hospital shifted from an older neonatal ICU ward layout, one that had a dozen patients in a large room, to a more modern private room approach. The new space required different workflows and running simulations in the space helped the team solve particular problems involving communication, visibility, and the need for nurses to help each other across rooms before the space was built. Biekmann reflected, "The hospital had a lot more buy in from creating an ideal state instead of just using a design from someplace else. We could help them see a vision of something they hadn't looked at before" through that process.

Building mockups has helped some hospitals prevent mistakes that might have occurred as the result of wanting to directly copy another hospital's design. The same design that works well in one setting might not work well for another hospital with different volumes, patient acuities, and staffing patterns. One hospital reported trying to copy the Seattle Children's Bellevue layout and learned, through the mockups, that "it didn't work for them culturally, the way they treated patients," so "it was scrapped," and they went forward with a different design. In a traditional design process, it would have been built, and "instead of a one day problem, it would have potentially had to spend millions in rework costs." This goes to show that there is not a single "best practice" layout that always works in all settings. More important is the right fit and alignment between layouts and workflows in a particular situation.

Lean Design at East Tennessee Children's Hospital

East Tennessee Children's Hospital (Knoxville) has been using Lean design for a new tower that will open in September 2016 that is designed to provide a better patient experience and improve efficiency for everybody involved.

The existing outpatient surgery process flow includes parking a block or two away, walking to registration and then to the lab (on the same floor). The patient goes to two additional floors for surgical prep, in a semi-private room, then to a holding room, in a large open bay, and finally to surgery. The Post-Anesthesia Care Unit (PACU) is on the same level, but the patient returns to the fourth floor for "phase two" recovery before going home.

In the future design, parking will be underneath the building, with spots reserved for surgery families. Patients will be preregistered, meaning they can get the rest of their care in a single floor, with the pre- and postsurgical rooms being directly next to the operating rooms. The PACU space is designed to be multi-function, meaning patients can be prepped or recovered in the same space. Patients will now be in a private room pre- and postsurgery, except for the most critical patients who will still be recovered in an open bay PACU. The need to keep some open bay space was a design criteria that came from the anesthesiologists and PACU nurses based on their need to "swarm" a patient if something is wrong.

The hospital's architecture firm, Shepley Bulfinch, proposed Lean design, including input from user groups and mockups. "The architect was open to us experimenting, doing measures, getting feedback, and modifying layouts," said Isaac Mitchell, director of Lean for the hospital.[9] On weeks alternating with the architects' biweekly meetings, Mitchell led a series of improvement sessions with different groups of hospital staff. The following week, he would meet with the architects to determine how to support these changes architecturally. User groups were involved from the beginning, including the outline of the space, the rough-cut layout, and the physical floor plan. The hospital frontline staff used spaghetti diagrams to understand all of the flows, all of the places people were going, and how to accommodate their needs. Additionally, architects completed direct observations with hospital providers and staff to better understand their operating requirements and hospital culture.

Initial full-scale mockups were done in a small 800-square-foot space, which limited them to individual rooms. But it allowed them to look at the detailed design, including getting input from parents (whose requests included a power outlet near their chair for charging a phone).

What did the hospital learn from the mockups? They learned that 11 of the 40 rooms would have been "unusable for full size beds because of columns centered on the headwall of the room." That "would have been an expensive and frustrating mistake," said Mitchell, had they not changed the design at that early stage. The hospital also changed the door design to a tri-fold design, as they learned a dual sliding door would not have left enough clearance for everything including emergency equipment. Some relatively simple spreadsheet modeling also showed that the hospital could feel comfortable reducing the number of pre- and postsurgical beds and operating rooms because "patients will be flowing instead of just sitting there."

Based on this initial experience, the hospital is now developing a more formal 3P, or production preparation process. This includes creating a full-scale unit mocked up in rented warehouse space, as shown in Figure 10.2. The department can "see not just how it's going to look, but how it's going to operate," which has reassured people that the vastly different design will work. This is in contrast to the old approach of saying "here's your space, figure it out" once it was already built.

Figure 10.2   A full-scale mockup, showing the view of a patient room from the nurses' station.

They have worked through scenarios and learned how things will work "so they are ready to go on day one." As part of an interesting partnership with a local manufacturing company, employees of Denso visited the mockup space to give input from an "outside eyes" perspective.

While some organizations' first exposure to any Lean concepts is through design efforts, East Tennessee Children's Hospital was building upon prior Lean experience, as did Seattle Children's Hospital. "Lean design was a natural extension of Lean daily management," said Mitchell, "and the culture helped people feel comfortable in speaking up instead of just nodding their heads and agreeing with the plan that was being presented." Lean thinking is also driving the hospital to work toward smoothing and leveling the schedule and flow of patients instead of asking them to all arrive early. And, they are improving their processes to make sure the right information is available in advance of procedures, rather than discovering a problem the morning of surgery.

As with all things Lean, Lean design and daily Lean management (discussed more in Chapter 11) are about focusing on the patient and involving everybody continuously improving workflows and the design process itself. Those efforts certainly won't end when the first patient arrives to the new tower for surgery.

Integrated Lean Project Delivery at Akron Children's Hospital

The history of Akron Children's Hospital dates back to the late nineteenth century, and they have, by the end of 2014, expanded to become a 421-bed hospital with more than 5,000 employees and medical staff. The hospital found itself, by 2011, needing "additional space for physician practices, operating rooms, emergency department services, and neonatal intensive care beds," along with the need for an independent outpatient surgery center.[10] Without years of experience and success with Lean and Six Sigma being used for operations improvement in the hospital, "this project would have followed a course of a traditional building project."[11]

The approach used was called "Integrated Lean Project Delivery®" (ILPD®), as developed by Akron Children's construction company, Boldt. Integrated project delivery, or IPD, is an approach that "integrates people, systems, business structures, and practices into a process that collaboratively harnesses the talents and insights of all participants to optimize project results, increase value to the owner, reduce waste, and maximize efficiency through all phases of design, fabrication, and construction."[12] IPD might already sound a lot like Lean, with the contractual collaboration and risk or gain sharing between the health system, architects, general contractor, and others. But, Boldt says they are "rigorously integrating Lean into IPD" by using Lean methods to reduce waste in building projects completed at Akron Children's, Sutter Health, and other healthcare organizations.[13] The Akron Children's approach combined Lean operations, Lean design, and Lean construction and was inspired by a visit to Seattle Children's Hospital and the Bellevue surgical center.[14]

Akron Children's involved "patients and families, as well as staff" from "day one" of the project.[15] Compared to a traditional construction project, a large number of people (300) were involved in value stream mapping, spaghetti diagrams, and the evaluation of "full-scale cardboard mockups in a warehouse." Flexibility was an important concept, as private neonatal ICU rooms were built so that they could be converted to pediatric ICU rooms or regular inpatient rooms, as needed. In the iterative Lean style, Akron Children's leaders insisted on not "settling for less than seven iterations" of any design or concept. Early designs "always look perfect at first glance, but they can be improved," the hospital learned.[16]

Through these methods, along with a lot of creativity, teamwork, and hard work, Akron Children's ended up with a building that was built

- Two months ahead of schedule
- For $47 million less than anticipated (a 20% reduction)
- 21% smaller than originally expected, resulting in $20 million of the savings[17]

Their chief operating officer, Grace Wakulchik, said, "The integrated Lean design approach helped Akron Children's realize cost and space savings that have enabled additional technology and resource investments throughout" the new pavilion.[18]

Conclusion

Lean hospitals focus on reducing waste, improving flow, and providing a better experience for patients and staff, all while minimizing costs. Traditional approaches for designing and building (or renovating) healthcare spaces are often full of waste, delays, and unnecessary expense. And these methods, unfortunately, do not properly engage the people who then have to work in or manage those spaces. Lean design helps organizations to build better spaces that are on time and under budget by improving space and workflows in an integrated and mutually supportive way. It's not often that a health system gets an opportunity for major construction, with the expense and effort that's required. That's why it's important to design and build a space that minimizes waste in ways that set the organization up for smooth operations and continuous improvement over time. Instead of just copying another hospital's design, it's possible to use Lean thinking, along with the input and creativity of our staff, to build spaces that truly meet the unique needs of our organization and our patient populations.

Lean Lessons

- "The way we've always done things" can always be challenged, including the way we design and build healthcare spaces.
- Understanding the current state is an important step in designing an improved future state.
- Involving staff and physicians early is better than trying to force "buy-in" once a design has already been created.
- Iterative design, through mockups and simulations, might take longer up front, but it leads to more effective designs and ends up saving time through later design and construction phases.
- Lean design leads to spaces and workflows that work better for staff, patients, physicians, families, and all stakeholders.
- Lean design allows for construction to be "better, faster, and cheaper" while delivering the highest quality and fitness for use.

Points for Group Discussion

- What new spaces are going to be built or significantly redesigned in the next few years? What is our vision for how Lean design can help?

- If departments or leaders are planning for new space, are we sure we have first done everything we can to maximize the use of the existing space and capacity, using Lean methods for improvement?
- What can we do to free up staff time to participate in current-state analysis, mockup review, or similar activities?
- Why is it important to have actual patients and families participating in these efforts?
- How can we determine if architecture and construction firms are seriously committed to Lean design or if they are just using the buzzwords?

Notes

1. Biekmann, Bernita, personal interview, September 2015.
2. Grunden, Naida, and Charles Hagood, *Lead-Led Hospital Design* (New York: Productivity Press, 2012), 19.
3. Grunden and Hagood, 16.
4. Sell, Jon, Lean Applied to Designing a Dialysis Unit, http://blog.array-architects.com/kc/lean-applied-to-designing-a-dialysis-unit (accessed October 23, 2015).
5. Grunden and Hagood, 157.
6. Biekmann, personal interview.
7. Wellman, 231.
8. Biekmann, Bernita, Lean Design, http://www.hksinc.com/insight/lean-design/ (accessed October 22, 2015).
9. Mitchell, Isaac, personal interview, September 2015.
10. Vinas, Tonya, *Lean Operations, Lean Design, Lean Construction* (Akron: Akron Children's Hospital, 2014), 12.
11. Vinas, 27.
12. The American Institute of Architects, Integrated Project Delivery: A Guide, http://www.aia.org/groups/aia/documents/pdf/aiab083423.pdf (accessed October 26, 2015).
13. Boldt, Integrated Lean Project Delivery, http://www.theboldtcompany.com/page/integrated-lean-project-delivery/ (accessed October 26, 2015).
14. Silvis, Jennfer Kovacs, Using Mixed Methods to Build Akron Children's New Pavilion, http://www.healthcaredesignmagazine.com/article/using-mixed-methods-build-akron-childrens-new-pavilion (accessed October 26, 2015).
15. Vinas, 31.
16. Vinas, 69.
17. Silvis.
18. Akron Children's Hospital, Akron Children's Hospital Shares Secrets to Building a Lean Facility in New Book, https://www.akronchildrens.org/cms/news/book-shares-how-to-build-lean-hospital-facility/index.html (accessed October 26, 2015).

Chapter 11

Engaging and Leading Employees

Improving the Way We Manage

Lean is not just about tools. It is also a distinct management method that guides what we do as managers and how we lead our employees. Convis wrote, "Management has no more critical role than motivating and engaging large numbers of people to work together toward a common goal. Defining and explaining what that goal is, sharing a path to achieving it, motivating people to take the journey with you, and assisting them by removing obstacles—these are management's reason for being."[1] Is that true, today, for all leaders in your organization?

The Lean challenge goes beyond getting through an initial project. Once that phase is over, we still have people and processes to manage on an ongoing basis. That is why Lean is a never-ending journey—we have to guard against slipping back into old methods, and we have to push for additional improvement or, more accurately, create an environment where people want to continually improve. An engaged workforce, in which everybody is participating in identifying and implementing improvements, is the best way to achieve long-term success.

The traditional management mindset looks at a set of standard operating procedures and thinks, "We put a lot of thought into these processes, so they must be perfect." Assuming otherwise might be considered a sign of failure or incompetence. Lean thinkers, on the other hand, assume that a process can always be improved, even if it seems to work fine today. The adage "If it's not broke, don't fix it" does not apply in a Lean setting. Lean leaders accept that they are not perfect. Not being perfect is acceptable as long as the team is continuously working toward perfection. Lean thinkers might say, "It's not broke, but it's not perfect, so let's make it better!" Continuous improvement applies to everyone and everything, including the way we lead.

People often attribute this quotation to a senior Toyota executive, comparing themselves to their Detroit competitors: "Brilliant process management is our strategy. We get brilliant results from average people managing brilliant processes. We observe that our competitors often get average (or worse) results from brilliant people managing broken processes."[2] Hospitals typically have brilliant people (and they're caring and hardworking). Imagine how much better things could be with brilliant processes. They are not mutually exclusive.

Before Lean, managers might not be aware of what is broken. With the best of intentions, employees might hide problems by working around them. It might look like people are busy, but they are busy dealing with waste. By learning to recognize waste, by getting out of our offices, and by encouraging people to speak up, we can finally start to see what is broken in the details of our processes. If employees are afraid to speak up, the burden falls on management to create an environment where people feel safe.

It is not enough to tell our employees they have to find and eliminate waste in their own work. We also have to commit to managing differently. Many supervisors and managers have difficulty making the transition to managing in the Lean workplace. Just as employees might fear layoffs, supervisors often fear losing their power or becoming irrelevant in a culture of employee engagement. Some managers (or executives) might have to be replaced, but most can be taught and coached in the Lean approach. David Mann said, "What makes Lean difficult is not that it is so complicated but that it is so different from what we've learned."[3]

A few years into their Lean journey at ThedaCare, the hospital kept staff and leaders busy with "rapid improvement events" and other projects focused on the details of the work. One day, a "brave soul," as former chief executive officer (CEO) John Toussaint, MD, describes them, asked a senior executive, "How are we supposed to change when you are managing the same way?"[4] A question like that is a good sign that people are willing to speak up (and feel safe doing so).

In a culture of fear, a person would have to be very brave to question their leaders. In a Lean culture, leaders and staff can and do question and challenge each other in the name of improvement. Kim Barnas, former president of ThedaCare's two largest hospitals, wrote that a manager observed, "The ultimate arrogance is to change the way people work without changing the way we manage them."[5] The question and comment served as a bit of a wake-up call for ThedaCare's leaders to create a management system and a new culture.

Traditionally, organizations tend to be very hierarchical and top-down in their approach, many hospitals included. One hospital director said, "We struggle with this. We still have a very command and control middle management workforce who are extremely protective of their departments and their problems." Managers in a Lean environment do not make all the decisions or solve all the problems. Lean managers avoid giving directives to their employees. Many managers do not know how to operate in any other way.

Toussaint humbly talked about his efforts to shift his own personal leadership style to set an example for the rest of the organization. Table 11.1 shows his comparison of Lean leadership styles to what he calls traditional "white coat" leadership.[6] The white coat, not limited to physicians, signifies formal position-based authority. The attributes of white coat leadership tend to stifle open communication and quality improvement. "CEOs and other leaders are not generally rewarded for being humble," says Toussaint, adding, "No one person has all the answers, however, and humility demands that we recognize this ... in humility there is great freedom. We can stop pretending to know everything."[7]

Table 11.1   A Comparison of Leadership Styles

"White Coat Leadership"	*"Improvement Leadership"*
All knowing	Patient
In charge	Knowledgeable
Autocratic	Facilitator
The buck stops here	Teacher
Impatient	Student
Blaming	Helper
Controlling	Communicator

One U.S. hospital was a few years into its Lean journey, yet the CEO still made many top-down decisions. Patient surveys showed that late-night noise was the biggest cause of complaints. Inpatient unit managers were, needless to say, surprised when workers arrived to install carpet in the hallways. Unfortunately, the new carpet made it physically harder for nurses to push computer carts down those hallways, so they spent more time at the nurses' station. One executive mandate (use technology to get out from the station) ran into conflict with the other mandate (carpeted hallways). Instead of following a plan-do-study-adjust (PDSA) cycle, the carpet was introduced to other floors before the impact on the first unit was fully determined.

Ironically, patient satisfaction data showed that noise complaints dropped starting the month before the carpet was installed. Why? Nurses had taken initiative to make a number of small improvements, such as closing doors and turning TV volumes down at night. So, as nurses were learning Lean principles and their executives said they supported that effort, the senior leaders were not yet thinking Lean themselves.

What Is a Manager's Role?

In a Lean culture, we don't view employees as just a cost. We view them as partners in accomplishing our goals and mission. Some organizations, in the name of cost-cutting, have eliminated a level of management. However, one organization that was not yet practicing Lean was left, after layoffs, with managers each having 80 direct reports, which made it extremely difficult to engage with that many people. While even the best managers don't "add value" from a Lean perspective, they certainly can (and should) play an important role in improving operations, systems, and outcomes.

To support the change to a Lean culture, ThedaCare realized they "needed a different leadership structure, with leaders driving change," said Theresa Moore. ThedaCare actually added a manager level back in, between supervisors and directors, with specific role definitions for each level. This allows supervisors to spend more time at the *gemba* and allows managers to work on more strategic improvements, such as capital spending requests.

What, then, is the role of an effective manager in a Lean culture? Managers have a responsibility to set direction and lead the way, making sure their employees understand customer needs, organizational priorities, and how the pieces fit together. Shook described the role of a manager at Toyota as having two objectives:

1. Get each person to take initiative to solve problems and improve his or her job.
2. Ensure each person's job is aligned to provide value for the customer (or patient) and prosperity for the company (or hospital).[8]

How do we get people to take initiative? It is tempting to force people to take initiative through direct orders and formal, positional authority, but that is not very sustainable. Leaders often try to provide financial incentives and rewards, but the best Lean cultures rely on intrinsic motivation and allowing people to thrive. While we want staff improving their own work, managers and higher-level leaders play an important role in helping staff not suboptimize or lose sight of the bigger system and interactions within the organization and broader health system. Local goals should be aligned with the larger organization's goals through a "strategy deployment" process, as described below.

Gary Kaplan, MD, CEO of Virginia Mason Medical Center, believes in the power of intrinsic motivation and leaders creating the right environment instead of forcing participation, writing, "*Kaizen* can't be imposed from above. Leaders should introduce, teach, and encourage the adoption of *kaizen* methodologies, but it is only sustained when employees are engaged—because they have found that it makes their work easier and more satisfying. Employees become champions of *kaizen* when they see it reduces the burden of work and the waste of rework and waste of time that come with inefficiency. It frees them to do the important things that add value for our patients and helps them recapture the passion that drove their original career decisions to work in healthcare."[9]

Fujio Cho, former chairman of Toyota, summarized the "three keys to lean leadership" as

- Go see ("Senior management must spend time on the shop floor")
- Ask why ("Use the 'why?' technique daily")
- Show respect ("Respect your people")[10]

David Verble learned four points from Cho during his time at Toyota, saying leaders should coach others to

- Give them the job as their own
- Let them think; let them try
- Help them see
- Force reflection[11]

Managers, especially in hospital departments that do not have direct patient contact, need to ensure that their people are oriented around providing value-added activity for the customer, our patients. This can be done through departmental mission statements, goals and measures, and other gestures that remind staff of their important work. One hospital posted signs that reminded staff of their indirect role in patient care. For example, the nutrition services department emphasized, with a smiling employee photo, that they often "have oncology patients who have lost all interest in food" so they "take the time to chat with them—then I make them a custom meal. Milkshakes are my specialty."[12] They are not just delivering food; they are contributing to the patient's well-being, recovery, and satisfaction.

It can be more effective, in the long run, to challenge your people to come up with solutions, even if it initially takes longer or they stumble along the way through the PDSA process. However, managers often have difficulty empowering their employees to come up with solutions and answers of their own. Many managers define their value by their own firefighting or problem-solving abilities; after all, they were made the boss for a reason. This resistance to "give up control" tends to become stronger as you move up the organizational chart. Senior leaders often have decades of bad habits, such as the "white coat" behaviors, and it can be difficult, if not impossible, to change.

ThedaCare's Theresa Moore coaches leaders to understand that their role is to "help people see the system and connect the dots," to "let staff think things through rather than telling them not to do something," and to ask "what did you learn?" after improvements are made. One ThedaCare manager said, "The job of a manager is improvement, and that's not true everywhere!"

One hospital chief operating officer (COO) lamented that his new pronouncements that "firefighting is bad" ran in conflict with how people knew him from his 30-year career in that organization. While he knew, logically, that everybody needed to focus on improving systems and preventing fires, he said that people knew he rose through the ranks to COO because he "was always the best at fighting fires and figuring out how to get things done through workarounds." This is an understandable personal challenge.

Lean managers are neither dictatorial nor extreme delegators who are hands-off leaders. As Shook said, Lean managers are not the "modern, enlightened leader" of the 1980s empowerment or total quality management styles. Lean managers do not say, "I don't care how you do it, as long as you get results."[13] Lean leaders care about the process and the results, realizing that the right process brings you the right results. But, managers in a Lean culture don't dictate how the work is done, as we discussed in Chapter 5. Leaders should find a balance, knowing when to delegate, empower, and challenge their staff and when they should step in to be a servant leader. Although we rely on frontline staff, some systemic problems must be escalated to higher-level leaders in order to get a fix put in place.

Setting objectives and boundaries is something a manager must do, but objectives are not a "make-the-number-or-else" target, with the common dysfunctions that were discussed in Chapter 9. Lean leaders don't just pressure people to somehow care more or try harder. Lean managers say, "Follow me. Let's figure this out together," working to improve processes and systems.[14] In a Lean organization, goals, objectives, and strategy tend to flow top-down. Ideas and solutions should generally flow from the bottom up, with the assumption that frontline (or "value-adding") employees are closest to the process and the customer so they are, therefore, the experts. Lean organizations have frequent feedback loops between the levels, as information flows in both

- Executive/Senior Leaders
- VPs and Directors
- First-Level Managers
- Frontline Supervisors
- Charge/Senior Staff and Clinicians
- Value-Adding Staff and Clinicians

Figure 11.1   Illustration of how goals and ideas flow up and down in a Lean organization.

directions. As upper managers set direction and vision, they ask employees to confirm that it seems correct (or to give input to make it better). As ideas flow up, managers may question and challenge ideas, testing the thought process involved in the solutions. This is illustrated in Figure 11.1.

At Baylor Scott & White Health (Texas), daily huddles take place at every level of the organization, starting with frontline teams and ending with the executive staff. Through these "tiered huddles," important information about immediate risks or challenges can flow up as needed within a few hours. Important updates can likewise flow down to frontline staff and middle managers by the next day.[15] That, along with their strategy deployment process, is an example of how a Lean culture is both top-down and bottom-up.

Engaging Employees in Change

Far too often, leaders try to force change on physicians or staff, then complaining that staff are being "resistant." The best strategy for getting "buy-in" about change is to engage the people who are actually doing the work, realizing they are the experts and that they must be respected.

When Avera Health was about to implement a new computerized physician order entry system (CPOE), Kathy Maass reminded leaders that "when we make major changes, we go back to the frontline staff rather than having a few people off in a conference room deciding what needs to be done." Senior leaders at Avera typically insist that staff be involved in the design of a new system or process. "That's been very successful for us," says Maass. While CPOE "changes nearly every process in the hospital," they were "successful from start" because they involved people early.

Avera involved physicians, nurses, pharmacists, and health unit coordinators in designing and testing 25 different patient scenarios before the CPOE "went live." This allowed them to "problem solve those scenarios" before broader training started. This approach has led to "90% compliance" with "very few workarounds" being required.[16]

Strategy Deployment

A growing number of healthcare organizations, including Virginia Mason Medical Center (Seattle, Washington), ThedaCare (Appleton, Wisconsin), Baylor Scott & White Health (Texas), and St. Boniface General Hospital (Winnipeg, Manitoba), are using a Lean management methodology called "strategy deployment," also known as "policy deployment" or *hoshin kanri* in Japanese.

Following the top-down and bottom-up model, strategy deployment aims to create alignment at all levels of the organization. Seniors at an organization help define four or five "true north" directions and objectives that cascade all the way down to first-level supervisors and their staff. As the name is meant to suggest, the true north of an organization should be pretty consistent from year to year, although the precise measures might change more frequently.

For example, the four true north objectives at ThedaCare came from the question, "What are the most important problems and opportunities?" They are as follows, along with the high-level measures that correspond to each true north:[17]

- Safety and quality (preventable mortality and medication errors)
- People (workplace injuries, employee engagement index, and wellness scores)
- Customer satisfaction (access, turnaround time, quality of time)
- Financial stewardship (operating margin and productivity)

The senior leadership team establishes and reviews high-level metrics and helps ensure that each level in the organization has local metrics that are aligned with true north. For example, a medical/surgical unit might track patient falls as a safety and quality metric, while an outpatient clinic might measure employee strains and sprains. Frontline managers and staff in a mature strategy deployment setting can readily explain how their local metrics are important to their patients and how they contribute to the overall goals of the organization. They can also point to specific *kaizen* or PDSA initiatives that are helping improve those metrics. ThedaCare categorizes measures as either a "watch indicator" that is being monitored or a "driver," which is something they are currently working to improve.

Aligned does not mean identical. At one hospital, the labor and delivery (L&D) department recalled how the initially proposed top-down metric for patient safety was the number of falls in each unit. The L&D manager said, "Meeting a goal of zero falls would have been easy. Our patients are young and generally don't fall." L&D pushed back and substituted a patient safety metric that was more relevant to their patients and their care.

Going beyond measurement, strategy deployment also ensures that improvement ideas and projects are not just top-down mandates. While a small number of strategic projects might be identified and prioritized by senior leadership, staff and managers also help determine what to do (the how) to meet the goals of the organization (the what). The "catch ball" process ensures that top-down goals are adjusted based on feedback from managers, and improvement ideas from employees also receive feedback and input from their leaders. This collaboration distinguishes strategy deployment from older "management-by-objectives" or "goal deployment" methods that were only top-down. As ThedaCare discovered, it is important to "break the cycle of hierarchy."[18]

Strategy deployment also creates focus by forcing an organization to prioritize key improvement initiatives instead of trying to do everything all at once. One health system had the senior leadership team identify the "top priority" projects and initiatives; it totaled over 400! As they started with strategy deployment, a number of long (and sometimes heated) discussions identified the top 20 initiatives that were truly "must do, can't fail" and would be monitored by leadership. ThedaCare's senior leadership "visual room" has walls displaying rapid improvement events and ongoing strategic initiatives, but they also have a process for formally "deselecting" initiatives that are not part of that year's priorities. The deselected items, what some call the "yes, but not now" list, are left on the wall so they can be reconsidered in the future rather than forgotten. Strategy deployment helps executive teams focus, meaning it's more likely that the top 20 projects can actually get done instead of every project being distracted or losing resources to other projects, with nothing getting done.

Toussaint said, "Strategy deployment is forcing a continuous improvement look at the world, whereas the traditional way is just a batch, which is a project." Previously, ThedaCare's annual planning process was "a big batch where we'd have a board retreat for four or five hours." By the time the plan was completed, it was "out of date," said Toussaint. ThedaCare now has a planning cycle that can be continuously revisited, following the PDSA mindset.[19]

Common Management Problems

We can find common management problems across most hospitals. Hospitals often take their best, most successful, or most personable nurse, for example, and make that person a supervisor overnight. People are often thrown into supervisory roles without formal training, forcing them to learn on the fly rather than being taught to follow a management model that is consistently applied throughout the health system. This informal approach leads to some employees struggling and removing themselves from the management chain forever (another example of the waste of talent).

Many individuals who are promoted based on success in their individual contributor role lack certain skills and experiences that are necessary for success as a supervisor. For example, we may promote a supervisor who is uncomfortable having tough, necessary conversations with employees. Rather than confronting them constructively or holding them accountable, supervisors often look the other way. Or, they are so busy in meetings or reviewing reports and paperwork in their office that they do not have a chance to see waste at all. We cannot assume all managers have basic supervisory skills, such as knowing how to effectively train an employee in a task. By comparison, Lean and its foundational Training Within Industry methodology offers time-tested methods for teaching supervisors how to effectively train employees, as mentioned in Chapter 5. New methods combined with new Lean cultural mindsets can make management more appealing to our most talented people, setting them up to be more successful as leaders.

This is not to say that all hospital supervisors, managers, and leaders are ineffective. Hospital supervisors have many positive traits that can help them become even better managers. Unlike other industries, supervisors and other leaders in hospitals tend to be promoted into their roles, usually within the same organization. While this can create some challenges, such as how to effectively manage former peers, the big systemic advantage is that the supervisors are more likely to understand the daily value-added work. This advantage, however, may degrade over time, as the supervisor is away from the daily work longer, and tools and technology change.

Much as we try not to blame individual employees for process problems, Lean thinkers avoid blaming individual managers for their past practices. Adopting a Lean management approach requires us to admit there are problems with the old system (or lack thereof). Without blaming individuals about how we got this way, we should focus on improving our management system for the sake of patients, employees, and the hospital. Hospitals can change their selection criteria for supervisory and leadership roles, define more specific "standardized work for leaders," and do a better job of training and mentoring leaders throughout their careers.

Lean as a Management System and Philosophy

As the 1990s ended, Toyota leaders wanted to document more detail about their management system. An internal document called "The Toyota Way" led to the publication of a book of the same name. *The Toyota Way* spells out four major principles and 14 additional principles, as shown

Table 11.2   Principles from *The Toyota Way*

I. Long-term philosophy
1. Base your management decisions on a long-term philosophy, even at the expense of short-term financial goals.
II. The right process will produce the right results
2. Create continuous process flow to bring problems to the surface
3. Use "pull" systems to avoid overproduction
4. Level out the workload (*Heijunka*)
5. Build a culture of stopping to fix problems to get quality right the first time
6. Standardized tasks are the foundation for continuous improvement and employee empowerment
7. Use visual control so no problems are hidden
8. Use only reliable, thoroughly tested technology that serves your people and processes
III. Add value to the organization by developing your people and partners
9. Grow leaders who thoroughly understand the work, live the philosophy, and teach it to others
10. Develop exceptional people and teams who follow your company's philosophy
11. Respect your extended network of partners and suppliers by challenging them and helping them improve
IV. Continuously solving root problems drives organizational learning
12. Go and see for yourself to thoroughly understand the situation (*genchi genbutsu*)
13. Make decisions slowly by consensus, thoroughly considering all options; implement decisions rapidly (*nemawashi*)
14. Become a learning organization through relentless reflection (*hansei*) and continuous improvement (*kaizen*)

in Table 11.2.[20] Some of these principles are, unfortunately, ignored by organizations that say they are "implementing Lean." For example, how many organizations would look at the first principle and say they are "implementing long-term decision-making?"

A Daily Lean Management System

Successful hospitals and departments implement a management system to maintain improvements as well as drive *kaizen*. This management system consists of methods that include

- Process audits, or rounding
- Performance measures
- Daily stand-up team meetings, or "huddles"
- *Kaizen* and suggestion management

This approach has been successfully practiced by many hospitals as they begin their journeys, or it has been adopted after struggling with the aftermath of a tools-driven approach to Lean. The University of Michigan Health System calls its approach "Lean in Daily Work," which includes what they describe as "key visual metrics, daily team huddles, daily problem solving through the "Everyday Lean Idea" (ELI) process, and leadership gemba walks." One of the goals with this process is to "redirect reactive firefighting to a systemic, proactive process." The leader's role in this process is to support improvement work by freeing up time and coaching people, helping everybody have "two jobs"—doing the work and improving the way work is done.[21]

ThedaCare defines their "Business Performance System" (BPS) management method as interconnected components that include

1. Daily status (stat) sheets
2. Daily huddles
3. Monthly scorecards
4. Monthly performance review meetings
5. A3 thinking and countermeasures
6. Leader standard work
7. Visual management
8. Sustaining improvement through training and managing to standard work[22]

Stepping back to the question posed in Chapter 1 ("what problem are we trying to solve?"), ThedaCare defined problems such as "Teams were not positioned to see, prioritize, and pursue thousands of identified improvement opportunities" and "Unit leaders had significant variations in management styles with no structured management reporting system."[23] Before copying methods that you might see when visiting ThedaCare or reading their books, think about the problem statements you might define regarding your own management approach. It's important to realize that these are holistic management *systems* and that copying one or two components might have a limited effect or sustainability.

Process Audits or Rounding

As discussed in Chapter 5, process audits are necessary to ensure that standardized work is being followed (and that it *can* be followed). It is also necessary to observe the process to see what opportunities for continuous improvement exist. In some hospitals, the term *audit* has negative connotations, so the terms *rounding* or *daily checks* might be used instead. Supervisors and managers do not audit the process to catch employees doing something wrong, like a policing function. This rounding, a type of "*gemba* walk," is meant to uncover problems and focus on improvement, not fault-finding. Audits and rounding are also often considered part of "standardized work for leaders," as embraced by many health systems in their Lean approach.

Some organizations use *kamishibai* boards, a form of visual management, to prompt managers to audit certain processes on certain days. The board shows which standardized work processes should be checked each day, in the spirit of "inspect what you expect." *Kamishibai* cards typically specify what details to look for in the work and the process. Each card is displayed on the board with the top of the card showing as white if the process has not been checked, green if it was checked and standardized work was being followed, and red if it was checked and standardized work was not being followed. If a card is red, "supportive leadership is provided," says Didier Rabino, a HealthEast vice president and "Lean Sensei."[24] The board also contains a log and a chart that are used for tracking standardized work adherence over time.

Standardized Audits of the Standardized Work

Lean hospitals implement a hierarchy of audits and standardized work checks; the frontline charge, supervisor, or team leader is the primary auditor. Standardized work for conducting the audits includes a checklist that is carried around the department. The checklist identifies standard questions that should be asked; a list that can be customized to the needs of a particular area. ThedaCare leaders call these "stat sheets" that vice presidents, directors, and managers carry to the *gemba*.[25]

The list might include items related to the following:

- Are there any observed or reported safety risks or problems?
- Were equipment maintenance and other key tasks done according to schedule?
- Are there any patient complaints or concerns?
- Is standardized work being followed?
- Are metrics current and posted?
- Are 5S practices being followed?

The completed audit sheets are typically posted on a wall for all to see. This helps communicate what problems are found and creates some accountability to leaders to follow their own standardized work. If we intend for an audit to happen once each shift or once each day, leaders have to follow that standard to set a good example for their employees. The audits can help emphasize that standardized work is not just for frontline employees.

Audits should not be done just to "check the box." Audits are meant to be a primary input into the problem-solving and improvement process. It does no good to identify the same problems every day, continually writing them down on the audit sheet. Problems that are identified should be fixed right away, if possible. Or, the sheets can be discussed with employees during team meetings. If a problem is not being solved immediately, the planned action can be recorded on the audit sheet or team board for communication and visibility purposes.

In some hospital or department cultures, people are afraid to write down problems. Often, there is a feeling that it is unacceptable to admit having problems. Remember the Toyota expression of "no problems is a problem." Leaders have to ensure that their supervisors are not overlooking problems in an attempt to make their audit sheets look good. Likewise, leaders have a responsibility to react to problems in a constructive manner, focused on solving problems and removing barriers to getting things fixed.

A Hierarchy of Rounding

In some areas, a senior staff member or charge nurse might be the one to audit the department each shift. The manager of the frontline auditor also does audits then audits the audits and so forth up the organization, as shown in Table 11.3. Ultimately, the responsibility for standardized

Table 11.3 Rounding and Auditing Hierarchy

Level/Role	Frequency of Audit	Frequency to Audit the Audits
Frontline supervisor	Shift or day	N/A
Manager	Week	Day
Director	Month	Week
Vice president	Quarter	Month
C-level	Quarter	Month

work rests with the hospital CEO and other top leadership. It is not an acceptable excuse for senior leaders to say, after a patient safety incident, that their employees did not follow policies or procedures, especially if not following policies was a common occurrence. In the National Health Service (NHS) Releasing Time to Care program, the hospital CEO visits each ward, the *gemba*, on a monthly basis to see firsthand how things are working and to provide assistance, signing his or her name on a board to indicate the visit and that the CEO is checking that lower-level leaders have completed their checks.

Second-level leaders serve a dual purpose: to audit the audits and to conduct audits of their own, albeit less frequently than frontline leaders. A department manager who has multiple supervisors is responsible to do a daily check to see if the supervisors have completed their audits. Hanging all of the audits for an area on a single display board can make it easier for the manager to do a quick daily review while walking through the department.

The manager also should do a firsthand audit, with or without the frontline supervisor, of each area once per week. Doing audits with frontline supervisors provides opportunities for the manager to ask questions and to be available to the staff. Discussions about problems and possible improvements can be held during the audit, right in the *gemba*.

If it's a problem in our organization that senior executives stay away from the *gemba*, we can ask "why?" Often, the physical layout of a building or health system campus is designed with executive offices in a far corner away from the patients and care providers. Rather than blaming executives or labeling them as "resistant to going to the *gemba*," work together to make it easier to manage the right way. Set up a satellite office or desk that an executive can use when they are away from their main office. At New London Family Medical Center, CEO Bill Schmidt intentionally parks so that he has to walk through the emergency department and inpatient units on the way to his office. "Leadership is very visible," he says.

Going to the *gemba* to do rounding cannot be an opportunity for leaders just to put a new name on old practices and behaviors. Blaming individuals, yelling at them for not following the process, looking the other way when core safety methods are not practiced, or chastising people for not reaching goals are behaviors that have no place in a Lean culture.

As we move up in the organization, these audits should still occur. They provide a way of encouraging leaders to go to the *gemba*, to be out of their offices or the executive suite. Having upper-level executives conduct audits can be helpful. For one, it gives them an accurate picture of what is happening day to day in different departments. Second, it makes them visible to the employees and provides accessibility for people to ask questions or make suggestions; many frontline employees rarely, if ever, see their vice president or C-level executives in their own workplace. Third, it sends a powerful message to the employees to see that higher-level managers are asking questions about standardized work and Lean methods. An upper-level manager should not be directive, as asking questions about goals and work methods can send a powerful message about what is important.

Leaders who are new to the Lean process will often resist the need to oversee their employees' standardized work. They might argue that they have good employees or they should be trusted. Other times, managers might resist because they do not have time (if so, time should be freed up) or because they do not like conflict. These managers should be given training and skills for constructive interactions with their employees, as well as ongoing coaching from their leaders.

Performance Measures

The ability to measure performance effectively is necessary for continuous improvement. Employees often do not know how their department is performing in a quantitative way. It may be that performance measures (or metrics) are not tracked or that metrics are not shared by managers. Some managers want to shield their employees from the pressure that performance measures might bring. In a Lean environment, respect for people means we are honest with people about how the department is performing, and we work together to close any gaps between current performance and desired or required performance levels.

Before Lean, there are common dysfunctions with existing metrics. First, metrics are typically tracked using monthly averages, which hampers improvement efforts. Second, metrics are often focused on financial or accounting measures, such as work units or labor cost, which seem irrelevant to staff. Third, information is often posted in hallways outside the department, where it goes unseen.

A Lean culture must ensure that goals do not become inflexible targets that people must reach at all costs. In 2014, a major scandal highlighted the problem of U.S. military veterans waiting too long for appointments. At least 40 veterans died while waiting for care at the Phoenix Veterans Affairs (VA) Health Care System. Many of them were on a so-called "secret waiting list" that was created as managers "were trying to hide" the fact that about 1,500 veterans were "waiting months to see a doctor." The target for appointment waiting time had been 30 days but was lowered to 14 days in 2011.

A VA undersecretary admitted that the 14-day target was "unrealistic." With that pressure, a number of dysfunctional practices and "gaming" became common, not just in Phoenix, but also allegedly in 25 other cities around the country. Patients' requests might be written down on a hidden paper list until their appointment could, later, be entered into the computer once the target was possible. Or, people in the scheduling office would try to steer the patient to request a date that they knew was achievable, instead of letting the request occur naturally. That would make the gap between "desired date" and "scheduled date" be zero days, well under the target. In other cases, pressure from supervisors led schedulers to falsify the "desired date." The VA identified these "schemes" in 2010, but the bad practices and, more importantly, the waiting times were not eliminated.

Similar dysfunctions occur whether leaders make threats of punishment (for not hitting targets) or offer rewards (for hitting them). As author Brian Joiner wrote, there are three things that can happen when people are placed under pressure to hit targets: (1) improve the system, (2) distort the figures, or (3) distort the system.[26] Lean leaders make sure it's the first that occurs, not the last two.

Timely Measures Can Drive Timely Improvement

Timely measures give us much more helpful information than infrequent averages. How useful would the speedometer on your car be if it only displayed your average speed when you arrived at your destination? We need more continuous feedback to make sure we are not driving too fast at any given time.

Likewise, viewing process performance measures as monthly averages makes it difficult to drive process improvement. For one, averages tend to mask the detail of what happened on given days during the month. In the middle of a month (when the metrics are often tabulated as a batch and posted), lab staff might look and ask, "Why was turnaround time poor last month?" At that point, memories might be fuzzy regarding specific reasons, making it difficult to do anything beyond trying harder and hoping for better results. The average might have been skewed by a few bad days, resulting from "special causes." If the monthly average is just slightly worse, it does not necessarily mean the underlying process is any worse than before, in a statistically significant way.

It is better to measure performance on a daily basis, once a shift, or more frequently (through ongoing visual management). This immediate feedback facilitates root cause problem solving and the prevention of problems. When we can ask the team a timely, specific question such as, "Why was our chemistry turnaround time much worse than usual yesterday?" we are more likely to get accurate reasons and root causes. When, through visual management, a charge nurse can ask, "Why did rounding not occur last hour?" that is more helpful than looking at a report that says hourly rounding occurred 87.2% of the time last month. Of course, in either situation, we should be looking to see if the problem appears as a "special cause" situation (truly caused by a particular event we can identify) or if it appears to be "common cause" (just part of the usual system that sometimes leads to bad performance).

It is important that metrics are used to identify improvements in a blame-free environment. Performance measures can be used, unfortunately, in a context and method that does not show respect for people. If managers were to use the metrics as a way of merely pressuring employees to do better without a means for improvement, this would be unfair and might give Lean a "mean" reputation.

Even when performance has improved or is better than expected, leaders at ThedaCare will ask "why?" and "what's your hypothesis about why this occurred?"[27] Bill Boyd, their surgery value stream director, says that leaders "don't just focus on outcomes, but look at the process ... the goal is not just to improve but to understand how to." At ThedaCare, if a team hits a goal, leaders might say, "Great, how much better can you get?" in the spirit of pursuing perfection. New London Family Medical Center's Bill Schmidt says, "Even if a metric is in the green [performing better than a goal], we're still working on improvement."

At a different health system, one that was earlier along in their Lean journey, hospital leaders were happy that they were exceeding their goal to increase surgical admissions by 10% by the end of the year. Before the start of that year, as part of their annual strategy deployment cycle, they had chosen three major projects (managed as A3s) that were supposed to lead to the increase. Unfortunately, none of those projects had even been started yet. We say "unfortunately" because it showed that the hospital didn't understand its system well enough to know why admissions were up (and it was a problem that they were not executing their plan). Without understanding why performance had improved, it was just as likely to later fall without explanation.

A Balanced Scorecard Focuses on All Stakeholders

Lean metrics focus on more than just accounting measures. For example, before practicing Lean, the managers at one lab focused on an accounting-driven productivity metric of hours worked per tested specimen. This was the primary measure for the department, viewed monthly. Through the Lean process, the lab instituted daily measures for turnaround time and started viewing the productivity metric daily, instituting more frequent improvement activity. Although the primary objective was turnaround time, labor efficiency and productivity also improved by 10%.

In addition to viewing averages, many departments start looking at the variation in their service levels. For example, a hospital might look at the average "door-to-balloon" time for chest pain patients but might also look at variation or outliers to understand why every patient did not get the most timely care. What most customers remember is not the average performance, but the worst or the best. Measuring the time under which 90% of your patients are treated might more accurately reflect what your customers are feeling.

In a Lean environment, we focus on more than just cost. The mantra is typically SQDCM—safety, quality, delivery, cost, and morale. In manufacturing, "delivery" usually refers to the on-time delivery of products; in healthcare, this can relate to patient access or other forms of turnaround times or on-time measures. This balanced approach, often reflected in the strategy deployment true north goals, emphasizes that cost is not the primary motivation for improvement. If safety, quality, and delivery (as seen in the turnaround time performance of a lab) are improved, then cost tends to follow. Table 11.4 shows some typical metrics adopted by departments.

Another management principle that can be incorporated into this system is explaining why each metric is important. For example, in a lab where they measured the "percentage of tests resulted before 7 a.m.," the metrics sheet explained, "This is a key measure that physicians use to judge lab effectiveness. Physicians get dissatisfied if results are not on the patient chart when they do morning rounding, and this can delay patient care decisions or discharges." Even if employees are experienced, they often do not understand the true impact of certain measures on their patients or internal customers.

Table 11.4 Example Metrics for Measuring Lean Improvements

Metric Area	Pharmacy Example	Laboratory Example	Inpatient Care Example
Safety	Number of adverse drug events	Number of unsafe or near-miss behaviors seen	Number of patient falls
Quality	Number of reworked prescriptions Number of med cabinet stockouts in units Nurse satisfaction surveys	Percentage of time "critical values" are called Number of lost/missing specimen cases Number of mislabeled specimens	Percentage of patients who fully understand their discharge instructions
Delivery	Response time for "first-dose" orders	Turnaround time average for key tests Percentage of morning draw test results on patient charts by 7:00 a.m.	Number of patients discharged before 10:00 am
Cost	Inventory levels in pharmacy	Cost per test Overtime hours per week	Length of stay Cost per patient
Morale	Employee satisfaction surveys	Number of suggestions submitted each month	Sickness call-off or voluntary turnover rate

One hospital lab implemented all of the Lean approaches to metrics, except that instead of a broad set of metrics, each one was focused only on turnaround time (TAT). After a few weeks, an employee asked if management was saying that quality was not important. They were afraid that some coworkers, having competitive personalities and wanting their TAT measures to look good, would cut corners on quality. The managers of the lab responded by emphasizing that safety and quality were certainly priorities. Employees would not be (and had not been) blamed or made to feel bad when TATs were worse than their goals. Lab managers reminded staff that, in their context, fast TATs meant better clinical quality for the health system as a whole. In addition, though, the lab looked for direct lab quality measures that could be quantified and began tracking those as well.

Metrics Should Be Visible, Visual, and Statistically Meaningful

Metrics should be posted in high-visibility locations, where they can be seen as people are doing their work. Since employees might not take the time for a detailed look at the charts and metrics each day, visual management elements can be used so everyone can gauge department performance at a quick glance.

In many pre-Lean environments, department results are posted in the form of tables of numbers. The tables typically show comparisons between two data points, as in performance versus last month or last year. These simple comparisons can be misleading, particularly when compared to more visual ways of displaying multiple data points. If in the average emergency room, the "left without being seen" metric was down from 3% to 2% this month, for example, there are still many unanswered questions:

- What does that tell us about the process other than one data point is lower than the other?
- Will the number be the same in the next month, meaning we have a predictable process? How much variation should we expect month to month?
- Did we really improve, or did normal or "common cause" variation in the data make it look like an improvement that is likely to disappear when the data fluctuate upward again?

Some departments have existing scorecards with densely packed tables of numbers. One perioperative services department, before Lean, had 50 different metrics, each measured for the last 12 months, all squeezed into a single page called a "dashboard" (can you imagine driving a car with that type of dashboard?). While there was no shortage of data available, their presentation was overwhelming. Lean metrics (those that are displayed visually for the employees) are often a critical few key indicators of the overall health of the department. Many organizations have each department track one key indicator that aligns with each of the four or five true north objectives. We might track more measures, for financial reporting purposes or to meet the requirements of upper management, but we do not have to post everything that we track.

Lean metrics are made visual through the use of trend charts and color coding. Trend charts show patterns so we can see if a metric is just fluctuating (as shown in Figure 11.2) or shifting in a statistically significant way where there is a new process average (as shown in Figure 11.3).[28] Being able to view trends is an improvement over simple comparisons to goals (our turnaround time is better than our 30-minute goal) or comparisons to the past (our turnaround time is three minutes better than yesterday).

These trend charts can use a formal statistical process control (SPC), or control chart methodology, that allows managers and teams to avoid overreacting to every fluctuation in the metrics. SPC gives us tools to know when those ups and downs are just "noise" (common cause) and when

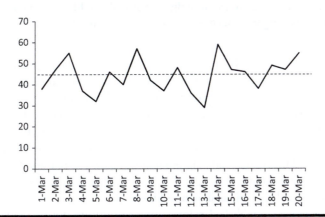

Figure 11.2 Example of a trend chart, where data points appear to be fluctuating randomly around an average (the dashed line).

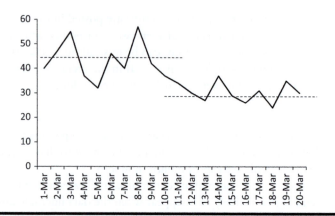

Figure 11.3   Example of a trend chart, where the data show a statistical shift from a higher average to a new lower average (the dashed lines).

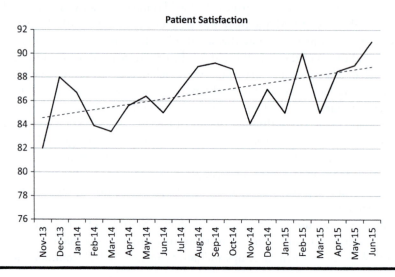

Figure 11.4   Example of data that are actually statistically stable and in control, but appear to be improving in a misleading way because of the linear trend line.

we have a significant change to which we should react, or a "signal" (special cause). With SPC, we take process data, such as daily turnaround times for a particular test, and determine if the process is "in control" statistically. If a process is in control, it means we can reliably predict how that process will perform tomorrow. When we make a significant process change, seeing a process shift, as in Figure 11.3, helps us confirm if we made a statistically significant change or not.

SPC charts also help us avoid situations for which we think we are improving based on an Excel linear trend line. Having one bad data point at the start and one good data point at the end can create an upward linear trend, making it look like we are improving when the process is actually stable and in statistical control, as shown in Figure 11.4.

Some departments have established color coding to indicate if a particular metric is better, slightly worse, or much worse (green, yellow, red color coding, respectively) than a goal or customer requirement. We must take care that the goals are not arbitrary, and that employees are

Figure 11.5 A clinical laboratory posts its turnaround time metrics and volume levels each shift. The display board is in the department, so all employees can see, and team meetings are held in front of the display.

not blamed or pressured for being consistently in a yellow or red zone since that is a reflection on process capability, not the people. One laboratory, as pictured in Figure 11.5, posted three sets of daily metrics, one for each shift, in a high-visibility area within the lab.

If employees walk by the metrics board or can see the board from their workspaces, they can use the color coding as an indication of how the process is performing. Seeing a lot of green is a visual indicator that they are meeting customer and patient needs. It is not, however, a reason to stop looking for *kaizen* opportunities.

Daily Stand-Up Team Meetings or Huddles

Another way to engage employees is the use of daily update and communication meetings. These meetings are structured using a standardized work approach in terms of the agenda used for each day on each shift. Huddles should be held in a stand-up format, often around the board where metrics, process audits, or suggestions are posted. This helps to keep the meeting short, to keep the team close to the workplace, and to focus on the results of efforts and improvements. Depending on the type of department, the huddle might include all staff (if work can be set aside for a few minutes), while other departments might only include those who are available at the moment. Departments often tweak and adjust their huddle start times to ensure the highest possible attendance.

At ThedaCare, teams huddle around what they call "tracking center" boards. Theresa Moore says that the teams have experimented with the format and that there is "not a published standard." "More important," explains Moore, "is the coaching approach more so than the board itself." The author has seen other organizations that spent a lot of time designing a board that was perfectly identical in each unit, or they have literally copied one they saw at ThedaCare. But, more often than not, those boards are not used as actively or are not used at all. The point is not to have nice-looking huddle boards; it would be better to see a board that is slightly different and even messy, as long as it is being used and is proving helpful to a team and their performance.

The huddles need to remain focused and be kept at 5 or 10 minutes, avoiding the tendency for them to lengthen over time. In a meeting of this length, it is not possible to discuss every issue or to do complex problem solving. The intent is quick communication, prioritized around immediate needs. As problems or suggestions are brought up, they can be captured on a whiteboard (or in a *kaizen* system, discussed further in this chapter) for more detailed discussion as time allows later in the day. If we have six or seven people at a team meeting, we might only need two or three specific people for investigating a particular root cause, so the full group meeting needs to be kept short to avoid wasting people's time.

Sample Huddle Agenda

1. Safety reminder of the day; review safety issues or risks
2. Immediate problems to be aware of (instruments down or people called in sick)
3. Review of yesterday's metrics and trends
4. New employee suggestions or ideas; updates on previous ideas
5. Share any positive feedback

There are variations in huddle agendas, as organizations experiment and do what works best for them. New London Medical Center starts with celebrations, which they think is an improvement over their initial practice of ending huddles with a celebration.

Harvard Vanguard Medical Associates is among the organizations using this daily huddle approach. For example, their Kenmore Clinic in Boston has a 10-minute huddle each day in the orthopedics clinic; the huddle includes physicians, physician assistants, nurses, and medical assistants. They follow a standardized format, discussing recent problems in a very nonhierarchical team environment. Problems and ideas for improvement are posted and tracked on a whiteboard where the huddles are held, with clinicians and staff members at all levels taking the lead on different improvements. To help build collaboration across departments, the huddles initially included a representative from the radiology clinic that was located down the hall. This facilitated open and honest discussion about patient flow and other possible issues throughout the value stream. Based on that initial success, the standardized huddle process has been spread across multiple clinics in the Boston area.

An increasing number of organizations are conducting daily safety huddles at the hospital or health system level. At Mary Greeley Medical Center, the huddles are always attended by, and often facilitated by, the CEO, Brian Dieter. ThedaCare holds a 13- to 20-minute daily safety call that includes leaders from all of their different sites. One of the goals is to "affirmatively confirm that each part of the system has what they need to have a safe day," says Mark Hallett, MD, MBOE, the COO for Appleton Medical Center and Theda Clark Medical Center. Safety includes patients and staff, as the system measures the number of days without a lost work time injury.

One pitfall to avoid was highlighted by a manager, who said his hospital had gotten away from having regular huddles. The corporate staff was inadvertently punishing managers for holding team meetings because the time spent in them hurt their productivity metrics. Managers became reluctant to pull frontline staff away from direct patient care for this reason. This highlights another example of how, unfortunately, the best local Lean efforts can be undermined by a lack of alignment with corporate or senior leadership attitude, policies, or metrics.

Kaizen *and Daily Continuous Improvement*

The acronym TPS has traditionally stood for the Toyota Production System. In recent years, Toyota executives have started calling TPS the Thinking Production System to emphasize the important role of employees' creativity and thinking in continuous improvement.[29] Toyota needs its employees to be engaged and thinking, rather than "checking their brains at the door."

In healthcare, people are sometimes afraid that Lean will somehow turn them into robots, as they misunderstand the role of standardized work. In my experience, healthcare professionals often complain, before Lean, that their ideas aren't heard. Lean hospitals fully engage the creativity and efforts of their employees and physicians, improving processes and patient care, while creating a more fulfilling workplace. A Lean thinker recognizes that people want to improve; their leaders need to let them.

A growing number of health systems are using *kaizen* strategies for continuous improvement. Franciscan St. Francis Health (Indianapolis) has implemented and documented about 25,000 staff-driven ideas since 2007, with 40% staff participation rates each year.[30] Franciscan does not require a financial benefit to be measured for each improvement, but finance has validated more than $6 million in hard savings. There are other benefits as, for example, their neonatal intensive care unit (NICU) patient and family satisfaction scores have increased to the 99th percentile, and their manager attributes this to the hundreds of *kaizen* improvements they have implemented.

Their CEO, Bob Brody, says, "Saying yes to *kaizen* was easy for me. As a leader, I recognize my role is to lead others to create the future of our organization. I knew our future required the continuous development of the improvement skills and abilities of all our staff and their engagement in continually improving the services we provide to our patients and their families."[31]

Other health systems have impressive levels of daily continuous improvement efforts. By 2012, ThedaCare employees were implementing over 20,000 small improvements per year.[32] HealthEast (St. Paul, Minnesota) implemented over 28,000 ideas in 2014.[33]

Toyota highlights the importance of employee engagement, stating, "Every Toyota team member is empowered with the ability to improve their work environment. This includes everything from quality and safety to the environment and productivity. Improvements and suggestions by team members are the cornerstone of Toyota's success."[34]

We have already briefly introduced how *kaizen* is a key Lean strategy. *Kaizen* allows us to build on our standardized work. *Kaizen* is meant to be a daily process by which many small improvements are implemented in an ongoing basis. *Kaizen* should not be a bureaucratic process by which ideas are generated or approved only by managers, senior leaders, or a far-off suggestion committee. *Kaizen* is not just a series of formal, weeklong improvement events or workshops. It should be a process that engages employees in fast improvement cycles, allowing them to take ownership of improving their processes instead of just lobbing complaints at their leaders. Employees should be encouraged to bring up problems or ideas directly to their coworkers or supervisors in a face-to-face manner as often as possible.

Wherever an improvement idea comes from, it should be treated as a PDSA experiment. Not every new idea will work in practice, so a trial must take place in a limited area (one unit or one room, rather than the whole hospital) and over a limited time frame, a "small test of change." During and after the trial period, all participants need to evaluate if the change really improves the system or if there were side effects caused in adjacent areas. If the change is deemed positive, it can be accepted as the new process. If not, the team can go back to old methods or continue looking for a new one.

A classic example of small *kaizen* took place at New London Medical Center. Leaders wanted to improve patient satisfaction scores for cleanliness, so they asked housekeeping staff for ideas. One housekeeper said they often clean rooms while the patient is away for therapy, so the patient doesn't know the room was cleaned. The housekeeper designed a card to leave for the patient to inform them about cleaning taking place. After the idea was tested, a further *kaizen* led to a dual-language card being created instead. CEO Bill Schmidt says, "It thrills me that the housekeeper ran with this" and implemented the improvement.

Since the scientific method and the Lean change process allow for a hypothesis ("This change will improve the system") to be proven incorrect, leaders must create an environment in which rapid experimentation is encouraged. Rather than pondering the problem forever and trying to come up with the perfect solution the first time, it is better to try something, in a limited way, to see if it works. Part of the approach is that employees must not be shamed for making a suggestion that does not work as expected. It is something that provides learning. As the PDSA cycle suggests, the team can try a different idea, starting with rethinking the problem statement and going through the rest of the improvement cycle. On the other hand, this environment of rapid experimentation should not be considered an excuse to try ideas that are not well thought out just for the sake of trying something new.

General agreement on this approach often leads to specific questions about how we actually implement *kaizen*:

■ How do we manage suggestions?
■ How do we evaluate ideas?
■ How do we keep continuous improvement from being uncontrolled or chaotic?
■ How do we get input from everybody and keep everybody informed without being too bureaucratic?

- How do we make time for staff and managers to work on *kaizen*?
- What if people change things they should not have changed?

Questions like this should be discussed within your team and organization. Instead of expecting the practice of *kaizen* to be perfect from the start, it is more realistic to follow a high-level PDSA cycle: ***Plan*** your method for improvement, ***Do*** some improvements, ***Study*** what is working or not working, and ***Adjust***. Again, see the *Healthcare Kaizen* book for more examples of how health systems have adopted *kaizen* methods, improving their approaches over time.

Toyota Kata

Mike Rother's book *Toyota Kata* has been embraced by many health systems as way of teaching and practicing a scientific approach to improvement. "*Kata*" is a Japanese word that means both "way of doing" and "form," or choreographed patterns that are practiced repeatedly as in the martial arts. In the *Toyota Kata* approach there are two patterns or ways, called the "improvement *kata*" and the "coaching *kata*." Each of these has a series of routines or forms that are practiced in a deliberate way in the workplace. The goal is to build strong scientific-thinking habits through repetition and real practice, rather than relying on theoretical training alone. Our brainpower has infinite potential, if we manage it well, says Rother.[35]

The improvement *kata* pattern prompts and teaches people to:

1. Understand the overarching challenge
2. Grasp the current condition
3. Establish your next target condition
4. Experiment toward that target condition[36]

Figure 11.6 shows the improvement *kata* model, illustrating a process for setting a high goal (the challenge) and then conducting experiments that are intended to iteratively close the gaps between the current condition and the next target condition that's been set in the direction of the challenge. When we make an improvement, that new level of performance becomes our new current condition. Every experiment is not necessarily a step forward, but something is learned through each experiment, which is an important contributor to the development of our skill with the scientific method.

The coaching *kata* pattern provides practice routines for the manager, once they have learned the improvement kata pattern, to act as coach, asking employees

1. What is the target condition?
2. What is the actual condition now?
   - Reflect on the last step taken: What did you expect? What actually happened? What did you learn?
3. What obstacles do you think are preventing you from reaching the target condition, and which one are you working on now?
4. What is your next step (next experiment)? What do you expect?
5. How quickly can we go and see what we have learned from taking that step?[37]

When the two *kata* pattern routines are practiced together across the organization, it can form the core of a daily management system around which more advanced practices, such as strategy

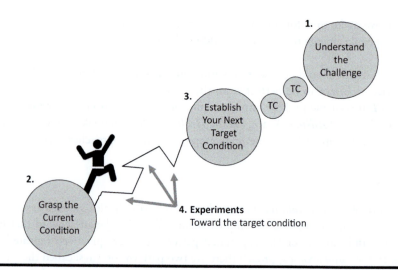

Figure 11.6 Illustration of the improvement *kata* thought process and approach. (Adapted from Rother, Mike, The Improvement Kata, http://www-personal.umich.edu/~mrother/The_Improvement_Kata.html.)

deployment, can be built. Ideally, managers at all levels are able to play the role of coach, while also playing the role of learner, being coached by the level above them.

The *kata* approach, with its focus on measurable challenges and target conditions, reminds one of Ohno's "start from need" advice and Shook's question of "what problem are we trying to solve?" from Chapter 1. In Lean, process and routines matter, but so do organizationally relevant results. Lean leaders don't just demand results; they work with people, teaching an effective process and routines, through regular practice, to drive results that matter.

Michael Lombard, senior director of operational excellence for Cornerstone Healthcare Group (United States), explains the success he has seen as a result of practicing the *Toyota Kata* approach, saying, "In late 2014, Cornerstone Hospital of Broken Arrow, Oklahoma, was struggling with a major patient care challenge and, like many hospitals, didn't have a strong management system for tackling such large endeavors. To address the challenge, the hospital senior leadership team began practicing *kata* routinely, with my support as their coach, for about three solid months. By early 2015, *kata* practice had become the nucleus of the hospital's Lean management system, the patient care challenge had been achieved, and as a direct result, the hospital's net profitability had tripled. Even more importantly, by engaging in such intensive *kata* repetition, the hospital's senior leaders became equipped with strong new habits and mindsets that they can now direct toward whatever the next major challenge may be."[38]

Craig Koele, CEO of two of Cornerstone's specialty hospitals, says, "The application of the Improvement kata is limitless. It helps cut through the noise around the many variables impacting the health care business ... by identifying ever smaller incremental steps that we can evaluate, one after the other, in rapid succession."[39]

The Problems with Suggestion Boxes

Organizations often use suggestion boxes as the primary means of employee involvement. While well intended, these boxes often impede the flow of ideas, leading to frustration and cynicism among employees.

Suggestions tend to accumulate in boxes, with long periods of time elapsing before they are actually read as a batch. At one hospital laboratory, managers had misplaced the key to the box and did not know the last time it was opened. The team jokingly asked if the hospital had been afraid that their ideas would be stolen by a competing hospital. After asking facilities personnel to cut off the padlock, the managers decided the box could remain unlocked until a better method was put in place.

Traditional suggestion systems often feature a monthly (or less frequent) suggestion review meeting, at which managers or a designated team read and evaluate the merits of each suggestion. This is often done without any direct interaction with the person who submitted the suggestion. If the team is reviewing anonymous suggestions, there is no opportunity to give feedback or to dig deeper into the idea.

One advantage of real interaction over suggestion boxes is that some suggestions are not practical. An example might be, "We should hire five more people for the night shift." With a suggestion box and review meetings, all we can do is say no, especially when the suggestion is anonymous. When an employee brings us an idea verbally, we can thank him or her and explain why that particular solution might not be practical, due to budget or technology constraints, for example. The discussion can then turn to finding a solution that would work. Toyota's high percentage of suggestion approval is a sign that they work toward finding something that can be implemented; that sometimes takes effort, but it is for the good of the organization and shows respect for people by being engaged with them instead of just saying no.

The Role of Leaders in Kaizen

Supervisors and managers should be appreciative of employees coming forward with a complaint or a problem. Exposing and embracing problems instead of covering them up or avoiding them is a positive step forward. When a complaint is brought to their attention, such as "We are too busy between 8:00 and 10:00 a.m.," supervisors should challenge the employees to come up with a solution or a suggestion. A simple, yet effective, question is, "What should we do to address that?" The question should be asked in an open, honest tone rather than in an accusatory tone that suggests there is no solution to be found.

Asking employees what they think might catch some people by surprise, given common pre-Lean environments. Some supervisors find it threatening not to be the ones coming up with answers all of the time. Supervisors and managers are not necessarily to be excluded from the problem-solving process, but they are not the ones who must come up with all of the answers. The frontline employees doing the actual work are more likely to have effective, practical solutions. Eric Dickson, MD, president and CEO at UMass Memorial Medical Health Care, said in the context of their "Idea System" program, "Managers have this feeling that good ideas can only come from the managers. That has been the hardest thing, getting managers to believe that people on the front lines have better ideas than they do." Over 2,200 ideas have been implemented to date, so Dickson told a group of leaders, "You have to embrace this. [The *kaizen* approach] is not going away. This will become a part of our culture."[40]

In some cases, employees do not have the authority required to solve problems themselves or within their team. For example, if a laboratory employee brings a complaint or a problem forward, saying nurses in the emergency department are not properly labeling specimens, that is a problem outside the employee's control. In situations such as these, leaders must step forward to take action on behalf of and in support of their employees. Leaders should play the dual role of encouraging and empowering employees by challenging them to develop their own solutions and stepping in to help when needed, particularly with value stream problems that cross department boundaries.

The surest way to stop the flow of employee ideas is to respond negatively to them. How many times is our initial reaction to an idea one of the following statements?

"That's a dumb idea."
"That won't work."
"We can't do that."
"We tried that before."

Supervisors have to go out of their way to be positive when suggestions or ideas are presented. Even if the idea seems like a "dumb" one, supervisors should respond by asking questions. Ask the employee to step back and state the problem. Do anything other than saying no. Since employees are not required to speak up and participate, in a formal sense, supervisors must treat suggestions like a gift.[41] This also ties back to assuming that people are trying to do a good job. When presented with a seemingly inappropriate suggestion, a manager should try to understand why the employee thinks it is a valuable idea and then use it as a developmental opportunity.

Imai wrote that there are three stages that an organization goes through in learning how to have a *kaizen* culture. This progression is important because we want to push people to be more effective problem solvers while not discouraging their participation. In the first stage, supervisors must make every attempt to help them with even the most basic of ideas. Once people are interested in *kaizen*, the second stage allows us to educate employees about how to provide better suggestions, such as emphasizing better root cause analysis and not jumping to solutions. Only in the third stage, after gaining interest and educating people, should managers be "concerned with the economic impact of the suggestion."[42]

Finding a Better Method for Managing Kaizen

Having standardized work for managing suggestions can help create the proper balance between bureaucracy and completely uncontrolled changes. Many departments have implemented a method in which ideas are brought to supervisors or coworkers face to face, ideally in the daily stand-up meeting.

One version of a standardized *kaizen* card, or idea card, is shown in Figure 11.7. Rather than just listing what should be done, the form prompts the employee to define the problem and think about what the measurable impact would be for the patients or the department. The cards are meant to follow the same PDSA cycle used in the A3 method, as mentioned in Chapter 7.

One hospital lab, at the start of its initial Lean project phase, generated 151 employee suggestions in the first eight weeks, most of which were acted on almost immediately. Over time, this lab generated an average of one formally documented suggestion per person per year. By comparison, one of the best automotive parts suppliers, Autoliv, went from 0.5 implemented ideas per person per year to 63 in 2009 and eventually 123 per person per year.[43,44]

After a suggestion is made, action should be taken as soon as possible. While having a bias for action is good, we need to temper against the temptation to rush into fixes without checking to see if things really improved (skipping the study step of PDSA) or without properly communicating the change to others (skipping the act step). If we move too quickly, we might lose the opportunity to get input from others or to check to see if we are fixing the right problem (skipping the plan step). While in the case of minor, local, and isolated changes, we might be able to "just do it," in many other cases we are better off "just PDSA-ing it."

The *kaizen* card prompts the employee (often along with his or her supervisor) to write a problem statement. Often, when we give a suggestion, we jump to an answer (such as "We need a

Front of Card	Back of Card
Problem _____	Implementation Steps _____
_____	_____
_____	_____
Idea _____	_____
_____	_____
_____	_____
_____	_____
Date Originated _____ By: _____	_____
Expected Benefits _____	_____
_____	Results Verified? YES / NO
Input Needed From _____	New Method Standardized? YES / NO
_____	Completed Date _____

Figure 11.7   An idea card template used in health systems.

new centrifuge"). By forcing a statement of the problem, we must focus and define what is wrong. Instead of jumping to an answer, we are not locking ourselves into a single solution to evaluate. The supervisor can ask questions about what is wrong with the current centrifuge. Maybe there are other options instead of signing a purchase order (the Toyota ideal of "creativity before capital").[45] The goal of the discussion between employee and supervisor is to find something that can be implemented, even if it is not the original idea.

The *kaizen* card also prompts the employee to write a proposed countermeasure, to explain it in terms of outcomes. We need to list not only the idea but also how we expect the idea to improve safety, quality, time, or cost. These might be rough estimates or even just qualitative understanding of the benefits, but it gets employees thinking about results, not just what they want to implement.

Instead of jumping to just one solution, leaders in a mature Lean environment will ask employees what alternatives they considered. John Shook, an early American employee at Toyota, told a story about how managers at Toyota never just said yes to an idea. They always asked why the employee thought that was the best solution, in the name of probing and finding better solutions, not to second-guess the employee.[46] The manager can ask questions like the following:

- What makes that the best countermeasure?
- What alternatives did you consider?
- Are we solving the root cause of the problem?

When Jim Adams was senior director of laboratory operations at Children's Health in Dallas, Texas, he implemented a suggestion system in which employees were encouraged to verbally bring suggestions to the new team stand-up meetings held at the beginning of each shift. In the meeting, the team reviewed the previous day's metrics on turnaround time. After just a few weeks of reviewing data that measured service quality for the patients and the physicians, Adams noticed a clear trend, saying, "The suggestions made a sudden shift to ideas that were focused on how to improve care and quality for our patients instead of being inwardly focused on what the employees wanted or needed. It was an amazing change, as Lean helped improve our customer and patient orientation."[47]

The *kaizen* card and the method also prompt employees to obtain input from coworkers or leaders. Some ideas can be implemented quickly with just some input from coworkers (such as the organization of a workstation). Other ideas might have an impact on clinical results or patient care, so managers or physicians might need to be consulted. A team might formally list and post the types of suggestions that can be done with feedback from coworkers and which types of changes require manager or medical oversight.

Many, including Toyota, have experimented with giving financial rewards or incentives for employee suggestions. Toyota pays employees in some locations modest incentive payments for implementing (not just making) suggestions.[48] Many would argue that we should rely on people's intrinsic motivation as *kaizen* is supposed to make your own work easier, so that is the incentive. In healthcare, we have a strong intrinsic motivation to make improvements that benefit patients. Many organizations have successfully engaged employees in a *kaizen* approach while offering only token financial rewards or incentives. The recognition aspect of "rewards and recognition" can be very powerful, as leaders at different levels sincerely thank employees for their contributions.

Leaders need to be careful that the financial reward does not become the goal in and of itself. Depending on the culture of the organization, employees might get no financial reward, a small token reward for implementing suggestions, or some percentage of cost savings shared with them. There is no blanket answer to the question of whether we should pay people for suggestions. There are benefits and drawbacks to each approach, so the answer is best left to your own judgment based on the existing culture in your organization. Even well-intended gestures or rewards can be complicated. At one hospital in Ontario, leaders had been selecting an "idea of the month" in an inpatient unit. One suggestion came in that read, "Stop selecting an idea of the month. It's demoralizing to those who don't get chosen."

One of the gurus of *kaizen*, Masaaki Imai, compared the traditional Western view of suggestions with a "Japanese" view (which we could read as meaning the Lean view), "The Japanese-style suggestion system emphasizes morale-boosting benefits and positive employee participation over the economic and financial incentives that are stressed in a Western-style system." Not every small improvement has a specific return on investment (ROI), and ROI is not the only important reason why we would do *kaizen*.[49]

Visual Tracking of Kaizen Ideas

In a Lean environment, suggestions are posted visually on a board for all to see.[50] Some organizations use websites or different web-based apps or intranet sites to create this visibility.[51] As ideas are

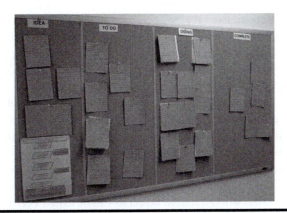

Figure 11.8 An idea board in the laboratory at Children's Health.

being considered, employees and leaders can review the board to see what ideas are in progress, as illustrated in Figure 11.8. With that visual method, employees who see concerns or want to have input into a suggestion can do so. Managing the process visually avoids situations where either a selected few employees or the managers are the only ones who have input. This also helps avoid charges of favoritism that often come from less transparent systems.

The visual tracking board also allows the team to see what is being implemented. As ideas are piloted and accepted (or rejected), progress is tracked visually as the cards are moved to columns further to the right. The four columns are typically labeled:

- New idea
- To do
- Doing
- Done

As people walk by the board, they often stop and read the cards, adding their thoughts to the idea or taking that idea (or a variation) to their part of the workplace. With this board or another visual method (like tracking software), people can see if ideas are being submitted but not being acted on by the team. Hospital leaders, in their rounding, can also see this and follow up with department managers to better respect their employees' ideas by encouraging employees to take action, helping them as needed.

After our planned trial period for the change on the card, the submitter and the team can evaluate the results of the experiment (moving into the study phase of PDSA). If the piloted process had positive results, we can work to formalize that as the new standardized work method, formerly documenting and sharing the improvement. Or, the team can go back and try something new, after working to better understand the system and why the original idea did not work as predicted.

Communicating Kaizen Improvements

Organizations often struggle with communicating process changes to employees, especially in a 24/7 workplace like a hospital. A Lean organization will create standardized work for how to update the standardized work documents and how to communicate that change to employees. Informal methods that often do not work well include posting signs, using change logbooks, or updating the standardized work document without telling anybody. Signs can be ignored, and change logbooks can go unread. Even if employees are supposed to initial changes in the logbook, supervisors often do not formally track who has read and initialed those changes.

Whether an improvement has gone through a formal *kaizen* tracking process or was a small "just did it" change, the department and its employees can benefit from taking time to document what they have accomplished or even what they have tried.

The *kaizen* card has places to record what communication has taken place and if the relevant standardized work has been updated. The exact communication channels used for standardized work changes may vary, depending on the culture at your hospital, but the daily team meeting is a good way of communicating that a change has occurred. Formal standardized work documents should be updated, with changes highlighted. If any training resources are required for the change, managers should make them available.

Another approach that has worked well in hospitals can be called a celebration wall (some sites call it a "*kaizen* wall of fame"). For any improvement made in the department, no matter how big or how small, employees or supervisors create a quick one-page summary that is displayed for all to see. Posting successes (and even some well-intended "failures" that did not work as predicted) gives recognition to employees for their efforts, helps share ideas across work areas, and creates a permanent record of your *kaizen* activities. An example *kaizen* report is shown in Figure 11.9.

The goal is for this to be a simple process, with improvements documented in just a few minutes—simple and quick, not time-consuming and detailed. The completed forms can be

Figure 11.9 An example of a *kaizen* wall of fame sheet filled out by laboratory employees at Children's Health.

posted on a wall, near where team meetings are held or in another common, high-visibility location.

For more detail about *kaizen*, see my books *Healthcare Kaizen: Engaging Front-Line Staff in Sustainable Continuous Improvement* and *The Executive Guide to Healthcare Kaizen: Leadership for a Continuously Learning and Improving Organization*, both co-authored with Joe Swartz.

Conclusion

Healthcare has many traditional mindsets and approaches to management, many of which frustrate staff and providers. Lean is not an approach that focuses only on staff members redesigning their work; leaders need to redesign their management system. Team huddles and management *gemba* walks help increase communication and teamwork while reducing blame. Performance measures help teams understand if they are meeting customer and organizational needs while inspiring and focusing continuous improvement efforts. By managing differently, we can start a virtuous cycle in which employees feel good about making changes that improve patient care and improve their own work environment. As this enthusiasm grows, employees will want to make more improvements. Employee engagement and *kaizen* are the keys to improving quality and safety, reducing costs, and improving employee morale.

Lean Lessons

- Lean is not just about asking our employees to change; managers need to change their methods as well.
- Managers must inspire their employees to take initiative to improve the system, while keeping them aligned with the big picture.
- Standardized work applies to managers and how we manage; auditing the standardized work is a form of standardized work.
- Employees should know how their processes are performing, but we should not pressure them to improve results by working harder.
- Daily, visual metrics are more effective than monthly averages.
- Employee ideas and suggestions should be managed in a way that avoids chaos, yet is not bureaucratic.

Points for Group Discussion

- Why might our supervisors and managers be afraid of empowering their employees?
- Is our organization very top-down or command-and-control? If so, what problems are caused by this?
- How does a new frontline supervisor or manager get trained in our organization today?
- Why do we need to audit the audits?
- What are some reasons why our employees might not speak up or make more suggestions for improvement? Why might employees not take action? What can leaders do to encourage a culture of continuous improvement?
- Is our current culture more of a helpful coaching leadership style or a corrective and punitive style?

Notes

1. Convis, Gary, Role of Management in a Lean Manufacturing Environment, Society of Automotive Engineers, http://www.sae.org/manufacturing/lean/column/leanjul01.htm (accessed March 26, 2015).
2. Jones, Dan, The Beginner's Guide to Lean, Lean Enterprise Institute, http://www.lean.org/common/display/?o=15 (accessed March 26, 2015).
3. Vasilash, Gary S., "David Mann and leading Lean," *Field Guide for Automotive Management*, http://www.thefreelibrary.com/David+Mann+%26+leading+lean.-a0151922358 (accessed August 29, 2015).
4. Toussaint, John, and Roger Gerard, *On the Mend: Revolutionizing Healthcare to Save Lives and Transform the Industry* (Cambridge, MA: Lean Enterprise Institute, 2010), 81.
5. Barnas, Kim, "ThedaCare's Business Performance System: Sustaining continuous daily improvement through hospital management in a Lean environment," *The Joint Commission Journal on Quality and Patient Safety*, 2011, 37(9): 387–399.
6. Toussaint, John, presentation, Lean Healthcare Transformation Summit, June 9, 2010.
7. Toussaint, John, *Management on the Mend* (Appleton, WI: ThedaCare Center for Healthcare Value, 2015), 55.
8. Shook, John, Lessons from Toyota for Healthcare Management?, Lean Enterprise Academy, http://www.leanuk.org/pages/event_summit_2007_speaker_shook.htm (accessed March 26, 2015).
9. Graban, Mark, and Joseph E. Swartz, *The Executive Guide to Healthcare Kaizen: Leadership for a Continuously Learning and Improving Organization* (New York: Productivity Press, 2013), xxxi.
10. Shook, Lessons.
11. Shook, John, Coaching, http://www.lean.org/shook/DisplayObject.cfm?o=2686 (accessed October 16, 2015).
12. Graban, Mark, What's Your Role in Hospital Quality?, http://www.leanblog.org/2011/03/whats-your-role-in-hospital-quality/ (accessed October 16, 2015).
13. Shook, John, presentation, First Global Lean Healthcare Summit, What Toyota Can Teach Us about Lean Leadership, June 25, 2007, http://www.leanuk.org/events/previous-events/lean-summit-2007-1st-global-lean-healthcare-summit.aspx (accessed August 29, 2015).
14. Ibid.
15. Hoeft, Steve, and Robert M. Pryor, *The Power of Ideas to Transform Healthcare: Engaging Staff by Building Daily Lean Management Systems* (New York: Productivity Press), 249.
16. Maass, Kathy, personal interview, September 2015.
17. Toussaint, John, and Roger Gerard, *On the Mend: Revolutionizing Healthcare to Save Lives and Transform the Industry* (Cambridge, MA: Lean Enterprise Institute, 2010), 76.
18. Ibid., 78.
19. Taninecz, George, Strategy Deployment, ThedaCare Center for Healthcare Value, 4. (Appleton, WI: white paper, 2011).
20. Liker, Jeffrey K., *The Toyota Way* (New York: McGraw-Hill, 2004), 37.
21. University of Michigan Health System, Daily Lean Management: Your Role as a Leader, unpublished presentation, http://www.leanblog.org/UofM-leanmgmt (accessed October 16, 2015).
22. Barnas, Kim, *Beyond Heroes* (Appleton, WI: ThedaCare Center for Healthcare Value, 2014), x.
23. Barnas, ThedaCare's Business Performance System.

24. Rabino, Didier, personal correspondence, September 2015.
25. Toussaint and Gerard, *On the Mend*, 172.
26. Joiner, Brian, *Fourth Generation Management* (New York: McGraw-Hill, 1994), 9.
27. Moore, Theresa, personal correspondence, May 2015.
28. Wheeler, Donald J., *Understanding Variation: The Key to Managing Chaos* (Knoxville, TN: SPC Press, 1993), 28.
29. Public Affairs Division, The "Thinking" Production System: TPS as a Winning Strategy for Developing People in the Global Manufacturing Environment, October 8, 2003, http://media.toyota.co.uk/wp-content/files_mf/1323862732essenceTPS.pdf (accessed August 31, 2015).
30. Graban, Mark, Gemba in the NICU: More Notes from Our "Kaizen Live" Experience at Franciscan, http://www.leanblog.org/2015/05/gemba-nicu-notes-kaizen-live-experience-franciscan/(accessed October 16, 2015).
31. Graban, Mark, and Joseph E. Swartz, *Healthcare Kaizen: Engaging Front-Line Staff in Sustainable Continuous Improvements* (New York: Productivity Press, 2012), 235.
32. Graban, Mark, and Joseph E. Swartz, *The Executive Guide to Healthcare Kaizen*, 55.
33. ThedaCare Center for Healthcare Value, Healthcare Value Network Members Share New Quarterly Results, http://www.benzinga.com/pressreleases/15/06/p5606947/healthcare-value-network-members-share-new-quarterly-results#ixzz3dW7OMAlD (accessed October 24, 2015).
34. Tozawa, Bunji, and Norman Bodek, *How to Do Kaizen* (Vancouver, WA: PCS Press, 2010), 299.
35. Rother, Mike, personal correspondence, October 2015.
36. Rother, Mike, The Improvement Kata, http://www-personal.umich.edu/~mrother/The_Improvement_Kata.html (accessed October 16, 2015).
37. Rother, Mike, The Coaching Kata, http://www-personal.umich.edu/~mrother/The_Coaching_Kata.html (accessed October 16, 2015).
38. Lombard, Michael, personal correspondence, October 2015.
39. Ortiz, Tyson, and Jeffrey Liker, A Family's Growth Fueled by Crisis: The Power of the Improvement Kata, http://www.ame.org/target/articles/2015/familys-growth-fueled-crisis-power-improvement-kata (accessed October 24, 2015).
40. Nicodemus, Aaron, What's Good for Toyota is Good for UMass Memorial, http://www.telegram.com/article/20140518/COLUMN73/305189982/.U3iYBClSwNE.twitter (accessed October 16, 2015).
41. Bodek, Norman, personal interview, December 30, 2007.
42. Imai, Masaaki, *Kaizen: The Key to Japan's Competitive Success* (New York: McGraw-Hill, 1986), 113.
43. Tozawa and Bodek, *How to Do Kaizen*, 301.
44. Robinson, Alan G., and Dean M. Schroeder, *The Idea Driven Organization* (San Francisco, CA: Berrett-Koehler Publishers, 2014), X.
45. Smalley, Art, and Isao Katō, *Toyota Kaizen Methods: Six Steps to Improvement* (New York: Productivity Press, 2010), 4.
46. Shook, Lessons.
47. Adams, Jim, personal interview, June 2007.
48. Magee, David, *How Toyota Became #1* (New York: Portfolio, 2007), 34.
49. Imai, *Kaizen: The Key*, 112.
50. Mann, David, *Creating a Lean Culture* (New York: Productivity Press, 2005), 149.
51. Graban and Swartz, *Healthcare Kaizen*, 286.

Chapter 12

Getting Started with Lean

How Do We Start?

Some awareness and understanding of Lean concepts is just the beginning. Knowledge without action will not bring results for patients and other key stakeholders, so it is time to look at how to get started with Lean in your hospital.

The goal should be learning from the examples set by others rather than blindly copying Toyota or leading hospitals. For any organization, be it a factory or a hospital, there is no simple programmatic approach for adopting and practicing Lean methods and transforming a culture. Every health system or individual hospital has its own starting point, its own starting point culture, and its own goals and needs.

> Richard Zarbo, MD, DMD, senior vice president and chair of pathology and laboratory medicine at Henry Ford Health System (Michigan), has led the Lean transformation efforts at their lab since 2005. Zarbo stated, "There is no cookbook approach to Lean," as organizations and leaders must create a program that is their own. Zarbo emphasized that Lean must be introduced in a way that is not driven through traditional "top-down leadership," as he admits to having tried and failed with that approach, initially. "The tools you can read about, the results you can read about, but how Lean is applied is different [in each environment] because Lean is a living thing—it's the people," he said.[1]

As important as thinking and planning are, we also need action, experimentation, and learning. What is stopping you from getting started today? Start small with your Lean efforts, and learn as you go. Identify a problem or two to solve, rather than asking what tool to use first. Find out what works (and try to understand why). Keep doing the things that work, and share the ideas with others in your organization (and even those outside), without expecting them to copy blindly. If something does not work, ask why, and learn from the experience. Hospitals that have been working with Lean the longest are the most likely to say, "We still have so much to learn!"

Hospitals cannot wait until some sort of mythical perfect plan is figured out; we have to start taking action now.

The LEI Lean Transformation Model

In 2014, John Shook and the Lean Enterprise Institute (LEI) published a "Lean Transformation Model" that is helpful for organizations and leaders who are trying to get started.

The five key questions Shook recommends asking are

1. "What is the purpose of the change—what true north and value are we providing, or simply, what problem are we trying to solve?
2. How are we improving the actual work?
3. How are we building capabilities?
4. What leadership behaviors and management systems are required to support this new way of working?
5. What basic thinking, mindset, or assumptions comprise the existing culture, and are we driving this transformation?"[2]

Using the analogy of a house (different than the models shown in Chapter 5), the roof of this house is the goals that matter in the particular situation and the "value-driven purpose" of the organization. The model builds upon the question posed by Shook in Chapter 1: "What problem are we trying to solve?" The pillars of the house are process improvement and the idea of developing the capabilities of everybody who works in the system, including leaders and management. The management system that Shook describes is "driven by leadership behaviors." The foundation of the house includes the basic thinking, fundamental assumptions, and mindsets and culture as that "underlies the entire system and drives the transformation."[3]

Where Do We Start?

It is not practical to start using Lean across the whole organization, all at once. Some have struggled to get results by trying to train or influence 5,000 employees in a hospital or 50,000 across a province. The resources and attention required to support broad action with coaching and mentoring are often too high, and our focus is spread too thin. Instead, it is preferable to find a single area or value stream in which to start—but where?

To help identify priorities for Lean, look at your strategic drivers or ongoing challenges that are not being met. A health system is less likely to succeed if it is pushing Lean on an area, as opposed to people "pulling" on resources and support. Success is also hampered by focusing on implementing tools instead of solving problems. Questions that leaders might ask to help prioritize Lean efforts might include

- What is a patient safety problem or risk to solve?
- What are the most pressing complaints from patients?
- What major issues do physicians or other employees bring to your attention?
- What departments have been struggling?
- Who is proposing large capital purchases or new construction projects?

Table 12.1   Motivations for Lean

Motivation	Percentage
Patient satisfaction	76
Employee satisfaction/engagement	66
Patient safety (proactive)	65
Culture change	61
Overall cost pressures	56
Quality and rework costs	51
Patient discharge delays	51
Emergency department waiting time	46
Operating room utilization	41
Employee retention	35
Patient safety (in response to incident)	35
Emergency room boarding	33
Need for growth	29
Labor costs	25
Need for revenue increases	25
Payer reimbursement reductions	25
Labor shortages	20

In a non-scientific survey conducted for this book, 79 respondents stated their motivations for starting Lean, as shown in Table 12.1, with multiple responses accepted for each respondent. Patient-focused goals, including safety and satisfaction, rank high on the list.

The initial direction and goals might have to be set by the senior leadership team based on their understanding of the strategic needs of the health system. If employee satisfaction levels among nurses are very low, and turnover has soared, there might be no need or time for debate about where to start. This might lead to a project in one inpatient unit, with the goals of reducing waste and eliminating roadblocks and problems that frustrate nurses, leading to better patient care and reduced turnover. Successes and lessons learned can be spread to other units and other hospitals, taking care to modify or adapt approaches as needed.

Parrish Medical Center (Titusville, Florida) emphasizes the following balanced high-level performance measures in its "Lean Six Sigma" improvement work:

Service: patient satisfaction
People: employee satisfaction and employee initiatives

Quality: quality goals and initiatives
Growth: any new program's market growth initiatives
Finances: the financial condition of the hospital[4]

Another method for prioritizing needs would be to conduct a high-level Lean overview seminar for departmental directors and senior leaders. After there is a shared understanding of Lean, ask for an initial volunteer. Who is pulling on Lean as a solution more enthusiastically than others? Especially for a first implementation, it is best not to force Lean on a leader who is not ready to admit there are problems or does not believe Lean methods can help. Avoid the temptation, though, to think the organization can start by giving a one-hour Lean overview class, or just a workshop on 5S, to all employees and then expect improvements just to happen without coaching or support. There is a proper time for such widespread training, but this comes later in the Lean journey, after success in a few departments or value streams. Lean success requires desire, leadership, action, and persistence—things that training cannot provide. People must learn by doing, but with the coaching of an experienced mentor. Some would call this mentor a *sensei*, a Japanese word for teacher or one who has gone before.

Starting in the Midst of a Crisis

When Eric Dickson, MD, took the job as chief executive officer (CEO) at UMass Memorial Health (Worcester, Massachusetts), the system was "at the brink," in the midst of a severe financial crisis, in early 2013. The system had a "minus 5% operation margin," was losing $10 million a month, and was "very close to defaulting" on their publicly traded debt, which had been downgraded to "junk bond" status. The system had "a horrible relationship with organized labor," and the nurses went out on strike at the main hospital. Service and quality scores were "average, but average quality scores in healthcare are pretty bad," says Dickson. He wondered if that crisis was really the right time to get started with Lean.

In Dickson's own words:

> We never announced that we were going to institute a Lean program here. We started with things that were inarguable—values, principles, how we were going to do the work. For us, we define True North in the organization is the best place to give care, the best place to get care.
>
> Intentionally, for our caregivers we put "Best place to give care" first. Not that it was more important, but that it was sequential. It was never going to be a great place for our patients until it was a great place for our caregivers.
>
> Then we defined the role of management as, "We take care of the people who take care of patients, and that's our job." We did some symbolic things to represent that. We took out all the reserved parking spots that people would walk by every day as they came in to work and moved them to the very back of the parking lot.
>
> We thought about just taking them out completely, but it was more important for us to put them at the very back of the parking lot, so that people knew they were there, and those stories started to be told around the organization. We looked for ways of symbolizing this.
>
> We cleared our plate in an exercise of key prioritization. We took everything that people were working on and we built ten A3s, the must-do, can't-fail projects of the year, things that we had to get done. We brought the discipline of A3 thinking to our projects,

so that we didn't have these déjà vu meetings where we'd come in, and you'd hear about the same problem over and over again, with no clear progress being made on any.

Perhaps most importantly, we built a foundation of engaging everyone, every day, through our huddle system. We made that the base of our Lean program, what was the frontline groups getting together with their manager, going over metrics, primarily in and around the experience of care and the experience of giving care, and instituting the frontline staff's ideas.

We set that as one of our True North metrics, the number of ideas implemented, and we tied every manager's compensation, in part, to that.

By 2015, about two and half years into their efforts, the system is implementing 20,000 staff ideas per year. The system improved its quality and patient safety metrics and had a "$110 million swing in operating performance." Dickson adds, "Finances are all green now. I've trained the board, I think, to focus on the quality, and not on the finances."[5]

Assessing and Choosing Where to Start

When not in the middle of a crisis, another approach to identifying and prioritizing Lean opportunities is to conduct short assessments of multiple areas, among those who have identified themselves as candidates for Lean. An assessment is a focused effort that might last anywhere from two days to two weeks, depending on the complexity of the department or value stream being assessed. Value stream mapping, process observation, and discussions with employees and patients can be used to identify waste, delays, rework, and other non-value-added activities in a process. Quantitative data can be collected to help determine which improvements are possible, including

- Patient safety
- Turnaround time or patient flow improvements
- Quality improvement (reductions in rework time or costs that result from errors)
- Labor cost savings (through attrition or reductions in overtime)
- Inventory savings (from reductions or consolidation of inventory and supplies)
- Revenue growth opportunities (eliminating backlogs, improving utilization, or expanding services)
- Avoiding or delaying capital expansion or construction

Areas in which hospitals first used Lean methods include virtually every clinical or non-clinical department, such as

- Laboratory
- Phlebotomy
- Food services
- Home health division
- Outpatient clinics
- Outpatient surgery
- Medical records
- Pharmacy
- Materials management
- Ambulance services

- Emergency department (ED)
- Inpatient medical/surgical units
- Wound care
- Catheterization lab
- Patient scheduling
- Sterile processing departments

This wide range of responses comes from a set of just 50 hospitals (responding to the survey for this book) and shows there is no single best place to start; it depends on the needs, culture, and existing situation for each particular organization. Many health systems start with departments that seem more production oriented in nature, including the laboratory and pharmacy, where employees interact with physical products and machines or instrumentation more than patients. Support or ancillary departments, like pharmacies and laboratories, have an impact on many value streams and patient pathways, so one project can initially have a broad impact on the hospital. Some hospitals choose to start with a high-volume patient care value stream, such as outpatient surgery or the ED, looking to make a very visible impact that can inspire Lean efforts in other departments.

What Do We Call It?

The word *lean* often has many negative connotations in everyday usage, as people often associate the word with not having enough people or money. Headlines about living in "lean times" are usually not positive news stories. Even so, some healthcare organizations will brand their approach as Lean, making sure they educate employees about the Lean management system and what it really entails.

Many organizations, though, will give their overall improvement program a different primary branding, using a term such as process improvement, performance excellence, or operational excellence. Leaders and implementers certainly will talk about Lean as a methodology, but the name of the department and posters on the wall do not use the term. Another advantage of a more general term is that something like operational excellence as an umbrella can encompass Six Sigma and other methods, as discussed in Chapter 2.

Other organizations create their own primary branding around the name of the organization, with examples including the ThedaCare Improvement System, the Virginia Mason Production System, the Michigan Quality System, or the Bolton Improving Care System. Using the name of the organization emphasizes that they are creating something of their own, even if it borrows from Toyota and earlier healthcare examples. Some of these terms keep the focus on the end result, such as quality or the patient.

Getting Started with *Kaizen*

Rather than starting with a grand plan for systemic transformation, many health systems start by practicing *kaizen* in limited tests. While *kaizen* generally means "continuous improvement," as discussed in Chapter 10, there are different types of improvement that all use that term. Table 12.2 summarizes the three levels of *kaizen* improvements. All three types of *kaizen* are required and fit together as shown in Figure 12.1, a version that was adapted by Franciscan St. Francis Health (Indianapolis) from the *The Toyota Way Fieldbook*.[6]

Table 12.2   Types of *Kaizen*

Kaizen *Method*	Scope of Problems	Duration to Work On	Examples
Point *kaizen*	Small	Hours or days	Using 5S principles to reorganize a nurse's station; solving an equipment downtime problem
Kaizen events	Medium	One week (often longer, including planning)	Reducing operating room changeover time, pharmacy mistake proofing; standardizing automated inventory cabinets across units
System *kaizen*	Large	9–18 weeks	Layout and process redesign of a department, such as clinical lab, pharmacy, or ED triage process

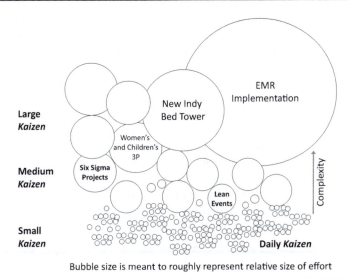

Bubble size is meant to roughly represent relative size of effort

Figure 12.1   The three levels of *kaizen*.

It is important to choose the proper scope of problems to be solved with each of the methods. Toyota tends primarily to use "point *kaizen*" in its factories because they already have stable, well-designed processes after decades of improvement. Toyota teaches that the plan-do-check-act (PDCA) thought process is the same across all types of *kaizen*, regardless of the scale of the problem. Toyota uses their infrequent "*kaizen* events" to teach people how to make smaller point *kaizen* improvements on a more continuous basis in their workplace.[7]

The same is true in hospitals, including ThedaCare, where they shifted from initial reliance on events to a balanced approach that also allows for what they call "continuous daily improvement," or smaller improvements that follow the PDCA (or PDSA, plan-do-study-adjust) model.[8] Some hospitals rely exclusively on *kaizen* events to drive change and improvement. The overall approach of a hospital can incorporate events but should also train and encourage employees and supervisors to make small improvements every day (through point *kaizen*). Some problems are large and broad enough that a system *kaizen* approach would be most effective.

Dickson recalls that, during his first experience with a Lean transformation at a previous organization, "It felt like it was all about, 'Let's start doing lots of *kaizen* events and finding efficiencies in the system.'" He learned that Lean is "really about respect for the people and continuous improvement … especially the respect for people part." UMass conducts some events, but Dickson emphasizes the need to engage "everyone, every day, in continuous improvement and doing it in a way that shows respect for people."[9]

At one of ThedaCare's critical access hospitals, New London Family Medical Center, CEO Bill Schmidt says they, like the larger sites in the system, started with improvement events but also added larger strategic initiatives and smaller process improvements.[10] While some critical access hospitals (with 25 or fewer beds) say they are too small to practice Lean, New London Medical Center was one of the first to try. New London got educated about improvement events and had a *sensei* from a consulting group help them. New London was able to draw on ThedaCare's pool of facilitators before developing their own. Schmidt said an advantage of being smaller was that a higher percentage of staff could be quickly touched by Lean, but a downside was "when we [made a mistake in our approach], it took longer to recover."

Schmidt said there was not a great fear of layoffs, given the system's "no layoffs philosophy"; the bigger fear among staff was how their own role would change in a Lean system. He said, "Word spread quickly about people being reassigned. They might not have been thrilled to be doing something different, but at least they were doing something."

One systemic challenge related to waste and cost reduction in critical access hospitals is the "cost-plus" reimbursement model from the federal government. In that context, the hospital loses 50 cents of reimbursement for every dollar saved. Yet, Schmidt said, "There was never any question that reducing cost, and doing so appropriately, wasn't the right thing to do."

Kaizen Events

It may seem confusing that the term *kaizen* means continuous improvement, yet so many organizations use weeklong quick-hit *kaizen* events to solve problems. Running a few events here and there might be more sporadic or episodic, instead of continuous, improvement. *Kaikaku* is a different Japanese word that can be translated as "radical, revolutionary improvement," a description that might be more accurate for this type of change.[11] *Kaizen* events are somewhat misnamed but can be an effective approach to certain types of problems. While the phrase "*kaizen* event" is popular in the manufacturing world, many hospitals use terms such as rapid process improvement workshop (RPIW) or rapid improvement event (RIE), but the concept is the same.

An event is conducted by a team formed specifically for this purpose and disbanded afterward. The team is often cross-functional, led by a *kaizen* leader experienced with Lean principles. Events are typically structured in this schedule, shown in Table 12.3.

Many of the early improvements at ThedaCare were a result of their RIEs. Their Friday "report out" sessions often have six event teams presenting to senior leaders and up to 100 other people in an auditorium. The session is described as "part teaching session, part evangelical Lean revival."[12]

Table 12.3 *Kaizen* **Event Structure**

Day	Purpose/goals
Monday	Conduct Lean and *kaizen* event training Observe the current process firsthand, collect data, talk with employees
Tuesday	Brainstorm, identify, and discuss opportunities for improvement Establish performance improvement goals
Wednesday	Start implementing changes to layout or process Experiment with changes, follow PDCA
Thursday	Finalize what works and standardize the new process Design management methods for sustaining change
Friday	Document results and improvements, compare to plan Present event to management, celebrate success, plan for future changes

While ThedaCare sets a goal for 50% improvement of a key metric during the event, the audience cheers loudly just the same for teams who do not reach that stretch goal. That 50% goal is meant to spur creative breakthrough thinking, as opposed to being a strict target.

Further into their journey, ThedaCare continued to conduct some RIEs most weeks, but by 2011, leaders set an expectation that 80% of improvement would come from what they call their "continuous daily improvement" (CDI) process, driven by huddle boards in different departments.[13] The system reported implementing more than 20,000 improvements in 2012.[14] John Poole, senior vice president for the ThedaCare Improvement System, said CDI is "the hard work in the Lean world: culture change, day by day."[15] Poole added, "For several years, we were harvesting the low-hanging fruit, doing *Kaizen* Events and RIEs that took obvious waste out of value streams. It felt gut wrenching at the time, but in hindsight, it was the easy 20% of needed change. We hadn't yet created a culture of continuous improvements."[16]

Pitfalls of **Kaizen** *Events*

One pitfall with *kaizen* events can be the lack of focus after the intense weeklong event. If decisions and changes were driven by just a few staff members or outside experts rather than the people doing the work on a daily basis, there is a greater risk that the old process might reappear (if the new process was even adopted at all). If the entire team and their supervisors have not been taught or encouraged to continually improve their new process, performance might degrade. One hospital manager said, "We have a lot of 'do-over' RPIWs because the results disappear as soon as the team does. We only do RPIWs; there is very little culture building."

Even Virginia Mason Medical Center (Seattle, Washington), with their impressive Lean results and culture change, reported that in 2004 they were "only holding the gains on about 40% of those changes, partially because it is easy to slip back into old ways of doing things if there is a lack of accountability and follow through."[17] One could say they applied *kaizen* to their RPIW process, as by 2011, their leaders reported that 90% of projects showed sustained results after 90 days, but only 50% held results and methods 6 or 12 months out.[18]

Having a strict weeklong deadline can drive risk-averse organizations or leaders to choose problems that are easy to solve, to help ensure they can complete the event in a week. This fear could lead to events that are severely underscoped, leading to unimpressive results. In addition, an individual event without an overall "big picture" focus might only improve a single area, causing problems in other areas beyond the scope of the event.

Kaizen events do not have to be four or five days long. Some problems do not require a full week, and it is often difficult to get physicians or other clinicians to devote an entire week away from patient care. Barnes-Jewish Hospital (Missouri) has developed a shorter "6–3" event that has a smaller scope. As described by Dr. David Jaques, vice president of surgical services, "The team is prepared to determine the solution during the six hours and has at least one day in between the two work days to try and verify their solution. The last three hours is spent analyzing and finalizing the outcome of their solution."[19]

Lean Transformation Projects

A system *kaizen* approach, sometimes called Lean transformation, consists of a larger project, or series of projects, that solves a broader set of problems than is typically addressed in a *kaizen* event. In each project, a transformation is made from the current state to a future-state process, using methods that can include

- Improving the physical layout and structure
- Improving the work processes to increase flow
- Error proofing and quality improvement
- Improving the scheduling process
- Standardized work
- Inventory management and control (*kanban*)
- 5S and visual management
- Initiating a daily *kaizen* process
- Starting a broader daily Lean management system

These transformation projects usually take 9–18 weeks. With an extended project, we can solve bigger and more systemic problems by implementing a wider range of Lean methods than can be achieved in just one week (or a series of weeks). Lean transformation projects focus not only on quick improvements, but also on sustained success and continuous improvement. This approach allows for giving a broader set of employees more extensive training and experience with multiple Lean tools. It also allows the extended time needed to train supervisors and other leaders to start managing in a Lean manner. This was the primary improvement model used at Children's Health (Dallas, Texas) and Avera McKennan (Sioux Falls, South Dakota), as discussed in Chapter 1.

When an initial project department or value stream has been selected, it is important for the project to be properly defined and scoped. One has to find the balance between a scope that is too large (which will take longer and might increase complexity) and one that is too small (which might not have a significant impact).

A formal charter document can be created by department leadership and the Lean project team to ensure that goals and objectives are aligned. To further emphasize that the project is about improving performance more than just implementing Lean methods, the team should determine what metrics it plans to improve. A baseline set of metrics should be gathered so the team can measure improvement during and after the project. Goals for improvement should be established for each metric based on customer needs and the potential for waste reduction that was identified during the assessment.

A formal problem statement, as with any Lean problem solving, is important so that the goals are understood, along with understanding why the project or improvements are critical to the hospital. The charter should include a statement about how the project aligns with the strategic plan of the hospital. The document should also show the expected timeline and key milestones for the project.

The initial project is just the starting point, as our goal is to transition from a project mentality to a new way of working and managing, every day. Progressing through transformations in multiple departments or value streams allows the health system to form a critical mass of Lean thinking and success, which can set the stage for incorporating Lean into all processes of the organization. Many Lean transformation efforts are followed up with continued point *kaizen* efforts as well as formal *kaizen* events. No department or hospital becomes "fully Lean" after a Lean transformation project; problems remain, and some amount of waste will always be present since perfection is a difficult goal to reach.

Many *kaizen* event efforts start resembling the transformation or system *kaizen* approach. Virginia Mason uses multiple planning and data collection weeks to prepare for the workshop week in their RPIW methodology. Virginia Mason also builds in plans to reevaluate metrics multiple times after the project to test for sustainment. Table 12.4 shows some highlights of the event preparation that takes place.[20]

Rather than having a debate about which *kaizen* method works best, hospitals should incorporate all methods, using them appropriately depending on the type of problem that needs to be solved. In some organizations, working with *kaizen* events across many departments is the best way to spread Lean broadly across the hospital, but at the risk that deep understanding and system *kaizen*-level change do not occur quickly in any one department. Other hospitals use system *kaizen* to make fundamental and sustained changes in one department or a few departments, but at the risk of not introducing the rest of the hospital to Lean concepts and methods. There are many trade-offs and therefore no easy answer about which approach is best.

The Lean Project Team

People often lament, "We don't have time for improvement." Employees are often struggling just to get through the day due to the waste, rework, and workarounds. They're often staying late and

Table 12.4   *Kaizen* Event Preparation

Timing	Activities
8 weeks before	Identify area of need
6 weeks before	Document current process, create value stream map, collect data
4 weeks before	Form team, identify metrics
2 weeks before	Finalize target metrics, complete observations of current state
1 week before	Finalize planning
Workshop week	Create changes to current state and implement, measure results
Post workshop	Remeasure gains at 30-, 60-, and 90-day intervals

having trouble getting their work done. Having the time to do some root cause problem solving seems like a luxury. It is often thought to be easier to keep putting fires out than it is to take the time to put preventive measures in place.

If we were to ask people to improve on top of their daily duties, the initial effort might be strong; however, the temptation is always there to let Lean become a lower priority than getting the daily work done. Managers are tempted to pull employees off Lean work when other employees are sick, causing efforts to lose momentum or stop altogether. It is a classic catch-22—needing to improve, but not having enough time to work on improvement.

One approach that works well in hospitals is to dedicate a full-time process improvement team to kick-start Lean, pulling participants from frontline staff roles. When leaders free up personnel, the improvement team can be trained in Lean methods, then analyze the current process and take time to work on designing new and improved processes. Organizations must identify Lean team members and leaders who are change agents, those who can work well with others and those who can influence their coworkers.

Clay York, formerly the laboratory manager at Children's Health (Dallas, Texas) reflects on their Lean success, as highlighted in Chapter 1, saying, "We saved $419,000 annually in labor cost, without layoffs, as a result of our initial Lean implementation project. These savings would not have been possible without the continual flow and implementation of ideas and suggestions from the people who do the real work. Freeing up their time to actually write up and follow through with their plans is absolutely necessary to achieve these types of results."

Stephanie Mitchell, laboratory services director at Riverside Medical Center (Kankakee, Illinois) adds, "For Lean to be successful, you need dedicated staff and dedicated time to accomplish the goals of a project or improvement. They can't give the attention needed while still doing their regular job. So, we had four staff members dedicated to Lean for about 12 weeks as we redesigned our lab and we still occasionally schedule days for staff to process improvement and redesign. It takes time to work on improvement, but in the end the return on the investment was well worth it."

To create a dedicated team, hospital leaders must ensure employees are not pulled back into daily work; they must have 100% of their time dedicated to Lean. People can be freed up by spending on agency or PRN (as needed) staff or overtime to cover the absence of the team from the department. This is a short-term investment that allows the team to drive improvements that will reduce waste, reducing the need for as many employees in the future.

The process improvement team should be cross-functional and diverse. Successful teams typically consist of four to six employees who are mainly drawn from inside the home department for the project. Having a long-time employee on the team with a new employee creates an effective combination of perspectives. Having an employee who has worked in other hospitals is helpful for bringing an understanding of the ways different hospitals operate.

It is also helpful to have a team member or two from outside the home department. These internal outsiders bring fresh eyes to the process. For example, a nurse from an inpatient unit might be selected for a pharmacy project team. The nurse brings the perspective of an internal customer, someone who interacts with the pharmacy. The nurse would have an understanding of process defects and problems that cause waste and rework for the inpatient units. Building a team of insiders and outsiders can help bridge communication gaps between hospital departments, leading to joint problem solving and a reduction in finger pointing. The outsider can ask honest questions about the process, asking why as often as possible. When internal team members have to explain their processes to an outsider, it helps surface waste better than when everybody on the team has the same background and understanding of the old methods and processes.

An internal outsider might intentionally be a member of a department that expects to soon use Lean methods. For example, a radiology technician might be made available for the initial lab project team. This provides an outside perspective for the lab team and gives the radiology technician experience with Lean. Lean hospitals often plan team staffing resources "one ahead and one behind," carrying over a person from the previous department in addition to pulling ahead one from the next.

At one hospital, an ED nurse was placed on the Lean team for the laboratory. During initial team-building meetings, the nurse introduced herself as from the ED and immediately apologized. Most of her interactions with anyone from the lab had been angry phone calls, made in an attempt to find the status of test results. She explained that she was not normally like that, but the pressure of the ED led people to yell and be short with others. The nurse had a strong motivation to help improve the lab, as both she and her coworkers in the ED would benefit from her work when she eventually returned to her normal job.

Regardless of the exact makeup, the Lean team requires a project leader and coach, either an outside consultant or an internal Lean leader from a process improvement department. Responsibility for Lean transformation cannot be delegated or outsourced. The coach should not be expected to come up with all of the answers or be expected to "make you Lean" without any effort of your own. In fact, many coaches will, after training the team in Lean concepts, insist on not giving answers. Instead, the coach, or *sensei*, will guide the team by asking questions and having the team develop its own solutions. Having a new process developed by the people who work in the department leads to greater buy-in compared to a case where the answers come from an outside expert. Even if the outside expert has the right answers, there will be less ownership (or none) over the Lean changes and the improved process.

Executive Sponsorship and Leadership

Systemic hospital-wide Lean improvements will only succeed with the strong support, involvement, and leadership of top hospital leaders and influential physicians. Lean efforts will be less likely to reach their full potential if executives are not willing to tackle difficult cross-functional issues that will be identified in events or transformation projects. Another failure mode is leadership not understanding Lean principles, leading them to ask for suboptimization of departments or laying off people as a result of productivity improvements.

John Toussaint, MD, former CEO of ThedaCare, writes, "The most common problem I see is that leaders fail to recognize the magnitude of change that will be required and that change extends to the leaders on a personal level." He adds that when "leaders have simply handed over the keys to the consultants or the improvement staff," that approach "does not work."[21]

Jackson-Madison Laboratory at West Tennessee Healthcare first gained Lean experience in its clinical lab areas. The lab improved turnaround times, reduced head count requirements, and saved $1.2 million from reduced construction and space requirements at a new facility.

Moving to microbiology, the lab applied the same concepts and lessons learned from the first project. They improved the flow through the accessioning and plating areas from batch processing to single-piece flow. As in many labs, West Tennessee had previously only read and provided results for plated specimens during the day shift. Looking at their value stream and patient needs, the lab realized there would be benefits from reading specimens 24 hours a day, so that change was made.

Microbiology also found an opportunity to make a major improvement that, while costing the lab more, would benefit the hospital as a whole. Leadership embraced the Lean principles of not suboptimizing that one department at the expense of the whole. The lab identified an opportunity to adopt a slightly more expensive, but faster, test for methicillin-resistant *Staphylococcus aureus* (MRSA). The new test could detect an estimated 28 cases a year of MRSA before they became full-blown. Since it costs an average of $35,000 to treat each active MRSA infection, this saved the hospital an estimated $983,000. Without top leadership support, the lab might have been prevented from making the decision that was best for the whole hospital.[22]

Beyond the lab, the hospital saved $5 million in its first three years of using Lean and Six Sigma together.

Since process changes challenge people, leading to discomfort for many, top executives need to be consistent in their support for local leadership and the Lean process. Executives need to be effective at articulating the answer to the "Why Lean?" question, articulating the need for change and the problems that need to be solved. Understanding the need for change is critical, and executives must play a major role in communicating that to the rest of the organization.

Some people make excuses that their employees or leaders do not buy in to Lean, meaning employees slowly or subtly sabotage the efforts or outright refuse to participate. An LEI survey about Lean obstacles illustrated the amount of finger pointing that happens when organizations struggle with Lean. Three of the top four obstacles were exercises in blaming, including "middle management resistance" (36%), "employee resistance" (28%), and "supervisor resistance" (23%).[23] When problems arise, the best approach is to ask why. If you start looking at root causes for why employees might not be on board with Lean, they might include fear, anxiety, or a lack of understanding, all of which can be addressed by executive leadership. As Chip and Dan Heath write in their book *Switch*, "What looks like resistance is often a lack of clarity."[24]

It is not enough for executives to say they are behind Lean. Executives have to be out in front, leading the charge, communicating and taking visible action.[25] As executives, you have to keep articulating your Lean vision and continually explain why Lean is an important strategy for your hospital. Leaders need to aim for true commitment from employees, a choice they make, rather than forced compliance. As author and professor Peter Scholtes said, "People don't resist change, people resist being changed."

Even better than support and understanding is direct involvement from leaders. It is often eye opening for senior leaders to spend time at the *gemba* observing the process themselves. This should not be a quick walk-through; a *gemba* walk should be a prolonged observation of a single area or a walk through an entire end-to-end value stream. Observing the process firsthand will highlight waste and problems that people struggle with daily. Who seems frustrated? Who is racing around because of time pressures? Where can you see batching and disorganization? Who does not have the supplies and equipment they need to do their job? Observing and listening to your employees will bring a fuller view of the need for Lean than scorecards or financial measures alone.

Executives also have to identify fears that employees might have about Lean. If Lean is not seen as good for the employees, they will be less than enthusiastic. One common fear is that Lean and the resulting efficiency improvements will be used to reduce head count. Executives must be visible and vocal in their commitment that Lean will not be used to drive layoffs; otherwise, rumors and fears will spread, undermining Lean. Even if senior leaders have no intent of laying off employees, the lack of a public statement can cause rumors to spread and morale to drop. At Silver Cross Hospital (Joliet, Illinois), David Schlappy, then vice president, quality and medical staff service, made this pledge, saying, "We're not going to lay off anybody, nobody loses their job because of process improvement initiatives. I am committed to that personally, that if we were going to go forward with Lean, I would put my personal reputation on the line that we weren't going to do that." A pledge like this is usually one of the keys to Lean success in a health system. A number of leading hospitals, including Avera McKennan and ThedaCare, have similar no-layoff policies or commitments.[26]

Starting from the Middle

It is possible for Lean to start in a single department when driven by local leadership. In a survey conducted for this book, 46 respondents who have Lean hospital initiatives were asked who initiated Lean efforts for the hospital, as shown in Table 12.5 (multiple responses were allowed). Results show that director-level leaders are just as likely as, or more likely than, C-level executives to initiate Lean efforts. Starting in the middle could mean that the Lean efforts end in the middle, if senior leaders never take interest in Lean. But, there are times when the initial spark for a health system comes from a middle manager who suggests Lean or starts with the approach in their area.

In the case of Riverside Medical Center (Kankakee, Illinois), Stephanie Mitchell, administrative director of laboratory services, initiated the Lean efforts. She made the case to her senior leadership team to get help for the first project and directly oversaw the effort. While leaders were willing to hire a consultant, they were not yet completely sold on the idea. CEO Phil Kambic said while he believed in the "sound management practices of Lean" and was willing to let the lab try, he was "skeptical" it would be successful based on experiences with other improvement methodologies.

Table 12.5 Initiators of Lean Efforts

Role	Percentage
CEO, CFO, or CIO	32.6
CMO or CNO	10.9
VP, administrative	28.3
VP, clinical/medical	19.6
Director, administrative	37.0
Director, clinical/medical	30.4
Manager or supervisor	15.2
Physician or nurse	4.3

After initial success in the lab, where turnaround times were reduced dramatically and internal customers (like the ED) were happy with the improved performance, the executive team became excited to be out in front leading the effort for the whole hospital. Even though Kambic and chief financial officer (CFO) Bill Douglas oversaw the Lean efforts in the lab, through participation in regular steering committee meetings, their interest in Lean training for the entire senior leadership team grew after the first project. They also sponsored continued Lean education throughout the hospital and worked to spread the methodology to other departments, such as pharmacy and inpatient care settings.

After the initial skepticism, Kambic became sold on incorporating Lean into the core strategy of the hospital: "Lean is the approach that makes the most sense. It's not benchmarking, where it's hard to find apples-to-apples comparisons. Lean is focused on improving our own processes, right now, with our people and their creativity."

Mitchell later added "Lean and continuous process improvement" to her title and responsibilities, helping spread Lean and coach people throughout the hospital. She conducted daily continuous improvement (*kaizen*) training for 85% of managers and directors, who then started leading these efforts in their areas.

Establishing a Model Line and a Road Map

Some hospitals have started with Lean by teaching and using a single tool, such as 5S, across all departments. An effort like this risks spreading your coaches or trainers too thin. This approach also increases the risk that the hospital is not solving the problems that matter to patients and employees. Sure, using 5S alone will eliminate some waste, but nurses might get frustrated if they are asked to spend time organizing their station when the poor patient flow through the ED has everyone at a breaking point. Lean might get a reputation as the latest "flavor of the month" if more significant results are not achieved through initial efforts.

Toyota's Bonini coaches organizations to start with a model line that is an "inch wide and a mile deep," which means being "narrow in scope" and "implementing that full Toyota Production System (TPS) triangle in great depth, using the right philosophy, the right tools for the process at hand, the right managerial approach where we develop people who can sustain and spread these practices" to other areas.[27] In this approach, "the whole triangle is being implemented," referencing Figure 2.1.[28] Sustaining and spreading this approach requires people who "deeply understand, through experience, how the philosophy, tools, and managerial approach can be applied in their organization," adds Bonini.

Bonini says, "TPS is learned 90% through experience," adding, "It's hard to understand until they've lived and built an organization with that philosophy. It's hard to understand the tools unless they've been used. It's hard to understand the managerial approach unless they have developed people by coaching them through many problem solving cycles or activities ... so they can learn by doing."[29] Bonini uses an analogy of learning to ride a bicycle or play golf, in that the basic concepts are simple and can be learned from a book. "But, you'd never think to learn to swim (or become a surgeon) through lecture alone," as these "must be learned through application under the guise of a very skilled coach (with many years of experience) and deep reflection."

Rather than trying to implement a Lean method (or set of methods) throughout the entire hospital, an effective approach is to establish a model line in one department (such as the pharmacy or a laboratory) or one particular patient value stream (such as patient flow starting at arrival to the ED). Creating a limited model line scope reduces the time required to adopt and practice a full set of Lean methods and management systems. The goal of a model line is not to use some superficial Lean tools, but to fully embrace a broad set of Lean practices and mindsets. The goal is to be a shining example of what is possible for the rest of the organization.

The model line can be selected based on prioritizing a number of factors, including the needs assessment (which problems need solving?), current-state assessment (what waste can be eliminated?), and readiness assessment (do the managers, staff, and physicians agree that change is needed and possible?). Bonini suggests selecting a model line area with a strong business need that can feasibly be significantly improved in 9 to 12 months and strong organizational leaders who are humble and eager to learn by doing, not just reading books. If Bonini can't get two to three hours of top management time during his time on-site, it shows that it's "not the right priority or strategy at that time," which makes it "very difficult" to transform the area.[30] Bonini adds, "If it's part of the strategy and has the attention of very top management and the board, then it's logical to spend two to three hours on each [of the ongoing workshops]. They need a strong commitment to make this happen."[31]

The senior leadership team may start with a plan or road map for implementing Lean transformation projects beyond the initial department as a way of working toward a Lean culture and management system. Hospitals often plan their first two or three projects, based on the current view of goals and priorities. For example, in the first year of the Lean journey at a hospital, it might plan to complete two projects, for example, in the lab and in radiology, since each transformation project takes approximately three or four months.

Toussaint advocates for a "model cell" approach in his book *Management on the Mend*, based on his own experience and firsthand observations of other health systems around the world. He writes that, when done well, a model cell "is a revolution instead of the usual evolutionary change in work processes," but there is "danger that your revolution can go terribly awry."[32]

Toussaint's five tips for a successful model cell approach are

1. Must be focused on a business problem that is important, relevant, and clear.
2. Scope must be limited.
3. "Create a new system based on standard work" that is "clear, useful, and accepted by the people who will use it."
4. Tie the work to "true north" directions and goals.

5. "Involve senior leadership [CEO and COO] if at all possible," not as full-time participants, but checking in regularly. "The hand on the helm must be willing to change, as well."[33]

Toussaint also highlights the seemingly contradictory goals of a model cell. First, it's an area to test new ideas and "embrace failure as a path for learning." Secondly, the model cell is also a place to demonstrate "the results of your finest efforts" that will help motivate others to embrace Lean and spread the practices developed in the model cell.

ThedaCare's well-known "collaborative care" model for inpatient care was not launched throughout the entire organization all at once. Collaborative care was developed and then piloted in a single unit, where care was redesigned and standardized. In the initial tests, the model cell showed an improvement of patients who said they were "very satisfied" from 68% to 90%. Costs also fell by 30% in the model cell. Therefore, this became "the standard for inpatient care at all ThedaCare hospitals."[34]

Bonini says the role of top management in the model line process includes

1. Passionate commitment, the transformation is "fostered and led by top management"
2. Learn TPS principles in detail, well enough to teach them
3. Build an organizational culture that surfaces and solves problems, as "problem solving is the root of this culture"
4. Be active in the *gemba*, go and see

The spread, or what some might call *yokoten* in Japanese, of model cell methods might move sequentially at first, from one unit to a second. The second unit doesn't just blindly adopt what was developed in the first unit. Rather, they evaluate the new approach and decide whether to adopt the new method or adapt it to their needs. If the second unit improves upon what the first unit did, those ideas should be shared back with the first. Then, maybe the methods are spread to a third unit. This methodical rollout might seem tedious. It might seem tempting to save time by making a top-down mandate that forces every other unit to adopt the model cell practices. But, experience shows that the "go slow to go fast" approach is more effective, even if it is slower. After spreading practices to a few departments, the organization might have enough confidence to suggest that everybody adopt the new standards, leaving open the need for adaptation (rather than copying) and continuous improvement.

Some organizations have announced a system-wide "rollout" of continuous improvement practices. It's easy for a hospital to buy 75 large whiteboards and have them installed (although it's harder than it should be in the more bureaucratic institutions). It's more difficult and requires more leadership to get 75 units to enthusiastically embrace the boards, huddles, and other practices. It's especially difficult to do so all at once.

A Model Cell for Kaizen

In comparison, in December 2014, the author helped Mary Greeley Medical Center (Ames, Iowa) to implement and test a model line approach to *kaizen* and daily continuous improvement. Two departments, each having enthusiastic leaders, were chosen as pilot areas: materials management and a surgical inpatient unit. This made it easier for the author and Mary Greeley leaders to teach, coach, and observe. Ron Smith, a process improvement coordinator, was trained to be the internal coach and key person to help spread *kaizen* practices. At the same time, vocal and visible support came from their CEO, Brian Dieter, and their vice president and quality improvement officer, Karen Kiel-Rosser. They provided recognition and support for early improvement efforts, along with local departmental managers and directors.

After some initial success was confirmed, Smith put together a plan that would introduce *kaizen* methods to two departments every two weeks. Based on lessons learned from the model unit, Smith created a standardized training and coaching plan for the new areas and their leaders. By April 2015, *kaizen* practices had spread to 14 departments, with new areas being prioritized based on "pull from department leaders." This pull was created by sharing improvements from early adopters and the CEO talking about *kaizen* and the need for improvement.

To speed up the initial rollout wave, which was completed in July 2015, Ron developed and coached a second process improvement facilitator who could introduce these practices to new areas. That allowed them to launch three or four units every two weeks. In addition to their ongoing coaching, a "second wave" of formal training is planned to help each department progress from relatively simple "just do it" improvements to also focus on more complex problem solving and root cause analysis.

One advantage of a model line approach is the reduction of risk. For example, if mistakes are made in an initial launch of a new practice, the impact of that small test of change is limited. Additionally, if you're buying and designing a huddle board or other materials (or software) to support new practices, lessons learned from the model cell can be used to tweak the design. At one hospital, where over 80 boards had been purchased and installed, the first week's use led the process improvement team to realize the boards should be modified. That would have been easier to do with a single board or two, rather than the whole lot of them.

Pros and Cons of a Road Map

Many organizations ask for (or expect) a detailed three- or five-year "Lean road map" that tells leaders exactly what will be happening each month. In dynamic, fast-moving environments, this is pretty close to impossible to do. That doesn't mean that an organization should "wing it" and be completely reactive. Senior leaders can work with middle managers to develop a longer-term vision for the organization and *what* they want (or need) to accomplish, in terms of goals and direction, along with articulating the *why*. The details of exactly *how* the transformation will progress or take shape will be figured out over time. Leaders should expect that any plan that is created will have to be tweaked and adjusted over time. As former U.S. president Dwight D. Eisenhower said, "Plans are nothing; planning is everything."

As Fuijo Cho, honorary chairman of Toyota, said in 2002, "There are many things one doesn't understand and therefore, we tell them why don't you just go ahead and take action; try to do something. You realize how little you know and you face your own failures and redo it again and at the second trial you realize another mistake or another thing you didn't like so you can redo it once again. So by constant improvement, or the improvement based upon action, one can rise to the higher level of practice and knowledge."[35] That same mindset can apply to high-level Lean transformation efforts or the practice of daily *kaizen* within a team.

Dedicating People to Lean Beyond Projects

While the goal is for Lean to eventually become the culture, daily management system, and way of thinking, Lean usually starts off as an artificial program or initiative. Health systems in the early days of their Lean journeys usually make frontline staff and managers available to work on Lean through rapid improvement events, transformation project teams, or dedicated departments.

The Lean Department

Many organizations have created an internal department that is called the "Lean department," or other names such as

- Business transformation office
- *Kaizen* promotion office
- Lean promotion office
- Process excellence department
- Operational excellence group

People in this department might be referred to as internal consultants, coaches, or facilitators. Their role is not to make the organization Lean or to come up with every idea or improvement. The department should be tasked with teaching and coaching others, leading or facilitating some improvement events and projects (teaching others in the process), and developing future leaders for the organization through their education and participation in Lean.

What's the right size for a central Lean department? It depends partly on the size of the organization and the roles and responsibilities of the team members. A transformation of any reasonably large size requires more than a single person. Some hospitals have tried having a "lone wolf" or a department of one, an approach that most often leads to that individual leaving the role or the health system in frustration. If the ideal number is greater than one, Toussaint advocates having a department that's the size of 1% of the organization's FTEs, based on his experience and past advice from his mentors and consultants. For a health system with 3,000 FTEs, that would be 30 full-time Lean staff members. It's more common to see a team ranging from four to eight in a hospital of typical size.

One approach would be to start with a relatively small team, as required to support a model line area. Then, keep adding staff (and finding constructive things for them to do) until it seems that adding more would be unhelpful or counterproductive. Call it the PDSA approach to sizing a Lean department.

It is common for a health system's Lean department to consist of a mix of insiders and outsiders. Hiring an engineer or operations manager from a good Lean manufacturing organization can be a great partner for a nurse, pharmacist, or unit manager from within your hospital. The insiders and the outsiders can learn from each other about concepts and terminology that are new and useful to the other. Often, an insider and outsider are paired up to facilitate a rapid improvement event or to teach a class together, playing off each other's strengths and experiences until they are, perhaps, to a point where they can work more independently.

Over time, a health system might add an equal mix of outside hires (from other industries or healthcare organizations) and internal staff. Healthcare professionals often get excited about Lean through an initial project or event, identifying themselves as change agents who want to focus on improvement and work with other areas. If productivity improvements are made in the hospital, staff can be redeployed to the Lean office rather than laying them off. Ask managers to give up "their best people" for the Lean group—those who have the energy and people skills to be effective change agents.

Hospitals, through hiring managers and human resources departments, sometimes confuse different certifications and indicators of Lean experience when hiring for Lean facilitator roles. Job postings for a Lean or process improvement role might specify that a particular color of "Lean Sigma" or "Six Sigma" belt is required for the role. If that is a hard requirement, a hospital would err in screening out, for example, former Toyota employees who would not have any sort of belt certification. Arguably, the person from manufacturing who has years of experience and demonstrated success with Lean would be a better candidate than somebody who has merely passed an online test to receive a formal belt credential. It's important to understand what type of person and what experience you really need for your Lean journey.

It's also important to have a leader for this group or effort who is experienced with Lean, either within healthcare or from an outside industry. One hospital appointed an experienced project manager to be in charge of their "Lean Sigma" program. She promptly asked "What's Lean Sigma?" and exclaimed, "I'd better get trained on that right away." True story. Yes, project management is an important part of a Lean journey, but the most successful Lean health systems have hired the key internal Lean leader away from manufacturing, an outside consulting group or another health system that is further along with Lean.

While the position in the Lean department is full time, many organizations expect time in that role to be a developmental assignment rather than a permanent position or career path. TheadaCare, for example, generally has two-year terms on the central improvement team. Toussaint refers to the flow in and out of the team as "the bloodstream of the organization," gaining and spreading Lean knowledge as if it were oxygen, in his analogy.[36] Within TheadaCare, there are more than 100 executives and leaders who spent time as Lean facilitators. "We have learned that when management is deeply entrenched in Lean thinking, the culture moves quicker in the right direction."[37]

Gary Passama, CEO of NorthBay Healthcare (Fairfield, California), reflected on the start of their Lean journey by saying, "Our approach to inculcating Lean at NorthBay was deliberate in nature. We were not interested in a 'big bang' approach. We wanted Lean to become part of daily life at NorthBay. We also wanted our team members at all levels to feel empowered to apply Lean principles at the work site level. That is what we have worked hard on over the past three years.

We now have three Lean Facilitators on staff who act as a resource for implementing projects and changes. We have seen changes ranging from how we stock supplies in various departments to how we schedule patients in our outpatient settings. In some instances we have achieved measurable savings. In other instances patient satisfaction has improved.

While cost savings are nice we did not set out in our Lean activities with that as a primary goal. Our staff understands this and therefore does not fear Lean. We have had no significant layoffs since embarking on our Lean journey. It may be a coincidence but since we started using Lean principles we have had our best years in terms of financial results and employee satisfaction scores."

The Importance of Change Management

Implementing large-scale change, including the adoption of Lean, is difficult. It consumes a great deal of energy and requires persistence, dedication, and a formal change management plan. It is commonly said that 80%–90% of the Lean implementation challenge is related to people and the acceptance of change. The remaining 10%–20% of the challenge is the implementation of technical tools and methods.

A McKinsey study estimated that the "success rate" of "transformation programs" is "less than 40%."[38] No clear estimate exists for how often this occurs, but there have been failed attempts to adopt Lean practices in some healthcare organizations, leading to their cancelation or abandonment over time or when a change in leadership occurs. Some might blame Lean as being a poor fit for healthcare, but success at other organizations proves that Lean *can* work; it's just not *guaranteed* to work (nor is it guaranteed to be easy). Hospitals often struggle with other large-scale changes, including merger integration, electronic medical record system adoption, or new hospital construction. Hospitals that struggle with Lean often had previous struggles with total quality management (TQM), Six Sigma, or other methodologies. This begs the question about the root cause of these failures.

As many people say, "change is not an event; it's a process." Leaders are often tempted to rush change, using top-down mandates to try to make adoption of a new idea or new practice into an instantaneous event. An organization, and each individual, comes to accept changes (or not) at their own pace. The ProSci® ADKAR® Model for change management shows how each individual might progress through these phases at a different pace:

- "**Awareness** of the need for change
- **Desire** to participate and support the change
- **Knowledge** on how to change
- **Ability** to implement required skills and behaviors
- **Reinforcement** to sustain the change"[39]

Much so-called resistance to change is a manifestation of something being missing, such as the first four phases in the ADKAR model. Leadership and communication can help move people along that progression.

Different models help illustrate how large-scale change occurs at an organizational level. ExperiencePoint has published a model that is a slight tweak to the famed "8-Step Process for Leading Change" from professor and author John Kotter. The ExperiencePoint model's seven steps are

1. **Understand** the need for change
2. **Enlist** a core change team
3. **Envisage**, build a vision and strategy
4. **Motivate**, create a sense of urgency more broadly
5. **Communicate** the vision to the organization
6. **Act**, take action
7. **Consolidate** gains[40]

Many Lean transformation efforts struggle because leaders jump straight into action, or the sixth step in that model. The idea of starting by understanding and defining the problem or the

Figure 12.2   Change curves, showing how performance may change over time, with or without effective change management practices.

need for change should be familiar as "start from need," from Ohno and Chapter 1. Forming a core change team can be a "steering committee" for a health system or a "Lean team" for a department or value stream, as discussed earlier in this chapter. Executives often err in assuming that employees and managers understand the current crisis or situation, along with the urgency for change. Choose a change model that your team can relate to, think about it, and think of transformation as a process (or a journey), not an event.

One challenge with even many successful transformations is that key performance measures may get slightly worse when new processes are put into place or changes are made, as shown in Figure 12.2, whether measured in terms of labor productivity or customer service measures (such as patient satisfaction in an ED or turnaround time for a laboratory). If training on new processes or communication is poor or haphazard, organizations run the risk of introducing chaos and further hurting performance. Even if training and communication are effective, the "learning curve" effect shows us that it takes time to become comfortable with a new process and performance will improve over time.

That dip in the measure will be smaller and of a shorter duration, however, if there is effective change management in place. Employees, especially Lean team members, need to understand that system improvements that might seem undeniably better from a logical standpoint will still cause a sense of loss or grief among employees. Changing and dismantling old processes can sting, particularly among those who had put those old processes in place. After all, today's wasteful process often used to be somebody's great idea.

During a Lean implementation, the hospital department and employees typically go through a cycle of denial, fear, and stress before gaining belief that the improvements will actually happen and will improve their working environment. Employee satisfaction scores may decline before they recover and improve beyond the baseline number. Family therapist Virginia Satir described a five-stage change that is reminiscent of Figure 12.2, as individuals go from the status quo, to resistance, to chaos, then to integration, and a new status quo.[41] It's natural for people to be afraid of change, as psychologist Robert Maurer describes in his discussion of how the amygdala section of our brain and our "fight or flight" instinct kicks in for a large change, even if it should be considered a positive change.[42] It ignores human nature for executives to lecture people to not fear change. A healthy respect for people would recognize the need to engage people and to make changes small, especially at first, so as to make change less scary and avoid the "fight or flight" response.

Teams need to be prepared that their coworkers may go through such a cycle with its ups and downs. This cycle can be dampened through constant communication and feedback. There are cases when nothing but time and experience with a new process will build support, acceptance, and enthusiasm for Lean and new systems. Employees and coworkers may give strong, sometimes emotional, feedback that the old system and layout "works for me," saying that they do not feel the need to make changes. Leaders need to support their team and remain involved throughout the project.

A Snapshot of Hospital Success: Avera McKennan Hospital & University Health Center

Starting in the Lab

Avera McKennan Hospital & University Health Center (Sioux Falls, South Dakota) is a 545-bed facility that is the largest tertiary hospital in the Avera Health system. The hospital started its journey in 2004 in its laboratory.

Moving ahead to 2015, the laboratory has maintained or has continued to reduce its turnaround times while increasing its testing volume by 40% with a lower staffing level than before Lean. "Collect-to-result" turnaround chemistry panel times were reduced 44%, from 62 minutes to 35. Continued improvements have dropped these times to 31.5 minutes. Complete blood count (CBC) "collect-to-result" times have been reduced by 25%, to 17.5 minutes, with the introduction of auto verification in 2014.

"We continuously re-evaluate our lab for improvement opportunities. Whether we install new instrumentation, add construction, or review existing processes, Lean is at the center of the evaluation process," said Mike Black, assistant vice president for laboratory services. "Our employee satisfaction continues to excel. As new staff are added they are trained in the Lean process as well."

As a testament to the Avera McKennan laboratory's mission to strive for improvements, it was the first lab in the nation to become CAP ISO 15189 certified in 2004, which combines quality management and continuous improvement. Avera McKennan is currently the longest-running lab in the nation to hold that standard.

Avera McKennan has applied Lean in many departments, including

Laboratory and histology
Pharmacy
Emergency department
Operative services
Surgical case cart builds
Housekeeping
Behavioral health
Women's center
Inpatient units, including medical, surgical, nursing, and telemetry
Long-term care
Primary care clinics

Materials management/supplies
Marketing
Specialty clinics access
Neonatal intensive care unit
Breast center
Dialysis
Hospital operations (medication safety and electronic physician order entry)
Home medical equipment
Business office and health information management

Improving Inpatient and Emergency Flow and Care

Beyond the lab, Avera McKennan applied Lean concepts to the design of its new ED in 2006. Improved patient flow, along with other process improvements, led to lower construction costs. The ED expansion was cut from a planned 24 rooms to just 20, resulting in a savings of $1.25 million in construction costs. The rooms and the department layout were designed to be more effective for the physicians, nurses, and other employees, saving space without negatively impacting patient care. The department is laid out with the rooms arranged in a U-shaped configuration, with department personnel working in the middle. This improves communication, teamwork, and visibility while reducing walking distances. Patients can enter and depart from the hallway outside the "U," being spared the typical ED noises and sights. Each room, other than trauma, is completely standardized, which improves patient flow because patients no longer wait for specialized rooms. The team created specialty carts, such as a cast cart, that can be wheeled into rooms as needed for a specific patient. A nurse can get needed supplies from a cupboard in each patient room. These cabinets have doors that are accessible from both the patient room and the centralized staff area, so restocking can take place without interrupting patient flow.

"While some of these improvements seem like small things, they resulted in big wins. They cut down on the number of steps staff must take each day, and allowed nurses to stay at the patient's bedside," said Dave Kapaska, DO, regional president and CEO of Avera McKennan.

This design was so successful that Avera is duplicating it with very few changes in a freestanding ER that is part of a new primary care clinic in west Sioux Falls. Construction will take place in 2016 on this project, which will be South Dakota's first ER that stands alone from a hospital campus.

Avera McKennan's new ED processes and design in 2006 to 2007 boosted patient satisfaction scores from the 60th percentile to the 90th on Press Ganey surveys. Average length of stay was reduced to just over two hours, well below national (4:07) and state (2:59) averages at the time. As of 2015, length of stay remains at or below benchmark averages at 2:26. Today, under the more recent HCAHPS patient experience survey, the ED consistently scores at or above top performing hospitals. Lean principles allow Avera McKennan's ED to handle ever-increasing volumes. In the last fiscal year, ED visits numbered 29,029, a 6% increase from the prior fiscal year.

Lean Design for Long-Term Care

Avera also used Lean methods to design a new long-term care (LTC) facility over the course of three years, involving staff including nurses, certified nurse assistants, food service, housekeeping, and others in the iterative layout and design process. "You can't just design in a conference room and hope that it works out," says Kathy Maass, director of process excellence.

The new LTC site was designed with multiple "neighborhoods" of 16 rooms that all have self-contained dining and activities areas and other services, such as laundry done in the neighborhood. Going from semi-private rooms to private rooms with showers impacts housekeeping and their workflows. Process changes were tested out in the old space before the new LTC site opened, as they now have to serve lunch at four different times instead of serving everybody at a centralized dining room at the same time. Medications and supplies are kept in each patient room, even though every resident has slightly different supplies. For the first time, there were no deficiencies found through the state nursing home survey process, thanks to standardized processes and Lean.[43]

Lean is a Turning Point for Home Medical Equipment

Home medical equipment (HME) is a segment of healthcare that is highly regulated, with constantly changing regulations for Medicare reimbursement. For years, Avera Home Medical Equipment had struggled with reporting structures, billing, and dissatisfaction among referring providers and patients. Lean was the vehicle of change for HME, led by Steve Crim, director of operational strategy. "We started out by distilling down the 100 things that needed to happen to fewer than five things that would be the most noticeable changes, in order to have some 'wins.'"

One example was an improved process for patient follow-up on CPAP devices. At one point, claims were missing some information, which prevented or slowed reimbursement. Frontline employees knew best what needed to happen, but they just needed guidance as to how to get there, Crim said. It was vital to communicate clear expectations and due dates to employees with constructive feedback and follow-up to reinforce that change was not optional. The team then designed a process to collect all required information upon order. Collecting the information the first time the order was touched eliminated extensive rework and the delays that occurred when CPAP devices were ordered.

Due to the struggles this department had faced, employees no doubt feared that their jobs were in jeopardy. Employees needed to feel safe or "that we had their backs," Crim said. "As long as they were willing to give us their commitment to work with us, we let employees know it was OK to fail—we'd figure it out." "The tremendous thing was that we did it with the people that were there, and we didn't lose anyone through this process. They have embraced a new way to meet the needs of patients and expectations of the organization," Crim said.

Improving Clinic Scheduling and Appointment Availability

In clinic care, Lean principles paved the way for Avera to offer same-day appointments at many of its clinics. When unexpected illness strikes, it's preferable for patients to see their own primary care provider. Yet, when the patient wants an appointment the same day for acute symptoms, that's not always possible.

Previously, patients were given another clinic number to call if their particular clinic's schedule was full for the day. "The result was that we were losing patients or patients were dropping off," said Deb Soholt, director of women's health and administrative liaison to Avera's Primary Care Innovation Council. "Our goal became to give patients what they want when they call—and that's a same-day appointment with a provider."

A Lean team helped providers streamline their own schedules so they could take same-day appointments for their own patients whenever possible. At the end of each day, the provider and nurse review the schedule for the next day to identify schedule slots that can be used for same-day appointments. These slots are marked with a visual indicator and schedulers have permission to fill the slot without calling the RN to "work in" another patient. Work was also done to standardize the length of appointments for specific chief complaints across the system so schedulers know how much time to allow per visit.

Patients are offered an appointment with their provider, if the schedule allows. However, if their own provider has no available time, the scheduler can see the schedules across the entire enterprise and can then offer the patient an appointment with another provider. Those appointments at another clinic could be scheduled without asking the patient to hang up and make another call. The patient can choose to wait for a time with their own provider or see another provider same day.

"We asked schedulers to consider themselves as salespeople who are selling our physicians' time. When patients call for an appointment with one of our physicians, we want to make sure they have that appointment by the end of that call," said Todd Townsend, a process excellence consultant. "Schedulers have never seen their role in quite this way before."

When this project was launched in September 2012, the number of customers who did not receive an appointment on their first call plummeted from about 70 per week to less than 10. Physicians are busier, are more productive, and appreciate having a streamlined schedule. New physicians get more opportunities to work up to their capacity as well.

"The outcome has been spectacular. Patients are grateful to be seen, and we are using our primary care system to its fullest. Previously, we had capacity and capability that we were not leveraging," Soholt said.

Improving Inpatient Care and Implementing EHR and CPOE

Hospital units also streamlined processes to reduce waste and free up time, making the workload more manageable, reducing overtime, and allowing staff to take needed breaks instead of constantly being on the go. "The breakthrough was that nursing began to look at Lean principles as an ongoing problem-solving tool," said Maass.

Additionally, Lean principles were put to work in preparing for meaningful use requirements of computerized physician order entry (CPOE) and bedside medication verification. Thanks to successful implementation of its electronic health record, Avera McKennan has won the HIMSS Stage 7 award, which recognizes a healthcare environment where paper charts are no longer used.

A year before going live with CPOE, a nurse, a health unit coordinator (HUC), and a pharmacist from every hospital unit went through all potential orders to find changes that needed to happen in advance for a seamless go-live. "At go-live, we made the change very visible. We took away the familiar plastic folder for patient charts and replaced them with a paper folder containing only a minimal amount of information," said Maass. "Doctors couldn't write orders because there was no paper. This visible change signaled to them, 'this is a different day.'"

Staff also scanned and archived existing documents to create single-piece flow. "The changes in the process were all thought through and sketched out. We didn't have to wait until the go-live date to find any issues. A lot of hospitals struggle with utilization, but our use was high enough to qualify for HIMSS Stage 7," Maass added. Pervasiveness of inpatient CPOE since July 2015 has remained above a steady 90%–91%, compared with the national benchmark of 90%.

On the heels of CPOE came medication bar coding. A group studied possible pitfalls, and nurses tested bar coding equipment in a simulation lab. "We let them be involved with the decision up front, so they felt ownership of the change," said Doreen Hardy, a process excellence consultant. Hardy and her team found solutions to the more than 20 pitfalls that were identified in advance.

"Once again at go-live, we had an amazing compliance rate," Maass said. Inpatient bedside medication verification utilization has measured 96%–97% since July 2015. Likewise, medication scanning has measured at 95% and above since July 2015, compared to the 95% national benchmark for both measures. Scanning of transfusion products at Avera measures 100%.

Instead of having to fear any negative repercussions for errors or near misses, staff have been rewarded for a "good catch" with a little bag of goldfish crackers for fun. Weekly "good catch" participants were invited to a fish fry at the home of the chief nursing officer.

"We would not have had successful CPOE and medication barcoding implementations without applying Lean principles in advance to prepare for this monumental change. This has saved us millions through Meaningful Use incentives," said Dave Kapaska, DO, regional president and CEO of Avera McKennan.

Lean Transformation Projects and Other Forms of Improvement

Process excellence consultants at Avera McKennan follow up the projects with ongoing coaching for departmental leaders, who own the new process and continue to improve it as part of the new management approach. Projects help jump-start change, but sustainability requires ongoing effort and new leadership styles. "It's a continuous improvement process," Maass said. "We are managing the process rather than the outcomes."[44] For example, the team identified an opportunity to create standardized work to ensure that central lines and intravenous lines are changed properly, as needed.

The transformation projects are selected by senior leaders, but projects can also be initiated out of employee suggestions. These longer projects are important, as Slunecka said, "I believe that doing just *kaizen* events is like applying so many Band-Aids. A weeklong event is extremely helpful in improving a process that has been completely redesigned using a Lean design process. But the full redesign must be completed first. Healthcare design is too complex to accomplish in a week and it takes far longer than that to change a workplace culture."[45]

Respect and a Leadership Commitment to Staff

Avera McKennan showed that productivity improvement and cost savings could be accomplished in ways other than layoffs or head count reductions. Early on in Avera McKennan's Lean journey, the hospital made a promise to employees that they would not be laid off as a result of Lean or other improvements. Fred Slunecka, former regional president of Avera McKennan and now the chief operating officer of Avera Health, said, "We basically promised employees we would do everything we can to protect their careers, but not their specific jobs, if they in turn do everything possible to keep the organization economically secure." Jobs and roles might change.

Filling the role formerly played by external consultants, Avera now employs three full-time internal consultants, all of whom have nursing backgrounds, led by a director. Avera's consultants do not run weeklong "*kaizen* events" as many hospitals do. In earlier years of their Lean journey, Avera typically held longer 10- to 16-week transformation projects, making more radical changes than could be accomplished in a week. In recent years, they have run shorter projects due to time pressures, as it is difficult to free up staff to be dedicated to the long projects.

Avera is placing a growing emphasis on observation or modeling projects. Discrete-event simulation (DES) software was used to model the real system to predict various performance metrics, for example, patient wait time and resource utilization. In addition, simulation allows decision makers to model "what if" scenarios to improve metrics, for example, better patient care in terms of response time, along with better utilization of resources and staff time.

In the ED, DES was used to ensure that the RN-to-patient ratio is appropriate at all times of the day, any day of the week. At the Avera Heart Hospital, DES was used to schedule system resources more efficiently and prevent the need for purchasing new equipment.

Avera McKennan's experience shows that Lean is not about cutting heads—it's about having the right staffing levels. In the 2006 ED project, analysis of current processes showed that the work could not be effectively accomplished with current staffing. So, in that case, the hospital actually added to the head count to improve patient throughput. Slunecka summarized the goal of optimizing the entire system rather than just suboptimizing labor costs by saying, "Every project has saved money more than the cost of the project—not all show labor savings."

A key to Avera McKennan's success has been the recognition that Lean is about people. Slunecka said employees—the human factor—are the key. Employees are engaged in the process, submitting improvement ideas, and persevering through the difficulties of implementing change.

Other results from Lean at Avera McKennan include

- Assessment time in ambulatory surgery reduced from 45 minutes to 25, reducing nurse walking distance by 90%.
- Mammography waiting room time reduced from 40 minutes to 12.
- Babies in the neonatal intensive care unit are no longer awakened to be given medications, as teams changed to a process to better consider their natural sleep cycles.
- Operating room inventory was reduced by $182,000; 600 nurse hours per year were saved by eliminating an end-of-shift inventory count.[46]
- The size of standard surgical instrument sets was reduced, saving purchasing costs, reducing reprocessing work, and improving ergonomics for staff.
- A new women's center and outpatient surgery center were designed and built using Lean principles.
- By adjusting scheduling, they were able to delay the purchase of a new MRI until 2018, delaying a $2 million expenditure.

A Commitment to Lean Thinking, Better Management, and Continuous Improvement

Julie Ward, vice president of innovation and strategy, said, "Health care workers as a whole are in it for the mission. They're in it for the satisfaction they get from making a difference in someone's life, and the great thing about Lean is it's always from the customer perspective," she said. "The byproduct is that we become more efficient and our costs go down. What we often see is that when people experience being part of a Lean team and achieve these transformative outcomes, they become Lean converts," Ward said. "They begin to see how they can change on the fly to achieve those improvements."[47]

Since process excellence began at Avera McKennan in 2004, the innovation team has worked on 130 Lean projects.

"It's undeniable that change is coming to health care. Outside, competitive pressures will force a delivery system that's different than we're used to. Changing as the marketplace changes is imperative to our mutual success," said Dave Kapaska, DO, regional president of Avera McKennan. "I can't underemphasize that innovation is absolutely essential, and Lean concepts continually help us to find new efficiencies. We must find ways to work smarter with fewer resources per task."

Other industries have undergone complex change, including the food industry. "We're interested in what we can learn from those who have gone before us, so we're tapping into that wisdom," Kapaska said. In fact, Steve Crim, retired general manager of John Morrell, the largest food production facility in the United States., located in Sioux Falls, joined Avera McKennan as director of operational strategy in 2013. Crim has spoken at employee forums to help employees prepare for and accept change, making these practical points:

- Understand that change is a journey. We're not striving for perfection. Rather, we're striving to be better each day, and get that much closer to reaching our goals.
- Become a student of your work. Know it inside and out.
- Be an opportunity seeker. Don't just hunker down and hope that all this talk of change will "blow over." Look for ways in which you personally can grow and change, and at the same time help our organization improve.
- Work together. In order to thrive in the future, we'll need to collaborate and achieve consensus. No one person has all the answers.
- Participate. Change will take all of us. We can't sit on the sidelines.

"Our top goal is providing great care for our patients. But we're also concerned about the success and security for each of our employees. To accomplish this, we must remain competitive, excellent and innovative," Kapaska said.

Conclusion

There is no single road map or cookbook for a hospital to follow in its pursuit of Lean. Certain key elements are necessary, including identifying problems to be solved, direct participation by executive leadership, and the willingness of frontline employees and managers to make improvements to their own processes. Starting with the transformation of a model line area can help demonstrate the potential of Lean to the rest of the organization. Focusing on the management system and sustaining improvements is important for making sure that Lean is not just the new flavor of the month, but instead is part of the vision and strategy for the future at the hospital.

Lean Lessons

- Hospitals should focus their Lean efforts based on need and the readiness of area leaders to drive change.

- There are different styles of *kaizen* that may be appropriate depending on the problem that needs to be solved.
- Executive leadership and involvement are critical for Lean success.
- Lean success requires action, hard work, and discipline.
- Lean cannot be done everywhere all at once; start with a model line area that can set an example for others.
- Having a dedicated cross-functional process improvement team is vital to success.
- Training cannot be ignored, yet training is not a cure-all.
- While a few quick fixes are positive steps, do not lose sight of the bigger picture and a more strategic plan.

Points for Group Discussion

- What problems really need solving? Where should we start? Is there broad agreement about the need to improve and our ability to improve?
- How would you answer Shook's five Lean Transformation questions?
- Why is a pledge of no layoffs due to Lean so important for engagement and success?
- How can we transition our Lean efforts from a tools and project mentality to a way of thinking, managing, working, and improving every day?
- What skills or personalities make the best Lean team members?
- How do we get our senior leaders engaged and involved with Lean if they are not already?

Notes

1. Lusky, Karen, Laying Lean on the Line, One Change at a Time, http://www.captodayonline.com/Archives/0709/ 0709h_laying_lean.html (accessed October 21, 2015).
2. Rapoza, Joshua, A Lean Transformation Model Everyone Can Use, http://www.lean.org/LeanPost/Posting.cfm?LeanPostId=135 (accessed October 23, 2015).
3. Lean Enterprise Institute, John Shook Explains the Lean Transformation Model, https://www.youtube.com/watch?v=kEcdliWZH30 (accessed October 23, 2015).
4. Ruhlman, Jeannie, and Cheryl Siegman, "Boosting engagement while cutting costs," *Gallup Management Journal*, June 18, 2009, http://gmj.gallup.com/content/120884/boosting-engagement-cutting-costs.aspx (accessed March 26, 2015).
5. Graban, Mark, Podcast #231—Dr. Eric Dickson, Starting with Lean at UMass Memorial, http://www.leanblog.org/2015/09/podcast-231-dr-eric-dickson-starting-with-lean-at-umass-memorial/ (accessed October 21, 2015).
6. Liker, Jeffrey K., and David Meier, *The Toyota Way Fieldbook* (New York: McGraw-Hill, 2006), 310.
7. Meier, David, presentation, Lean Enterprise Institute Workshop, October 6, 2009.
8. Toussaint, John, and Roger Gerard, *On the Mend: Revolutionizing Healthcare to Save Lives and Transform the Industry* (Cambridge, MA: Lean Enterprise Institute, 2010), 67.
9. Graban, Mark, Podcast #231.
10. Schmidt, Bill, site visit, May 2015.
11. Marchwinski, Chet, and John Shook, *Lean Lexicon* (Brookline, MA: Lean Enterprise Institute, 2003), 34.
12. Toussaint and Gerard, *On the Mend*, 66.
13. ThedaCare Center for Healthcare Value, *Thinking Lean at ThedaCare: Strategy Deployment*, DVD (Appleton, WI: ThedaCare Center for Healthcare Value, 2011).

14. Toussaint, John, email exchange, January 2013.
15. Tonkin, Lea A. P., and Michael Bremer, "ThedaCare's culture of continuous daily improvements," *Target* 2009, 25(1): 8.
16. Ibid., 7.
17. St. Martin, Christina, Seeking perfection in health care: Applying the Toyota Production System to medicine, *Performance and Practices of Successful Medical Groups: 2006 Report Based on 2005 Data*, Medical Group Management Association, 20.
18. Patterson, Sarah, presentation, Institute for Healthcare Improvement National Forum, December 7, 2011.
19. Graban, Mark, LeanBlog podcast #76—Dr. David Jaques, Lean in Surgical Services, LeanBlog Podcast, October 14, 2009, http://www.leanblog.org/2009/10/leanblog-podcast-76-dr-david-jaques/ (accessed March 26, 2015).
20. Nelson-Peterson, Dana L., and Carol J. Leppa, "Creating an environment for caring using Lean principles of the Virginia Mason Production System," *Journal of Nursing Administration*, 2007, 37: 289.
21. Toussaint, John, Management on the Mend (Appleton, WI: ThedaCare Center for Healthcare Value, 2015), 3.
22. ValuMetrix Services, West Tennessee Healthcare Case Study, http://www.valumetrixservices.com/sites/default/files/client_results_pdf/CS_WestTennessee_Jackson%20Madison_Lab_OC4020.pdf (accessed March 26, 2015).
23. Lean Enterprise Institute, New Survey: Middle Managers are Biggest Obstacle to Lean Enterprise, July 18, 2007, http://www.lean.org/WhoWeAre/NewsArticleDocuments/Web_Lean_survey.pdf (accessed March 26, 2015).
24. Heath, Chip, and Dan Heath, *Switch: How to Change Things When Change Is Hard* (New York: Crown Business, 2010), 5.
25. Flinchbaugh, Jamie, *The Hitchhiker's Guide to Lean* (Dearborn, MI: Society of Manufacturing Engineers, 2006), 39.
26. Graban, Mark, How Lean Management Helped Hospitals Avoid Layoffs, FierceHealthcare.com, October 1, 2010, http://www.fiercehealthcare.com/search/site/story%20how%20lean%20management%20helped%20hospitals%20avoid%20layoffs%202010%2010%2001 (accessed March 26, 2015).
27. Bonini, Jamie, presentation at 2014 Lean Healthcare Transformation Summit.
28. Bonini, Jamie, interview, December 2015.
29. Bonini, Jamie, interview, December 2015.
30. Bonini, Jamie, presentation at 2014 Lean Healthcare Transformation Summit.
31. Bonini, Jamie, interview, December 2015.
32. Toussaint, *Management on the Mend*, 29.
33. Toussaint, *Management on the Mend*, 31.
34. Toussaint, *Management on the Mend*, 29.
35. Ortiz, Tyson, and Jeffrey Liker, A Family's Growth Fueled by Crisis: The Power of the Improvement Kata, http://www.ame.org/target/articles/2015/familys-growth-fueled-crisis-power-improvement-kata (accessed October 24, 2015).
36. Toussaint, *Management on the Mend*, 71.
37. Ibid.
38. Isern, Josep, Mary C. Meaney, and Sarah Wilson, Corporate Transformation Under Pressure, http://www.mckinsey.com/insights/organization/corporate_transformation_under_pressure (accessed October 21, 2015).
39. Prosci, A Model for Individual Change, http://www.prosci.com/adkar-model/overview-3/ (accessed October 21, 2015).
40. ExperiencePoint, "What's the deal with all these change models?," unpublished manuscript.
41. Smith, Steven M., The Satir Change Model, http://stevenmsmith.com/ar-satir-change-model/ (accessed October 21, 2015).
42. Maurer, Robert, *The Spirit of Kaizen* (New York: McGraw-Hill Education, 2012), 16.

43. Maass, Kathy, telephone interview, October 2015.
44. Maass, Kathy, telephone interview, February 2011.
45. Slunecka, Fred, personal correspondence, December 8, 2009.
46. Schawn.
47. Schawn.

Chapter 13

A Vision for a Lean Hospital and Health System

Introduction

So far, we have seen the roots of Lean thinking: Henry Ford, W. Edwards Deming, and Toyota, among others. The core concepts, philosophies, tools, and leadership styles have been defined and introduced. We have shared real examples of health systems that have already used these methods to make improvements that matter for the patients, employees, physicians, and hospitals. The questions that are sure to follow are "How do I get there?" and "What will I look like when I'm done?"

First, there is no "done" or "there" as a final destination with Lean. There is always a problem to solve, a waste to eliminate, and a new form of value-adding work to create. After about 70 years of developing and using what we call Lean, Toyota still has waste and problems to solve. Toyota is, however, significantly better than their competitors in many ways, and they continue to improve. There is no perfectly Lean organization, so the term *Lean hospital* might really be shorthand for "a hospital that is using Lean methods in a systematic way to improve and manage." Using the term "Lean implementation" or "Lean transformation" implies that a health system can be "done" with this work. We're all just practicing Lean, perhaps, and we can keep improving how we improve, continuously over time.

Earlier editions of this book talked about a "Lean hospital." In an era when independent hospitals and physician practice groups are becoming part of increasingly large integrated health systems, we have a new opportunity to define and optimize a "Lean health system" instead of just a "Lean hospital." If patients define value as maintaining health and quality of life, a Lean health system can accomplish that goal, keeping people home instead of just treating them more safely and more efficiently.

When Is a Health System Lean?

Using the original definition of Lean from *The Machine that Changed the World*, is there a hospital anywhere that operates with half of everything, compared to other hospitals? A Lean hospital in those terms would have, among other measures:

- Half the errors
- Half the infections
- Half the patient harm
- Half the waiting time
- Half the length of stay
- Half the head count (or more likely, half the employee turnover)
- Half the cost
- Half the space
- Half the complaints from patients and physicians

Health systems might not improve to a Toyota-like point of being literally twice as good as their competitors (that gap has been closed by their competitors over time, anyway). That said, we should set the bar high for our organization. History has shown that Lean concepts allow breakthrough thinking, leading to dramatically better performance, rather than modest incremental gains, such as the 95% reduction in central-line associated bloodstream infections at Allegheny General Hospital.[1] ThedaCare and Gundersen Lutheran (Wisconsin) have each demonstrated 25% to 30% lower costs for inpatients and cardiac surgery patients.[2,3] Even if we had half the defects or half the patient injuries as another hospital, is that good enough? No, but we have to strive for perfection, even though absolute perfection might seem difficult or impossible.

We might even reach outside the boundaries of the hospitals, looking to improve the larger healthcare system. Lean health systems would work to reduce emergency department visits by half by better coordinating the entire continuum of care in their communities. Group Health (Washington) reduced emergency visits of its members by 29% through its patient-centered medical home approach, based on Lean principles.[4] Lean hospitals can also work to prevent readmissions, as did UPMC St. Margaret Hospital (Pennsylvania), which reduced readmission rates for chronic obstructive pulmonary disease (COPD) by 48%.[5]

Health systems are getting results with Lean, in hospitals, surgery centers, specialty clinics, and primary care offices. The challenge now is to spread those ideas so every site that delivers healthcare services can improve. We should learn from the leaders and the example they are setting, adapting their methods to our own health system or location. We can also share ideas and collaborate with others who are learning as they go. An example of this is the Healthcare Value Network, a joint effort of the Lean Enterprise Institute and the ThedaCare Center for Healthcare Value, where over 60 organizations across North America share and learn from each other in a collaborative environment. The Pittsburgh Regional Health Initiative, initially led by former Alcoa CEO and United States Treasury Secretary Paul O'Neill, is an example of a regional effort; it is hoped it will be duplicated in other regions, states, or countries. Within Lean and process improvement circles, groups have formed for individuals and health systems to learn from each other, including the Massachusetts Hospital Lean Network, the Bay Area Process Improvement Network (San Francisco and Silicon Valley, California), and a nascent group that bridges Austin and San Antonio, Texas.

What Would a Lean Health System Look Like?

Having a chance to tour or walk through a hospital or clinic that has embraced Lean, you might look for visible Lean methods in use. Visible indicators might include 5S and visual controls, marking and labeling where items are supposed to be stored. You might also see standardized work or *kanban* cards or bins posted and in use. Employee *kaizen* ideas, performance measures, or A3 reports might be displayed on walls. The physical structure and layout might be compact, logical, highly visual, and neatly organized. A Lean hospital building might be new and architecturally striking, with thoughtful design elements improving the efficiency and quality of care. Or, it might be an older, humble building that is full of Lean spirit and practices that make all the difference.

Much of what makes a Lean health system, however, cannot be directly observed during a tour. Can we directly observe the thought processes and mindsets of the organization? Can we see how people solve problems? Given enough time, we might be able to directly observe supervisors interacting with their employees, but we usually do not get that chance on a tour. Toyota has been very open in letting other manufacturers, even direct competitors, tour their factories. Other companies have typically copied the tools and the visible methods, often coming away not understanding the true nature of the Toyota Production System.[6]

What Would a Patient Experience in a Lean Health System?

A good exercise might be to think through what the perfect patient care experience would look like and how it would feel. For example, for an outpatient surgery patient, what would be an experience of perfect service and perfect care? This might seem similar to the creation of an ideal state version of a future-state value stream map. We can challenge ourselves on how things should work to set goals for our Lean improvements.

The patient would be able to promptly get an appointment or procedure scheduled, with the health system doing everything it can to minimize delay by increasing capacity and throughput with low-cost process improvements. Having the right sized capacity means that patients are more likely to get the right care in the right place at the right time. The hospital provides a clear estimate of total expected cost for the payer and out-of-pocket costs for the patient (if applicable), relying on transparent standard prices for routine procedures and not asking the patient to pay for the results of any errors or process problems.

The patient's Lean experience begins before arrival, which can include presurgical steps such as scheduling, surgical consults, and making sure everything is communicated properly (such as the need to arrive for labs or presurgical fasting) to avoid miscommunications, rework, or delays. Think through the patient experience from the time the patient drives up to the hospital. Is everything clearly labeled for where to park and where to come for registration? Is the patient able to get registered without repeating the same information to multiple people? Is the patient able to avoid excessive delays before the procedure starts?

From a clinical and surgical standpoint, does the hospital ensure that all proper preparation and quality steps are followed before the procedure, including confirmation of the patient identity, marking of the site, and the time-out of the universal protocol? In a Lean hospital, the so-called universal protocol is actually universally followed, to the spirit of the guidelines rather than just going through the motions. How is the process error proofed to protect the patient from harm? Are all of the participants (nurses, physicians, anesthesiologists, etc.) aware of their role, interactions, and standardized work? Is there a team environment in which everyone is focused on the patient instead of hierarchy and titles? Are clinicians following evidence-based practices that are best for the patient? A Lean hospital would have good answers to these questions and would, additionally, make sure all instruments or scopes have been properly sterilized because processes are always followed as the result of effective training and supervision.

Beyond the surgery itself, what service is provided to any family or loved ones who are waiting? Are parents of a child allowed to stay with the child as long as possible and then be there when they wake up? Are they kept informed of the patient's status to ease their worrying? Is the patient able to get through the postoperative recovery area and discharged without any avoidable delays beyond the required recovery time? Beyond avoiding delays, a Lean hospital ensures that patients are not rushed home too quickly for any reason. Has clear and unambiguous communication been made about the patient's postoperative responsibilities to help in recovery and to prevent infection? Have appointments been scheduled for postoperative therapies and follow-up? Does the patient receive a billing statement that is 100% accurate and easy to comprehend (again, if applicable)?

Whatever vision you create for perfect care, be sure to include both the clinical care and the service aspects of the patient's experience. Starting with fresh eyes and thinking toward perfection will drive better improvements than looking for incremental improvements over today's practices and waste.

Beyond day surgery patients, what would ideal care feel like for patients arriving in the emergency room or staying in the hospital for a few days? Patients, in any Lean setting, should experience minimal delays, or at least fewer delays than they are accustomed to. In fact, many aspects of the patient journey through a Lean health system might seem unusual or surprising as things are improved and reinvented. Talk with your colleagues, leaders, and employees to create a vision of what a patient would experience (or not experience) in a Lean health system. How can you measure or otherwise gauge progress toward those goals?

What Would It Be Like to Work in a Lean Health System?

Working in a Lean hospital or clinic should be a positive experience for employees, leaders, and physicians. After seeing many cases of morale and employee engagement improvement with Lean, employees should not want to leave a Lean hospital to work someplace else. In some cases, work life has become so fundamentally different (and better) that employees who have left to go to a traditional health system have come running back, no longer able to (or wanting to) operate in a traditional non-Lean environment and culture.

Employees in a Lean environment should expect, among other things,

To be listened to by supervisors and other leaders, to have their ideas solicited, to have the freedom to make improvements for the betterment of the system, and to be treated with respect, repaying that respect with a commitment to help the organization improve

To have managers and leaders who are skilled teachers and coaches of Lean and problem-solving methods and who invest a large portion of their time in developing these skills and abilities with their own staff

To be provided with everything they need to do their work to the highest level of quality, including the proper equipment (in working condition), the right space, staffing levels, training, and management support

To focus on holistic patient needs instead of rushing through a list of tasks

To be properly trained on how to use new technologies and how to follow new policies and procedures, rather than be expected to figure things out for themselves

To develop the discipline to work within a system, but also to maintain the creativity required for *kaizen* and more radical improvement efforts

To not be overburdened with more work than can be done in a high-quality manner or to be standing around with nothing to do (and not sent home early because the health system is more interested in saving money in the short term than they are in engaging and developing their employees)

To have the time to take breaks and have a proper meal during their shift

To be able to speak up and ask for help if they are overburdened or have questions and to get a prompt, helpful response from management

To be challenged to grow, personally and professionally, always striving to learn and improve personal technical, leadership, and problem-solving skills

To not be blamed for systemic problems; to not be set up for failure

To feel a sense of pride for contributing to a high-performance organization, for understanding their personal roles and how their work has an impact on patients, coworkers, the hospital's bottom line, and the community

Again, Lean is not a system that is soft on people or an environment where everyone is superficially nice to each other, avoiding conflict. The Lean culture of "respect for people" also demands a sense of responsibility, as true respect challenges employees, and each other, to get better for the sake of the patients and the organization.

Managers and leaders could expect an environment in which the direction and goals from senior leadership are clear and actionable. Managers at all levels would have a voice in shaping the strategy of the hospital, also working with their employees to develop improvement plans to meet these true north goals. Managers could expect that staff members will be open about problems, waste, and near misses, creating an open blame-free environment for improvement. Managers and leaders in a Lean environment would expect to have goals that are not suboptimizing, allowing them to focus on goals other than meeting their budget.

How Would We Describe a Lean Health System?

To create a vision, can we define in aggregate how to describe a prototype Lean hospital or health system? One good starting point might be for a hospital to follow the general 14 principles of *The Toyota Way*.[7] A Lean hospital might also be characterized by the following traits: strategy and management system, patients, employees, waste and *kaizen*, and technology and infrastructure.

Strategy and Management System

A Lean health system and its leaders have a clear understanding of *why* Lean is a necessary methodology and how Lean will not just improve key measures, but also help the organization be more competitive and successful over time.

A Lean health system has leaders who actively seek to learn and apply Lean lessons from within and outside their organization and industry, often receiving assistance or mentoring from manufacturing leaders who are on their board or in their community.

A Lean health system has goals and improvement efforts that are tightly integrated with strategy and vision, moving beyond the isolated use of tools to the engagement of all employees and leaders in the building of a Lean culture. The Lean strategy and the health system strategy are one and the same through the strategy deployment process, being communicated widely and consistently from the corporate executive suite to the frontline employees and physicians.

A Lean health system realizes that success comes not only from technology and clinical excellence, but also through employee engagement and operational excellence. Lean hospitals help stakeholders understand that spending money on new technology and new space is not the only way to demonstrate a commitment to serving the community.

A Lean health system has a leadership method and model that is taught to supervisors and managers and is practiced by all leaders. Lean behaviors, such as going to the *gemba*, rounding and auditing the process, collaborating on improvement efforts, and being a servant leader, are used as criteria for employee and leader selection, performance reviews, and advancement.

A Lean health system is not overly dependent upon a few key leaders or other individuals for lasting improvement and culture change. Leaders contribute through strengthening the organization as a whole as compared with striving for individual achievement.

A Lean health system strives for improvement in every area and not just where there are patient interactions. Support and administrative areas including human resources, accounting, finance, and community relations will all be focused on applying Lean methodologies to their areas.

A Lean health system creates collaborative relationships for all partners and stakeholders, including physicians, vendors, and payers. Patient safety practices and quality data are shared openly with other hospitals and the community, rather than using those methods as a source of competitive advantage.

A Lean health system works diligently to reduce costs so that they can be profitable at the lowest levels of reimbursement, rather than complaining that reimbursements are too low.

A Lean health system competes vigorously to attract new business through its superior quality and value, signing "centers of excellence" contracts and attracting patients and payers from long distances who appreciate the quality and value provided.

A Lean health system has a small, centralized group that maintains consistent Lean practices and training. This group coaches leaders and staff to drive improvements and to own their processes, rather than doing it for them. This central team, along with senior leadership, continually mentors and develops managers in Lean behaviors and management philosophies.

A Lean health system has specific leaders who are responsible for the overall flow, management, and improvement of key patient care value streams.

A Lean health system determines proper staffing levels based on patient volumes, actual workloads, and the time required to do work in a safe, high-quality way. Best attempts are made to match staffing to volume in different time periods. Reliance on benchmarking or budget constraints as a primary staffing driver decreases.

A Lean health system sees problems as opportunities for learning and considers proficiency with the learning and problem solving as key competitive advantages in fast-moving times.

A Lean health system operates as a cohesive system rather than being a collection of independent hospitals and clinics. Staff and leaders collaborate and learn across sites, solving problems together and sharing best practices as appropriate. Patient flow is optimized across sites, with patients being transferred as necessary to meet their needs, rather than a particular hospital worrying about losing reimbursement.

Patients

A Lean hospital is passionately and meticulously focused on the patients, families, and guests, aiming for perfect, harm-free care, while respecting patients and their time. The patient comes first in all activities, decisions, and priorities. Leadership helps create that expectation with all stakeholders.

A Lean hospital involves patients, as the ultimate customers, and their loved ones in process improvement efforts. New designs and processes are tested to make sure they meet patient needs. A Lean hospital understands patient needs by asking them, rather than assuming, and realizes different patients have different needs and wants.

A Lean hospital provides excellent service in addition to the best clinical care. The patient is surrounded by a warm, caring environment in which staff and clinicians have the time to fully attend to their physical and emotional needs.

A Lean hospital asks patients for real-time feedback rather than just relying on formal surveys. Feedback is used to improve processes and prevent future patient satisfaction problems, not just to make the immediate patient happier.

A Lean hospital sets goals of zero preventable errors that cause patient harm, as any other goal is unacceptable. The staff and leaders work tirelessly toward that goal through standardized work, root cause problem solving, and error proofing, rather than relying on individuals to be careful or relying on inspection. When preventable errors occur, patients and payers are not charged for the work required as a result, and employees are not blamed.

A Lean hospital minimizes waiting times for patients, using scheduling practices that respect patients' time. A Lean hospital works tirelessly to improve flow and reduce waiting times, both for appointments and during visits and episodes of care. A Lean hospital has discharge processes that smoothly get the patient home without delay once they are medically ready to leave.

Employees

A Lean health system recognizes that employees are the true source of value for patients and the hospital, rather than viewing them strictly as a cost to be reduced. Top leadership makes a consistent commitment to all employees that Lean improvements will not lead to layoffs and, instead, lead to new opportunities and growth for people.

A Lean health system helps employees understand that not all activity is value-added. Rather than defining waste as being "our job," everybody works to eliminate it so more time can be focused on the patients.

A Lean health system fully engages every employee in improving their work, supporting the innate desire to provide perfect care to patients. Leaders help employees understand how their work fits in to the value stream and work collaboratively with them in *kaizen*. Employees are not sent home every time census drops, as that is seen as an opportunity for *kaizen*.

A Lean health system does not overburden employees with more work than can be done in a high-quality manner or pressure people to work harder or be more careful as a means to quality, safety, or efficiency.

Waste and Kaizen

A Lean hospital recognizes that there is waste in every process, focusing on continuous improvement and root cause problem solving instead of workarounds and firefighting. Individuals (employees or leaders) are not blamed for the waste or problems.

A Lean hospital proactively identifies and fixes problems and reduces waste, rather than being strictly reactive. Employees are encouraged to speak up, expose waste, and make improvements to the system, instead of hiding problems and making things look good.

A Lean hospital breaks down departmental silos to focus on improving care and preventing delays for patients, allowing employees to feel pride in their work, by being able to cooperate across value streams instead of suboptimizing their own area.

A Lean hospital values the judicious standardization of work methods in the name of improving safety, quality, and productivity, rather than allowing people to develop their own different methods for doing the same work or precluding one patient from the best-identified method of care.

A Lean hospital is never satisfied with being better than average, being in a top percentile, or winning awards; it always strives to get better. Perfection is a difficult goal to reach, but it is the only acceptable goal to a Lean hospital.

Technology and Infrastructure

A Lean hospital is physically designed to minimize waste for patients and for all who work inside its walls. It is designed with direct input from staff and patients to support efficient workflows and value streams, rather than forcing departments and employees to adjust their work to the space. A Lean hospital focuses more on what is functional and effective for the patients and staff rather than glossing over bad processes with marble entryways and lobby fountains. Lean hospitals use collaborative and iterative design and build practices like Lean design, 3P, and integrated project delivery.

A Lean hospital has process technology, automation, and information systems that solve a real problem, making work less difficult or less error prone (or both). The hospital does not install automation or new systems for the sake of having new systems. Employees and physicians are deeply involved, early on and throughout the process, in the selection of technologies that meet their needs. A Lean hospital takes the time to properly train all stakeholders in new technologies, ensuring they can be used most effectively rather than blaming individuals for not using the systems.

In Conclusion

In 2001, the healthcare industry started to say, "We want to see a Toyota in healthcare."[8] At that point, there was no clear leader in terms of a hospital that had dramatically different processes or results from the others. Even if some clear leaders in Lean healthcare are becoming widely known, Lean success stories can be found at hundreds of hospitals around the world. It is more likely that, over time, a top tier of hospitals will emerge—hospitals with results that are much better than the industry as a whole. Lean advocates would assume that many in this top tier will be the ones who are most effectively using Lean principles. This top tier will continue to learn from each other, improving continually. The hospitals outside that top tier will likely fall further and further behind—some will likely be forced to close or will be pressured into mergers. We all have the opportunity to aim high, working hard every day to reduce waste, respect our people, and provide better and better care for our patients, through Lean methods. Let's seize that opportunity.

Points for Group Discussion

- ■ What core measures can we improve by half in our organization?
- ■ How might people react to a goal of "zero" or "perfection"?

- How are some of these patient-centered goals complicated by the payer system and financial incentives in our country?
- What is your own long-reaching vision for a Lean hospital, within your department, your hospital, and more broadly?

Notes

1. The Commonwealth Fund, Case Study: Perfecting Patient Care at Allegheny General Hospital and the Pittsburgh Regional Healthcare Initiative, September 30, 2008, http://www.commonwealth-fund.org/Content/Innovations/Case-Studies/2008/Sep/Case-Study--Perfecting-Patient-Care-at-Allegheny-General-Hospital-and-the-Pittsburgh-Regional-Health.aspsx (accessed July 1, 2011).
2. Toussaint, John, "Writing the new playbook for U.S. health care: Lessons from Wisconsin," *Health Affairs*, 2009, 28(5): 1343–1350.
3. Boulton, Guy, "Integrated systems hold down costs while keeping up quality," *Milwaukee Journal-Sentinel*, September 12, 2009, http://www.jsonline.com/business/59087997.html (accessed March 26, 2015).
4. Reid, Robert J., Katie Coleman, E. A. Johnson, et al., "The Group Health Medical Home at year two: Cost savings, higher patient satisfaction, and less burnout for providers," *Health Affairs*, 2010, 29(5): 835–843.
5. California Health Advocates, Creative Interventions Reduce Hospital Readmissions for Medicare Beneficiaries, October 7, 2010, http://www.cahealthadvocates.org/news/basics/2010/creative.html (accessed March 26, 2015).
6. Taylor, Alex, How Toyota defies gravity, *Fortune*, December 8, 1997, http://archive.fortune.com/magazines/fortune/fortune_archive/1997/12/08/234926/index.htm (accessed April 3, 2015).
7. Liker, Jeffrey, and David Meier, *The Toyota Way Fieldbook* (New York: McGraw-Hill, 2005), 35.
8. Appleby, Julie, "Care providers slam health system," *USA Today*, May 9, 2001, p. A01.

Glossary

3P: *see production preparation process.*

A3 report or "A3": A standard Toyota method for planning and problem solving, taking its name from the use of a single sheet of A3 paper, which is approximately 11 × 17 inches.

Andon cord: A method for signaling that a problem has occurred, alerting supervisors that assistance is needed. Often a physical cord hanging down from a production line. If the problem cannot be solved immediately, the process or work activity is stopped to ensure *jidoka*, or quality at the source. More generally, any method for empowered employees to stop the work temporarily to ensure quality.

Baka yoke: Japanese phrase that translates as "fool proofing" or "dummy proofing," not preferred in Lean usage. *See poka yoke.*

Batching: Doing work or moving material in quantities greater than one, such as running batches of tests or producing batches of medications. In a batch of cookies, we make more than one at a time, given the size of cookie sheets and the oven. Batching usually connotes waste but may be necessary given constraints in the system.

Boarding: Keeping patients waiting in an emergency department, often in a hallway, after being seen because there is a problem preventing them from being admitted and physically moved to an inpatient room.

Bottleneck: The stage in a process or value stream that is the constraining step for overall flow.

Current state: Version of a value stream map that shows how things work today.

Defects, waste of: A type of waste where something was not done right the first time, or the steps required to inspect for or correct defects. Can apply to products in a process (a defective blood specimen) or to the process itself (a treatment order is not sent by a physician's office, delaying treatment). Defects often lead to rework.

Diversion: The practice of a hospital asking ambulances to take patients to other hospitals, unless the patient would be put in jeopardy by the delay, which is often caused by downstream capacity constraints.

Downstream: The next step or department in a value stream. For example, after a patient is ready to be admitted from the emergency department, the inpatient unit to which he or she is being admitted to is the downstream department. The opposite of *upstream*.

Error proofing (poka yoke): The practice of designing or modifying systems, processes, or equipment to prevent errors from occurring or make it harder for errors to occur. Also includes practices that make errors more apparent or make systems more robust to tolerate errors.

Errors: Describes the result of something that has gone wrong, even if all participants in the system had the best intentions and were performing properly. Types of errors include skill-based errors, for which an unintended action took place; lapses, a mental error; and slips, or physical errors.

FIFO: First in, first out. Describes the flow of materials or people in a system; the item that has been in inventory the longest is used first, or the patient who has been waiting the longest is seen first.

Fishbone (Ishikawa) diagram: A visual diagram that shows multiple contributing causes for an event. The bones of the fish typically represent categories such as people, methods, machines, materials, or environment.

Five whys: The method of continuing to ask why to reach a root cause (or root causes) for an error or problem.

Flow: The absence of waiting in a value stream. *See also* one-piece flow.

FMEA: Failure Modes and Effects Analysis. A method for brainstorming and analyzing potential defects or errors in a system for the sake of prioritizing improvement activities.

Future state: Version of a value stream map that shows how things can, should, or will work in the future.

Gemba: Japanese word that means "the actual place" or "the place where the work is done."

Genchi genbutsu: Japanese phrase that means "go and see."

Heijunka: Japanese word that means "level loading," either demand for a service or the workload for people in a system. A level-loaded system would have the same patient volumes or workloads in every time increment.

Hoshin Kanri: *See* strategy deployment.

Ideal state: Version of a future-state value stream map that shows how things should work, given ideal circumstances and processes.

Inspection: Looking for defects or quality problems after the fact, inspecting products one at a time or in batches. Error proofing is more effective for ensuring 100% quality.

Jidoka: A Japanese word meaning "quality at the source," which is done by visualizing and highlighting problems so they can be solved and prevented.

Just in time (JIT): One of the two pillars, along with *jidoka*, of the Toyota Production System. JIT refers to the idea of making what is needed, when it is needed, in the amount needed.

Kaikaku: Japanese word meaning "radical or transformational change."

Kaizen: A Japanese word meaning "continuous improvement" or "small changes for the good."

Kaizen event: Also known as "Rapid Improvement Event" or "Rapid Process Improvement Workshop." A formally defined event, typically one week long, with a team that is formed to analyze the current process and to make improvements in a process or value stream, with the team being disbanded after the event.

Kamishibai: A Japanese word meaning literally "paper drama," meaning in this context a visual board that is used to track the audits and oversight of standardized work methods.

Kanban: A Japanese word, now adopted in English, that is translated as "signal" or "card"; a method for managing and controlling the movement and ordering of materials in a system.

Kata: A Japanese word, meaning "form," referring to a repeatable routine that is practiced. It is used in the context of a way to learn the scientific method and become better problem solvers, through the practices of the "improvement *kata*" and the "coaching *kata*" routines.

Lean: A quality and process improvement methodology and management system, based on the Toyota Production System, that emphasizes customer needs, improving quality, and reducing time delays and costs, all through continuous improvement and employee involvement.

Level loading: *See heijunka.*

Metrics: Performance measures that are tracked or charted to gauge the effectiveness of a department or process.

Motion, waste of: Type of waste related to employee motion, particularly walking.

Nemawashi: A Japanese term that means "laying the groundwork," often used in the context of sharing and discussing A3 documents.

Non-value-added: A term that describes an activity that fails one or more of the three conditions for being value-added.

One-piece flow: A Lean ideal by which patients or products are treated, worked on, or moved one at a time. Also *single-piece flow*. One-piece flow is a direction or goal, more than an absolute mandate.

Overprocessing, waste of: Doing more work than is necessary for good patient care or for customer needs. For example, spinning tubes of blood longer than necessary in a centrifuge does not lead to better test results; the unnecessary time is overprocessing.

Overproduction, waste of: Doing work earlier than is needed by the customer or creating items or materials that are not needed. An example might include drawing tubes of blood that might not be needed for testing.

PDCA (PDSA): Plan-Do-Check-Act (or Plan-Do-Study-Adjust). A continuous improvement cycle, similar to the scientific method. Originally credited as the Shewhart cycle, after an influential quality improvement statistician. It became more widely known as the Deming cycle, after W. Edwards Deming.

Phlebotomist: A hospital employee who draws and collects patient blood specimens.

Piecework: A system of paying employees based on their production of a manufactured product or per unit of service performed. Frequently used in the garment industry (dating to the sixteenth century AD) and in healthcare (dating to the eighteenth century BC). Piecework is meant to provide incentives to employees, but also creates incentives for overproduction.

Point *kaizen*: An improvement that is small, impacting just one person or one part of the process, taking a short period of time to complete.

Poka yoke: Japanese phrase that means "error proofing" or "mistake proofing."

Policy deployment: *See* strategy deployment.

Practical state: Version of a future-state value stream map that shows how things can realistically work after some process improvements. The process will be better than the current state, but not as good as it could be in the ideal state.

Product: Term that generally refers to the one being acted on in a process or value stream. Can be a patient or a physical product, such as a medication or patient specimen.

Production preparation process (3P): A space and process design methodology that is characterized by staff involvement, a focus on flow, and iterative designs that are tested in physical mockups.

Pull: Moving products or supplies only when they are needed, based on a signal from a downstream department or process. The opposite of *push*, which triggers movement whether the downstream is ready or not. For patients, pull means the patient signals when they need the next aspect of care, such as a procedure or room. It's not pull to move the patient when the room is ready.

Quick changeover: *See* setup reduction.

Rework: Work and activity done to correct a defect or replace defective work. Example: A pharmacy order incorrectly missed a patient allergy, so the order was reworked to then prepare and send the right medication.

RIE: Rapid improvement event (*see kaizen* event).

Root cause: A fundamental cause for a problem, error, or defect in a system. Called a root cause because you often have to look beyond the surface of a problem to find it. Related to the five whys approach.

RPIW: Rapid process improvement workshop. *See kaizen* event.

Safety stock: Inventory of supplies or materials held specifically to protect against expected vendor delays or against usage that is higher than normal.

Setup reduction: A methodology for reducing the amount of time required to change over a resource, such as equipment or a room, from one use or patient to another.

Single-piece flow: *See* one-piece flow.

Six Sigma: A quality improvement methodology that is driven by statistical analysis and other tools, led by specialists called Green Belts and Black Belts. A Six Sigma quality level refers to a process with just 3.4 defects per million opportunities.

SMED: Single-minute exchange of dies, another term for setup reduction or quick changeover.

Spaghetti diagram: A pictorial representation of movement of an employee or product through a physical area, drawing its name from the way a plate of cooked spaghetti might look. Also spaghetti chart.

Standardized work: A Lean method that documents the current one best way to safely complete an activity with the proper outcome and the highest quality. Also refers to the management method for ensuring that standardized work is followed and improved on.

Stockout: Having zero on-hand inventory available for a needed item, tool, or supply.

Strategy deployment: A management methodology that combines annual strategic planning cycles and the alignment of goals and measures across and throughout the organization, further aligning improvement activities and priorities with the organization's goals and direction.

System *kaizen*: A longer-term (often 12–16 weeks) improvement project or series of projects, with goals to improve a broader area than a point *kaizen* or *kaizen* event. Also known as Lean transformation projects.

Takt: The pace of customer demand or workload, expressed in time units. *Takt* equals the available working time in a period divided by the number of units of work to be completed. Example: If a clinic has 240 minutes to give a projected 100 flu shots, the *takt* time is 2.4 minutes.

Talent, waste of: Type of waste referring to not fully utilizing the talents and potential contributions of employees.

Total quality management (TQM): A quality management system based on statistical methods and variation reduction, popular in the 1980s and 1990s.

Transportation, waste of: Type of waste related to the movement of a product in the value stream.

True north: Used in strategy deployment, the four or five consistent directions that form the long-term vision and goals for the organization, for example: safety, quality, people, and financial stewardship.

Turnaround time: The elapsed time between an order being written until a result or other product (such as a medication) is ready. May also be measured from the time the order is received or from the time a specimen is received in a laboratory.

Two-bin system: A type of *kanban* system in which an item is kept in two equal-size bins. An empty bin acts as the signal for a replacement bin's worth of items to be purchased or moved to replace what was consumed.

Upstream: The preceding step or department in the value stream. The opposite of *downstream*.

Value-added: Activity that meets all three rules: (a) the customer must be willing to pay for the activity, (b) the activity must transform the product or service in some way, and (c) the activity must be done correctly the first time.

Value stream: The entire end-to-end process for patient care or the flow of a product, typically crossing multiple health system sites or departments.

Value stream map: A diagram that shows a value stream, including the process steps, waiting times, and communication or information flows. Also illustrates time elements and value-added or non-value-added designations for activities.

Violations: Intentional actions that go against accepted practices, as opposed to errors, that may occur even if everybody was following the correct method.

Waiting, waste of: A type of waste for which there is no activity for the observed employees, patients, or products in a system.

Waste: Activity that does not add value for the customer or patient. Synonymous with non-value-added.

Workaround: A reaction to a problem that is focused on minimizing the short-term impact without doing anything to prevent the same problem from occurring in the future. For example, if a medication is missing, a workaround would be the nurse walking to other cabinets to find a dose for the patient. This action does nothing to prevent the medication from being missing the next time.

***Yokoten*:** A Japanese word that means the horizontal sharing of best practices in an organization, with the intent that others see the practice firsthand and adopt and improve the new method, if they wish.

Index